Y0-DWP-042

RECREATION AND LEISURE

RECREATION AND LEISURE
The Changing Scene
THIRD EDITION

Reynold Edgar Carlson
Janet R. MacLean
Theodore R. Deppe
James A. Peterson

Wadsworth Publishing Company, Inc., Belmont, California

Recreation Editor: Roger Peterson
Production Editor: Connie Martin
Designer: Katie Michels
Copy Editor: Carol Reitz
Technical Illustrator: John Foster

The previous edition of this book was published
under the title *Recreation in American Life*.

Printed in the United States of America

3   4   5   6   7   8   9   10—83   82   81   80

Photo Credits

Part One: John Running/Stock, Boston.
Part Two: Rose Skytta/Jeroboam.
Part Three: Karen R. Preuss/Jeroboam.
Part Four: Clay Templin/Jeroboam.
Part Five: Elizabeth Crews/Jeroboam.
Part Six: Robert Burroughs/Jeroboam.
Cover: George Gerster/Photo Research, Inc.

Cross-country skiing, a major sport in Europe, has
become increasingly popular in the United States.

Library of Congress Cataloging in Publication
Data

Main entry under title:
Recreation and leisure.

    Previous ed. by R. E. Carlson, J. R.
MacLean, and T. R. Deppe published in 1972
under title: Recreation in American life.
    Includes bibliographies and index.
    1.   Recreation—United States.
2.   Leisure—United States.   I.   Carlson,
Reynold Edgar.   II.   Carlson, Reynold
Edgar. Recreation in American Life.
GV53.C3   1979   790.13   78-6901
ISBN 0-534-00585-3

To Garrett G. Eppley,
a pioneer in recreation education,
whose personal encouragement and professional guidance
have enriched the lives of each of the authors.

CONTENTS

FOREWORD

The last few decades have seen tremendous changes in the world.

Population has grown at a tremendous rate. We are told that 25 percent of all the people who ever lived are alive today.

As the population has grown, so has the spread of urban development. It is possible to travel for hours through urban areas and not see trees or green spaces.

We have seen a change from an agrarian, rural life-style to a world where technology is the standard. Today we can go to the moon and back, get on an airplane in London or Paris and arrive in New York ahead of the time we left. Transistor, laser, and heart transplant are common words in our vocabulary. Our horizon is no longer the edge of the farm or the end of the village street; we see events that happen thousands of miles away instantaneously on our television sets. Today we know more about the leaders and events in other countries than we do about our own community or even about our neighbors.

At the same time, we have been involved in a leisure revolution. As the authors point out, leisure is no longer for the privileged few. We have shorter workweeks, longer vacations and leaves for recreation pursuits. The Puritan work ethic is being replaced by a demand for creative opportunities for leisure time.

We are spending more money on leisure activities, and the provision of leisure equipment and services is a major economic factor today. In sports, performing arts, and outdoor recreation activities, participation is the norm. Parks and recreation programs are a high priority government expenditure based on strong citizen demand.

The new technology and the resulting changes offer many new opportunities. But at the same time we are presented with many problems. We are polluting the air we breathe, the water we drink, and the food we eat. We find there is not enough food to feed the growing population. There is great concern that the earth will soon be out of the fossil fuels needed to produce the energy required by the technological systems.

On the other hand, with the opportunity of abundance, there is a worldwide demand to get some of the action. There is a surge of nationalism with new countries continually springing forth. Nations, industry, business, and individuals are pushing to excel, to be the best, to be in control. As others try to hold on, to resist change, conflicts develop and the pressures on the institutions and the people are great.

Today the world is full of new challenges. Great leaders are needed, but the real success will come from the spirit and dedication of people. *People* are the greatest assest in this world. *Recreation is people*—working with and for people.

Recreation will provide outlets from pressure, stimulate creativity, and help promote worldwide understanding. For the recreation professional there is the opportunity for a great contribution and the reward of great personal satisfaction in helping others.

This book provides a solid base of understanding of the leisure field. It should be the starting point for those who choose to serve others in the field of leisure. The talents of the authors Carlson, Deppe, MacLean, and Peterson have been skillfully combined to produce an outstanding text. They have experienced firsthand what they have written, and, most importantly, they have been instrumental in many of the things that have happened in this profession.

It has been my privilege to work as a student under Rey Carlson, Ted Deppe, Janet MacLean, and Jim Peterson and to continue to be involved with them as a colleague and friend in recreation.

Robert F. Toalson

PREFACE

Recreation and Leisure: The Changing Scene is an extensive revision of our former book *Recreation in American Life.* In the years since the first edition, the social, economic, and political climates in which park, recreation, and leisure services professionals move have considerably altered. The authors have tried to reflect those changes and their impact on the recreation and park professions.

We live in a transitional period in which social issues and concerns have surfaced that form the basis for professional decisions and opportunities. The power structure and the general public are increasingly aware of the rights of special populations (the handicapped, the aged, the educationally or socially deprived), the need for appropriate use of depleting natural resources, the effects of environmental or psychological pollution, the broadening meaning of, and inferences from, equal rights ideology, the widening spectrum of acceptable life-styles, and the increasing need for education for total living in an accelerated, technologically sophisticated world.

Within those changing climates and foci of attention, we firmly believe that recreation has a positive contribution to make to the quality of life, not only in individual, but also in societal, welfare. This book confines itself primarily to the United States, not because the authors willfully chose to ignore the increasing international scene, but because they felt they could not do justice to both national and international concerns in one introductory volume.

This edition endeavors to present recreation in modern life in a broad, comprehensive manner—its philosophy, environments, historical antecedents, service delivery systems, special settings and populations, leadership, program, and professional challenges. It is designed to serve both as a textbook for introductory survey courses in recreation curriculums and as a reference book for park and recreation practitioners.

The American scene is one in which leisure and its uses have become a central issue. This edition describes conflicting philosophies; current economic impacts; government, private, and semipublic agencies' influences; and current status and predictable futures. In the last ten years the roles and contributions of the recreation, park, and leisure services professions have been recognized as considerable factors in the nation's attempts to satisfy human needs. The leisure movement has gained national attention. The profession has grown, not only in numbers and in status but also in its specific efforts to provide acceptable standards in personnel, environment, and management. Its role in advocacy, interagency cooperation and coordination, interpretation, leisure education, and provision of recreation programs and settings has greatly enlarged. We have tried to provide an overview of the breadth and scope of that impact.

We are indebted to many for the contents of this book: the many fine authors whose works have served as guideposts in the professional preparation of personnel; the park and recreation practitioners from whom we have received practical information and ideas; and the national professional organizations whose conferences, publications, and workshops have allowed us to test ideas.

We are proud to have had in our classes many men and women who now occupy professional positions of influence and responsibility in the United States and in several foreign countries. Their fresh enthusiasm and challenging input have helped to keep us abreast of changing times.

We acknowledge the contribution of Tony Mobley and Roger Lancaster, who reviewed specific chapters and made excellent suggestions. We are indebted to the following people whose reviews for Wadsworth Publishing Company helped to form the base for revisions: Joseph Bannon, Paul Price, Larry Williams, William Boldt, Clarence Pendleton, Donald Buchanan, and David Ng.

We are most appreciative of the individuals and agencies who gave us permission to use their graphics, contracts, or photographs. For information regarding youth-serving organizations, we thank the following national staff representatives: Meghan Blakemore Eaton, Camp Fire Girls, Inc.; Barclay M. Bollas, Boy Scouts of America; Sue Benedetti, 4-H; Carol B. Stroughter, Girl Scouts of the United States of America; Kit Mahon, Girls Clubs of America; Leonard M. Snyder, Young Men's Christian Association; Kit Kolchin, Young Women's Christian Association; and especially, Frederick T. Miller, Boys' Clubs of America.

Last, but certainly not least, we give special thanks to our immediate families, for whom we had less leisure during the revision of this book. A very special salute goes to Ruth Carlson, who gave up many of her own leisure hours to review, proofread, or analyze copy; debate issues; and feed hungry authors during many long sessions.

For us, this book represents an up-to-date, practical account of the challenges, contributions, and opportunities that exist in the exciting, rewarding profession in which we are privileged to serve.

RECREATION AND LEISURE

Part One
The Impact of Recreation and Leisure

The bow cannot always stand bent, nor can human frailty subsist without some lawful recreation.

Cervantes

As the United States moves into its third century, recreation and leisure will assume an ever-increasing role in the quality of our lives. We have lived through two hundred years of dramatic change, which has exploded in the last few decades into diverse life-styles, values, expectations, and ideals. Not the least of those complexities is the large amount of free time for populations not yet educated to its use or convinced of its potential value.

Part One of this book looks at conflicting philosophies, the emergence of the park and recreation movement, and the economic impact of leisure use and misuse in an affluent country.

What is recreation? Is leisure as meaningful as work? What factors influence recreation environments? Each of us makes some leisure choices. Why? What influence do these choices have on us? On our society? On the nation's economy? On the environment in which we live?

1
Leisure and Recreation in a Changing World

For there are three forms of life, of which the first is the practical, the second, the contemplative, and the third, the life of enjoyment.

Plutarch

A twentieth-century folk tune said, "The times they are a-changin'." A nineteenth-century poet wrote, "The old order changeth, yielding place to new." Change, it seems, is the only constant in history. Why should we be so concerned with its effects today?

We have always experienced change, but the speed of transformations around us today is socially, physically, and psychologically disruptive. It tends to keep us off balance. Yet that same disequilibrium gives the recreation and leisure service professions challenges and opportunities undreamed of at the turn of the century. Leisure services may have a significant role throughout the life continuum—from providing opportunities for exciting innovation and preventing stagnation to relieving tensions caused by drastic, rapid change.

Setting the Stage

We live in a troubled world of conflicting value systems; economic struggles between the "haves" and "have-nots"; dissolution of geographic barriers; increased free time (chosen or enforced) for larger segments of the population; diminishing opportunities for, or decreased satisfactions in work; loss of permanence in a transient society; technology's dehumanizing influences; and altering physical, moral, social, and emotional involvements. In such a world, intelligent and satisfying use of leisure may ultimately condition not only the quality of life, but also survival itself, in terms of psychological balance and physical well-being—the chance to be human in complex environments.

Let's remind ourselves of a few contributors to that complexity:

New industrial machines, which decrease demands on human physical energies

Sophisticated computers, which not only remove the boredom of routine calculations or data treatment but can become monitors, teachers, and critics

Knowledge revolutions, which create mental stress

Incredible mobility, both horizontal and vertical (*up from* and *down into* the earth and sea as well as across them)

5

Consciousness raising for many segments of the population, which creates a panorama of alternative life-styles or expectations

Advanced communications technology, which can literally make the world one neighborhood with instant mutual accessibility

Sensory information overload (more than we really want to know and frequently more than we can assimilate with real understanding)

Miracle drugs, which prolong life or condition its quality

Legislation that dictates or influences individual choice

Have influences such as these had any impact on what you yourself choose to do for recreation?

In the midst of accelerated change, human beings remain essentially unchanged. Although medical technology has given us means to prevent or control stress with biofeedback, drugs, or remedial therapies, we have the same elemental urges, physical needs, and psychological or social yearnings that our ancestors experienced centuries ago.

However, the social and physical environments in which we live have faced radical changes, some irrevocable. Our environments include a rising crescendo of nerve-racking noise, overcrowding, mandatory social interdependence, economic imbalance, altered demands of the work arena, and elongation of life expectancy coupled with compulsory retirement (now under attack in many areas). Perhaps the greatest contribution to potential humanness under these conditions will come from our efforts to develop in ourselves the ability to choose behavior in our discretionary time that will enhance ourselves or the social and physical environments we inhabit.

The Past as Prologue

Throughout history, people have sought leisure. Once it was the prerogative of only the upper classes or primitive tribes who dwelt where nature was bountiful. Today, particularly in the Western world, leisure is available to all classes in ever-increasing amounts. Modern technology has provided extended hours of leisure for many. Never before has there been so much discretionary time or such varied outlets for its use. Never before have the opportunities and challenges in education for rewarding use of leisure loomed so large.

In leisure may lie the final test of our degree of civilization. This free time provides the means either for improving the quality of our lives or for destroying ourselves; and science and technology have given us the tools for both tasks. Although our economic and industrial progress has always depended upon productive work, our cultural, moral, and spiritual development—our quality of life— depends in large measure on how we use or misuse our leisure. Thus, leisure is a two-edged sword. It carries no guarantee of Utopian happiness, however described. It may bring opportunity for enjoyment of art, music, or science; for development of physical and psychological health and strength; or for acquisition of inner resources which lead to tranquility. On the other hand, it may bring boredom, idleness, escape through drugs, overindulgence, social deterioration, or corruption.

What or who can make the difference? In a democratic society, the uses of leisure will always remain the prerogative of the individual; however, the great increase in the availability of leisure for large segments of the population places upon society some responsibility for making adequate provision and education for its use. Skills and interests developed through leisure choices are significant not only to the individual, but also to the society that may be affected by the quality of those choices. Society as a whole, therefore, must be concerned with leisure and recreation and their potential contribution to, or influence on, societal welfare.

Terminology—What's in a Name?

Leisure is a term fraught with many connotations and conflicting conceptualizations in the literature. What do we mean by the term? How does leisure relate to work? To recreation? To play?

If we were to ask lay and professional persons to explain the terms *leisure* and *recreation*, we would probably get a variety of responses, each within a personal philosophy, each influenced by past experiences. Although there is some agreement about the nature and function of leisure and recreation, definitions for either concept are not readily forthcoming. In the following pages, we will explore several conceptualizations, provide some rationale for our choice of terminology, and let the reader agree or disagree.

Leisure

The explanations of leisure fall into four general categories, although some authors have proposed fine differences that split such classifications.

Leisure as contemplation—high intellectual and cultural involvement; a state of mind or being. Leisure is pictured qualitatively as an ideal, a collection of positives. Kaplan described this as the humanistic model.[1]

This concept also seems to include those definitions that describe leisure in terms of the pace at which we do things. We may perform our work or our recreation in a *leisurely* manner. The idea paints a picture of slow, easy, free involvements, regardless of the activity involved.

Here are examples of this approach to leisure:

> Leisure and free time live in two different worlds. . . . Leisure refers to a state of being, a condition of man. —de Grazia[2]

> Leisure is a state of being in which activity is performed for its own sake or as its own end. —de Grazia[3]

> Leisure, like contemplation, is a higher order than the active life. . . . it involves the capacity to soar in active celebration, to overstep the boundaries of the workaday world. —Pieper[4]

Leisure as activity, usually qualified as "nonwork" activity. Many park and recreation professionals are inclined to broaden this definition of leisure to include self-fulfillment values, and label the experience *recreation* instead of *leisure*.

Here are examples of the nonwork concept:

> Leisure is activity . . . apart from the obligations of work, family, and society . . . to which the individual turns at will, for either relaxation, diversion, or broadening his knowledge and his spontaneous social participation, the free exercise of capacity. —Dumazedier[5]

> Leisure is that portion of human experience which, within the context of free time, is a potential source of values. . . . leisure consists of relatively self-determined activity experience that falls into one's economic free-time role. —Kaplan[6]

> This act (leisure) would have to be free of necessity of creating its own order; the mind's bias would have to be satisfied without exhausting effort, the threat of failure, the penalties of work. —Kerr[7]

> Any activity carried out freely without restraint or compulsion may be considered to be leisure. —Neumeyer and Neumeyer[8]

Leisure as free time, discretionary time, choosing time. This time can be used in a variety of ways and may or may not be linked to the work we do as paid employment. Examples of this concept include:

> Leisure is best identified with time . . . time beyond that required organically for existence and subsistence; a time to choose; discretionary time, when the feeling of compulsion is minimal. —Brightbill and Mobley[9]

> Leisure is that portion of an individual's time which is not devoted to work or work-connected responsibilities or to other forms of maintenance activity and which, therefore, can be regarded as discretionary or unobligated time. —Kraus[10]

> Leisure is increasingly recognized as that time available to be used at the individual's discretion—a self-deterministic condition. —Murphy[11]

The holistic view of leisure, which integrates the other three. It includes aspects of activity, attitude, and setting.

> Leisure is best defined as unhurried, pleasurable living among man's spontaneous and educated enthusiasms. —Douglass[12]

> Leisure as a construct with such elements as antithesis of work. . . . a perception of the activity as voluntary or free, a pleasant expectation or recollection, a full range of possibilities from withdrawal in sleep or drink to highly creative tasks. . . . From this view, nothing is definable as leisure, per se, and almost anything is definable as leisure, given the synthesis of elements suggested. —Kaplan[13]

We need to be aware of diverse views as we embark upon the study of leisure and recreation in our nation's third century. Neulinger's research indicated that seventy-seven percent of a representative sample emphasized leisure as "discretionary or unobligated time."[14] As Kaplan observed, "Leisure to the participant, like his religion and his love, is what he thinks it is."[15]

Amid the chasms of disagreement, the authors of this book subscribe to the following definition:

> Leisure is that portion of time not obligated by subsistence or existence demands. It represents discretionary or free time, time in which one may make voluntary choices of experience.

In their free time, people may choose to engage in recreation offerings. They may also decide to go back to work, to catch up on sleep, or to do nothing. Leisure represents a block of time, large or small, in which the individual is free from the necessities of personal maintenance, the demands of employment, and the obligations imposed by the family or some other institution. Leisure, then, of itself is neither good nor bad. But the uses we make of leisure have great potential for positive or negative influence on the quality of our lives. The authors make this choice of definition for the reasons given below.

1. With full realization of the complexities sometimes attached to the two words, *free* and *time,* we contend that in our daily lives we have segments of clock time or even psychological time (the rhythms of our own inner timing) when we are at liberty to make some choices of what we wish to do. We may choose to do nothing, a choice that would not be acceptable within the concept of leisure as an elevated state of being. Leisure is a challenge and an opportunity both for the individual and for society. With increased choosing time, society must be concerned with providing both a range of available experiences from which to choose and stimulation to develop appropriate decision making within that range.

2. The concept of leisure as an all-positive, ideal state of mind or being is extremely difficult to interpret to the public, which

Figure 1.1. Contemplation of natural beauty is a favorite form of recreation.

needs leisure services. If we are to make a leisure ethic possible, we must sell the plumber
as well as the philosopher. Defining leisure as
an intangible state of mind leaves no vocabulary with which to describe meaningfully the
many leisure services. We must be able to describe an identifiable territory or sphere of
commitment in order to convince taxpayers or
those in political power to support those services. Since the park and recreation profession is the only profession whose *sole* objective
is the development, maintenance, and monitoring of the nation's expenditure of leisure
with the expressed intent of improving the
quality of life, it needs to define its arena of responsibility in terms that the general public can
readily understand.

3. Defining leisure as discretionary time
does not necessarily link it irrevocably with
work. While industrial societies have traditionally seen leisure as the other side of work,
we are no longer in the old pattern of
work—and then leisure as a refresher to return to work. We are seeing large segments of
choosing time as a result of modern conven-
iences in transportation, communication, and
personal maintenance. Many people, including the retired, the disabled, the unemployable, and the unemployed, have no work yet
have large quantities of unobligated time.

4. Our definition does not intend to exclude all obligation. Our choices in leisure may
bring commitment and obligation as we
choose to volunteer in the hospital, serve on

political commissions, or care for younger brothers or sisters.

5. The descriptions of leisure as nonwork experiences with characteristics of perceived freedom, potential satisfactions and rewards, and pleasant expectations closely approximate the characteristics of *recreation* experiences as outlined by recreation professionals. Much of the advocacy of the nonwork, nonutilitarian descriptions of leisure comes from psychologists and sociologists who do not recognize or attempt to define recreation or its role.

Play

A term linked with recreation concepts, particularly by psychologists and the early philosophers, is *play*. Here we also have a gamut of descriptions.

> Play is the means whereby the child, in fantasy, comes to know reality.—Slavson[16]

> Play is any self-rewarding activity that is not necessary for the maintenance of life.—Havighurst[17]

> Play is a voluntary activity or occupation executed within certain fixed limits of time and place, according to rules freely accepted and absolutely binding, having its aim in itself and accompanied by a feeling of tension, joy, and the consciousness that it is different from ordinary life.—Huizinga[18]

> Play is commonly considered to be the behavior emitted by an individual not motivated by the end product of the behavior.—Ellis[19]

> Play is the purest, most spiritual activity of man. . . . It holds the sources of all that is good. It gives, therefore, joy, freedom, contentment, inner and outer rest, peace with the world.—Froebel[20]

> That which is neither utility nor truth nor likeness, nor yet, in its effects, harmful, can best be judged by the criterion of charm that is in it and the pleasure it affords. Such pleasure, entailing as it does no appreciable good or ill, is play.—Plato[21]

Concepts of play vary. Even Huizinga, with his structured rules and space and time restrictions for play, might not now accept his own description of play as the "all-inclusive base" of life itself. In contrast, many authors would emphasize the free aspects of play to deny any limitation that would obstruct creativity.

To some, play is spontaneous; to others, play is structured by orderly rules. To some, play is confined to children's activities; to others, it is the spirit or mood that accompanies the behavior. Some people use *play* to denote active physical participation as opposed to more passive involvements. Rather than play with semantics to further confuse already garbled terminology, the authors of this book choose to use the terms *play* and *recreation* interchangeably.

Recreation

As we explore the meaning of the term *recreation*, we again have divergent opinions. Here are a few illustrations.

> Recreation is not a matter of motions but rather of emotions. It is a personal response, a psychological reaction, an attitude, an approach, a way of life.—Romney[22]

> Recreation is activity that rests men from work, often giving them a change (distraction, diversion), and restores them for work.—de Grazia[23]

> The word recreation has come, however, without our willing it, to be the rallying word for those who work for a creative, cooperative expression of personality through sports, athletics, play, and certain art forms.—Braucher[24]

> Recreation is any activity pursued during leisure, either individual or collective, that is free and pleasureful, having its own immediate appeal, not impeded by a delayed reward beyond itself or by any immediate necessity.—*Dictionary of Sociology*[25]

In our society, leisure and recreation are often used synonymously . . . both denoting non-work activities that one engages in periodically as a necessary change from the routine or compulsion of work. —Kando[26]

Recreation consists of activities or experiences carried on within leisure, usually chosen voluntarily, either because of the satisfaction and pleasure he gains from them or because he perceives certain personal or social values to be derived from them. —Kraus[27]

Recreation is an emotional condition within an individual human being that flows from a feeling of well-being and satisfaction. It is characterized by feelings of mastery, achievement, exhilaration, acceptance, success, personal worth and pleasure. It reinforces a positive self-image. Recreation is a response to esthetic experience, achievement of personal goals or positive feedback from others. It is independent of activity, leisure, or social acceptance. —Gray and Greben[28]

Recreation has been defined as an activity, an emotional condition, a social institution, a means for retooling our energies for work, or a voluntarily chosen experience within one's leisure. Therein lies a large field of both extremely narrow or all-inclusive descriptions.

A Personal Philosophy

It is quite evident that concepts and philosophies vary. Although there is some trend in sociology and recreation professional circles to substitute the word *leisure* for *recreation*, it is the position of the authors that the terms are not synonymous. If we accept leisure as the time in which you are free to choose, then what is recreation?

Recreation is any *leisure* experience *voluntarily chosen* by the participant with the *expectation* of positive, enjoyable satisfactions *from* that participation.

Such a definition provides, first of all, a definable arena or sphere of responsibility for the park and recreation professional. Such a professional is committed to serve clientele not when they are on their jobs, not when they are engaged in self-maintenance, but when they have blocks of time whose use they may direct according to their desires. The challenge becomes one of (1) providing a broad cafeteria of choices to meet diverse recreation tastes; (2) making those choices available, exciting, and rewarding to meet the expectations of the participants as well as to meet their personal needs; and (3) helping individuals to attain their true potential through counseling, advocacy, and coordination roles with regard to their recreation choices.

There are other key words in the definition. Recreation is an *experience* that involves not only what the participant is doing but also how he thinks and *feels* about the activity—his attitude. Experience also encompasses the environments in which behaviors take place and the ramifications of such environments, human or natural. A middle-aged couple may not find the modern, free-form social dances pleasant but may still frequent the popular discotheque because of the surroundings. The person who is not an avid bridge fan may host bridge parties enthusiastically because of the warm or witty conversations that engulf the experience.

Another key word is *expectation*. We go into recreation experiences with the expectation of certain rewards. Realistically, for many reasons, those expectations may not be met. The participants still have choice—they may elect to disengage themselves from the involvement or they may find that other rewards not originally sought make it worthwhile to continue.

Implied also is that *enjoyment* is derived from the experience itself. Such an implication does not preclude delayed values and rewards. A stamp collector who enjoys his search also gains satisfactions from displaying his collection at the local hobby show. An artist who paints as a true amateur (for the love of the act) may get rewards removed from the actual creative act as her guests applaud the displayed works. Obviously, there can be dual rewards in many recreation choices—fun in the doing and in the enjoyment of the results sometimes long afterward.

The definition does not deny the attitudinal aspects of a recreation choice. As Ott Romney indicated long ago, recreation is not so much what you are doing as what you feel as you are doing it. Thus, no one experience or activity per se can be labeled recreation. What is recreation for one may be work or even drudgery for another. What is recreation for the same individual may be less than satisfying on a different day, with different individuals, or under different circumstances. For example, a tennis game may be more satisfying played with your friend than with your brother.

The definition is not limiting, except as it describes the *voluntary* aspects of choices and the *time frame* in which they are made. Definitions that tie the raison d'etre for recreation to restoring ourselves for work cannot apply to those who do not have employment that demands their time and energies.

At the same time, the definition of recreation does not connote a nebulous condition of well-being, euphoria, and an all-positive self-image, wherever and whenever such a flow of feeling takes place. In some instances, such a result may occur because of recreation experiences, but we also might find some of that exuberance and well-being in our chosen work. In recreation, as in work, there is a possibility of embarrassment, failure, or dissatisfaction from an experience, even though the initiator of the activity and the participant in it had pleasant expectations and goals.

Community recreation denotes those recreation experiences that society provides through vari-

How Is Your Leisure Ledger?

Keep a log of your activities (by half-hour units) for one week.

In the log, write *F* for free time, *W* for work, or *P* for personal maintenance beside each block of time. Indicate with *R* any time spent in recreation. You may find that you will have two letters on some time frames.

Chart your time consumption according to total hours in each category and the percentage of total available hours each total represents. (You have only 168 hours in the week, remember.)

Chart the numbers of hours that you indicated were spent in recreation. What was the percentage of total free time? What were your other free-time experiences?

Analyze your recreation experiences in the following categories:

How many hours in active participation? Spectator?

How many hours alone? With others?

How many experiences were free? Cost money?

How many experiences were primarily mental? Physical? Social?

How many hours indoors? Outdoors?

How many hours used transportation? No transportation?

How many hours used energy resources —gas, electricity, and others?

How many hours with peer groups? Others?

Critically analyze your week in terms of choices and resultant satisfaction. Is there any need for change? What are your conclusions?

ous social institutions such as the municipal park and recreation departments, the school, the home, religious institutions, private agencies, and the like.

The definition of recreation could permit an individual to engage in destructive, antisocial, or debilitating activities out of personal choice; however, community recreation programs tend to provide activities that embody positive values as defined by the community mores. The decisions are pragmatic rather than philosophic. If community recreation agencies, which are in many instances financed by taxes, do not operate within the accepted ethic of the community, the services are soon severed by the disturbed populace. Therefore, although drug parties or viewing the latest hard-core porno films may be within the confines of the definition of personal recreation choice, public community recreation agencies rarely attempt to meet such recreation expectations.

Profile of the Recreative Experience

Despite the difficulty in defining the essence of recreation, most professionals in the park and recreation field agree upon certain characteristics (though they may assign them to the terms *leisure* or *play*, rather than *recreation*). What is recreation? How do we describe it?

It is person-centered. The focus in recreation should be on the individual, not on the activity. How the child feels about making a clay elephant is more important than how much the glob of clay resembles a pachyderm.

Recreation is participation as opposed to inactivity. The activity may involve quiet discussion or contemplation, participation in the most rigorous sport, or any point on the continuum between. It may include low-level attention to television as well as explosive debate over political issues.

Recreation occurs in leisure. The time for recreation is the time when one is free from the demands of work or self-maintenance.

Involvement is voluntary. Individuals participate in recreation voluntarily and are free to disengage themselves.

Satisfactions are inherent in the experience. Recreation is its own paymaster; the rewards lie in the doing, although delayed values may also accrue (for instance, better physical fitness for the happy jogger or an enlarged vocabulary for the crossword puzzle fan).

Recreation usually involves a change of pace or focus. A person who has a routine job may choose adventurous risk in recreation as a change of pace. The worker who has been employed in heavy physical labor may enjoy a good book, listening to music, or going to a movie instead. The golf pro who has struggled to improve the skills of pupils all week may choose, for weekend recreation, a round of golf with a colleague—a change of focus. The same activity is involved, but with a different attitude and perspective.

Recreation provides enjoyment, fun, and personal satisfaction. Although there are many concomitant values, if enjoyment or some personal uplift is not experienced, the participant has little motivation to return to the activity. Some authors describe this feeling as a consummatory effect, the healthful losing of one's self in the doing. Skiers find it in the exhilaration of the downhill run, but they may also find it in recognizing their development when they have mastered the steeper trail. Individuals get their fun in a variety of ways. Worried parents fail to see the enjoyment in their child's dangerous motorcycle climbs. Those who are afraid of heights wonder at the sanity of the hang-gliding enthusiast or the sky-diver.

Recreation is broad in concept. Because recreation depends on the attitudes of individuals, it may apply to a large spectrum of experience. The types of recreation are as numerous as human interests and desires. They include offerings in drama, dance, arts and crafts, outdoor recreation, social recreation, sports and games, mental and linguistic activities, and volunteer services.

Recreation activities can involve all ages, from the preschool youngster to the older American, and all capacities, from the paraplegic or retarded to the vibrantly healthy. They range from vigorous backpacking to quiet, intellectual philosophic debate; from watching activity to creating it; from totally independent individual projects to those requiring highly skilled professional leadership or publicly financed facilities; from low-level intensity and purpose to total commitment of the participant.

The above characteristics do not operate in isolation. Many of these same attributes could apply to other experiences. Work may provide enjoyment. Worship may furnish a change of pace. Therefore, any isolated characteristic does not suffice as a definition of recreation. Recreation is a composite of all the concepts.

Some Lingering Misconceptions

Changing times demand changing attitudes, and the lag often causes erroneous ideas. As with any term, certain misconceptions still linger concerning *recreation*.

Recreation Only as a Refresher After Work

One popular misconception is to describe recreation as any kind of mental or physical change from work that enables you to work better. Examples might include a stenographer's coffee break, a professor's detective story, or a factory worker's weekend in the woods. Such a concept furthers the philosophy of the work–recreation cycle which fosters the idea of the sanctity of work and sees the purpose of recreation as a reward for work or as a

preparation for work. Although recreation often provides renewal of spirit and energy to return to a job, those who do not work are in even greater need of finding the satisfactions of life in their leisure hours. Certainly, for many, work provides the great satisfactions and purposes of life; but in a world in which work hours are decreasing and leisure hours are increasing, the values of recreation that are totally unrelated to work are mounting.

Recreation as Sinful or Evil

The Puritan, who held that work and piety were synonymous, denounced any form of recreation as evil. Whatever was pleasurable had to be sinful. In the past, when the production of necessities was the primary concern of society, the idea of the sanctity of work was understandable. The Puritan ethic was as much an economic as a moral ideal. In today's economy, which demands discretionary time for the masses if production rates are not to outstrip the ability to consume, recreation must be both respectable and necessary.

Recreation Only as a Time-Filler

To justify recreation as a mere escape from boredom or as activity to fill empty hours is to demean seriously its possible values. Large monetary expenditures by government and individuals for recreation opportunities are convincing evidence that recreation experiences are more than something to do when you have nothing to do.

Recreation Only as a Means to an End

Youth agencies, religious organizations, and retirement communities often characterize recreation as a means to an end. It is true that the involvement in recreation can foster some of the personal development objectives of the youth agencies. Attractive recreation opportunities can entice the elderly into private retirement developments. The church or synagogue's new gymnasiums or theaters may keep the parish more involved in the church. Institutions that still proclaim recreation as a channel to reach some other goal deny the essence of the potential value of the experience itself. Values emerge from the total experience in recreation, not just from the activity. Recreation may quite possibly be a means to a social, personal, or health end, but the experience is at the same time an end in itself, with attendant value and worth to the participants.

Recreation and Work as Dichotomous

All recreation is not good. All work is not bad or repulsive. The extreme views are the Puritan idea of work as piety and fun as sinful and the notion that every experience that provides satisfaction or a sense of feeling good about yourself or the world should be labeled *recreation.* With the present trends in both work and recreation, the elements of each view seem to be permeating the other. We find work attitudes in the overcommitment of some people to their recreation choices. Many people find real enjoyment and satisfaction in their employment as evidenced by greater numbers in service professions and the attempts by employers to provide job enrichment.

Recreation as a Panacea for Social Ills

Recreation is sometimes thought of as being valuable chiefly because it may help solve such social problems as juvenile delinquency, civil unrest, and the protests of deprived segments of the society. There has been much discussion, with a lack of conclusive evidence, regarding the relationship between antisocial behavior and the lack of recreation opportunities. Much of what is termed *juvenile delinquency* is based on misdirected urges for

adventure and recognition that might be satisfied through exciting recreation experiences. The thrilling sharpening of the senses that comes from pitting one's skill and intelligence against an adversary seems to be at the bottom of at least some forms of delinquency. Similar excitation can be found in healthful recreation pursuits, such as skiing, sailing, camping, skydiving, and some organized sports and games. Institutions concerned with delinquency can well look to recreation for ways in which to satisfy the urges that, when uncontrolled, lead to destructive consequences.

Although recreation may help to prevent antisocial involvements, recreation is not a cure-all for unacceptable behavior. Park and recreation departments are responsible for providing well-rounded, satisfying experiences through which both children and adults may develop and remain emotionally and morally stable. The values of recreation are in the enrichment of life for the majority; deterring the minority from delinquency is an important, but secondary, contribution.

A Look at Theory

When one attempts to explore from a historical perspective the varied explanations for why people engage in recreation experiences, diverse terminologies again raise problems. The psychologists or philosophers who were responsible for early theories were primarily trying to answer the question, "Why do we play?" Later explanations by sociologists and recreation personnel have used the terms *leisure* and *recreation,* rather than *play,* in their works. The following brief explanations will, at best, be an introduction. Reducing each theory to a few comments does an injustice to the intent of the theory's author. More complete explanations for most of the descriptions found below are in the works of Sapora and Mitchell,[29] Kraus,[30] and Ellis.[31]

Early Explanations

Here are some of the early attempts to explain why we play or engage in recreation experiences.

Surplus-energy theory. Play is the aimless expenditure of exuberant energy. German Friedrich von Schiller's concept, later expanded by Herbert Spencer, explains play behavior as a needed outlet for energies not used in productive activity. We have energy left over and we are impelled to use it in play.

Recreation theory. Recreation is necessary to refresh one after labor. Lord Kames' idea, adopted by Lazarus in Germany, proposed that recreation has recuperative effects. The theory still holds some credence with those modern writers who define recreation's value narrowly as a means of retooling one's energies in order to do a better job. G. T. W. Patrick in the early twentieth century supported an extension of this theory as he observed recuperative effects of large-muscle play activities after extended periods of small-muscle or intellectual involvement.

Instinct-practice theory. Play is a preparation for adult life. Karl Groos' turn-of-the-century studies of the play of animals and humans were based on the idea that certain basic instincts were inherent and served as a motivation for play behavior. Practicing the behavior prepared the child for later adult responsibilities. The kitten's pouncing on a moving ball was interpreted as preparing it for food hunting in cathood. The prolonged period of childhood in humans as compared to that in other species was explained as their need for more extended preparation because of the complexity of human adult life.

Recapitulation theory. Play is the result of biologic inheritance. In play, the growing child relives a series of cultural epochs through which the human civilization has come. Confronted with a two-year-old's tantrum or the three-year-old's tendency to stray as far as possible in a given thirty seconds, parents are somewhat inclined to believe that there is a savage stage or a nomadic stage being repeated. However, research with twins has tended to prove that environment has somewhat more influence than does heredity on play choices and actions.

Catharsis theory. Play is a safety valve for pent-up emotions. If you consider yourself a pressure cooker, play represents the release valve which keeps you from "blowing your top." The theory has been traced as far back as Aristotle's support of play as a means of relief from emotional tensions. Later research, particularly on the effects of aggression as a catharsis, has had conflicting results. William Menninger lauded the benefits of recreation as healthful sublimation of frustration or aggression. The research of Sipes[32] and Smolev[33] seemed to indicate that aggressive activities may actually increase or beget aggression, rather than drain off aggressive tendencies.

Self-expression theory. In contrast to the theories just reviewed, the self-expression theory, advanced by Elmer Mitchell and Bernard Mason, was founded on the assumption that as active, dynamic human beings, people seek to express themselves. Play is one result of that expression. The theory then tries to identify factors that influence play behavior. The factors include: (1) one's physical or anatomic structure, how one is built; (2) one's degree of fitness at any given moment; and (3) one's psychological inclinations or predispositions, which in turn reflect the influences of his or her social environment, physical environs, habits and attitudes, and the role of basic psychological needs, which they term *universal wishes*. In addition, the authors include the compensatory aspect of play, in which blocked

or thwarted motives are successfully subli-
mated into available or acceptable behavior
through recreation. For instance, a person who
would like to pummel an irritating roommate
may instead use his energies in a more socially
acceptable game of tennis.

Later Ideas

Theories of the past two decades have
been defined, supported, or denied by specific
attempts to apply research techniques to segments of more generalized explanations. The
results are not conclusive and are sometimes
conflicting, but the following have evolved as
extensions or refutations of earlier explanations. Again, oversimplification, for purposes of brevity, narrows the thrust of the
ideas in each.

Compensation theory. Leisure prefer-
ences are selected in order to compensate for
the inability to satisfy basic human needs in
other life involvements. This explanation
closely approximates the compensatory phase
of the self-expression theory.

Spillover theory or familiarity theory.
We tend to choose leisure outlets that are familiar to us and thus provide less risk and more
chance for success. In relationship to work,
then, a person would tend to choose in leisure
those experiences approximating the satisfying aspects of work.

Psychoanalytic theories. In essence, the
various versions describe play as either a rear-
rangement of circumstances that have been
unpleasant, so as to minimize their importance, or a reenactment of the situation with
the individual's role reversed to control the unpleasantness. For example, a study of children
in Vermont who played school found that
children who did least well in real school were
frequently the teachers in the play schools.
(The inference was simple. The child teachers

didn't ask any questions they couldn't answer.)

Balance theory. We choose in recreation
those kinds of experiences that will lend balance to our lives. The balance can be physical,
psychological, or social. A person who lives
alone may seek social interaction in recreation;
a person who does demanding intellectual
work may choose physical activity to sustain
balance.

Arousal-seeking theory. Play is caused
by the "need to generate interactions with the
environment or self that elevate arousal (level
of interest or stimulation) towards the optimal
for the individual."[34]

Each theory has an element of truth, yet
none is inclusive. Research progress, though
considerably accelerated in the last few years,
has not isolated one best explanation. Perhaps
this situation is understandable in light of the
fact that terms such as *recreation, play,* and *leisure* have not yet been definitively described
and the research world has only recently felt
that such entities might, in truth, be important
to human life.

How Do We Make Our Leisure Choices?

What, then, does condition or influence
the choice of our leisure behavior? Kaplan has
done perhaps the most erudite overview of the
pertinent components.[35] The following are factors that have some bearing on how we choose
to spend our leisure and what choices we make
for our recreation:

Time—the amount, the size of the block of
time (three-day weekend, five-hour day,
flexible work time, three-week vacation),
the season, the time of day, what preceded
the choosing time, what follows

Pressure of relationships—family, religious affiliation, community or institutional commitments, friends, community mores, work environment, social and physical surroundings

Economic support—availability of finance for travel, private or commercial outlets, needed equipment

Past experiences with specific activities—expectations, standards, alternatives available, pleasurability of rewards

Availability of recreation programs—variety of choices, leadership, transportation, or accessories needed to participate

Availability of areas and facilities—social and physical environments in which to perform

One's basic physical and mental capabilities and acquired skills

One's own philosophy of the importance of leisure and recreation

Society's attitudes toward the value of specific pursuits

How will you spend your weekend? Who will influence your choices? What is available within your time, money, and mental or physical capabilities? Will you repeat a past experience? Will you willingly choose an experience not acceptable within the mores of your community?

Potential Values

What potential benefits can accrue to you or to society as a result of your recreation choices? If recreation is an end in itself, why is there need for any justification beyond the satisfaction of the participant? Philosophically, it is tempting to defend the idea that recreation is a personal involvement and is no one else's business. Pragmatically, from the point of view of social institutions that provide money and effort to make recreation opportunities available, we must interpret concomitant benefits as they relate to the value systems in our communities. What are some of the potential contributions to life satisfactions that occur as a result of recreation choices?

Individual Rewards

Which of the following have been influenced by your choice of leisure expression, your recreation choices?

Physical well-being. Research has given us ample proof of the benefits of physical exercise. In our push-button lives, when work and the demands of daily living make fewer contributions to muscle tone and physical fitness, sometimes the only motivation for healthful exercise comes from the much-publicized perils of obesity—or—the stimulation of an exciting recreation outlet which just happens to be beneficial in the "battle of the bulge."

Emotional health. Recreation makes a significant contribution to mental and emotional balance. Psychiatrists Alexander Reid Martin, Paul Haun, and Karl and William Menninger have been perhaps the earliest supporters of the value of recreation as a therapeutic tool. Chapter 13 expands this topic.

The quest for identity, commitment, or "a piece of the action." Peter Martin makes a forceful case for the use of leisure choices to develop identity in disoriented patients.[36] The retirement literature also supports the idea that when the work years are over, the retiree must "become" through his or her leisure pursuits. In a world of rising expectations, there seem to be fewer outlets in work for ego fulfillment, commitment, and a feeling of individual contribution. Such conditions too often stimulate the uncommitted and alienated of any age to turn to *any* cause as a means of creating impact, being heard, and searching for something that gives them a "piece of the action." Teenagers, disgruntled laborers, and octogenarians alike, each with a diminished role in society, seek satisfactions in leisure to restore their positive self-image.

Sense of community. West and Merriam's research supports the view that outdoor recreation activities may contribute to family cohesiveness.[37] Other studies testify to the role of recreation in social solidarity.[38]

Learning. Piaget and others have indicated the influence of play experiences in childhood learning,[39] but recreation programs in community centers and the new thrust of community education efforts attest to the potential in freely chosen recreation experiences for adults to learn language, handcraft skills, or the latest political theories.

Self-image, self-esteem, and self-fulfillment. The contributions of leisure pursuits to self-definition and status recognition have been supported in several studies,[40] yet Maslow seems to tie self-actualization only to work. "The only happy people I know are the ones who are working well at something they consider important. This is a universal truth for all my self-actualizing subjects."[41] How do we reconcile such statements with today's diminishing work opportunities? Must society come to accept that self-realization may be attained in outlets other than those normally designated as work in our society?

Personality development. In recreation experiences, when the tasks are freely chosen

and when the consequences of actions may be less serious, there is a chance to test ourselves. We may come to know the joys of viable human interchange or the unpleasantness of shirked responsibilities. It is not accidental that character-building agencies use recreation experiences as a major tool for attaining their objectives.

Social interaction and social integration. There is evidence of a narrowing gap in the recreation choices of different socioeconomic classes. At the campsite, listening to a concert in the park, and participating in adult softball or bowling leagues, social and economic classes intermingle. Federal support and private philanthropies have made experiences once available only to the economically blessed (sailing, tennis, golf, symphony, dance, theater) open to all those who can be enticed into participation. The teamwork and common goals required in a sport, dramatic production, or festival parade may promote better understanding and acceptance among different race, age, economic, social, or sex strata. Slavson maintains that play experiences are practice grounds for better democratic living.[42]

Adventure. The typical American has lost the frontier. The pioneers, dissatisfied with their situation, could move west and start anew in an unsettled land. Today America has erased most of its physical frontiers. Technology has increased the safety of our environment and has taken the risk and even the excitement of decision making out of our daily lives. But human beings still need the thrill of adventure. Some get it in roller coasters, and some seek the risk of exposing their intellectual talents in a language class or debating club. Others seek their "kicks" in drugs. Would more opportunities to "shoot the rapids" minimize the temptation to shoot heroin?

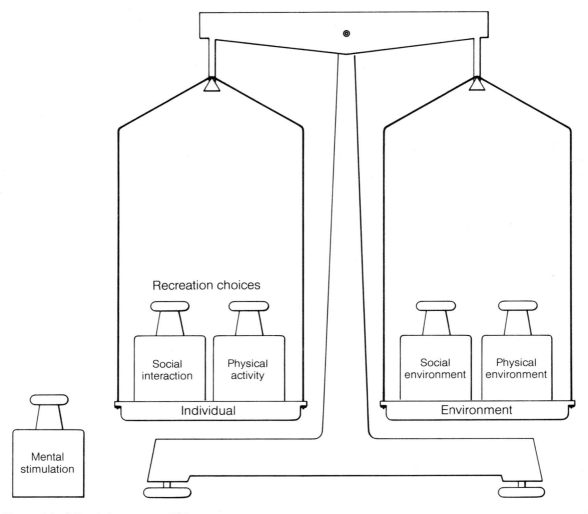

Figure 1.2. What balances your life?

The opportunity to find an acceptable balance. Perhaps the greatest value of recreation experiences is to make possible an acceptable balance in our lives. Imagine a scale such as the one in Figure 1.2. One side represents the individual, and the other side represents the environment, physical and social. Recreation may become the weights—the means to keep our lives in balance—not a perfect balance, for then we have inertia, but a swaying, dynamic balance that is acceptable to the individual. Let's take some illustrations:

Some social interaction to counteract the effects of transience caused by hypermobility.

A pinch of zest and risk taking for a routinized life—that disequilibrium that makes eventual stability like the satisfaction of coming home.

Solitude and a good book for the harried

Figure 1.3. Human interchange through recreation. Source: *Girl Scouts of the United States of America.*

homemaker or social involvement for the disengaged retiree.

Exhilarating physical exercise for the computer programmer or restful music or intellectual stimulation for the tired laborer.

A chance for decision making for the child or the adult who seems to be governed by others because of age, handicap, or economic or social status.

Community Rewards

Values derived by individuals may also benefit society, although, realistically, what the individual chooses as self-rewarding may be neither acceptable nor good for the community. There are, however, outcomes from recreation opportunities from which the entire community seems to gain.

A good case can be made for the economic assets. Chapter 3 will more carefully explore the impact of recreation on the economy. Additional rewards may come in attraction and retention of business and industry, in community attractiveness for tax-paying residents, in civic spirit and solidarity, and in safety both for individuals and for the environment.

Can We Change the Work Ethic?

The work ethic has been deeply ingrained in our culture, so deeply, in fact, that our residential location, our life-style, our pattern for social interaction, our economic well-being, our choices of recreation experiences, and even the education of our children have been dominated by what we did for a living. Technological, cultural, and social changes are making inroads on that dominance. Facility of transportation and communication allows us to live farther away from our work, but that same technology in the future may bring our work to wherever we choose to live. The only reason for leaving the comfort of our residences may be the exciting beckoning of a physical, social, or intellectual recreation experience.

What is work and how did it get such a hold on our psyche? Definitions of work as paid employment are common, although they ignore the large amounts of obligated effort put forth by today's homemakers.

How did we make the cycle from the Greek attitude of work as drudgery, heavy-heartedness, and exhaustion to the still-prevalent (though somewhat eroding) Protestant ethic, which invested work with meanings of goodness, morality, status, and consequent related dignity? Is the latter ethic still defensible when large segments of the population, through no fault of their own perhaps, are denied work opportunities, which seem to be so closely linked to self-worth, social status, and a sense of identity?

Note the change of emphasis pointed up in

Dynamics of Change: Although the Declaration of Independence mentioned the "pursuit of happiness" and the Constitution made no mention of work, 180 years later UNESCO'S Universal Declaration of Human Rights included the phrase, "Everyone has the right to work."[43] Will that right be attainable in the foreseeable future? Is it now? Unemployment percentages, inner-city unrest, and social protests of minority groups indicate that it is not. We profess one philosophy of the goodness of life and we create an environment in which that kind of goodness is impractical, if not impossible.

Daniel Yankelovich characterized the present work ethic by four themes that link with people's life values and satisfactions.[44]

1. The *good provider* theme, by which the breadwinner shows his masculinity. That theme has been considerably weakened as women have, from individual choice or economic necessity, moved into the world of paid employment.

2. The *independence* theme, through which an individual achieves autonomy and enough money to assure some freedom and control of destiny. Much of that freedom, even what one can do with monetary reward, has been reduced by government regulations and political decisions. Almost no one has the luxury of being his or her own person, even in leisure.

3. The *success* theme—hard work leads to success. Although social prestige is often linked to size of paycheck, the underlying assumption that the pinnacle is achieved primarily through hard work is not necessarily valid in our present labor environments.

4. The *self-respect* theme, which credits

hard work of any type with dignity—a means of maintaining self-image.

Yankelovich's research was done in the 1960s, but it is still valid, particularly in the independence and self-respect themes. The HEW Task Force on *Work in America* stressed the social status and self-esteem functions of work as it described the individual's personal need to perform services that are consequential and meaningful.[45]

Toward a Leisure Ethic

Is it possible to attain a leisure ethic in our generation, an ethic that would accept leisure, not as a replacement for work, but as a viable, acceptable alternative or complement to work? Certain social, technological, cultural, and attitudinal changes on the horizon may be instrumental in further eroding the dominance of the work ethic and effecting a leisure ethic. Can we put work and leisure on a horizontal value plane as equal contributors to the quality of life without a debit-credit or a mandatory interdependent relationship? Here are some changes in situation or attitude that are pertinent to the task:

Rising expectations, civil unrest, and citizen participation.   There is a spreading rise in expectations that one author calls the "psychology of entitlement." More segments of the population are demanding their "rights." Women, minorities, the aged, the poor, the disadvantaged, the disabled, and others are organizing to improve their psychological as well as physical environment. The voices are heard not only in the work arenas but in the leisure sphere as well.

The word *discrimination* has been applied to a variety of causes, from "everyone should swim free," to girls in Little League, to the Gray Panther liberation movement. The mass media have made the civil rights message so penetrating that a mentally retarded child in Florida faced her playschool teacher with the reaction, "I won't play today. I don't have to. I've got my rights, you know."

An erosion of materialism as an indicator of success.   Economist Robert Theobald insists that if we all *can* buy Cadillacs or live in mansions, there will be no significance attached to the good neighborhood or the prestigious "wheels." The "small is beautiful" syndrome brought on by depleting energy resources and diminishing natural resources seems to have given us additional impetus to turn from materialism as a symbol of "having made it" in today's society. Thus, work that brings affluence to buy bigness loses some of its power. The counter cultures of the 1960s helped accentuate a disdain for possessions as evidence of the good life. In contrast, many who lived through the Great Depression of the 1930s have not yet embraced these concepts, and there are some evidences that the youth of today in a tighter economy are also swerving from idealism to realism in their life-styles.

Willingness to risk economic security in order to improve the quality of life.   The dropouts from society who lived off the land or from handouts gave way to populations of "straight" individuals who have made a conscious decision that financial success is less important than better working or living conditions. Yankelovich indicated that "a substantial forty percent of adults say that they are now prepared to take certain risks with their own and the nation's economic security for the sake of enhancing the quality of life."[46]

Union workers strike for vacation benefits and recreation lounges as well as for higher pay and reduced working hours. Middle-aged men and women leave job security to look for more fulfilling employment. Women revolt against mundane housekeeping chores. Routine and dull jobs go begging while potential workers prefer welfare to drudgery. Larger portions of the work force take early retirement if it is available, and the notion of work as the reason for being is losing acceptance.

A widening acceptance of alternative channels for education. There is evidence that the traditional public schools are broadening their scope to include education for leisure. This subject is dealt with more fully in Chapter 7. In addition, there are alternative schools, freedom schools, community education and career education opportunities, external degrees, and continuing education offerings that emphasize leisure skills in enticing the dropout, the aged who never started, or the person who needs greater flexibility to pursue an educational dream.

Concern for the quality of the environment. *The Environmental Handbook,* prepared for the first National Environmental Teach-In, began with these words, "In 1968, the United States woke up to the fact that the richest country in the world is in the middle of an environmental crisis."[47] This observation accentuated the views of many recreation conservationists who had been concerned but less vocal about the ecological scene for several decades. In the 1970s the quality of the environment became a political and social issue of some magnitude.

Almost every aspect of environmental deterioration has relevance for the recreation needs of society. Air pollution in Los Angeles has at times closed the playgrounds. The murky clouds over many industrial cities make sun bathing or star gazing impossible. Water pollution diminishes opportunity for, and enjoyment of, fishing or boating. Noise pollution reduces our hearing capabilities and creates tension and frustration. Devastation of

the land by bulldozers upsets our watersheds. Our place to play is diminished as precious open space is used for skyscrapers and air strips, or parks are devastated by misuse or overuse.

The changing nature of work; the effects of cybernation. A century ago our nation devoted itself essentially to handcraft manufacturing methods or to agriculture. The worker could visualize the desired product and had considerable input into the channel for attaining it. Today, in an industrialized society, the scientific, technological, and electronic revolutions have helped transfer routine and physically exhausting drudgery from human hands and minds to machines. In the transition, the meaningful "whole" of work, creative and stimulating both physically and mentally, was frequently lost on the assembly line, which increased production but diminished the personal creative expression and/or physical exercise in labor. For a vast body of our population, even in service professions, there are dehumanizing effects of technological advances.

In spite of the efforts to increase job satisfaction with flextime (individuals arrange their own working hours), job enrichment, and team decision making, work falls short of being the sole or even the major contributor to an individual's self-image. Mee indicated, "There are strong signals indicating that the priority facing managers during the remainder of the century will be the human aspects of work rather than productivity."[48] Recreation for many must become the primary source for creative self-realization as well as for organic balance. Leisure may move from the former concept of a "reward for having worked" to a *partner* for work in developing a world that is good for people as well as for economic productivity.

Do we need to define a new philosophy of the meaning of life in a world in which leisure abounds and work opportunities diminish? According to psychiatrist Erich Fromm, the salvation of any people rests with their ability to desire those things that environmental factors require. So it is with acceptance and use of an abundance of leisure. A culture that has not learned to honor what it is actually committed to produce creates an uneasy population.

Our present increase in leisure forces leisure to be more than restoration or re-creation. Riesman predicted, "There may come a point where additional increments of leisure will prove more stultifying than satisfying to a mass of men who are incapable of absorbing any more."[49] That time has come for some segments of our population—the retired aged, the school dropout, the military veteran without a job, the unemployable, and the unprepared recipient of the thirteen-week sabbatical vacation in industry. Theobald warned, "The human muscle began to be disengaged from the productive process almost 100 years ago. Now the human nervous system is being disengaged."[50] We succumbed first to machines, then to computers. If two percent of the population by virtue of technological advances can produce enough for all of us to survive, then we shall become a nation of consumers; and the very real task of education must be to teach intelligent consumership of increased leisure, an arena not yet pursued by Betty Furness or Ralph Nader.

If we are to learn to live in a world we have helped to create, then we must accept the respectability of leisure itself so that free time may bring anticipation, not guilt; and recreation choices in that free time may be socially beneficial and individually rewarding. We need a closer link with formal education institutions to foster not only the teaching of leisure skills but also the changing of attitudes. The person who is no longer a member of the work force will have little peace of mind or sense of humanness until society comes to believe that what one does in leisure may be as significant and rewarding a contribution as what one does in work.

The Case for Recreation

How does recreation mesh with the leisure ethic? What positive role can it play in a world of increasing free time, changing mores, psychological uncertainties, and fast-paced living? In spite of its many potential values, recreation is not a cure-all for individual trauma or community ills. It is not a substitute for work, family, faith, or any other social institution. Recreation is a part of a whole.

The case can be made, however, for recreation as a dynamic force to allow people to really live, not just exist, in the complexity of today's society. Several factors focus sharply on the need for increased and innovative recreation outlets.

Increased Leisure

The twelve-hour day and the six-day week of a few generations ago have given way to the five- to eight-hour day, the three-, four-, or five-day week, paid vacations of from two to six weeks, and the thirteen-week sabbatical vacation. Predictions for the future indicate a work-year cut to 1,100 hours with four-day weeks and at least thirteen weeks of vacation. Leisure will come in larger amounts, which will condition its use. Such increased leisure has necessitated a change in the philosophy that work, of itself, is the real meaning of life.

Changing Home Life and Life-Styles

Work and play in early America centered in and around the home. All members of the family had many responsibilities; and when home chores were done, the children played near home. Although the home is still the basic institution in society, many modern conditions have weakened its influence. There is more time for recreation, yet there are fewer opportunities for obtaining it around the home and thus a greater necessity for seeking it elsewhere.

Population Factors Affecting Recreation

The growth of population has resulted in a change in the way people live. From a nation of fewer than four million people in 1790, we have grown to 216 million in 1977. The 1970 census cataloged a density of fifty-seven persons per square mile as compared with 4.5 in 1790. In areas like Harlem, with high population densities, living situations tend to become highly explosive. Whereas in the early days of our country every child might fish, hunt, and roam the woods freely, today, opportunities for such pastimes are restricted. It is now necessary for society, through government or other means, to set aside lands for recreation; yet with each passing year, intensifying population pressures make such lands more difficult to reserve.

If present trends continue, the bulk of our population will cluster increasingly in metropolitan sections. A change in recreation habits must necessarily follow. Recreation requiring space must give way to other forms of recreation, or else society must provide the space needed.

Cultural uniformity throughout the country has been accelerated through schools, newspapers, magazines, movies, radio, and television. Demands for recreation throughout the nation are likewise becoming more similar—subject, of course, to variations in climate, geographic factors, and the cultural patterns of some minorities. Recreation outlets must still provide for differences not only in ethnic groups, but also in age, sex, and disability.

Increased Income and Mobility

Recent years have brought higher incomes and higher purchasing power for most American people. Better health, increased vitality, and greater opportunities for education have accompanied the rise in income. When income rises above that needed for subsistence, there is more money to spend for recreation. Commercial recreation has grown in quantity and variety, and people have been able and willing to pay for it.

Good roads, automobiles, and rapid public transportation, accompanied by high incomes, have made the American people mobile and have placed within reach many recreation areas formerly of difficult access. Guaranteed annual income and raised floors of welfare may further increase appetites for recreation. But energy resource depletion may restrict those appetites.

Urbanization

At the time of the Declaration of Independence, only about 2.5 percent of the American people lived in cities of more than 2,500 population. Predictions for the year 2000 indicate that ninety percent of Americans will reside in urban areas.

As a result of the mechanization of agriculture, farms are larger and fewer individuals are needed to produce food, fibers, and lumber. The movement from country to city and the resultant change in living and working habits have had significant impacts on recreation. Commercial recreation has grown up in urban areas to meet the needs of city dwellers, and community recreation has had its greatest growth in cities. Coexisting with today's urban trend and somewhat counterbalancing it is the movement toward the suburbs, where families may have homes of their own with lawns and gardens and where the recreation pattern may differ considerably from that of the city dwellers.

Figure 1.4. Art is recreation for both creator and viewer. Sculpture by Robert Indiana, reproduced by courtesy of the Indianapolis Museum of Art.

The abandonment by the middle class of the city for the less dense suburb has left the inner city, in many instances, in a state of decay. The aged, the poor, and the educationally deprived form a poor tax base. Rising expectations of the poor, coupled with diminishing opportunities in both education and recreation, have erupted in riots, seemingly senseless destruction, and a determination to change the status quo.

The loss of space for recreation has sparked the creation of vest-pocket parks and mobile units to serve those who live in impacted areas; but in most large metropolitan areas the supply has not kept up with the ever more violent demand.

These factors, coupled with evidences of civil unrest, changing educational systems, and the effects of cybernation on the work scene, present a new perspective for the park and recreation movement.

The Present Challenge

In the present world, if recreation is to meet the potential values described for it, those who take the responsibility for individual and societal welfare through park and recreation choices have at least five important tasks.

1. The development of a value system

that will allow society to accept the dignity and worth of what an individual does in leisure not as a substitute for work, but on a par with work. Since the historical work ethic is deeply ingrained, this task will probably be the most difficult.

2. The development of skills, understandings, and appreciations that will promote leisure literacy and allow individuals a broader spectrum of leisure choices.

3. The development of leisure tastes and the practical experience of making decisions in leisure so that leisure choices will enhance, not deteriorate, the individual, the society, and the environment.

4. The availability of diverse program offerings. If an individual has limited selections, there is little chance of attaining broad perspectives.

5. The watchdogging of physical environments. If the agencies responsible for recreation experiences do not get involved as a community makes decisions that destroy or pollute natural resources, we will lose the places in which to make our recreation choices.

Thus, the park and recreation professional not only must be involved in the tasks of providing recreation outlets and maintaining areas and facilities, but also must deal with education for leisure decision making, interpretation of the value and worth of the opportunities recreation offers, and intervention as the community moves with social and political changes that are pertinent to human welfare.

The emerging central focus in life is the degree of humanism we may achieve. In spite of active programs of job enrichment, the work arena has not made tremendous strides toward minimizing the tensions of today's stressful existence. The challenge of the park and recreation profession may well be to afford individuals their real chance to feel human.

Responsibility for recreation services has been assumed by various commercial, educational, religious, and social organizations—public, private, and voluntary. This book is concerned with the challenges faced, the opportunities offered, and the responsibilities accepted or rejected by agencies within the community who are involved in recreation experiences. It is the story of community recreation.

Selected References

Anderson, Nels. *Man s Work and Leisure.* Leiden, the Netherlands: E. J. Brill, 1974.

Bellak, Leopold. *Overload, The New Human Condition.* New York: Human Sciences Press, 1975.

Berry, Adrian. *The Next Ten Thousand Years; A Vision of Man's Future in the Universe.* New York: Saturday Review Press, distributed by E. P. Dutton and Company, 1974.

Best, Fred, ed. *The Future of Work.* Englewood Cliffs, N.J.: Prentice-Hall, Inc., 1973.

Brightbill, Charles Kestner. *Man and Leisure, A Philosophy of Recreation.* Englewood Cliffs, N.J.: Prentice-Hall, Inc., 1962.

————, and Mobley, Tony A. *Education for Leisure-Centered Living.* New York: John Wiley & Sons, 1977.

Cheek, Neil H., Jr.; Field, Donald R.; and Burdge, Rabel J. *Leisure and Recreation Places.* Ann Arbor: Ann Arbor Science Publishers, Inc., 1976.

Cheek, Neil H., and Burch, William R., Jr. *The Social Organization of Leisure in Human Society.* New York: Harper & Row, 1976.

Craig, Timothy, ed. *The Humanistic and Mental Health Aspects of Sports, Exercise and Recreation.* Chicago: American Medical Association, 1976.

Dechert, Charles R., ed. *The Social Impact of Cybernetics.* New York: Simon and Schuster, 1967.

De Grazia, Sebastian. *Of Time, Work, and Leisure.* New York: Twentieth Century Fund, 1962.

Dunnette, Marvin D. *Work and Nonwork in the Year 2001.* Monterey, California: Brooks/Cole Publishing Company, 1973.

Ellis, Michael J. *Why People Play.* Englewood Cliffs, N.J.: Prentice-Hall, Inc., 1973.

Fabun, Don. *Dimensions of Change.* Beverly Hills, California: Glencoe Press, 1971.

Galbraith, John Kenneth. *The Age of Uncertainty.* Boston: Houghton-Mifflin Company, 1977.

Gordon, L., and Klopov, E. *Man After Work.* Moscow: Progress Publishers, 1975.

Haworth, J. T., and Smith, M. A., eds. *Work and Leisure: An Interdisciplinary Study in Theory, Education and Planning.* Princeton, N.J.: Princeton Book Company, Publishers, 1976.

Huizinga, Johan. *Homo Ludens: A Study of the Play Element in Culture.* London: Maurice Temple Smith Ltd., 1970.

Kaplan, Max. *Leisure: Theory and Policy.* New York: John Wiley & Sons, Inc., 1975.

———, and Bosserman, Phillip, eds. *Technology, Human Values and Leisure.* Nashville, Tennessee: Abingdon Press, 1971.

Levy, Joseph. *Play Behavior.* New York: John Wiley & Sons, 1978.

Linder, Staffan Burenstam. *The Harried Leisure Class.* New York: Columbia University Press, 1970.

Lundborg, Louis B. *Future Without Shock.* New York: W. W. Norton & Company, Inc., 1974.

Michael, Donald N., ed. *The Future Society.* Chicago: Aldine Publishing Company, 1970.

Muller, Herbert J. *Uses of the Future.* Bloomington: Indiana University Press, 1974.

Murphy, James F., ed. *Concepts of Leisure, Philosophical Implications.* Englewood Cliffs, N.J.: Prentice-Hall, Inc., 1974.

Neulinger, John. *The Psychology of Leisure; Research Approaches to the Study of Leisure.* Springfield, Ill.: Charles C. Thomas, Publisher, 1974.

Parker, Stanley Robert. *The Future of Work and Leisure.* New York: Praeger Publishers, 1971.

Pieper, Josef. *Leisure, The Basis of Culture.* New York: New American Library, 1963.

Rosen, Stephen. *Future Facts.* New York: Simon and Schuster, 1976.

Rosow, Jerome M., ed. *The Worker and the Job: Coping With Change.* Englewood Cliffs, N.J.: Prentice-Hall, Inc., 1974.

Sessoms, Hanson Douglas; Meyer, Harold D.; and Brightbill, Charles K. *Leisure Services: The Organized Recreation and Park System.* Englewood Cliffs, N.J.: Prentice-Hall, Inc., 1975.

Spekke, Andrew A., ed. *The Next 25 Years: Crisis & Opportunity.* Washington, D.C.: World Future Society, 1975.

Staley, Edwin J., and Miller, Norman P., eds. *Leisure and the Quality of Life; A New Ethic for the 70's and Beyond.* Washington, D.C.: American Association for Health, Physical Education and Recreation, 1972.

Tilgher, Adriano. *Homo Faber: Work Through the Ages*. Chicago: Henry Regnery Co., 1965.

Toffler, Alvin, ed. *The Futurists*. New York: Random House, 1972.

Van der Smissen, Betty, comp. *Indicators of Change in the Recreation Environment: A National Research Symposium*. State College, Pa.: The Pennsylvania State University, 1975.

Veblen, Thorstein. *The Theory of the Leisure Class*. Boston: Houghton Mifflin, 1973.

Weiskopf, Donald C. *A Guide to Recreation and Leisure*. Boston: Allyn and Bacon, Inc., 1975.

W. E. Upjohn Institute for Employment Research. *Work in America*, Report of a Special Task Force to the Secretary of Health, Education, and Welfare. Cambridge: MIT Press, 1973.

2
Recreation—Past and Present

What's past is prologue. A civilization knows where it is going only when it understands where it has been.

Alexander Winston

Whether we choose to agree with the poet Shelley, who said history is "a cyclic poem written by time upon the memories of man," or with the more earthy definition of Oscar Wilde, who said "history is merely gossip," we cannot ignore the fact that our future is inextricably tied to the past. In the field of recreation and parks, this is particularly meaningful; the evidence is overwhelming.

Prehistoric Era

Life in prehistoric times was a struggle for mere physical existence. In fact, the problems of daily survival are still a major concern in many parts of the world today. Yet examples of the continuing search for a more enjoyable life through forms of recreation are evident. Wherever or whenever humans have existed, they have found some time for recreation.

We can only surmise what types of activities occupied humans before recorded history; but by studying primitive cultures of the world, we strongly assume that children's play was essentially what it has always been. Children frolicked in streams and lakes; climbed trees; played with pets; planned mock battles against the enemy, both man and beast; and learned the art of survival—practically everything they did focused on the essential needs for food and shelter. Times of rest for prehistoric peoples were filled with sewing; stringing

beads; amusing themselves with songs, chants, and dances; and telling stories and myths around the campfire. In times of plenty, feasts and ceremonies lasted for days or months. Men perhaps enjoyed gambling, with the antecedent of knucklebones, and caring for the equipment needed for survival (much as modern people do today with their fishing, camping, and hunting gear—but without the urgency of survival at stake).

In primitive cultures, the lines between work and play were not sharply drawn; and, as conditions fluctuated, various activities changed from labor to pleasurable leisure pursuits. Many present-day recreation activities resemble those that had utilitarian or survival value somewhere in the history of the human race. Outstanding examples are the food-gathering activities such as fishing, hunting, gardening, and herb collecting. Few, indeed, are the recreation outlets today that had no utilitarian origins: skiing, boating, walking, swimming, horseback riding, combative activities, and arts and crafts such as pottery, weaving, and leather work—all were useful to primitive life.

Egyptian reliefs give evidence of interests in hunting, spearing, wrestling, and fencing. Kite flying provided a dual pleasure for the artistic talent and the physical energy of the Chinese and other Asiatic peoples 4,000 years before the Christian era. Expression of emotions in movement, or the interpretation of an occupation, formed dance patterns that were highly developed in early societies. Clay modeling and basket weaving were done for pleasure or practical purposes. Contests of speed and endurance were the early Persians' use of recreation to train their warriors, and the Japanese board game of "Go" existed 2,200 years before the birth of Christ. Singing, dancing, arts and crafts, sports and games, social activities, story telling, drama, music, and nature activities have given recreation satisfaction throughout the ages, affecting and being affected by the life of the times.

Cultural, social, and economic changes have always influenced the breadth and scope of recreation. As permanent communities were established, time for work and time for recreation became more clearly delineated, and the leisure classes emerged.

The Classical Age

From warlike Sparta to cultural Athens to the deteriorating Roman Empire, the importance of recreation pursuits was recognized, but the objectives varied. In the Golden Age of Pericles, the fifth century B.C., the Athenian democracy was dedicated to the idea that to live was not enough; to *live well* was the goal. "In corpore sano mens sana" (a sound mind in a sound body) was the harmonious balance expected from leisure. The cost of this leisure was high, however; even Aristotle condoned the enslavement of a large part of the population to allow leisure for a few. Attention to games in early Greek civilization constituted part of the education for the leisure class. The Athenian ideal integrated art, literature, philosophy, music, and sport into a unified concept. The concept of leisure as an opportunity for cultural development is evident in the Greek word for leisure, "schole," from which our English word "school" derived.

The Spartan civilization and its Roman counterpart viewed play also as a means of education, but its purpose was to physically and emotionally condition the people for the exigencies of war. Such a philosophy necessitated a heavy emphasis on physical feats of daring, accuracy, and endurance as recreation pursuits. Thus, both the military and the artistic attitudes toward play existed during the classical age.

Recreation Activities

Greek children must have led enchanted lives. They had terra-cotta rattles and figurines, marbles, hoops, balls, dolls, and kites to play with and engaged in tug-of-war, hopscotch, and other games similar to those found in any modern kindergarten. During these early years, the mother was in charge. It was a time of peaceful play, free from worry, grief, or pain.

At age seven, the boys and girls were separated. The girls stayed home with their mothers, while the boys attended private schools in which they studied music, gymnastics, oratory, drama, poetry, and politics. Their Roman counterparts were drilled in contests of speed and endurance and exposed to a scouting education comparable to the modern scouting program for Explorers.

The early Olympic games, the most celebrated of the Greek festivals, included foot races, wrestling, boxing, chariot racing, and oratory. The origins of the Olympic games are obscure. When the games were first recorded in 776 B.C., they were already firmly established as religious-athletic events. They reached their height in the fifth and fourth centuries B.C., when a victory at Olympia was one of the greatest honors attainable. Later, professionalization and bribery became rampant and the games declined, particularly after the Roman conquest of Greece. They were abolished in A.D. 394.

Other Greek festivals included symposia

and contests in singing, riddle solving, and drinking. Sixth century B.C. Panathenaic games included recitations, chariot racing, musical contests, and rowing. The Roman Ludi, or public games, provided spectator sports for scores of Roman citizens, who gathered to view the Ludus Troiae (a sham fight on horseback), chariot racing, gymnastic contests, gladiatorial combats, or military reviews. Both Greeks and Romans engaged in cockfighting, games of gambling, and board games of all kinds.

Facilities

The large stadiums and gymnasiums in Greece housed athletic activities, whereas open-air amphitheaters afforded areas for music, dance, and dramatic festivals. Friends of Plato bought a suburban recreation grove called Academus, where Plato founded an intellectual academy dedicated to "the means of living a life of philosophic leisure." There, cultural pursuits were directed for more than 900 years. The Academy fostered intellectual and aesthetic interests, whereas the Forum, or public square, provided an opportunity for public discussion. The public baths offered a setting for diversion, relaxation, or business transactions.

The Middle Ages

The "Middle Ages" is a modern term for the thousand years after the fall of the Roman Empire (A.D. 476–1492) when Europe was held together primarily by the unifying influence of the church. Many references have been made to the influence of excesses of leisure upon the downfall of Roman civilization. The new age, permeated by religion, turned its back on many of the play activities that had been a part of the social and cultural life of the classical period. The "good life" was the ascetic life of abstinence; worldly pleasures were not goals for this existence. Life was a preparation for rewards beyond.

Medieval civilization was characterized by class distinctions. Amounts of leisure and the media for its expenditure varied, as would be expected, with social status. The lords and nobility, between battles, had ample leisure. The serfs had little time for revelry after the fields were tilled, the animals cared for, and the grain pounded. The strong religious attitude of the church dominated choices of recreation activity, with a noticeable abstinence from the physical games and contests or arena spectator activities of classical times. Such authority had intermittent influences down through the Puritan period in American life.

That there existed during the Middle Ages a native vigor ready to burst the bonds of oppression is obvious, human nature being what it is; but the massive power of the church, sustained by the ignorance and superstition of the people, hung like a conscience over any who openly sought to make more pleasant the life that was "only a prelude to an infinitely worse or infinitely better future."

Recreation Activities

Outlets for recreation were varied, dependent primarily upon class distinctions, and were frequently related to the occupation at hand. The nobility, when not actively engaged in warfare for protection of home and country, played at mock battles in the jousts and tournaments of the lists. Women found pleasure in such domestic skills as embroidery or in watching the tournaments. The male child spent the first twenty-one years of life training for his role of protector. His play activities consisted of riding, hawking, lancing, singing, reading, and jousting, to perfect his ability as a chivalrous knight. His female counterpart learned music, embroidery, and other crafts. Indoor sports of the nobility included feasting, drinking, gambling, board games, and entertainment by the popular jester or the traveling bard of the day.

The poverty-stricken peasants also indulged in activities that related to their daily tasks. Communal dances portrayed their harvesting labors or mocked the life of their manor lords. Quarter-staff tilting or jousting was a favorite pastime for those who watched the flocks. Fairs, pageants, and racing; bowling, cockfighting, and archery contests kept the serfs outdoors where their work was.

Those involved in crafts or guilds shared recreation as they shared their work, owing allegiance to neither the lords nor the serfs. Fairs in which their work was displayed were popular. Singing work songs to glorify or to stimulate progress on their craft formed a bond in leisure and work hours. Possibly one of the most significant contributions of the guilds to the literature and entertainment of the day was the development of the guild carts, which moved through the streets to play mystery and miracle dramas on street corners. Play has been a theme of artists through all the ages (see Figure 2.1).

The church, too, added to cultural outlets in art, literature, and drama, although it did not condone the athletic contests and spectator sports of the day.

Facilities

Lists, the structures in which jousts and tournaments kept the nobility playing at warfare, were descendants of the Roman arena and forerunners of the modern football stadium. In the lists, spectators thrilled to dual contests or mass combat.

The guild wagons, built by craftsmen when the church moved the drama from the altar and the churchyard, formed the first traveling theaters. These wagons allowed persons standing on neighborhood street corners to witness the Corpus Christi plays or more banal offerings.

The Renaissance

The "Renaissance" is a term used to designate a well-known but indefinite space of time between the Middle Ages and the modern world (A.D. 1300–1600). The spirit of the age was questing and inquiring. The spread of popular education and the relief from the oppression of church authority brought about a revival of learning, a renewed interest in classical arts and activities, and a new philosophy of the meaning of life. In direct contrast to the former period, life during the Renaissance was lived, as Huizinga indicates, as a "game of artistic perfection."[1] The rules of the game were many and varied. The old identification with caste diminished, and new social, economic, and cultural strata were formed. The aristocracy and the bourgeoisie alike play-acted their leisure.

Recreation Activities

The formal court balls and parties of the aristocracy were mimicked in lesser style by the rising middle class. Fairs, exhibitions, banquets, operas, and theater were prevalent and popular; falconry, cockfighting, and sword fighting were as frequent, if less sanctioned, sports. Hunting and gardening occupied the leisure of adults, while children's games showed less emphasis on knightly combat.

Insecurity and instability characterized the age, but the relinquishing of static codes of living brought with it an inquiring spirit, which investigated the worth of pleasure and enjoyment. Play activities were finally looked upon as essential to the physical health of individuals and later took their place as aids to liberal education itself.

Facilities

Theaters, courtly ballrooms, arenas for fencing or other contests, and formal parks and gardens were outstanding in the Renaissance era. Open areas for festivals and fairs were also prevalent. Game preserves offered hunting paradises for the aristocrats and the adventure of poaching for the poor. Beer gardens and coffeehouses served as social recreation haunts or literary discussion centers for many classes.

Colonial America

While Europe floundered in its search for a balance of security and meaning for life, the exacting demands of existence in colonial America (A.D. 1492–1775) left little time for pleasure-seeking. The need to survive put a high premium on labor for all. Sustaining life in the wilderness was serious business, but it had its gratifications. People found their rewards in their own resourcefulness and skill.

Figure 2.1. Play as an artistic theme. Source: *Photo reproduced by courtesy of Museo del Prado.*

Making a living required long hours, but it offered satisfactions in social, creative, and physical achievements that are today often associated with recreation.

Because survival depended upon hard work, the early settlers in both Virginia and New England enforced rules against idleness. With the rigid zeal of their Puritan inheritance, New England laws prohibited all forms of amusement or misuse of time long after economic necessity for such abstinence had vanished. Thus, the earliest forms of recreation legislation were prohibitive rather than permissive. Governor Endicott of the Massachusetts Bay Colony decreed that "no person shall spend his time unprofitably," whereas the Virginia Assembly, early in the seventeenth century, issued the edict that persons found idle could be bound over for work. To be idle was to be evil, a concept so deeply instilled that its message has haunted the nation into the present time. The result of such a philosophy was not to eliminate recreation but to surround it with a sense of guilt.

The hardy pioneers, as human beings, needed release from their arduous labor, and their behavior often did not mirror their laws. Communal work projects were an excuse for merrymaking. The rewards of wrestling, dancing, and games after the tasks were completed were motivation for the work of barn raising, husking bees, and similar activities. Hunting and fishing were sanctioned; theaters were prohibited. As late as 1750, attempts to put on a play in Boston created a major riot.

Pleasure on a severe winter night confined itself to the social recreation enjoyed after the wedding or interment of friends or relatives. Many people turned in desperation to taverns and liquor for want of more wholesome recreation opportunities. Growing interest in card playing, dancing, bear baiting, and gambling produced more prohibitive laws and accompanying punishments. Only folk music and singing seemed to escape legal wrath. The wealthy of the South engaged in a renewal of English games and sports, enjoyed riding to the hounds, horse racing, and cockfighting. The Dutch settling in New York indulged in bowling, ice skating, and ice carnivals, and all the colonists played shuffleboard, participated in shooting matches, foot races, and marching reviews.

The eighteenth century brought economic prosperity, an increase in the population of coastal cities, and a widening of the western frontiers. Leisure had expanded for all parts of the country, but the slavery in the South gave the plantation owners the reputation for the most pleasure-loving society America had ever known. As increasing migration brought large numbers of non-Puritans to New England, rebellion against restraints began to mount. By the end of the eighteenth century, dancing classes in New York, the social gaieties of the Boston aristocracy, and the foxhunts and theatricals of Virginia were being viewed with less jaundiced eyes by a population that had become more economically prosperous and more prone to accept the inevitability of some recreation pursuits. Even Boston was beginning to remove the ban on theater, which New York and the South had enjoyed regularly during the last half of the eighteenth century.

Recreation in a New Nation

At the close of the Revolutionary War, the trans-Appalachian country was still largely unsettled, and the westward movement dominated the thinking of the American people. In spite of the growth of cities along the eastern seaboard and the development of urban culture, most American people still lived on farms or in small communities. (The first U.S. decennial census in 1790 revealed that ninety-five percent of Americans lived in rural places.) Recreation consisted principally of the simple pleasures of rural life—country dancing, social gatherings, mutual work projects, local fairs, hunting, and fishing. Recreation in frontier towns took on a rowdy character. People in the unrestricted, uninhibited frontier indulged in wolf drives, brutal ring hunts, shooting matches, logrolling, dancing, tomahawk throwing, gambling, and heavy drinking. Interspersed with these were occasional religious revivals, camp meetings, and shivarees, which helped to fill the recreational and emotional needs of the frontier folk.

In the slowly expanding cities on the eastern coast, people began to show a new dimension in their recreation choices. Gradually they threw off the Puritan cloak of inhibition and replaced the rural pleasures with commercial amusements and spectator activities. There was a shift from active to passive diversions with an emphasis on minstrel shows, circuses, amusement parks, and other forms of commercial recreation.

Cultural Awakening

A vogue for self-improvement, affecting all classes, set in during the 1830s and 1840s. In 1826, the National Museum paved the way for cultural interests. Public lectures were popular and drew large crowds. Despite the disapproval of religious leaders, the theater was growing. Farce and variety shows, circuses, and exhibitions mingled with stagings of the legitimate theater. Lyceum courses and, later, the chautauquas provided music and drama as well as lectures. The singing classes and dancing assemblies gave way to musical concerts and grand balls.

Early Park Development

The city park is a relatively recent phenomenon in America. Its beginnings are obscure, with some scholars agreeing that the plaza in St. Augustine, set aside in 1565, should be considered the first park in the continental United States. Others refer to the Boston Commons, established in 1634, as the first park. The Commons was originally set aside, in the English tradition, as a communal pasture. However, with the growth of the city and the loss of adjacent open space, the Commons came to be a recreation ground. The area had to wait until 1728 for the city to begin to develop its potential as a viable city park.

Although the Massachusetts Bay Colony created an ordinance opening bodies of water over ten acres to the public in 1640, it was 1850 before municipalities, in Massachusetts or anywhere, could legally form park or recreation departments. Since 1850, virtually every state has enacted legislation allowing local units of government to establish park and/or recreation departments.

The need for open space and park and recreation facilities was first felt in the larger cities. Changing life-styles, intensified by colonization of the eastern seaboard and the beginnings of the Industrial Revolution, were bringing rapid changes to thousands of new urbanites. As early as 1682, William Penn set aside five squares in the plan for Philadelphia, and in 1733 General James Oglethorpe designed public gardens, squares, and open spaces in Savannah, Georgia.

New York City and Mayor Ambrose C. Kingsland deserve credit for creating the 850-acre Central Park, beginning in 1853. Central Park was the example for future park expansion throughout the country. Frederick Law Olmsted, the first superintendent of Central Park, collaborated with Calvert Vaux to win the competition for the park design. Their plan, called "Greensward," was given the top prize and a cash award of $2,000. The designers, who envisioned a future in which New York's populace would be cramped for space, attempted to supply the joys of the country in the midst of the city. Central Park is still noted for those scenic and recreation objectives.

During the last half of the nineteenth century, the federal government became active in the park movement. Although a portion of Hot

---

The Civil War and Central Park

During the Civil War, the city of New York was compelled to suspend all construction projects in the interest of the war except the development of Central Park. The park commissioners declared that it would be uneco-nomical to suspend construction, since many structures were half completed and suspension would be wasteful. Their point of view carried, and work was not suspended.*

*Paraphrased from Charles E. Doell and Gerald B. Fitzgerald, "A Brief History of Parks and Recreation in the United States" (Chicago: The Athletic Institute, 1954), p. 29.

Springs National Park in Arkansas had been reserved for the public in 1832 because of the medicinal qualities of its water, it was not recognized as a national park until early in the twentieth century. The federal government's acquisition of Yellowstone Park in 1872, with the intention to preserve it for the enjoyment of future generations, marked the real beginnings of the national park movement.

In addition to those contributors to the early park movement already mentioned, no section on early park development would be complete without recalling the names of Major Pierre Charles L'Enfant, the planner of Washington, D.C.; J. Weidenmann, a Swiss who developed the Hartford Park System; H. W. S. Cleveland, who worked in Brooklyn, Minneapolis, and Chicago; John McLaren, who developed San Francisco's Golden Gate Park; and finally Charles Eliot, landscape architect who pioneered the Boston Metropolitan Park Commission and who had been an apprentice to Frederick Law Olmsted.

School and Recreation

Several other developments influencing recreation were taking place during the nineteenth century. This was the period of the rise of universal public education. Education's scope broadened and thus widened the horizons of individuals and increased their wants.

The use of leisure and the development of new skills began to interest more and more people.

As early as 1821, the Salem Latin School opened an outdoor gymnasium with crude equipment and no supervision. In the ten years that followed, outdoor gymnasiums were constructed in many of the eastern colleges (Harvard, Yale, Williams, Amherst, Brown), which introduced physical training into the curriculum. Many athletic and sporting clubs were organized. Subsequent developments were not forthcoming until health consciousness after the Civil War again focused attention on the school's role in physical health.

Rise of Voluntary Agencies

The nineteenth century saw the development of certain voluntary agencies, which took some responsibility for providing wholesome recreation opportunities and education for leisure use. In 1851, the Young Men's Christian Association was introduced in Boston from England; the national YMCA was formed in 1866. By 1860, the first Boys' Club had been established in Hartford to attempt to counteract the ills of the city. The first Young Women's Christian Association was established in Boston in 1866, although the national YWCA was not founded until early in the twentieth century.

Growing Interest in the Natural Environment

These years may be thought of as the golden age of the great naturalists. There were new species to be discovered and described as the land was explored and settled. Expeditions moving west contributed greatly to scientific knowledge and laid the cornerstone for the outdoor recreation movement of today. Educators, too, were beginning to see the values in outdoor education and recreation. In 1861, Frederick William Gunn of the Connecticut Gunnery School for Boys took his entire student body on a two-week camping trip for what is generally considered the first camping experience of its kind. Some twenty years later, Ernest Balch started the first private camp, and the YMCA initiated a camping program in its organization.

By 1867, concern for misuse of natural resources brought about the organization of commissions in Wisconsin and in Michigan to study conservation practices. Similar commissions followed in states on the eastern coast. By 1871, the Bureau of Fisheries had been set up in the Department of Commerce, and some fourteen years later, the Biological Survey became a part of the Department of Agriculture. In 1875, the establishment of the American Forestry Association helped unify the movement to save the forests. The end of the century saw the setting aside in the West of the first federal forest reserve. In a country that had been blessed with natural resources, there appeared to be a growing realization of their worth and of the need to take steps to preserve them for future generations.

Beginnings of Organized Sports

During the early years of the nineteenth century, organized sports were in their infancy, although the interest of schools in physical activities had awakened some realization of the need for such activities during after-school hours. Early participation in gymnastic games, tennis, foot races, and other rural pleasures had given way to spectator amusements, and the country's leaders began to lament the lost values. The social elite further spurred the revival of active sports by making them fashionable in the post–Civil War period, when America was beginning to worry about the physical fitness of its populace. "A basic need for outdoor exercise to conserve national health and the sponsorship of social leaders thus served in large measure to break down the barriers that had formerly stood in the way of the development of organized sports."[2]

The beginnings of modern baseball are sometimes traced to the 1839 diamond in Cooperstown, New York, or to the business and professional men's Knickerbocker Club, whose members played together in the Elysian Fields of Hoboken, New Jersey, in 1842. Baseball slowly spread until the public gave its stamp of approval by actually paying admission to watch the ball games. In 1869, when the Cincinnati Red Stockings were hired for a country-wide tour, professional baseball was born. Although the colleges took little active leadership in the growth of other sport activities, they introduced and developed football. The first intercollegiate game was played between Princeton and Rutgers in 1869. The sport aroused spectator interest from the start. The need for an indoor activity to replace the fair-weather enthusiasm for football and baseball prompted James A. Naismith, a YMCA leader, to develop basketball in 1891.

Skating, bicycling, tennis, and croquet grew in favor; but it was organized baseball, football, and basketball that stimulated the expansion that made attention to sports a significant development of the age. In 1885, new emphasis was placed on physical activities with the formation of the American Association for the Advancement of Physical Education, now the American Alliance for Health, Physical Education, and Recreation.

In 1896, 1,502 years after the close of the

ancient Olympic games, the modern Olympics opened in Athens to a crowd of 50,000 people. Held every four years since then, with the exception of war years, at locations scattered throughout the world, the Olympics today comprise a tremendous number of events, ranging from the traditional pentathlon to newer games such as basketball and water polo. With the aid of modern television, spectators number around 800 million persons.

End of a Century

Growth of urban areas (with accompanying social problems), increasing leisure, flourishing commercial recreation ventures of questionable reputation, and gross exploitation of the nation's natural resources characterized the later years of the nineteenth century, at the same time giving birth to today's emphasis on educating the public regarding the importance of provisions for acceptable recreation choices. Several innovations in organized recreation appeared before the turn of the century.

Boston Sandgardens

Most historians of the recreation movement give credit to the sandgardens of Boston as the true beginnings of the recreation movement. Dr. Marie Zakresewska, while summering in Berlin, noticed that youngsters were playing with heaps of sand in the public parks. At her instigation, the Massachusetts Emergency and Hygiene Association started a similar experiment in Boston in 1885. Whereas the Berlin project had been supervised by the police, the Boston sandpiles were supervised by interested volunteers until 1887, when people were paid for such duty. Similar activities extended to other Boston areas; and the idea was taken up by other cities, including

Philadelphia, Milwaukee, Pittsburgh, Denver, Minneapolis, New York, Chicago, Providence, and Baltimore.

Settlement Houses and Model Playgrounds

Voluntary agencies played a part in the onward movement of recreation as the Neighborhood Guild in New York City introduced settlement houses in 1886. Three years later, Jane Addams and Ellen Gates Starr established Hull House to serve Chicago's needs (see Figure 2.2). Addams later secured enough land around Hull House to start the first model playground in 1892. Similar play areas were provided within the next six years at the Northwestern University and the University of Chicago settlement houses. The pattern of apparatus play, sports activities for older youth, and supervised low organized games was a blueprint for similar efforts in other large cities. Early objectives of the settlement houses to meet the needs of the poor were soon broadened to include education, health, and recreation.

Parks and Recreation—An Unavoidable Merger

Although Washington Park had been opened in Chicago as early as 1876, it was little used for recreation purposes for another ten to fifteen years. In 1888, New York passed a law that appropriated $1 million a year for acquisition of land for parks and playgrounds. In 1889, the Boston Park Department converted ten acres along the Charles River into an outdoor gymnasium known as the Charlesbank Outdoor Gym. Here men, boys, and, later, women could wade, bathe, row, or use apparatus under supervision. Similar neighborhood parks with scenic and functional intentions were created in New York and Louisville.

Figure 2.2. Jane Addams and the original Hull House.

Such dual purpose joined the park and playground concepts.

Chicago's South Park playground system, initiated in the early years of the twentieth century, made a tremendous impact on the growth of the recreation movement. With their carefully planned fieldhouses and their spacious outdoor areas, the playgrounds represented the first acceptance of public responsibility for indoor and outdoor recreation facilities, varied interest programs, recreation outlets for all ages, year-round activities, and

leadership. The success of the small parks in meeting neighborhood needs was an inspiration, and the long-range thinking of the fieldhouse planners in providing structures adaptable to a variety of program types has stood the test of time.

In 1898, the New England Association of Park Superintendents was organized in Boston. It changed its name in 1904 to the American Association of Park Superintendents, and finally it became the American Institute of Park Executives in 1921. This organization provided outstanding leadership to the park and recreation management field and merged with the National Recreation and Park Association in 1965. Many of today's park and recreation leaders grew up in close affiliation with this landmark association.

The Recreation Movement

Isolated individual developments in recreation were made throughout the nineteenth century. It remained for the pressures of a changing industrialized society to force individual leaders, municipalities, and private and public agencies to unify those efforts. Neumeyer and Neumeyer described these social movements as follows:

> Analyzed from the point of view of development, social movements normally involve a number of more or less distinct aspects or phases, even though they overlap and tend to merge into each other. (1) Movements grow out of unsatisfactory and disorganized social situations causing social unrest and concerns. (2) The situation must be defined by competent observers as constituting a social problem and requiring adjustment. . . . (3) There must be a conscious effort to meet the situation. . . . A movement involves a type of social change that is produced by deliberate action designed to improve a given condition. (4) To become a movement, a conscious effort or event must be followed by others connected by a cause-and-effect relation and extended in time and space. . . . (5) The setting up of objectives and standards is evidence of maturation of a movement. . . . (6) The final phase is the gradual realization of the objectives as disclosed through the stages of its development, transitions in its policies and activities, and trends in its organization.[3]

The movement starts, then, with a felt need. Let us explore those events, conditions, and feelings that created an expressed need for better recreation opportunities and resulted in

an organization of the movement. Many of the conditions that gave rise to the modern recreation movement had their origins in the last half of the nineteenth century. The birth of the Playground Association of America in 1906 is most often named as the true beginning of the organized movement. Why did it occur? What happened before 1906 to alert people to the need?

Depletion of natural resources. At the close of the Civil War, the westward trend continued. In the East, practically all land had been turned over to private interests, although in the West there still remained vast areas of public domain that were to be held as a reserve. Characteristic of this period was the thoughtless exploitation of natural resources. Forests, grasslands, wildlife, and water resources were laid waste with a prodigal hand. Too late the cost of this careless policy was made apparent, and today America is still paying the cost of its early extravagance.

Effects of the Industrial Revolution. The Industrial Revolution, which changed America from an agrarian to an industrial society, developed in the early 1800s and mushroomed in the late years of the nineteenth century. The rise of industry and the development of machine power brought drastic changes in the life of the people. As the machine replaced manpower, work hours were decreased and new leisure became a right of all. The specialization of the assembly line and improved transportation made manufactured goods accessible to most people, and handcraft began to disappear as a means of livelihood. With the mechanized, mass-production approach to industry, the worker was deprived of the pride in achievement that was possible in earlier craft. A distinct need for outlets that would exercise the worker's creative energies and provide a sense of achievement and accomplishment became pressing for people who worked monotonous hours in tedious repetition of a small task. Industrialization had a further debilitating effect on workers who were once independent and self-reliant but now had to depend on an employer's paycheck and government services for their livelihood.

Urbanization. With the increase in industry came a decided shift to urban living, with accompanying problems in choice of, opportunity for, and space for recreation activity. Whereas in 1850 only 85 cities boasted populations of more than 8,000, by the end of the century almost 600 cities had more than 8,000 people and 28 cities had populations exceeding 100,000. Factories encroached on residential sections, and slum areas grew. With overcrowded conditions in the urban areas, the streets became the playgrounds. Organized efforts had to be made to set aside space for recreation opportunities.

Rise in crime and delinquency. The tremendous increase in the incidence of crime and delinquency in the latter years of the nineteenth century prompted such men as Jacob Riis in New York City to stimulate anti-slum campaigns to afford healthier living conditions, which he hoped would counteract the formation of delinquent gangs.

Increase in population. The steady growth in population demanded better organization for work, for living conditions, and for play. The Industrial Revolution, with its accompanying rural-to-urban population shift, had found the municipalities unprepared for servicing the needs of the influx of humanity.

Rise in the incidence of mental illness. It is not surprising that the social hygiene and mental hygiene movements in the United States evolved at approximately the same time and for some of the same reasons as did the recreation movement. The increase in the numbers of patients who needed psychiatric care gave ample proof of new tensions in the changing world. Recognition of the worth of recreation to relieve tension and serve basic psychological needs was late in coming but has blossomed into one of the strongest reasons for recreation programming.

Unsavory commercial recreation. Unwholesome commercial recreation opportunities fostered the need for their replacement by more truly recreative activities. The dime novels, pool halls, billiard rooms, dime museums with freak attractions, spicy nickelodeons (the forerunner of today's cinema), shooting galleries, and saloons were easily accessible to all. Vaudeville attractions, which combined melodrama and burlesque, gave the legitimate theater heavy competition. Even the theaters sold plenty of liquor on the premises. Horse racing, professional baseball, and prize fighting were popular, with heavy concentration on the gambling aspects of such spectator sports. Dulles points to the low status of commercial fare: "In 1898, the police of Gotham listed ninety-nine amusement resorts, including saloons with music and entertainment, on the Bowery alone. They classed only fourteen of them as respectable."[4]

Increasing mobility of the population. Although boat and train excursions had been available, at the end of the century the electric trolley and the motor car forecast the greater mobility of citizens and created a demand for recreation areas to which they could travel on weekends and holidays. The motor vehicle was soon to afford another means of spectator amusement; the first motor-vehicle race was run in Chicago in 1895. Two of six gasoline-driven cars finished a fifty-two-mile course, and the sport of auto racing was born.

Need for unification of individual efforts in recreation. The early, scattered attempts of various cities to provide space, leadership, facilities, or methods of control for recreation finally alerted those involved with such problems to the need for communication. The early Boston sandgardens; the model playgrounds of Chicago and New York; the provision of summer playgrounds in Philadelphia; the small-park systems in New York and Chicago; the initiation of Public Athletic Leagues by Luther Gulick in New York; the provision of a Board of Playground Commissioners as the first separate department of municipal recreation in Los Angeles in 1904; the use of school buildings as community centers in New York City, Rochester, and Pittsburgh; and early community recreation efforts in Oakland, Baltimore, Washington, and other cities all pointed to the urgency for some means of interrelating individual efforts and concerns and communicating information gained from experiences in different places. A plan for such interrelation was formulated when a few dedicated and visionary individuals, who "defined the situation as constituting a social problem requiring readjustment," met in Washington, D.C., in 1906 to plan what was to become the first true attempt at organization of the American recreation movement.

The Playground Association of America

The need for a social movement had been felt. The work of the Washington group in 1906, which culminated in the organization of the Playground Association of America, marked the "conscious effort to meet the situation." The organization of the Playground Association of America (renamed in 1911 the Playground and Recreation Association of America, again renamed the National Recreation Association, and merged in 1965 with other organizations to form the National Recreation and Park Association) is perhaps the

most significant event in the history of the recreation movement. With President Theodore Roosevelt as honorary president, Dr. Luther Gulick as president, and Dr. Henry S. Curtis as secretary and acting treasurer, the members of the association settled themselves to the following purposes expressed in their constitution: "To collect and distribute knowledge of and promote interest in playgrounds and athletic fields throughout the country, to seek to further the establishment of playgrounds and athletic fields in all communities and directed play in connection with schools."[5]

In June 1906, the association undertook the publication of *Playground* magazine, now *Parks and Recreation,* in an effort to help disseminate information. The following year, the first national meeting of recreation workers was held in Chicago to exchange ideas and information. This event marked the beginning of the annual conference, which today is called the National Recreation and Park Congress. Records show that 336 cities had organized programs by 1910. Joseph Lee, commonly known as the "father of the American playground," had been chosen president of the association; a normal course in play had been published; Lebert Weir had been named the first field representative; and Howard Braucher had taken his place as the first paid secretary (see Figure 2.3).

Since the formal organization of the movement, progress had been made in development of park and playground facilities, in improvements in the education of park and recreation leaders, in the contribution of youth-serving agencies and school-oriented recreation, in acceptance by municipal and federal governments as well as by private agencies of the responsibility for park and recreation opportunities, and in a concern for standards for facilities and leadership. Developments in the movement have continued, with a yearly meeting for evaluation of the present needs and concerns.

Figure 2.3. Lebert Weir, Joseph Lee, and Howard Braucher—pioneers in organized recreation.

Developments to Mid-Century

A Decade of Growth

In the second decade of the twentieth century, the disappearance of nineteenth-century attitudes toward leisure brought general agreement that park and recreation programs were necessary for all. In 1910, the Boy Scouts of America was incorporated. The earlier youth agencies, Sons of Daniel Boone and Ernest Thompson Seton's Woodcraft Indians, were absorbed into the new organization. In the same year the Camp Fire Girls was started through the efforts of Dr. and Mrs. Luther Gulick. The year 1912 brought the introduction of the Girl Guides, later to become the Girl Scouts of America. Each organization played a part in the recreation education of youth.

Increase in public responsibility. The federal government assumed its role in recreation in several ways during this decade. In 1912, the Children's Bureau surveyed recreation opportunities for youngsters; the Smith-Lever Act of Congress in 1914 called for demonstration and instruction in agriculture and home economics for those not attending college and made possible many recreation opportunities for rural residents. In 1916, the U.S. Congress formed the Bureau of National Parks, which grew into the present National Park Service.

The worthy use of leisure principle. Schools were exploring better means of providing recreation programs and facilities. In 1911 the National Education Association approved the use of school buildings for recreation services and social centers. A Russell Sage Foundation survey in 1914 found fifty schools giving courses for play leaders. The same year saw the inclusion of intramural sports programs in many schools, and during the next two years experimental play schools were initiated at the University of California and the University of Wisconsin. Laws were passed in many of the states mandating physical-training classes and areas for recreation in school systems. Possibly the most significant contribution of education professionals during the decade was the inclusion of the "worthy use of leisure" as an important objective for education in the National Education Association's Seven Cardinal Principles of 1918.

The 1913 yearbook of *Playground* magazine indicated that municipalities were continuing to build the playground systems peculiar to our country. The May 1915 issue listed eighty-three cities in eighteen different states that reported full-time recreation workers. Surveys by the Playground and Recreation Association and the Russell Sage Foundation reported a need for increased opportunities in music, drama, and the arts.[6] Social centers, settlement houses, and community centers had increased in such numbers as to stimulate the need for the formation of a National Community Center Association in 1916. Given impetus by both public and private agencies, the camping movement that had started in the previous century made great strides.

Before 1900, only a small percentage of the American people had vacations, and pleasure travel was extremely limited. After little more than one decade (1910–20), there were more than two million automobiles, which diminished the isolation of the country, changed the recreation habits of the populace, and literally altered the face of the United States as highways crisscrossed the land. The tourist and vacation industry got its start.

Effects of World War I. Before the entrance of the United States into World War I, there had been a heavy emphasis on decentralized neighborhood-center activities. As war camps flooded nearby communities with homesick soldiers, the physical and psychological strains on individuals and communities were great, and military statistics shocked the nation by declaring one third of the draftees physically unfit for active duty. The Playground and Recreation Association, at the request of the War Department, mobilized recreation resources into the War Camp Community Service, which initiated more than 600

community recreation programs near military centers and another fifty in strategic industrial centers. Although the organization was dissolved shortly after the fighting stopped, the value of recreation to the community had been clearly demonstrated.

The Predepression Years

The decade after World War I, a period of prosperity, brought a marked increase in appreciation of the importance of recreation. An upsurge of interest in recreation facilities, both private and public, was demonstrated by the prevalence of new parks, community houses, swimming pools, dance halls, beaches, golf courses, picnic areas, skating rinks, and bowling alleys. In 1921, the National Conference of State Parks was organized to further the state park movement. Activity fads swept the country, and commercial recreation mushroomed with the increased purchasing power of the population.

Henry Ford, with the assembly-line production of cars, gave easier transportation to the masses, and the tourist industry flourished. As early as 1922, motion pictures established a self-censorship to improve their services to the public and eliminate adverse criticism. With the advent of the "talkies" by the end of the decade, the movie theaters gained tremendous popularity for all ages, with weekly attendance figures estimated at 110 million in 1929.[7] Radio hams became engrossed in their new hobby, and the listening audience found effortless recreation at home with their wireless sets.

With the new appreciation of the assets that recreation could bring came greater adult participation. Spectator sports increased in popularity, and women began to join in sport activities without fear of reproof. There were publications on sports, art, drama, and music.

Use of leisure became a concern for research, and President Hoover's Research Committee on Social Trends in 1929 gave special consideration to recreation. Earlier interest in the development of outdoor recreation had prompted the National Conference of Outdoor Recreation, called by President Coolidge in 1924. The awareness of the need for special training for recreation leaders occasioned the start of the one-year graduate course, in 1926, by the National Recreation Association. Known as the National Recreation School, it carried the principal responsibility for educating recreation executives. By 1927, thirty-two states had passed laws for use of school buildings as community centers; and by the end of the decade, half the states had passed legislation to provide for extended recreation opportunities at the municipal level.

The Depression Years

One result of the depression of the 1930s was an increased emphasis on recreation. The modified workweek, shortened in order to spread available work among more people, gave more leisure. Commercial recreation programs closed for lack of business, since people no longer could pay the admission price for bowling, dancing, theater, and spectator events. A heavier demand was placed on facilities and programs of voluntary and municipal agencies, which were unable to handle the increased needs. This dilemma caused federal agencies to try to take up the slack, giving the recreation movement more impetus. Alerted to the seriousness of the situation, the administration furnished two different kinds of aid. First, through efforts to give jobs to those without work, the government started construction projects that involved building and extending recreation areas and facilities. Second, it provided finances for employing recreation leaders to initiate and supervise programs.

The blue eagle of the New Deal brought the "parade of the alphabet"; the Federal Emergency Relief Administration (FERA), the National Youth Administration (NYA), the Works Progress Administration (WPA), and the Civilian Conservation Corps (CCC) served to further the cause of recreation in a period of enforced leisure, at the same time aiding in the rehabilitation of the country. The FERA, WPA, and CCC gave people jobs and were responsible for the construction and improvement of centers, parks, picnic areas, roads, trails, and similar facilities. The WPA and the NYA hired recreation leaders and held institutes for educating volunteers and recreation workers.

Federal funds that were poured into state park and forest systems caused a great spurt in state outdoor recreation developments. Forty-six Recreation Demonstration Areas were initiated under the National Park Service in 1936 and were later turned over to federal and state agencies. Recognition of the state's function in providing areas and facilities to protect and improve game resources brought an increase in hunting and fishing.

The Federal Arts Project of the WPA stimulated interest in music, painting, theater, writing, and historical research. The Federal Theater Project became an active force in the theatrical world. At a time when the audiences in commercial theaters were dwindling because of forced economies, some 500,000 amateurs were acting on stages in community theaters. Thousands more were introduced to the joys of participating in choruses and orchestras or listening to public concerts.

The fads of the 1920s subsided and gave way to less costly pastimes such as contract bridge, backyard gardening, inexpensive hobbies, Chinese checkers, and bingo. The Big Apple and the Lambeth Walk had replaced the Charleston for the dance enthusiasts. Americans were still spending five percent of their total income on travel and vacationing.

The effects of the depression colored the recreation picture during the 1930s; but there were other significant events, which also had an impact on the forward push of the recreation profession. The White House Conference, called by President Hoover in 1930, firmly established through its Children's Charter that the American child could expect places and rights to play as a deserved heritage.

In 1933, the American Library Association included recreation in its three-point program. The American Physical Education Association adopted as one of its principles the "promotion of play and recreation as aspects of fine living." The International Recreation Department of the UAW-CIO, organized in 1937, emphasized the acceptance of employee recreation as part of the labor union's concern.

Perhaps most significant in the development of the recreation profession was the recognition on the part of colleges and universities that recreation is a profession that demands special education. The first College Conference on Training Recreation Leaders, sponsored by the University of Minnesota and the Recreation Division of the WPA, was held in 1937.

During the same year, at the request of Howard Braucher (then executive secretary of the National Recreation Association), a small group of recreation leaders assembled to discuss the need for a national organization for full-time professionals in recreation. The following October, the Society of Recreation Workers of America, which became the American Recreation Society and later merged in the National Recreation and Park Association, was formed in Atlantic City. It attracted over 500 charter members its first year.

The World War II Years

Duplicating and extending the concern that it had felt for its soldiers in World War I, the U.S. government renewed emphasis on recreation and its values on both the fighting and the home fronts during World War II. Statistics of the numbers of draftees judged unfit for service spurred interest in promoting better mental as well as physical health. The USO, American Red Cross, Army Special Services Division, the Welfare and Recreation Section of the Bureau of Naval Personnel, and the Recreation Service of the Marine Corps promoted programs on the battlefront, in the rest centers, in the hospitals, and in the camps. Their main concerns were relieving tensions of war, bolstering morale, and decreasing the psychological impact of the separation from home.

The United Service Organizations incorporated in 1941. They consisted of six agencies (Jewish Welfare Board, Salvation Army, Catholic Community Services, YMCA, YWCA, and the National Travelers' Aid), whose purpose was to serve the leisure needs of the armed services in community settings and to provide recreation for industrial workers engaged in the war effort. USO community centers enlisted thousands of volunteers for their drop-in centers, in which a lonesome or bored soldier might find food, dancing, a good book, or simply some friendly conversation.

Heavy demands were placed upon the recreation profession when the armed services alone needed some 12,500 recreation directors. The profession did not have adequately educated leaders, and soldiers' stories filtered back, telling of overemphasis on sports, lack of imagination in programming, a dearth of cultural opportunities, and other deficiencies. Yet there were some excellent experiences as evidenced by the 1951 report of the President's Committee on Religion and Welfare in Armed Services, a study of special services, which credited recreation with "shaping character, promoting national understanding and support of Armed Forces, and increasing efficiency of job performance."

American Red Cross services were carried to every part of the globe occupied by U.S. troops. On the home front, the American Junior Red Cross filled a desire on the part of teenagers to help with the war effort. Some seventeen million members produced articles for army recreation rooms.

Other significant progress occurred during the war years. The year 1941 saw industry taking a responsibility in recreation as it organized the National Industrial Recreation Association. The Federal Interagency Committee was formed in 1946 to coordinate the efforts of federal government organizations that relate to recreation.

The Federal Security Agency (now the Department of Health, Education, and Welfare), initiated in 1939 to "promote social and economic security, educational opportunity, and the health of the citizens of the nation," operated through its Community War Services program. It employed consultants for recreation programming and helped set up 250 to 300 new community programs. The Federal Works Agency made funds available for construction and operation of child-care centers and recreation centers. Through funds provided by the Lanham Act, the FWA took over some of the recreation functions of the defunct WPA.

Increased war tensions and the restlessness and uncertainty of the times created a soaring rate of delinquency among children and youth, which stimulated the Conference of the Children's Bureau, in 1943, to concentrate on prevention of this social ill. Lack of gasoline for travel necessitated a return to neighborhood activities. Teen centers, neighborhood adult programs, victory gardens, and increased industrial recreation opportunities flourished.

The consolidation of the Los Angeles administration into a Park and Recreation Department was the start of a series of similar community actions. At the state level, three states (North Carolina, Vermont, and California) had established state commissions of recreation.

The 1948 Jackson's Mills Conference and the 1950 Pere Marquette Conference evidenced the concern for better preparation of professionals at both undergraduate and graduate levels.

The war years had initiated and instigated many community programs. They had created an environment in which development of programs could be made with people who had seen the need for such efforts. More tangible evidence of the dying away of nineteenth-century attitudes came with the introduction of living war memorials. In place of the monuments in the square or the towering obelisks offered in memory of the dead of previous wars, swimming pools, civic centers, parks, picnic areas, and playgrounds are today's evidence of the respect communities have paid to the heroes of World War II.

Mid-Century to Present

The early 1950s were a time of dramatic change in America. The population was beginning to explode, new schools were under construction, people were on the move, and they had more disposable income and discretionary time than ever before. It was during this period that shortages of housing in the urban areas and the desire for breathing space forced thousands of families to move to the suburbs. The resulting demand for municipal services of all types, including parks and recreation, caused severe budget strains.

Upsurge in Outdoor Interests

Outdoor recreation burgeoned in the 1950s. The demand for recreation lands and facilities, combined with increasing deterioration of the environment and diminishing land resources, led to innovations through which the federal government could provide more space and improve environmental quality.

Through "Mission 66" (1956–66) of the National Park Service and "Operation Outdoors" of the U.S. Forest Service, facilities for visitors to national parks and forests were rehabilitated and expanded, but they still fell short of the demand. The results of a report on outdoor needs and interests initiated in 1958 were presented to Congress by the Outdoor Recreation Resources Review Commission. The Bureau of Outdoor Recreation, changed to the Heritage Conservation Recreation Service (HCRS) in 1978, was created to implement its recommendations. Ironically, this report omitted urban problems and children under 12 years.

The Land and Water Conservation Fund, created in 1964 to provide federal aid in outdoor recreation to states and local communities, had far-reaching effects. Because obtaining these funds required comprehensive planning by participating units of government, the fund became a tremendous spur to planning, particularly near urban centers. Within the next few years, every state had prepared acceptable plans; cities and counties that had never before explored their outdoor recreation potentials did so. The monetary impact of this program is particularly significant since it is a matching fund, with state and local units paying half the cost of the outdoor orientated capital improvements. During 1977–81, the federal government was to double and then triple the funds.

Other memorable government actions included the Open Space Program of the Department of Housing and Urban Development, begun in 1961, through which funds may be granted to communities for park and recreation sites; the establishment of a unified wilderness system in 1964; the Federal Project Recreation Act of 1965, which makes recreation co-equal with other purposes for which federal water-resource projects may be developed; the 1966 Historic Preservation Act; and the creation of a Wild and Scenic Rivers system and a National System of Recreational and Scenic Trails in 1968. Special cabinet-level councils concerned with water and air pollution, natural beauty, and recreation were organized, including the Council on Recreation and Natural Beauty set up in 1966 and the En-

vironmental Quality Council established in 1969.

In 1973 the Department of Interior produced a nationwide outdoor recreation plan called "Outdoor Recreation—A Legacy for America." It emphasized planning for people and called for enhancing the quality of American life by assuring opportunities for outdoor recreation in the city as well as in rural areas, for the disadvantaged as well as for the advantaged, for the young, the old, and the handicapped.

In 1976 Congress mandated the Secretary of Interior to submit a comprehensive review and report on the needs, problems, and opportunities associated with urban recreation in highly populated regions, including the resources potentially available for meeting such needs. This report will have considerable effect on the quality of urban recreation during the late 1970s and 1980s.

Concern for Fitness

The decade of the 1950s saw new concern for the emphasis on mental and physical fitness. With the unveiling of the Kraus-Weber tests for muscular strength and flexibility, which tended to prove American youths physically inferior to their European counterparts, national interest was centered on finding ways to correct this condition.

Interest in fitness has remained high since then. The National Collegiate Athletic Association, the Lifetime Sports Foundation, the Amateur Athletic Union, and the American Alliance for Health, Physical Education, and Recreation are active in promoting fitness programs. President Eisenhower initiated the President's Council on Youth Fitness and each succeeding President has supported the Fitness Council and active sports involvement. The phenomenal increase in the numbers of people participating in exercise programs, health clubs, diets, jogging, tennis, swimming, bicycling, backpacking, and many other activities is evidence that fun and fitness have become integral parts of our culture.

White House Conferences

The 1960 White House Conference on Children and Youth marked the golden anniversary of the first such conference and chose as its theme the slogan "For each child an opportunity for a creative life in freedom and dignity." The 1970 White House Conference on Children focused on the need for federal protection of children, and the 1971 White House Conference on Youth allowed youth themselves to spell out their concerns.

The first National Conference on Aging took place in 1950 and was initiated by the Federal Security Administrator in the Truman Administration to explore the growing problems of the aging. Two other conferences (the Conference of State Commissions on Aging in 1952 and the Federal-State Conference on Aging in 1956) preceded the first White House Conference on Aging held in Washington in January 1961. A group dealing with free-time activities acted upon state recommendations that pertained to recreation, voluntary services, and citizen participation. The nation again turned its attention to the challenge facing the aged at the White House Conference on the Aged and Aging in 1971.

In 1977, the first White House Conference on the Handicapped was held. The White House Conference on Conservation (1962) and the White House Conference on Natural Beauty (1964) focused national attention on concerns pertinent to the responsibilities of the recreation profession.

Increased Emphasis on Performing Arts

The 1958 act of Congress that made possible the National Cultural Center for the Performing Arts is evidence of the increased national impetus given to the performing arts as leisure outlets. Later renamed the John F. Kennedy Center for the Performing Arts, the $66 million complex, dedicated in 1964 and opened in 1971, has two theaters, a symphony hall, and a hall for opera, ballet, and musical comedy. In 1965, a bill was passed creating the National Foundation on the Arts and the Humanities, thus authorizing some federal subsidy of cultural and artistic activities. Lincoln Center in New York continues to expand, although financial bases for opera, symphony concerts, and other productions have been less than optimal.

Progress in Professional Education

Curriculums in professional preparation have expanded rapidly. Two-year curriculums in junior colleges and community colleges have added the associate degree program to the four-year undergraduate degrees and the master's and doctor's degrees. Specializations have arisen in therapeutic recreation, college student-union management, municipal park and recreation administration, wildlife management, natural resource management, park management, industrial and commercial recreation, and other areas.

Professional committees and conferences have dealt with the need for personnel standards and controls. Certification and registration plans are being completed. The National Recreation Education Accreditation Project, initiated by the American Recreation Society Professional Development Committee in 1961 and sponsored by the Federation of National Professional Recreation Organizations from 1963, completed pilot studies in 1969 for finalizing accreditation procedures in the early 1970s. The Board on Professional Education was empowered by the Board of Trustees of the National Recreation and Park Association in 1971 with the responsibility for implementing accreditation through the National Council on Accreditation. The Council on Accreditation, formed in 1974, started accrediting institutions in 1977. With the upgrading of professional preparation and the implementation of certification and registration procedures, the recreation and park profession is better able to ensure qualified leadership for the profession.

Encouragement through foundation and federal funding of more and better research has considerably expanded the body of professional literature. The Education Amendments Act of 1974 (Community Schools Act) focused attention on the use of public schools by establishing a program to provide educational, recreational, cultural, and other related community services through the use of the community education program as a center for such activities in cooperation with other community groups.

Increased Cooperation in the Profession

The recreation and park profession has long been plagued by the splintering of its energies into a myriad of professional organizations, each with a special focus. A significant attempt to coordinate these diverse efforts was made in 1954 when the Federation of National Professional Organizations of Recreation was established. It was not, however, until 1965 that the efforts of many dedicated leaders culminated in the merging of five national organizations. The American Institute of Park Executives, The American Recreation Society, the National Recreation Association, the National Conference on State Parks, and the American Association of Zoological Parks and Aquariums joined to form the National Recreation and Park Association, with headquarters in Washington, D.C. The first congress of the merged organizations was held in Washington, D.C., in 1966. The park and recreation profession had reached a significant milepost. Since then, further adjustments in the makeup of the National Recreation and Park Association have occurred. In 1971, the American As-

sociation of Zoological Parks and Aquariums returned to being a separate organization.

In 1976, a unique cooperative development took place when three independent national service organizations, the National Recreation and Park Association, the National Community Education Association, and the American Association for Leisure and Recreation, joined in a program to enhance recreation services at the community level.

Increased Concern for the Quality of the Environment

The recreation professional's concern for protection of the environment heightened in the late 1960s and the early 1970s as the entire nation became painfully aware of the price of technological progress in terms of vanishing forests, air pollution, water pollution, inner-city decay, noise pollution, and the problems of population explosion and implosion. President Nixon's first official act was the approval of the National Environmental Policy Act of 1969, which declared that it was the policy of the federal government, in cooperation with other levels of government and public and private organizations, "to create and maintain conditions under which man and nature can exist in productive harmony."

It was during this period that national interests and priorities gradually shifted from the social issues of the 1960s to the environmental issues of the 1970s. Attention focused on our vanishing wilderness; endangered animal species; noise, air, and water pollution; the ban on bottle and beer can tops; the worldwide population explosion; and the energy crisis. In 1977, President Carter established a new cabinet-level agency, the Department of Energy, to deal directly with many issues that continue to threaten present lifestyles.

In 1977 leisure spending became the nation's number one industry according to the Economic Unit of the *U.S. News and World Re-*

port. The dollar figure used for 1977 was $160 billion and was expected to climb to $300 billion by 1985. From 1966 to 1976 participation at sporting events rose forty-five percent, with corresponding increases in cultural arts activities.

In 1971–72, the President and Congress expressed their concern for establishing recreation resources close to where people live when they directed the National Park Service into the urban park field. The Gateway National Recreation Areas near New York City and the Golden Gate National Recreation Areas near San Francisco were established.

Social Concerns, Social Justice, and Civil Unrest

The late 1960s and the early 1970s found depression amid affluence, rising expectations amid poverty, rebellion with or without a cause, an unpopular war, and changing moral standards. Recreation professionals found themselves on the cutting edge of new lifestyles as parks were commandeered for love-ins, rock festivals, and political rallies. Research teams indicated that the lack of adequate recreation opportunities and challenging leisure pursuits was to blame for some of the difficulties in the decayed inner cities. Many of these problems are still with us.

The Road Ahead

The recreation and park movement has made significant progress, but it must continue to move as the face of the nation and the world changes. Problems of land encroachment, loss of natural resources, lack of long-range planning in housing developments or in expansion of municipalities, duplication of effort by public and private agencies, increased mobility of the population, early retirement from the work force, energy crises, and pollution are but a few of the challenges still facing us. National magazines and newspapers have taken up the cause of recreation to focus the public eye on leisure needs as never before. The expanded leisure of the future is a challenge to America to educate now for the recreation literacy of future generations. We have passed many milestones; but in the road ahead the American public must assume further responsibilities if the park and recreation needs of the emancipated citizen are to be met.

Selected References

Braucher, Howard. *A Treasury of Living.* New York: National Recreation Association, 1950.

Butler, George. *Introduction to Community Recreation.* 5th ed. New York: McGraw-Hill Book Co., 1976.

Curtis, Henry S. *The Play Movement and Its Significance.* New York: The Macmillan Co., 1917.

Doell, Charles E., and Fitzgerald, Gerald B. *A Brief History of Parks and Recreation in the United States.* Chicago: The Athletic Institute, 1954.

Dulles, Foster Rhea. *America Learns to Play.* 2d ed. New York: Appleton-Century-Crofts, 1965.

Grunfeld, Frederic V. *Games of the World.* New York: Holt, Rinehart and Winston, 1975.

Hampton, H. Duane. *How the U.S. Cavalry Saved our National Parks.* Bloomington: Indiana University Press, 1971.

Kraus, Richard. *Recreation and Leisure in Modern Society.* New York: Appleton-Century-Crofts, 1971.

La Gasse, Alfred B., and Cook, Walter L. *History of Parks and Recreation.* Wheeling, W.

Va.: American Institute of Park Executives, 1965.

Lee, Joseph. *Play in Education.* New York: The Macmillan Co., 1916.

Rainwater, Clarence E. *The Play Movement in the United States.* Chicago: University of Chicago Press, 1922.

Steiner, Jesse F. *Americans at Play.* New York: McGraw-Hill Book Co., 1933.

Van Doren, Carlton S., and Hodges, Louis. *America's Park and Recreation Heritage, A Chronology.* Washington, D.C.: U.S. Department of the Interior, Bureau of Outdoor Recreation, 1975.

3
Economics of Leisure

The difference between men and boys is mainly in the price of their toys.

Unknown author

How Americans spend their leisure and how they spend their money during leisure have profound economic consequences. As much as one fourth of the national income is based on recreation, and in many states it is the major source of income. The appetite for recreation seems unlimited, and expenditures on it bound upward year by year.

Productivity, Income, and Leisure

How has recreation become so important to the economy? There are three important factors: the productivity of society, personal income, and the amount of leisure. When these three are abundant—that is, when production is high, personal income is high, and leisure is abundant—the demand for recreation soars. The impact reaches all sectors of the economy—retailers, wholesalers, manufacturers, miners, foresters, government workers, and many others who at first glance may seem to have no connection with recreation.

U.S. agriculture and industry today produce goods in quantities far exceeding our survival needs. Consequently, it has been possible to reduce working hours and still pay wages that permit most people to purchase recreation goods and services. At the same time, education has broadened our mental horizons and increased our personal wants,

so that we demand and buy these goods and services.

Productivity, income, and leisure are in an intricate and delicate balance. A healthy economy depends upon their relative stability. For example, we cannot reduce the amount of leisure without throwing the economy out of kilter; if people worked longer, they would lack time in which to use the extra money they might earn. They would buy fewer boats, books, televisions, and cars; and they would patronize fewer resorts, movies, and sporting events. Industries dependent upon leisure use would wither, and their employees would be thrown out of work. Conversely, if the amount of leisure increased (with no speedup in production), people would produce and earn less; even with time to spare, they would not have the money with which to buy recreation goods and services. In a balanced situation, workers have enough leisure and money to enjoy recreation.

Provided that everyone who wants work can find it, workers themselves balance their desires for income and leisure. Some people with short workweeks may take second jobs or some people may work extra hours, thereby choosing increased income over leisure. Like the value of material objects, the value of leisure to a given person depends in part on the quantity available. The less leisure an individual has, the more he or she usually values it. Industry's custom of paying time-and-a-half or double-time wages for overtime work reflects the view that loss of prized leisure deserves extra compensation.

Productivity

Imaginative management, computerization, and automation have made it possible for today's worker to produce more than eight times as much per hour as the worker of 1850. Despite shortages of fossil fuels, improved methods of work and new forms of energy promise that the average worker's productivity will continue to grow, though perhaps more slowly, in the years ahead.

The gross national product (GNP), which is the total market value of goods and services in the United States as determined annually by the Department of Commerce, has mounted at a rate of about 3.5 percent per year, reflecting steady growth in economic output. The rate has varied with differences in business conditions from year to year, but expectations are that it will remain approximately the same. The percentage of the population in the labor force has also increased. In 1977, despite a worrisome jobless rate of 7.6 percent, more than ninety million people were in the labor force. This large number is explained in part by the growing percentage of working women, although the trend is offset somewhat by the growing percentage of persons over 65 years old, most of whom are not working.

Since today's workers require fewer hours to produce essentials, they spend more hours producing goods and services that contribute to comfort and pleasure, such as gourmet foods, luxurious homes, and fashionable clothing. Other workers provide professional services in education, law, medicine, dentistry, and social welfare, which a less productive society could not afford. A growing number of workers produce goods and services used in recreation.

Productivity is of course related to demand. If nobody wants a product or cannot af-

ford to buy it, there is no reason to produce it. Clever promoters, however, may create demands where none existed before.

Discretionary Income

Recreation wants are expanding, and the time and money available to satisfy these wants seem to be keeping pace. Personal income, despite the ups and downs of the economy, has been climbing over the long run, making more *discretionary income* (money one may spend as one pleases) available.

Although definite figures are not available, studies indicate that anywhere from five to twenty percent of family spending goes toward recreation. There is surprising evidence that lower-income families spend a larger percentage of their money on recreation than middle- or upper-income families do. Skyrocketing expenditures on recreation make the industries and services based on leisure among the fastest growing segments of the economy. A recent study indicated that spending for leisure far exceeded outlays for national defense or home building.[1]

Discretionary Time

Free time and the demand for recreation go hand in hand. The standard workweek has shrunk from almost seventy hours in 1870 to approximately thirty-eight hours today. With four-day workweeks beginning to take hold in some industries, frequent three-day weekends, and longer vacations, consumers now have large blocks of free time. Even during the workweek, one fourth of the average worker's time is free for choices of activity.

Recreation and Economic Health

The recreation opportunities offered in a community can contribute to its desirability as

Figure 3.1. Disney World in Florida is an outstanding commercial recreation success.

a place to live. Businesses and industry like to settle in such communities, and in so doing they create employment and raise property values. As a result, hard-headed public officials and civic leaders now give recreation serious attention as an economic asset. (See Figure 3.1.)

Recreation and Employment

People employed in work concerned directly with recreation include all those in the entertainment field, supervisors of recreation, managers and workers in parks and forests, those who construct or maintain recreation facilities, and the like. Many more people are indirectly employed through mining raw materials, manufacturing, wholesaling, retailing, and transporting goods used in leisure. By far the largest number of workers whose employment depends on recreation are those who produce the goods used in leisure, ranging alphabetically from stuffed aardvarks to zithers.

The entertainment industry employs not only some of the most highly paid people in the country but also countless behind-the-scenes workers in television, radio, concert halls, stage, movies, nightclubs, and amusement parks. Professional sports are likewise big business with highly paid performers. Resorts, camps, bowling alleys, pool halls, bars, dance halls, amusement arcades, gambling, and vacation travel agencies also have recreation for sale and employees to make the sale possible.

In addition, thousands of people work in park and recreation departments, wildlife and forestry services, youth agencies, settlement houses, industrial and business recreation programs, religious organizations, private recreation centers, leisure communities, hospitals, and institutions for the aged.

Recreation Products

The products used in recreation are pervading in their influence on many aspects of the economy. To illustrate the economic ramifications of recreation, let us examine just one important product.

No form of recreation takes a greater bite out of the average family budget than the recreation use of the automobile. At least one third of the driving is done for pleasure or for the purpose of reaching a recreation destination.

In 1977 about eighty-one percent of all households owned one or more cars. [2] With 110 million cars and small trucks in operation and with the average recreation usage equaling 3,000 miles a year at a cost of around seventeen cents a mile, the expenditures for recreation are staggering. The cost in many families exceeds the cost of food. A substantial number of motor cars, such as the specialized recreation vehicles, are used exclusively for recreation. Most family cars serve both for business and pleasure. About eighty percent of vacation travel is by car; and, even where public transportation is available, the car is often preferred for convenience, comfort, and status.

Estimates indicate that one out of every six jobs in the United States is related to the automobile. [3] Businesses heavily dependent upon the motor vehicles include retail agencies, garages, service stations, insurance companies, mining and manufacturing industries (iron, copper, aluminum, plastics, textiles, oil, paint, rubber, etc.), transport companies, advertising agencies, the mass media financed by advertis-

ing, and the many parks, camps, and resorts that can be reached only by car.

The secondary effects generated by the use of the car extend even further. For example, the $100 spent on car repairs in a local garage will help the garage owner to pay the grocer, the grocer to pay the plumber, and so on, thus stimulating business far exceeding the original $100.

Like other industries, the automobile industry is subject to economic fluctuations. The recession and the Arab oil embargo imposed in October 1973 sharply decreased the sales of both family cars and recreation vehicles. With the easing of fuel restrictions, sales jumped immediately, and the recreation vehicle business began to boom. Yet the worldwide energy shortage threatens not only the automobile but also work and leisure. Unless an adequate substitute for gasoline is found, drastic changes in the American way of life may be in store.

From time to time, something new, like the electronic game or the citizens' band radio, appears on the market. If it captures the public fancy, it forges a whole new industry and gives a new spark to the economy.

Continual improvements in old products and changes in models keep businesses humming and consumers buying. Backpacking became a rage with the young when new, lightweight equipment appeared. New models in trailers and motor homes create new demands from potential buyers. Increases in purchases of stereos, cassettes, and musical instruments are, at least in part, the result of improvements in recordings and equipment. Bicycling recaptured the public interest; and sophisticated, lightweight fifteen-speed models with unbelievable accessories—and unbelievable price tags—hit the market.

Recreation and Industry

Who would like to live where there are no parks or playgrounds, no halls for drama or music? The recreation climate of a community affects its ability to attract and retain residents and industries. Families who have a choice select communities in which both children and adults can find engrossing things to do. In selecting a site for plants, an industry studies not only the labor market, sources of raw materials, and transportation, but also the religious, educational, and recreation atmosphere of a community. Industries are more apt to prosper in communities in which their workers are satisfied. These are points to ponder for city officials, chambers of commerce, and others bent on improving a community's economy.

Recreation and Property Values

Land values often change drastically because of recreation developments. Large, attractive parks usually increase the value of adjacent property, such as the land adjacent to Central Park in New York, Lake Shore Drive in Chicago, and Golden Gate Park in San Francisco. In some cases the highest-priced residential property in a city adjoins parks.

While a heavily used playfield may decrease the value of adjacent property, particularly if it is lit at night and noisy, property just a few blocks away may benefit from proximity to the field. If play areas are carefully planned, with plantings to muffle noise, protect privacy, and please the eye, adjacent property may rise in price. The value of lands near newly developed reservoirs has sometimes multiplied fifteen to twenty times within a few short years. Commercial enterprises—a bowling alley, for example—might enhance the value of property in one section of a community but injure the value in another. Adult bookstores, topless bars, and X-rated movie theaters might be injurious to property values in most areas yet might increase values in a section devoted to such entertainment.

The best economic use of some areas is for recreation. Many lands that were regarded as nearly worthless until real estate promoters developed and advertised their recreation potentials are now expensive resorts. Palm Springs, California, a wealthy winter playground in the desert, and Sun Valley, Idaho, a popular mountain skiing resort, are outstanding examples. Similarly, some poor ranch lands in the West have brought better prices as vacation homes and guest ranches than they did as working ranches. Developers have salvaged many eroded and abandoned acres, such as despoiled strip mines, by planting trees and constructing lakes. At least one state park has been established on a former strip mine.

Many submarginal lands serve the economy best if left undeveloped. For instance, the attempt to drain the Horicon Marsh of Wisconsin for agricultural use proved economically disastrous, and the marsh was reflooded to serve its more valuable function as a wildlife refuge.

Recreation and Government Revenue

Revenue from income taxes, sales taxes, and property taxes rises or falls as recreation businesses and industries thrive or fail and as the incomes of the millions of workers employed in recreation enterprises go up or down. In addition to taxes applied to the public in general, governments raise special revenue from the following recreation-related activities:

1. Taxes or license fees levied on bars, nightclubs, pool halls, bowling alleys, and other private businesses.

2. Fees for hunting, trapping, and fishing licenses and taxes on hunting and fishing equipment. This income is used to improve fish and game habitats.

3. Taxes on admissions to various forms of entertainment.

4. Taxes affecting automobiles, recreation vehicles, and boats, such as registration fees, license fees, property taxes, driving license fees, and gasoline taxes. State taxes on motor fuels approximated $8.3 billion in 1975, reaching ten cents a gallon in Connecticut and Rhode Island.

5. Special taxes added to customers' bills in hotels and resorts.

6. Excise taxes on certain imported recreation goods.

7. Taxes on liquor and cigarettes, usually very high, which provide revenue to the government and also discourage their use. State revenues on alcoholic beverages in 1975 were $2 billion, and on tobacco, $3.3 billion. Seventeen states operate liquor stores themselves.

8. Fees for the use of government-owned recreation services and facilities.

9. State lotteries, pari-mutuel betting, and other forms of gambling. Gambling is legal in some form in forty-one states.[4]

Recreation Expenditures

Although we discuss expenditures for recreation, we do not imply that recreation values can be measured in dollars and cents. Some of the greatest joys in life are free, and what participants gain from recreation depends more upon their own receptivity than upon the money they spend. Nonetheless, when you spend money on recreation, you expect satisfaction; and if you increase your expenditures, you may expect increased satisfaction. Why else would you buy a $10 theater ticket rather than a $3 one, or a $200 bicycle rather than a $50 one?

Why Do Estimates Vary?

Exact figures on the total expenditures for leisure and recreation are impossible to obtain, although authorities make estimates of family expenditures and of particular areas of recreation. Several difficulties explain the variation in estimates. Should money spent on luxuries be included? If so, what is a luxury? Should the cost of magazines and books be considered a recreation expenditure? How about money spent on raising a garden? Or on smoking and drinking?

There is also considerable duplication in the figures for total national expenditures. For example, estimates of vacation costs might include costs for fishing, boating, or other activities for which separate estimates are made, so that when total costs are added, the same item might be included twice. The fluctuating value of the dollar presents further problems. If expenditures from year to year are to be fairly compared, it is necessary to interpret the figures in terms of the purchasing power of the dollar.

Some estimates approach $200 billion a year or nearly $900 per person. A 1975 figure of the Department of Commerce was more than $60 billion, but it did not include the cost of travel and vacations, recreation use of the automobile, and other leisure-related items. A thoughtful study by Kraus in 1970 placed the total at $132 billion a year.[5] The Economic Unit of *U.S. News & World Report* has made several estimates, ranging from $58.3 billion in 1965 to $160 billion in 1977, and a predicted total of $300 billion by 1985;[6] but these figures do not include money spent by government or private and voluntary agencies.

Recognizing these pitfalls, we venture nonetheless to present some estimates of the economic impact of leisure as indicated by the extent of participation and money spent. When the sources used have given conflicting estimates, the authors have had to use their own best judgment in selecting the figures.

Recreation Supplies and Equipment

A glance at a recent mail-order catalog of a large chain store revealed the extent of preoccupation with recreation supplies. There were ninety-nine pages devoted to automobile tools and equipment, including car stereos, tape players, and citizens' band radios; fifty-nine pages of tools, including home workshop supplies; twenty-three pages of televisions, radios, and cassettes; thirteen pages of bicycles and accessories; twelve pages of tents and camping equipment; four pages of musical instruments and supplies; four pages of photographic supplies; twenty-one pages of boats and accessories; six pages of motorcycle supplies; and numerous other pages describing roller skates, ice skates, home and garden needs, pool tables, game and sports equipment, leisure furniture, and toys.

The U.S. Bureau of Economic Analysis gives estimates totaling $44.9 billion spent for personal purchases in 1974 of the following recreation-related items: books and maps; magazines, newspapers, and sheet music; nondurable toys and sport supplies; wheel goods, durable toys, sports equipment, boats, and pleasure aircraft; radio and television receivers, records, and musical instruments; radio and television repair; and flowers, seeds, and potted plants.[7] Close to $5 billion are spent on toys alone.

About 1.5 million motor bikes and motorcycles, some of them primarily off-road vehicles, are sold each year in the United States. In addition, there are great numbers of four-wheel-drive cars and dune buggies. The Council on Environmental Quality estimated in 1974 that there were five million off-road vehicles in operation.[8] There are more than two million snowmobiles. Obviously recreation supplies and equipment are big business.

Travel and Vacation Businesses

The largest single item in leisure expenditures is the tourist travel and vacation business. Over $65 billion a year are spent on nonbusiness foreign and domestic travel, including transportation, food, lodging, sightseeing, entertainment, supplies, and guide service.

No aspect of leisure has been changed as markedly by the improvements in transportation as has the vacation. Cars, highways, and planes bring most of America within easy reach, and the wildlife parks of Africa or the mountains and tundras of Alaska are only slightly less accessible. These transportation miracles, combined with the availability of leisure, ample spending money, and travel tastes whetted by education and advertising, explain the vast travel and vacation businesses.

For some countries travel is the most important source of income. Forty-six American states indicate that the travel and tourist business ranks in the top three sources of income. Florida ranks it first, with one out of every four persons in the work force dependent, directly or indirectly, on tourism.

Sports and Outdoor Recreation

After the travel and vacation businesses, outdoor recreation and sports account for the largest expenditures in recreation. There has been a new emphasis on physical activity for the preservation of health, promoted by doctors, educators, and programs such as that of the President's Council on Physical Fitness and Sports. Commercial businesses, such as bowling alleys, winter sports complexes, skating rinks, fitness gymnasiums, and sporting goods stores, are thriving.

Most children and youth engage to some

extent in sports and outdoor recreation; and the burgeoning interest in these activities for women and girls swells the ranks of players. The large numbers of school teams and teams sponsored by park and recreation agencies require a considerable monetary outlay for equipment, playing fields, courts, and gymnasiums.

It should be remembered that some outdoor activities have little economic effect beyond the indirect benefit of mental and physical well-being. Examples include jogging, running, and the most popular of all outdoor activities—walking.

The Bureau of Outdoor Recreation predicted a 142 percent increase in participation in outdoor recreation from the year 1965 to 2000.[9] If you consider inflation, the dollar expenditures should rise at a rate far faster than participation.

Nature observation. About thirty-five million Americans find recreation in nature walks. Another thirteen million watch birds, and five million photograph wildlife. Although walking in the parks and woods may not cost much, nature observation can be very expensive. Thousands of enthusiasts spend money on cameras, film, field glasses, spotting scopes, and telescopes; those who can afford it travel, often with guides, on safaris to see and photograph birds, animals, and plants from the Arctic and Antarctic to the equator.

Camping. In 1976 some 51.1 million Americans camped. This figure is a seven percent increase since 1973. Although some campers still prefer the "simple life," improved equipment designed for comfort and ease has increased the financial investment in camping. The greatest cost of more than $2.5 billion a year is attributable to the purchase of recreation vehicles, trailers, tent trailers, four-wheel-drive vehicles, snowmobiles, and motor homes. Over six million trailers and motor homes are now in use in the United States,

Figure 3.2. Trailer travelers in a campground.

with more than 423,000 purchased in 1976 alone (see Figure 3.2).

To accommodate the vast numbers of campers, investments in public and private campgrounds and service facilities have soared. Several large private national chains have constructed facilities as both overnight and destination campgrounds.

Some eight million children a year are attracted to nearly 11,000 camps, which represent a large financial outlay by both parents and operators.

Boating. There were 35.2 million boaters in 1976. About one household in ten owns some kind of boat, and about $5.6 billion a year is spent on them. When we include the expense of boat operation and maintenance, the marinas, and the many activities dependent in whole or in part on boats, such as water skiing, scuba diving, and fishing, we readily see the economic importance of boating. In some places boats seem to have replaced cars as status symbols.

Boat owners have been purchasing more expensive and powerful motors. In 1950 the average horsepower of outboard motors sold was 6.9; by 1973 it had increased to 40.8; but, possibly in response to the gasoline shortage, it dropped to 40.3 in 1975.[10]

The number of boaters will almost double by the year 2000. New reservoirs, dam-controlled rivers, launching sites, marinas, and boat-storage facilities have expanded boating opportunities. The fuel shortage may increase the use of sailboats, rowboats, and canoes.

Fishing and hunting. Around 65 million Americans of all ages and from all segments of the population fish, running the gamut from bank fishing with worms and cane poles to the most costly big-game ocean fishing. Expenditures for equipment, food and lodging, transportation, licenses, privilege fees, and related costs exceed $3 billion annually.

Close to twenty-two million Americans hunt, spending more than $1.2 billion annually. The numbers of hunters have not increased rapidly in recent years, possibly because many hunting lands have been converted to agriculture. Expenditures for guns, ammunition, special clothing, licenses, leasing hunting lands, and travel make hunting costs high.

Swimming. About 110 million people in our country swim. The Bureau of Outdoor Recreation estimated that swimming expenditures total $4 billion annually. The construction and maintenance of the 890,000 swimming pools, of which over two-thirds are residential, explain much of the cost. Other swimming expenses include suits and water-related gear, such as surfboards and equipment for skin and scuba diving.

Winter sports. Winter sports have extended outdoor recreation into a year-round industry, and a sparkling snow brings out nearly 50 million sports lovers. Skis, ski lifts, snow machines, artificial mountains, snowmobiles, and snowmobile trails are very expensive. The simple sports of children's sled-ding, skating, pick-up ice hockey, and the ubiquitous snowball fight prove that winter fun is not confined to the wealthy or to resorts far from home.

Golf. More than 12,000 golf courses are scattered across the land to accommodate over sixteen million golfers who have made their sport a $7 billion business. Clubhouses, membership fees, golf hardware, professional services, maintenance of the courses, and particularly the cost of the land account for the high expenditure. Golf courses are usually located near urban centers on land that commands a high price per acre.

Bowling. Bowling, which depends almost entirely upon commercial facilities, claims 8.7 million enthusiasts, almost half of them women. The proportion of women has been steadily growing in recent years.

Cycling. Bicycling has come into its own. Recent construction of special bicycle routes and trails and the interest in saving gasoline have given it great impetus. About 100 million Americans own bicycles. Total sales in bicycles reached $800 million in 1974 alone.

In 1966 Wisconsin completed a 300-mile bikeway, and in 1971 Oregon allotted one percent of its highway money for new bikeways. Federal assistance came in 1973, when Congress authorized $120 million for bikeway construction, with the states putting up some of the money; many more safe routes for cyclists were built.

Horseback riding. There are nearly twenty million horseback riders and 8.5 million horses in the United States. Most of the animals are riding horses, a few are racing horses, and an even smaller number are work animals. The costs for animals, stables, food, care, training, showing, and equipment make riding a rather expensive hobby.

Other sports. The popular competitive games of baseball, football, soccer, basketball, hockey, boxing, tennis, badminton, and others demand outlays of money in proportion to the extent to which they are formalized. A backyard baseball game costs little more than the price of a ball, bat, and catcher's mitt; but a league game, particularly if professional, involves a great deal more.

Cultural Activities

Many Europeans still consider the United States culturally barren. Yet, the interest in arts and literature, and in museums of art, history, and science is so widespread that cultural activities have outdistanced sports in some parts of the country, such as New York City, in the numbers of participants and spectators. Special events, especially in the summer months, cater to the cultural arts. Festivals of music, art, dance, poetry, and drama; regional arts and crafts fairs; festivals of ethnic folk arts; pageants; and celebrations attract large crowds.

Music, dance, and drama. There are said to be more than thirty-eight million amateur musicians in the United States, whose music lessons and instruments strain the budget. For those who listen rather than play, record players and tape recorders as well as radios and television sets bring into the home all types of music for all types of tastes and pocketbooks. Travel costs and admission fees for those attending large music festivals, from rock to classical, add to the cost of music. Dance, which requires music, has in itself a more limited economic aspect. Probably more money is spent on it as a participation activity than as a spectator activity.

In 1975, 805 opera companies gave more than 6,000 performances, and many more were presented by the 1,463 symphony orchestras—metropolitan, community, and college. Attendance for nineteen of the major sym-

phony orchestras totaled nearly twelve million people, and gross expenditures were over $96 million.

Interest in live drama has not diminished despite television and movies. The legitimate theaters and opera, including nonprofit institutions, brought in $717 million in admissions in 1974. On Broadway alone in that year, forty new productions were presented, and more than $46 million were grossed at the box office, while road shows grossed nearly $46 million. Local productions, summer stock, and little theaters added to the intake.

More than 100 performing arts complexes have been developed in the United States since 1960 at a cost of $1 billion. Washington's John F. Kennedy Center for the Performing Arts opened in 1971. The Lincoln Center for the Performing Arts in New York, a private, nonprofit institution that opened in 1962 at a cost of $190 million, contains six major buildings with thirteen auditoriums offering drama, opera, ballet, and music. Its audiences totaled about 4.6 million people in 1976.

Arts and crafts. Supplies and instruction cost large amounts for those who find expression through painting, sculpturing, needlework, woodwork, rock polishing, and the numerous other arts and crafts. Street sales, craft festivals, and art galleries have proliferated, and more homes contain original works of art, despite their high cost. Art by famous masters has brought record high prices at recent auctions, with large museums competing for ownership.

Books, magazines, and newspapers. Books are selling better than ever, although much of the rise in expenditures is due to inflation. The market value of magazines, newspapers, and books reached $11.6 billion in 1976. Paperback books have reached a wider mass market than the more expensive hardcover books. Book clubs, offering books at fairly reasonable prices, guarantee large sales and widespread distribution.

Museums. In the United States there are more than 1,800 museums of art, history, science, or a combination of these. Some are built and financed privately, some by government, and some by educational institutions. Government funds, private donations, fees, and charges bring their total income to $500 million. Museum visitors in 1976 totaled seventy-eight million people.

Home Expenditures

Many of the expenditures already discussed center around the home and family. Homes, apartments, and leisure villages often include playing courts, gardens, outdoor cooking and eating centers, children's playground apparatus, swimming pools, play rooms, and hobby workshops that add costs of thousands of dollars for building, equipping, and maintaining.

Amusement and Entertainment

Catering to almost every conceivable interest and taste, a host of services feed the insatiable demand for amusement and entertainment, providing employment for millions of people and transferring billions of dollars from the pocketbooks of consumers to the pocketbooks of promoters and investors.

Some forms of recreation discussed in the pages that follow are passive forms of amusement; others demand more active participation. Some are educational, and others are mere time-fillers.

Spectator sports. A typical scene in a typical home finds members of the family getting their exercise vicariously by watching televised football, baseball, basketball, boxing, hockey, tennis, bowling, golf, racing, or other sports. NBC's payment of $100 million to Russia for broadcasting rights for the 1980 Olympics was a recognition of the dollar value of televised sports.

Television has evidently not impaired attendance, however, for the crowds at most sports are larger than ever. The choice of sports, once limited to baseball, boxing, football, basketball, and horse racing, has likewise multiplied. The attendance chart on page 246 in Chapter 11 indicates the tremendous growth in recent years.

The gate receipts and money spent on food, lodging, and transportation of sports fans are important to the economy of the cities in which big games are held. Admission fees to spectator sports were estimated as $1.3 billion for 1974. Although admission fees for amateur sports are usually not as great as for professional sports, the income is sufficient to finance the sports programs of colleges, universities, high schools, and many private sports clubs.

Amusement parks. A few of the old-style amusement parks still persist, traveling carnivals and circuses still move from city to city, and county and state fairs still have their midways. But the modern-day Coney Islands are the theme parks that developed largely in the 1960s and 1970s. They have spread from coast to coast and their very names illustrate their diversity: Six Flags, Opryland, Magic Mountain, Great America, Marineland, Kings Island, and others. Disneyland and Disney World, the best known, attracted twenty-two million visitors—foreign as well as American—in 1976.

A number of historic parks and reconstructed pioneer villages provide an interpretation of past cultures for visitors; safari parks, in which wild animals run free in pseudo-natural surroundings while visitors drive through or are transported by rail, as in Busch Gardens, Florida, offer the feeling of Africa without leaving home.

Radio and television. Pervading almost every home, rural and urban, radio and television have had indirect as well as direct effects on the economy. They have changed our tastes and increased our demands through both advertising and their depiction of affluent lifestyles. It is hard to imagine any Americans, with the exception of infants and some of the handicapped, who do not either see television or hear radio.

Television is in about 73 million homes. Over seventy percent of all households now have color television, and even in households with incomes of less than $3,000 a year, seventy percent have either color or black-and-white sets. Television broadcasting revenues in 1976 were about $6.5 billion.

Motion pictures. Antedating radio by twenty years as a form of popular entertainment, motion pictures reached an income height in 1945 with $1.4 billion spent for admissions. The advent of television cut sharply into motion picture attendance, and by 1964 receipts had dropped to only $913 million. Rising since then, but not as rapidly as for many other forms of recreation, box office receipts reached over $2.3 billion in 1977. Television use of movies, however, has added another dimension to their income. The televised presentation of *Gone With the Wind* in 1976 was viewed by about 110 million people and commanded a price as high as $260,000 a minute for advertising time during the movie. Still, the wide picture and better technical projection of the big screen provide an experience that even the new large-screen televisions cannot reproduce.

Other entertainment. Bars, nightclubs, and dance halls offer entertainment at a cost. For many people, particularly singles, the bar has become a social meeting place and recreation center, a function which the British pub has long served. Although expenditures for drink and entertainment are extremely high, accurate figures are difficult to obtain.

Commercial recreation centers catering to the public also include pool and billiard halls and centers for pinball and other games of skill and chance. Gambling is one of the fastest growing pastimes in the leisure field, with a turnover estimated at $75 billion a year. State lotteries give a profit to the states of about forty cents on every dollar wagered. Pari-mutuel betting produced state revenues of $586 million from horse racing in 1975 and $89 million from greyhound racing. In Nevada, where casinos gross $1.2 billion a year, gaming taxes pay half of the state budget; and state residents do not pay any income or inheritance taxes.

Entertainment in the form of dining out is more frequent than ever, and the foods are a far cry from those of yesteryear. Although the fast-food chains, like McDonald's, claim the bulk of patronage, restaurants catering to sophisticated tastes abound. Aided by frozen foods, electronic ovens, and fat pocketbooks, even small-town restaurants can offer famous gourmet dishes.

Motels, too, have become recreation-minded. Most of them offer swimming pools and color television. Some set aside areas for pinball machines, shuffleboard, billiards, sauna baths, miniature golf, and other attractions.

Many other forms of entertainment, legal and illegal, including drugs, prostitution, and pornography, increase the total spent on leisure.

Government Expenditures

At all levels of government, money is spent for recreation. The investment in land and facilities defies any effort at a dollar valuation. It includes land for parks, playgrounds, and special uses as well as the vast land and water holdings for forests, reservoirs, and wildlife preservation. It also includes developments for public use such as museums, community centers, stadiums, amphitheaters, zoos, auditoriums, shelter houses, camp-grounds, and hundreds of other items.

Local governments and schools. Most cities of more than 10,000 population provide recreation services. The 854 cities reporting 1975 operating and capital budgets indicated a total of over $965 million spent for recreation services.[11] To this sum should be added expenditures of other public agencies related to leisure, including museums, civic orchestras, cultural arts centers, and little theatres, to mention only a few, as well as expenditures for recreation in housing programs and programs for the handicapped, aged, and disadvantaged.

Schools at all levels spend money for recreation and leisure, including instruction for the use of leisure, teaching of skills, and the operation of extracurricular activities and facilities.

State expenditures. Numerous state agencies give leisure services; but, except in agencies whose primary function is recreation, it is difficult to determine from the budgets those items that can be labeled recreation. Periodic studies by the National Association of State Park Directors and the National Society for Park Resources branch of the National Recreation and Park Association give some specific figures on state park expenditures. Their studies indicated an expenditure of $670 million in 1975 as compared with $109 million in 1962 and $387 million in 1970. Park attendance grew 3.2 percent per year from 1970 to 1975, faster than the general population growth. The cost per capita in 1975 was approximately $1.40, with approximately twenty cents per visitor recovered through operating revenues.[12]

Federal expenditures. Many billions of dollars are involved in federal expenditures for recreation lands such as reservoirs, forests, refuges, and deserts in agencies such as the Bureau of Land Management, the Fish and Wildlife Service, the Army Corps of Engineers, the Bureau of Reclamation, the Tennessee Valley Authority, and the Forest Service. The National Park Service budget estimate for 1978 was $439 million, and the Land and Water Conservation Fund estimate for the same year was $637.8 million. It was anticipated that the LWCF budget would for some future years approximate $900 million a year, to be expended largely in grants to federal agencies, states, and local communities. These and other federal grants to states and communities comprise a large portion of their recreation budget.

Economic Problems in Recreation

Even though leisure expenditures have probably been the fastest growing segment of the economy, there are still some financial problems. During periods of recession, recreation services may be cut and families may reduce their spending. However, during the Great Depression of the 1930s, when local budgets were reduced, the federal government stepped in with an extensive recreation program that provided work for thousands of people. The recession of the mid-1970s brought severe cuts in the buying of cars, travel trailers, and some other recreation materials, but at the same time showed a substantial growth in the numbers of people wintering in Florida, attending amusement parks, and making other vacation expenditures. It also appears that after a recession, a pent-up buying demand is released, and spending for leisure goods and services begins to soar.

The volatility of public taste spells the doom of many recreation enterprises. Fads come and go, and today's expensive facilities may be closed down tomorrow. For example, when the miniature golf craze of the 1950s died down, along with it went the investment in miniature golf courses. The sport has since revived on a smaller but more stable basis. Financial headaches are also caused by the seasonal nature of many forms of recreation. How to turn a ski resort into a year-round vacation

What Do We Get for Our Money?

Joseph T. Williams has an annual income in six digits. Through the years he has accumulated a formidable estate, including bonds, stock in his company, an expensive home, and a fifty-foot yacht that cost him $100,000 and requires at least $20,000 a year in maintenance and crew. Because his free time is limited, he uses the yacht largely during summer vacations and sometimes in the spring and fall on weekends. Cold weather keeps him from using it during the winter.

Eighteen-year-old Jackson Jones lives with his family in a small town on a northern lake in a comfortable middle-class home. Jackson and a friend spent a winter in his basement building a fourteen-foot boat, following a pattern and instructions obtained from a catalog. The total cost, including fittings and oars, came to less than $200. Each spring the boat is launched; and in early evenings and on weekends and holidays it provides fun and fishing. The boys have rigged a small sail and try sailing.

Which of these people has the most satisfaction from his boat? Does the expenditure of money always increase satisfaction? Are some of the things in life that cost nothing more satisfying than some that are expensive? Does the desire for status enter into many recreation expenditures?

spot, how to persuade summer tourists to visit a resort during spring and fall, or how to encourage weekday use of beaches that are overcrowded on weekends are challenges that recreation managers constantly face.

There is probably no area of personal expenditure that shows less direct relationship between the amount spent and the value received than leisure spending. A walk in the woods may be more satisfying than a cross-country trip. A child may prefer a worn-out homemade toy to an expensive new doll. A person may cheerfully lose $10 in five minutes in a slot machine and then grumble about paying fifty cents for a magazine.

Selected References

Barlowe, Raleigh. *Land Resource Economics.* Englewood Cliffs, N.J.: Prentice-Hall, Inc., 1978.

Clawson, Marion, and Knetch, Jack L. *Economics of Outdoor Recreation.* Baltimore: The Johns Hopkins Press, 1966.

Epperson, Arlin. *Private and Commercial Recreation: A Text and Reference.* New York: John Wiley & Sons, Inc., 1977.

Jensen, Clayne R. *Outdoor Recreation in America.* 3d ed. Minneapolis: Burgess Publishing Company, 1977.

Jensen, Clayne R., and Thorstenson, Clark T. *Issues in Outdoor Recreation.* 2d ed. Minneapolis: Burgess Publishing Company, 1977.

Kaplan, Max. *Leisure: Theory and Policy.* New York: John Wiley & Sons, Inc., 1975.

Kraus, Richard. *Recreation and Leisure in Modern Society.* New York: Appleton-Century-Crofts, 1971.

"The Leisure Industries: Investigations of Commercial Recreation and Tourism." *Journal of Physical Education and Recreation*

46, no. 9 (November–December 1975); 33–48.

Recreation and Park Yearbook. Arlington, Virginia: National Recreation and Park Association, 1977.

The Recreation Imperative, A Draft of the Nationwide Outdoor Recreation Plan Prepared by the Department of the Interior. Washington, D.C.: U.S. Government Printing Office, 1974.

U.S. Bureau of the Census, *Statistical Abstract of the United States.* Washington, D.C.: Department of Commerce, published annually.

Vaughn, Roger J. *Economics of Recreation: A Survey.* Santa Monica: Rand Corporation, 1974.

Vickerman, R. W. *Economics of Leisure and Recreation.* Mystic, Conn.: Lawrence Verry, Inc., 1975.

Part Two
The Public Sector

Our government is not the master but the creature of the people. The duty of the state toward the citizens is the duty of the servant to its master.

Franklin D. Roosevelt

The relation of recreation to local, state, and federal government and to the public schools forms the substance of Chapters 4 through 7. The various levels of government, as we shall see, are intertwined yet distinct in their recreation functions.

The founders of the United States conceived a government based on the will of the governed and serving the needs of the governed, flexible enough to stretch across the generations. The phrase "life, liberty, and the pursuit of happiness" in the Declaration of Independence voiced the aspirations of the people, and the "general welfare" clause of the Constitution became in time the legal basis for federal action affecting leisure pursuits.

Even though most recreation is personal—self-directed by an individual, a family, or a small social group, government provisions are made for several reasons.

1. The primary function of government is to serve human needs, among which recreation is important.

2. Government is the means whereby people in a democratic society may choose to make services available.

3. Only government can provide services on an equal basis open to the entire population over a long period of time. Taxes provide the fairest way of making these services available.

4. Only government has the power to secure, hold, protect, and open for use the land, water, wildlife, and forests upon which much of our recreation depends.

Federal powers are limited by the Constitution, but broad interpretation of the Constitution by the courts has permitted federal activity to grow through the years. All powers not vested in the federal government remain with the states. Local governments must get their authority from the state.

In relation to recreation, it is the local government that serves the broadest needs and the greatest clientele. Because it is closest to the people, it is presumably more responsive and responsible to the people. The state influences local programs through permissive legislation, regulations, advisory services, and allocation of federal funds to cities, towns, counties, and districts. Except for the federal programs for the armed forces and federal employees, direct leadership of recreation programs by state or federal agencies is generally restricted to state or federal properties.

4
Role of Local Government

If you live in a town run by a committee, be on the committee.

Prelude to Bigness

A growing population and the movement of people to cities throughout America are dramatically obvious from the U.S. census data. Since census information was first collected in 1790, there have been three very significant milestones. The first, revealed in the 1790 census itself, was that ninety-five percent of the 2.5 million U.S. citizens lived in rural areas within 200 miles of the Atlantic seaboard. At that time, there were only twenty-four urban centers (2,500 population or more) in the nation, with only two having populations of 25,000 or more. The second demographic milestone came to light in 1920, when the decennial census showed, for the first time, that America's population had more urban dwellers than rural (51.2 percent urban). The third significant population bench mark was revealed in the 1970 census and supported by the 1975 update, which showed that during the first seventy-five years of the twentieth century, the U.S. population increased from 75 million to 215 million, with urban areas absorbing virtually all of the increase. In 1976, according to *National Geographic*, two out of every three Americans occupied less than two percent of the landscape.[1]

In other words, in just 200 years, America's population has been transformed from a predominantly rural, eastern cluster to a nation of more than 5,400 urban cities and towns. In such an urban society, people are often subjected to a deterioration of social controls, with the result that crime, poverty, the stresses of integration, and a multitude of other problems such as family breakups and delinquency acquire new dimensions. People crowded together can multiply the dangers inherent in the maze of human relationships.

Although people are living in ever-closer proximity, we find a gradual breakdown of the neighborhood. Urbanites living in our burgeoning cities find it increasingly difficult to sustain intimate contact; neighbors are virtually strangers. A deteriorating environment is threatening the very quality of human life in the city. Burdened with these many problems, city dwellers turn to local government as the instrument to aid them in improving life within the city.

Prior to the nineteenth century, U.S. cities performed few government functions. Public education, a function of New England colonial towns, was one of the earliest services performed by municipalities. In 1810, New York City, with approximately 100,000 people, spent only one dollar per capita for all municipal services.[2] It was not until the 1840s that police administration became a municipal function. Fire protection, first regarded as a private concern, appeared as a public service in the form of volunteer companies and finally became exclusively a municipal service during this same time. Public works administration started during the middle of the nineteenth century and developed rapidly in the second half of that century.

The greatest expansion of municipal functions came in the first half of the twentieth century. As families gradually changed from being independent to interdependent, increased demands were placed on local governments to provide additional services. It was under these conditions that health, welfare, parks and recreation, and similar items were added to the growing list of city services.

Park and Recreation Services—A Function of Local Government

Park and recreation services evolved as a municipal function under much the same circumstances as did the other services that the modern city provides. Starting first on a private basis, park and recreation services gradually became a municipal function when local governments were confronted with demands for open spaces and organized services, first in establishing parks and later in recreation. As the ever-increasing list of municipal services affected the taxpayers' pocketbooks, the need to justify these services became more imperative. Many people questioned the need for spending tax funds for an activity that they felt was a responsibility of the individual.

Many authorities of government feel that the functions of a local government should be justified only on the basis of felt need and expressed demand for a particular activity that individuals themselves cannot provide. According to James, the various functions performed by municipal governments "find their justification only in the fact that they contribute to the welfare of society and the individual in it. In fact, all government finds its raison d'être in that fact alone."[3] Certainly, recreation's contributions to the safety, health, morals, and welfare of the individual and society

merit community support along with such functions as education, public works, and police protection.

Legally, it can be shown that, by the enactment of state legislation authorizing cities to provide funds for recreation programs and by the judicial interpretation that follows such enactment, precedent has established parks and recreation as a rightful function of government. Although park and recreation services may be considered primarily an individual responsibility, the provision of areas and facilities and the conducting of an organized program for all to enjoy are certainly not within the means of all individuals.

Some things can best be done by government; other things are better accomplished by voluntary agencies or commercial groups. Experience tells us that community park and recreation programs should be a cooperative effort, with all agencies, both public and private, playing important roles.

Why should local governments provide park and recreation services?

1. People's use of leisure is an important social concern. In its provision of park and recreation services, a community contributes to the social, physical, and mental health of its residents.

2. Only through public park and recreation services will a large portion of the population have access to many recreation facilities, such as swimming pools, tennis courts, picnic areas, and golf courses.

3. Local government is best suited to acquire, develop, and maintain recreation space for the entire community.

4. Government sponsorship of park and recreation services assumes equal participation by all ages, races, and creeds, and for all seasons of the year; it is democratic and inclusive.

5. By providing a park and recreation agency, the combined wisdom of citizen participation on park and recreation boards can be assembled. A community can focus attention on protecting public lands and concentrate on long-range plans to assure proper growth of the system as the community expands.

6. Only through government is equitable fair-share financing available for the acquisition, development, and maintenance of park facilities and programs.

7. A park and recreation board can, through cooperative agreements with school boards, library boards, and other government agencies, energize and maximize the leisure and recreation potential of a community.

Organization of the Park and Recreation Department

When a community has identified and clarified its need for a municipal recreation program, it is faced with deciding whether an existing agency, such as the public schools or the park department, should conduct the program or whether it should establish a new administrative authority. Since recreation's scope is broad and its resources are varied, it is important not only to determine carefully the best administrative authority but also to consider the many interrelated arrangements that are essential if the best use of tax funds is to be made and the best possible services and program are to be offered.

A 1976 study of municipal services by the National Recreation and Park Association indicates that "the majority (sixty-six percent) of cities providing services function under a combined park and recreation agency. The same figure was reported in a 1970 NRPA survey and suggests a relative leveling off of the trend toward consolidation of park and recreation functions, which was most apparent during the 1960s."[4] Because of the complexities and styles of local government, in our judgment no one authority is best suited to administer all of the park and recreation services.

Factors Determining the Type of Administrative Authority

City officials must carefully study the following factors, which play an influential role in determining the best administrative authority for their community:

Enabling legislation. Since a municipality can perform only those functions authorized by the state government, it is important first to examine the existing state statutes to determine how such legislation will affect the local government in setting up a department. For example, in Wisconsin, state statutes make it desirable for local school systems to administer recreation programs. The Park and Recreation Law passed in Indiana provides definite advantages for a city and/or county to set up a recreation program as a consolidated department of parks and recreation. In Illinois, the park district law provides the best opportunity for a recreation program to be organized under the park department; in North Carolina, the advantages lie in a separate recreation authority.

Ability to obtain funds. It is also important to determine under what agency the most adequate funds can be provided. In some cases, legal requirements might influence the method or limitations of raising funds for yearly budgets or capital outlays. In other cases, personal bias might affect the possibility of financing a program. The attitudes of school boards or superintendents of schools, for example, might influence the amount of money they would be willing to set aside for recreation purposes. The factors concerning finance are varied and must be analyzed closely.

Influence of political pressure. The extent to which politics might have a detrimental influence on certain administrative bodies merits careful study. Recreation should not become a political football. The operation of the department should be devoid of outside political pressures in the matters of hiring personnel, purchasing equipment, and providing services. The park and recreation laws of each state should create a nonpartisan board, which should hire executives on the basis of qualifications and experience rather than for political reasons. Experience has proved that no administrative authority is immune to political pressures. Local conditions will determine the degree of susceptibility to such influences.

Availability of areas and facilities. No one organization controls all the areas and facilities necessary to operate a comprehensive community program. The agency, therefore, that controls areas and facilities or can develop policies, coordinate plans, and enlist cooperation with other community organizations might well be the logical authority to direct the community recreation program.

Community support. An organizing committee should be interested in determining the public's attitude toward the various types of organizations. The agency that is held in the highest esteem, has a reputation of providing quality service, and is looked upon with favor by other community and government agencies should be strongly considered to operate the municipal recreation program.

Quality of professional personnel. More than any other factor, the key to the success of any organizational structure is its leadership. Since the municipal recreation authority is often only one of the many organizations serving the recreation needs of a community, and since the success of the total community program is based primarily on the highest level of cooperative relationships, the organization that already has such leadership or the agency that will hire this leadership should be given strong consideration when choosing the proper authority.

Type of existing local government. Whether local government is administered by a professional city manager or an elected official will determine, to some extent, what type of authority will best serve the needs of the community. Traditionally, city managers do not approve of separate authorities with administrative boards or commissions. In addition, each city and town needs to assess carefully its own position in relation to the larger community, the district or region of which it is a part, to determine what effect, if any, these larger authorities may have on park and recreation services.

Types of Administrative Patterns

There are many ways to administer park and recreation services, and strong arguments can be found for all types of managing authorities. Examples of departments providing well-rounded programs and services under the guidance of qualified leadership can be found in each type of organization. Figure 4.1 shows the relative occurrences of administrative patterns. The main organizational patterns are briefly treated here.

Administration of recreation as a separate function. In the past, recreation professionals have looked with favor on organizing recreation under a separate commission, board, or department. Studies have revealed that this approach is still fairly common today. The organization of recreation as a separate department, comparable to other city functions and directly under the mayor or city manager, has received widespread support from students of government. Advocates of this procedure claim that more prompt and efficient management of the department results, with closer integration and coordination with other municipal departments. Lay participation can be

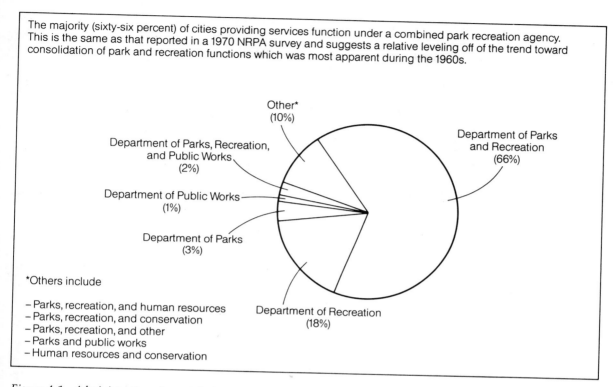

The majority (sixty-six percent) of cities providing services function under a combined park recreation agency. This is the same as that reported in a 1970 NRPA survey and suggests a relative leveling off of the trend toward consolidation of park and recreation functions which was most apparent during the 1960s.

Other*
(10%)

Department of Parks, Recreation,
and Public Works
(2%)

Department of Public Works
(1%)

Department of Parks
(3%)

Department of Parks
and Recreation
(66%)

Department of Recreation
(18%)

*Others include

– Parks, recreation, and human resources
– Parks, recreation, and conservation
– Parks, recreation, and other
– Parks and public works
– Human resources and conservation

Figure 4.1. Administration of municipal recreation services. Source: Parks & Recreation, *July 1976.* Reprinted by permission.

provided by establishing an advisory committee, which can act as a consultant and interpretive body to the department.

The majority of recreation professionals, however, advocate the establishment of recreation under a recreation board or commission, if there is to be a separate authority. Under this system, a board (preferably bipartisan), usually appointed by the mayor and approved by the council, guides the fortunes of the recreation program. Arguments for a board are many, but they chiefly center around the following: a board affords opportunities for more citizen involvement, it insures continuity of policy and program, it provides better opportunity for obtaining and reflecting public opinion, and it facilitates broad cooperative relationships in planning and coordinating pro-

grams with schools and other community agencies concerned with recreation.

The chief arguments against having a separate recreation authority are that park services can and should accommodate recreation activities because, after all, the basic purpose of a park is recreation. A separate recreation department would add to the complexity of local government and might even duplicate programs already sponsored by park departments and school authorities. A separate recreation department would have little or no property of its own and, therefore, would have to depend on the use of park or school property. In the long run, it would simply be more economical to integrate recreation into one of the existing agencies.

Excellent examples of cities utilizing recreation boards or commissions as the administrative authority for their programs are Long Beach, California; Cincinnati, Ohio; and Hutchinson, Kansas.

Park administration of recreation. In many cities, the recreation departments are outgrowths of existing park departments. Since the park movement was a forerunner of organized recreation and became well established in most communities before the concept of municipal recreation was recognized, it is natural that recreation joined forces with park departments. In the past, one of the main arguments against having park departments administer recreation programs was that park administrators were concerned mainly with caring for areas and equipment, and were more involved with maintaining beautiful lawns or shrubs than with stimulating use of the recreation areas. Present-day park directors are more recreation-minded and realize that public parks have basically one function: the leisure enjoyment of people. The gradual change in park leaders' philosophy has been instrumental in bringing park and recreation professionals closer together. The results have been a more cooperative relationship and efficient administration of community recreation. Minneapolis, Chicago, and Peoria, Illinois, operate their recreation programs through the park administration.

School administration of recreation. Madison, Wisconsin, presents concrete evidence that recreation can be effectively administered by school authorities. Because school administrators are becoming increasingly aware of recreation and realize that the school has definite responsibilities in this area, they are looking with favor toward fostering recreation programs. The federal government added credence to the school's role in recreation when it passed the Community Education Act of 1974. Objectives of this program

are to provide educational, recreational, cultural, and related community services in accordance with the needs, interests, and concerns of the community.

Proponents of this system point out that play is educational and should be taught and supervised by school authorities in an educational setting. A ready source of leadership is available. School systems are in daily touch with students and have easy access to parents for dissemination of information. In most cities, the public school board and administrators command a high degree of respect from parents and the public in general, and it is felt that the public would look with favor upon the school's direction of the recreation program. Schools also have buildings, playgrounds, and other facilities that play a key role in affording recreation programs for the community.

Those opposed to school administration point out that school programs omit large segments of the population, such as preschoolers, adults, and senior citizens. School facilities, with rare exceptions, are not designed for community recreation purposes. They are often unattractive and difficult to supervise. Opponents point out that school budgets are barely adequate for normal school programs, much less for taking on the responsibility for recreation. The pool of available teachers with recreation leadership skills is not as large as the proponents claim.

Combined department of parks and recreation. The consolidation of parks and recreation into one department, each receiving appropriate recognition, has received considerable attention in recent years and has emerged as the dominant authority for municipal park and recreation services. Under this type of organization, recreation tends not to be subordinated to the construction and maintenance of park areas and facilities; and certainly better overall integration of planning, maintenance, and programming results. By combining the park and recreation functions into one department, authorities hope that overlapping costs may be eliminated and that the combined functions may be organized into a unified and efficient effort. Under joint partnership, each function may be understood and appreciated for its respective role.

Those favoring other systems suggest that the combined department is too large to administer efficiently and that such departments become too powerful in the eyes of local politicians. Opponents say that the success of such authorities rests in the hands of the chief officer, and that it is too much to expect one person to be expert enough to do the job adequately.

Cities that have found success in combined park and recreation departments include Los Angeles, California; Kansas City, Missouri; Richmond, Virginia; and Dallas, Texas.

How these four major types of recreation administration are organized successfully in four U.S. cities is charted in the appendix.

County, district, and regional metropolitan systems. In recent years there is evidence that since 1975 the population growth is away from large metropolitan areas. Of the forty largest U.S. cities, twenty-nine lost population during the 1970s. A few of these people moved to other large urban areas, but the majority returned to small cities and towns. Paradoxically, most people are still within easy access of urban areas where work, leisure, and the amenities of life are provided.

As those living on the fringes of urban complexes started to demand park and recreation services, different methods of mobilizing the forces of government to provide such services began. In some instances, county units of government were established; in others a district or regional concept emerged. In some cases, the villages, towns, and cities were included in the large unit of government; in others they were not.

Strong arguments can be made in favor of larger units of government providing park and recreation services. Advantages include coordinated planning, an enlarged tax base, rendering of service to small towns in the area with an insufficient tax base for their own programs, and reduction of administrative overhead by wider use of expensive personnel and equipment. Those against such systems argue that local autonomy is lost when control is transferred to a larger and higher level of government, close identification and involvement of local citizens may be lessened, and it is difficult to maintain a close working relationship with schools and voluntary agencies.

In practice, county, district, and regional departments have been instrumental in solving many of the problems resulting from urban sprawl and have helped to serve the total recreation needs of all citizens in large metropolitan areas. Outstanding examples of such systems include: Miami and Dade County, Florida; the Oakland, California, East Bay Regional Park District; The Nashville–Davidson County, Tennessee, Park and Recreation Department; and the Huron/Clinton Metropolitan Authority in and around Detroit, Michigan.

Collective Wisdom of Boards

Citizen interest, knowledge, and action have been the foundations for growth of the park and recreation movement. Recreation is not formalized or stereotyped; it differs from city to city, from neighborhood to neighborhood, and from season to season. The park and recreation department must know the city and its people, be familiar with past programs in local recreation services, and develop a program based on knowledge of current local interests, habits, desires, traditions, and mores. It must make its program services known to all the people. The executive plays a vital role in all this, but he or she cannot do it alone. In this field, where relationships with community groups are many and continuous, and where the collective judgment of a carefully selected group is likely to be wiser than the decision of a single executive, diverse public interests must often be reconciled.

In addition to collective wisdom, the citizen's unique purpose, place, and value in serving on park and recreation boards and commissions may be further described.

1. Appointed park and recreation boards permit the elective authorities to provide more credibility for their vow to be responsive and accountable to the electorate. They appoint a policy-making board that represents, and is close to, several segments of the population.

2. Boards and commissions may investigate, in depth, problems that elected authorities have no time to examine.

3. The essence of recreation is dealing and working with groups, and the group action on such matters as determining policies and making regulations should be the product of group thinking.

4. Active boards discourage and prevent bureaucratic tendencies on the part of public officials.

5. The policies of a board are frequently more acceptable to the public than are those of a single department head.

6. A board can act as a board of appeal for the citizenry.

7. Board members are ambassadors to higher authority in government, business, and industry.

8. A board provides a layperson's view and advice in matters of broad public concern.

9. Boards, through overlapping terms of office, provide continuity of policy and thinking despite changes in administration.

10. A board provides liaison and a working relationship with other related public, private, and voluntary agencies.

11. Boards and commissions have wide acceptance throughout the country and provide a most significant avenue of preserving the democratic process.

Organization Means People

The human element must be paramount in considering any organizational method. Each individual in the organization must be assigned specific tasks, broad outlines of interrelationships must be established, and definite lines of authority must be created. All personnel, from the executive to the park gardener, must understand the unifying purpose of the organization. The question often raised is whether proper organization or quality of employees takes precedence. Even the best organizational structure will break down with uninspired, uninformed, dissatisfied workers; yet not even the best leaders, caught in the web of confusion resulting from poor organization, will achieve the goals of the department.

Community leaders should study thoroughly the various organizational patterns to determine the one that best fits their communities. The factors that will influence their selection should be examined. To the pattern eventually chosen should be added qualified personnel that have the ability to initiate, organize, delegate, and coordinate. Final success will be based chiefly upon the attitudes, enthusiasms, and loyalties of these workers. As Aristotle wrote: "The form of government is best in which every man, whoever he is, can act best and live happily. The test of ideal government is not its particular organization but the result of that organization in promoting the welfare and happiness not of any one class but of all classes."

Legal Authority for Recreation

Local government must receive legal authority from the state before a program can be organized and conducted. The city or county itself is a creature of state government. Its very existence, its type of government, and the kind and scope of its powers are derived from the state constitution and statutes. Recreation as a recognized government function must fit into this framework.

In its early history organized recreation did not require specific legislation from the state. School and park legislation was broadly interpreted to include recreation under school and park legal powers. In early years, cities based their authority on existing general welfare and police powers. As needs for recreation began to grow and more money was requested, local officials looked for more specific legal powers that would authorize their communities to operate recreation programs. Efforts were made to broaden the existing park and school legislation to include recreation services, but this did not prove to be entirely satisfactory, since many of the park and school authorities did not take advantage of the newly created powers. Recreation leaders stressed the need for specific recreation enabling laws.

State Enabling Laws for Recreation

In each state, a myriad of laws can be found pertaining to recreation and parks. Some laws have direct influence, whereas others indirectly affect local governments. Laws can be found that are general in scope or that pertain to a single community or to a specified class of cities. Laws in the fields of health,

welfare, parks, conservation, and education, to name only a few, provide certain limitations or controls on local recreation administration. For example, in one state, fifty-eight laws related to parks and recreation were on the books in the early 1950s. It is no wonder that this state was interested in establishing, in one act, broad enabling legislation to allow all communities in the state to establish municipal recreation programs. With such a complexity of laws, city and community leaders are perplexed as to what laws affect their cities in setting up community parks and recreation programs. Park and recreation authorities are in almost unanimous agreement that the passage of good state recreation enabling acts will do much to further the development of municipal recreation.

A desirable enabling act grants a considerable amount of home rule for recreation. It enables communities to establish and conduct recreation programs under any type of administrative authority (park board, school board, separate recreation board) that the community feels would be most effective for its local situation. Legislation of this type is *permissive* in nature.

Many states have initiated laws authorizing county, district, regional, or metropolitan park and recreation districts. Recreation agencies of this type are found principally in large urban areas. Under such conditions, recreation services can be provided not only to the major city itself, but also to the many suburbs surrounding it.

The provisions of state enabling acts vary, with no state having an ideal or perfect law. Since cities and politics differ and not all their features are considered desirable or pertinent for each situation, the existing laws are generally a matter of compromise. The following provisions are recommended for inclusion in all state enabling acts:

1. A method of establishing the managing authority and board

2. Powers of the administrative authority and executive

3. Fiscal procedures to be followed, including how money can be obtained, accounted for, and spent

4. Cooperative agreements among existing government agencies

5. Qualification and selection of personnel

Local Recreation Legislation

Once a city or county decides to establish a municipal recreation program, it must study the powers granted to the local community through state enabling legislation or home-rule provisions. It is up to the local government to establish the local recreation authority, based upon the specific powers authorized by the state. In a city under home rule, the local charter may need to be amended to provide recreation services. Where a state enabling act is provided, the city must pass an ordinance to initiate the program.

Financing Local Recreation

Money is needed to provide adequate recreation opportunities for all citizens; this concept must be generally accepted by the public and its elected or appointed officials before adequate funds will be provided. The increased number of recreation programs and the increased expenditures for parks and recreation indicate that more and more communities are accepting recreation as a government function. Sufficient and dependable financial support must be supplied, and the budget that is passed indicates the course of action that is felt necessary to provide an adequate program. This money determines the

magnitude, scope, and quality of services that can be offered. Funds are needed to acquire areas and facilities, to employ qualified leaders, to purchase supplies and equipment, and to maintain the parks, community centers, and other facilities that are essential for a well-rounded program.

How Much Should a Community Spend?

Parks and recreation are only two of many municipal functions. The amount that should be set aside for these purposes from the total tax dollar is difficult to ascertain. Because many local governments are faced with a financial crisis and there is competition among municipal departments, councils and boards are confronted with the problem of determining which functions are most important and then allocating sufficient funds to perform each function properly.

Many factors need to be considered when trying to answer the question, "How much should a community spend for park and recreation services?" Communities differ as to their park and recreation needs, their economic standards, the number of existing non-government agencies providing programs and facilities, cost-of-living indexes, the community's attitudes toward fees and charges, and other factors that influence the decision on expenditures.

Caution, too, should be exercised in comparing community expenditures for parks and recreation. There are varying policies of cooperative fiscal arrangements in using school facilities and personnel. In some cities, school areas are accessible to the park and recreation departments for athletic leagues and community-center activities at no cost. In other cities, a charge is made for the use of school facilities. In communities in which the school administration is the official recreation authority, many of the costs for operating recreation programs are borne by the school budget. Where the park and recreation departments are administered as separate functions, it is sometimes impossible to determine the actual costs for the recreation program. In some instances, the park department maintains all of the areas and facilities for the recreation department, with the cost charged to the park budget. In other instances, the park department provides the same services for the recreation department but charges the cost to the recreation budget. These examples illustrate only a few of the situations that make it difficult to determine what is actually being spent by cities for their parks and recreation programs.

Methods of Financing Recreation

Funds for financing municipal park and recreation services can be divided into two categories: those for the current operation of the department and those for capital development. Discussion of the sources of these funds will be categorized according to their main purpose.

Sources of current operating funds.
The following are considered to be the principal sources of current operating funds:

Appropriations from the general fund. One of the most widely used methods of securing money for recreation is submitting a budget to the appropriating body, normally the common council. Upon approval by the necessary reviewing boards, the money is drawn from the city's general fund.

The general fund is created and maintained to finance the overall functions of a municipal government. The park and recreation department endeavors to obtain its fair share of the city's tax funds, along with the police, fire, public works, and other departments. Where recreation is under the school

administration, the recreation director presents a budget to the school administrators, and the money approved is considered a part of the overall school budget. The amount of money received each year depends to a large extent upon the ability of the recreation board and administrator to win approval of their program from the council or school board, which must determine the budgets of several departments in relation to the anticipated revenue.

Special recreation tax. A special tax levy for recreation is authorized in a number of states, with the money derived being set aside in a special revenue fund. A fund of this nature is usually created through statutory provisions for definite revenues for such functions as parks, recreation, and schools. Advantages of this method include the facts that the money cannot be spent for any other government service except the purpose for which it was created, and that such a levy usually guarantees stability in the budget year after year.

In some states, the local park and/or recreation authorities have been granted complete fiscal independence, with the boards having the right to levy taxes and spend the money without receiving approval from the mayors or city councils. In other states, special levies for park and recreation purposes are subject to city council approval. It is possible in special revenue funds to receive additional appropriations to supplement the money received from the special park and recreation tax.

The special tax is usually expressed in terms of a certain number of mills on each dollar of assessed valuation or so many cents per $100 of assessed valuation of a community. The tax is determined as follows: The total cost of the recreation program for the coming year is calculated; then the anticipated revenues from all other sources, excluding the property tax, are deducted. The balance of the anticipated expenditures must come from the property tax. This remainder is then divided by the assessed valuation of the community, resulting in the recreation tax levy. For example:

Recreation budget request $100,000
Anticipated revenue from fees
and charges   40,000
Balance to be raised from
property tax $ 60,000

Tax rate = $60,000÷ $30,000,000 (net assessed valuation) = $0.20 per $100 assessed valuation

Fees and charges. Municipal recreation is partially supported by fees charged for certain services or facilities. It is important to realize, however, that parks and recreation, like public education, cannot be self-supporting. It is generally agreed that when certain facilities or services have a high initial cost and have limitations as to the number of people they accommodate, fees should be charged. Golf courses and swimming pools are two of the most common examples of facilities charging fees. Traditionally, playgrounds, parks, and community centers that serve large numbers of people in the community are free to the public. Most cities open their recreation activities to children at no cost. In recent years, because of budget limitations, more and more park and recreation authorities are increasing their fees and charges to encompass services previously provided out of the budget. Practices will vary, and a community that is determining new policies or reevaluating old ones should remember first that the recreation program is for all people in the community and that a stringent policy of fees and charges might exclude a large number who most need the benefits of the program.

Sources of capital development funds. The following are considered to be the principal sources of funds for capital outlay:

Bond issues. Borrowing for capital acquisitions and improvements by issuing bonds has been considered essential if large and costly projects such as swimming pools, camps, community buildings, or golf courses are to be provided by municipalities. The expense of such undertakings would be prohibitive if imposed upon a community at any one time. Bonds are a supplement to taxation and should not be considered actual revenue, since they create a liability that must be paid from future taxes.

There are two main types of bonds: general obligation bonds and revenue bonds. General obligation bonds are paid for by ad valorem assessments on real and personal property. Normally such bond issues are put to a referendum vote by the eligible voters to be taxed. In some states, park and recreation authorities can issue bonds within certain limitations without a referendum vote. Revenue bonds are issued with the idea that the facilities constructed will produce sufficient revenue to pay off the indebtedness.

Special assessments. Special assessments are used most commonly to finance permanent improvements, which are paid for in whole or in part by the property owners in the area especially benefited. This method is not used widely, nor is it highly recommended by community officials. The desirable feature is that it places the cost of services on those who benefit and are willing to pay. However, the poorer areas of the community, which often most need such facilities and improvements, generally are neglected if this becomes a common method of financing.

Donations and gifts. One of the main sources of funds for capital outlays for many semipublic agencies is gifts from philanthropic organizations and civic-minded individuals. Municipal park and recreation departments, possibly to a lesser degree, have also received valuable gifts from individuals. In their long-range plans, recreation authorities should be ever alert to this source of assistance.

Federal funds. During the past few years, there has been a plethora of federal programs

Figure 4.2. This water garden replaced a blighted section of downtown Fort Worth, Texas.

to aid communities in acquiring open spaces and recreation facilities (see Figure 4.2). Among them have been the Open Space Land Program of the U.S. Department of Housing and Urban Development (HUD), Model Cities, HUD's Community Development Block Grants, the "Legacy of Parks" Surplus Property Program, the Land and Water Conservation Fund of the Department of Interior, and General Revenue Sharing funds.

Many of these funding sources come and go as federal administrations come and go. The one with the best and most consistent track record has been the Land and Water Conservation Fund operated by the Department of Interior's Heritage Conservation Recreation Service. This is a matching fund requiring state and local agencies to produce half the cost. Expenditures are primarily restricted to land acquisition and outdoor-related activities.

Open Areas and Facilities

With rare exceptions, park and recreation departments have been plagued with a short-

A Questionable Gift

The finest estate in the most exclusive section of Bluetown belonged to the Garcias. They had made their fortune in the town's only major industry, a glove factory. Their will bequeathed the mansion and the land on which it stood to the town as a park and recreation center and provided $1 million for building a swimming pool and other necessary facilities. No money was included to maintain the estate and employ leadership.

Should the town accept this gift? Can it be fitted into the town's long-range plans to provide services to all members of the community? Is the location such that only the more affluent people would use the development? Would the town budget be strained by maintaining this facility so that other programs would suffer? What information do you need to make an intelligent decision?

age of land and facilities on which to provide the amenities of a dynamic park and recreation system. What led to such a dilemma? How did a nation so young allow itself to repeat many of the basic planning mistakes that hinder the quality of life in most cities of the world? Earlier, we stated that two out of every three Americans occupy less than two percent of the land; therein lies the problem. Development was so rapid that we did not have adequate planning to foresee the problems.

Fortunately, some of our ancestors had the knowledge and vision to set aside parks and open spaces for future generations. Can you imagine a New York City without Central Park or Los Angeles and Kansas City without their Griffith and Swope Parks? All of the grand parks, gardens, playfields, forests, wilderness areas, and recreation facilities we enjoy today are there because someone made them happen.

Responsibilities of Local Government

One of the major concerns of the modern city is the provision of properly developed recreation areas to meet the leisure needs of its citizens. The provision of land properly spaced and creatively developed according to the needs of the city or metropolitan area is essential if a well-balanced community park and recreation system is to be achieved. Experience tells us that local government is best suited to provide appropriate areas and facilities for the whole community. Following are some of the main responsibilities relative to this function.

Acquire, develop, and maintain sufficient land for all community needs. Statutory provisions for local park and recreation authorities make it possible for the city or county to require land to be set aside (subdivision control); acquire the land where it is deemed essential (powers of eminent domain); coordinate present as well as future planning for recreation areas in relation to total community needs (city or county planning); and finance the acquisition, development, and maintenance of such areas in the most economical way (bonding and taxing powers).

In spite of the powers available to cities and counties, many communities are failing to meet present and future needs. Because of our bulging cities, massive highway developments, and exploding suburbs, land is fast disappearing, and what is left is astronomical in price. We must, therefore, look beyond our present city boundaries and buy or reserve sufficient land, in desirable locations, for future development. This concept of reserving land in advance of urban sprawl is one of the hardest of all ideas to sell to elected officials who are struggling to meet existing budgetary obligations, much less speculate about future land needs. Once land is set aside or utilized for other purposes, it is almost impossible to reclaim it for public recreation. So, unless people are willing to pay the cost for land now, park and recreation authorities are powerless to meet the demands for recreation areas and facilities.

It is important that the land acquired be so located throughout the city and county that it meets the needs and interests of the neighborhood and community. It is not enough merely to set aside adequate acreage; it is important also that the land be developed and maintained in usable units so that a wide variety of activities can be fostered.

Provide an organized program or supervisory control. An organized program or supervisory control must be initiated according to the area's purpose and the community's needs and interests. In some areas, the main functions of the administrative authority are to establish appropriate policies and to exercise supervisory control to make the best use of the area. The municipal authority may also have a responsibility for providing an organized recreation program, so that the maximum use of the facility may be achieved, the objectives of the program fulfilled, and the best interests of the individuals met. A camp or playground without a well-organized program would be a waste of community efforts in providing such facilities. The provision of qualified leaders, more than areas, facilities, or equipment, will determine whether a well-organized recreation program will result.

Coordinate use of existing facilities. Cooperative relationships should be established between municipal park and recreation authorities and private, religious, industrial, and youth-serving agencies, and schools. These community organizations should be encouraged to utilize the areas, facilities, and services offered by the city. Recreation authorities should stimulate interest and give technical assistance to leaders of community groups who wish to use public property. Since cooperation is a two-way street, it might be necessary or economical for municipal park and recreation departments to use areas and facilities owned and operated by schools, industries, and other youth-serving community agencies. Such cooperative relationships will assure the fullest possible use of existing community resources and might decrease duplication of physical developments. Cooperation of all groups—public and private—will yield maximum returns to the taxpayer's or the philanthropist's dollar. If cooperation exists, additional facilities will be built only when facilities of all existing organizations are being used to capacity. (See Chapter 10 for specific case studies on this subject.)

Develop immediate and long-range plans. Comprehensive planning is essential to assure a varied and well-integrated system of park and recreation facilities. Proper balance, harmony, and order can be assured only if the plans of the many public and private recreation agencies in a community are coordinated.

Guard against encroachment. Not only are cities failing to acquire space fast enough for park and recreation purposes, but many are finding it difficult to hold what they already have. Schools, hospitals, libraries, highways, and factories are being built on land once acquired and, in some cases, developed for recreation uses. Using park and recreation land already owned by the city represents the line of least resistance and involves less work and expense than does acquiring other lands for a project. Reports from all sections of the country reveal that the encroachment problem is widespread. In Murfreesboro, Tennessee, the city's only park was traded for a new industry; in Louisville, Kentucky, a new superhighway devoured one complete park and pieces of two others. In St. Louis, Missouri, part of the famous Forest Park Zoo had to be relocated for highway improvements.

On the other side of the ledger, some cities have had the foresight and willpower to resist such attempts. Several years ago, widespread interest was focused on the Cook County Forest Preserve's successful battle against the University of Illinois, which sought to develop a Chicago campus on one of the Forest Preserve's choice sites.

Park and recreation lands, once lost, can rarely be replaced. It is imperative that cities resist encroachment attempts with vigor and force.

Basic Considerations in Planning

Some of the basic principles that must be considered by the park and recreation authority are listed here.

Integration. A large number of cities today have established planning commissions or boards to develop master plans for the total development of the cities. Where such planning agencies exist, park and recreation authorities should work closely with the planning authorities in integrating the recreation plan with the master plan. Such things as the acquisition of new school sites, the development of streets and highways, housing developments, and industrial growth and development must be taken into consideration in planning future park and recreation space and facility requirements.

Study and analysis. Area and facility planning should take into consideration the people to be served. The park and recreation agency must study such factors as the needs and interests of the individuals in each neighborhood, their nationality traits and customs, and the population indexes, and fit the plans accordingly. Since people, neighborhoods, and cities differ, it is reasonable to assume that a stereotyped playground, playfield, or park will receive mixed responses in different neighborhoods and communities.

Cooperation. Notable progress has been achieved in cooperative planning between school and park recreation administrators in the past decade. The location of playgrounds at elementary school sites and playfields at secondary school areas has proved to be one of the most economical and effective ways of providing adequate recreation opportunities in the average community. The use of these areas for recreation purposes has been effective only when the needs of both the school and the recreation leaders are jointly considered and when school facilities are planned with joint use in mind.

The park-school plan, in which the park and the school authorities acquire and develop adjacent areas as a single functional unit for mutual benefits, has received increasing recognition throughout the country. Minneapolis and Baltimore are among the cities that have demonstrated success of the park-school plan. Schools may serve as indoor recreation centers and may be used by community groups. Cooperative planning between these two government agencies seems imperative if the taxpayer is to receive maximum benefits from tax dollars.

Coordination. Voluntary and semipublic agencies, such as the YMCA, Boys' Clubs, or settlement houses, conduct programs that are similar to or interrelated in many respects with recreation programs conducted by school and municipal agencies. It is important that these agencies and the public authorities cooperatively plan program and facility developments so that duplication and maladjustments or, in some areas, deficiencies will not occur.

Interrelation. The relationships between county, district, regional, state, and national agencies should be considered. It is not enough to limit our thinking and planning merely to the many facets of recreation in our modern communities. Our new supersonic age, with higher family incomes and improved modes of transportation and communication, has placed our national parks, ski resorts, and seashores within reach of the mass of the American people. Our state parks are bursting at the seams. Under such circumstances, park and recreation authorities must broaden their planning to include these additional recreation outlets. Having state and regional parks within easy reach of our urban population influences local recreation offerings and opportunities.

There is growing evidence that the American love affair with the automobile could end abruptly, causing extraordinary burdens on local park and recreation facilities until such time as new energy sources are made available. This, once again, emphasizes the need for comprehensive planning.

Guidelines for Open Space Development

How much land and what types of developments are needed to provide a comprehensive system of recreation areas and facilities? These questions confront local officials concerned with providing organized park and recreation programs. Over a period of years, various national professional and service organizations, planners, and park and recreation leaders have developed guidelines for communities in establishing recreation areas and facilities. Attempts have been made periodically to revise these standards to meet the needs of our changing society.

One of the oldest standards, still used in some quarters, is that a city should have at least one acre of public park and recreation land for each 100 people in the community. In less sophisticated times, this standard was acceptable. However, it falls far short of what local authorities need to consider if realistic standards are to be met. Factors such as population age, diversity, and distribution must be considered along with the types of facilities and their locations within the community if such a standard is to have meaning. No longer is space alone enough. Each park and recreation facility must be creatively designed and developed to meet its intended purpose and be

properly maintained and managed to ensure its fullest use.

Types of Local Parks

Current practice suggests that each community should strive for three basic types of in-city parks. They are miniparks, neighborhood parks, and community parks (including protection of environmental corridors and flood plains). In addition, it is desirable for each community to have access to district and regional parks as well as special resource areas, including forests and nature preserves, wilderness areas, streams and trails, and fish and wildlife areas (see Figure 4.3). Obviously it is beyond the scope of even the most ambitious community to supply all of these facilities, but every attempt should be made by all com-

Figure 4.3. A uniquely beautiful beach preserved as a county park in Dade County, Florida.

munities to acquire, develop, and maintain such facilities.

Miniparks. Sometimes referred to as block parks, tot-lots, or vest-pocket parks, these areas provide a protected environment for young children in residential areas and space for adults in residential or commercial areas. They are usually designed for specific age groups and range in size from one-fourth acre to five acres. Normally ten to twenty percent of the total area is undeveloped and the park is usually within a five-minute walking distance of users.

Neighborhood parks. These areas provide active and passive recreation facilities for all age groups within normal walking distance of urban neighborhood residents. The parks range from five to fifty acres, with ten to twenty-five percent of the total undeveloped. Neighborhood parks should be developed in conjunction with school facilities where possible. Such parks support a wide variety of users with pools, active sports, playfields, playgrounds, and space for quiet meditation.

Community parks. Ranging in size from 50 to 400 acres or more, community parks have large amounts of land undeveloped, averaging twenty to forty percent. Such parks are capable of sustaining large crowds of users. Special features include golf, playfields, picnic areas, playgrounds, swimming pools, nature activities, and bicycling and hiking trails.

Environmental corridors and flood plains along stream and river valleys are unique resources found in most communities and should be an integral part of the community's open space system. Effort should be made by local governments to acquire and protect such properties.

Large parks and special resource areas. While local government has well-defined re-

sponsibilities for in-city parks, the responsibility for outlying parks (district and regional parks) and special resource areas is usually assumed by larger units of government, such as county, district, regional, or state authorities. There are some notable exceptions such as the mountain parks outside Denver and Boulder in Colorado; the Watchung Reservation in northern New Jersey; the East Bay Regional Parks in Alameda County, California; and the Cook County Forest Preserves in the Chicago area. Some of the main types of these parks are given below.

District parks. Preservation of natural resources is important in these facilities, which range from 400 to 800 acres in size and serve residents within thirty minutes of driving time. Usually forty to sixty percent of the land is left undeveloped. Features include biking, hiking, and walking trails; nature trails; golf; picnicking; water resources for swimming, boating, and fishing; and playfields of various types.

Regional parks. The emphasis here is strongly oriented to the outdoors. Minimum size is about 1,000 acres, and the parks serve those within one hour of driving time. Fifty to eighty percent of the land remains undeveloped. Facilities often include bridle, hiking, bicycling, and nature trails; a nature center; picnic sites; and provisions for boating, swimming, fishing, camping, and (depending on location) winter sports, rock climbing, and other activities.

Forest and nature preserves, wilderness areas, streams, trails, fish and wildlife areas. Kept primarily in a natural state, these areas emphasize the very things that give them their names: forests, trails, waterways, lakes, ponds, and wilderness. Such areas have limited access, usually comprise 10,000 acres or more, and are more than an hour's drive from most users. Some may feature scenic drives, and almost all have wildlife and waterfowl sanctuaries. Developments can include camps, trails, picnic areas, trailside museums, and water and winter sports facilities.

Guidelines for Facility Development

When attempting to establish guidelines for the type and number of recreation facilities that communities of a given size should have in order to complement the parks, professionals are confronted with the same kinds of questions they must ask when considering open space. How many tennis courts are enough? How many ball diamonds and swimming pools should a community have? There are no easy answers. Each community must determine its own standards after considering a variety of factors, such as population size, age, diversity, distribution, and ethnic character; the type and number of other public facilities available in the area; geographic location as it relates to climate; and available finances.

The following facilities are considered the minimum for medium and large communities and desirable for small communities:

Softball diamonds	Community center
Baseball diamonds	Auditorium
Tennis courts	Golf course
Swimming facilities, indoor and outdoor	Outdoor theater
	Basketball courts
Playfields	Playgrounds
Picnic areas	Undeveloped natural areas

Depending on needs, finances, leadership, interests, and climate, the following additional facilities may be found in communities of any size:

Aquariums	Bocci courts
Arboretums	Botanical gardens
Arenas and coliseums	Campgrounds
	Casting pools
Beaches	Coasting and tobogganing areas
Bike rights-of-way	

Cultural centers	Nature centers
Day camps	Nature trails
Environmental studies areas	Picnic areas
	Running tracks
Exercise/fitness trails	Shuffleboard courts
Fishing piers	Skateboard arena
Football fields	Skating rinks, ice and roller
Gardens—flowers, formal, vegetable	Ski centers
Handball/racquetball courts	Soccer fields
	Spray pools
Hiking and riding trails	Stadiums
Historic buildings	Surfaced play areas
Horseshoe courts	Volleyball courts
Jogging pathways	Wading pools
Lake and water sports	Wildlife preserves
	Zoological parks
Liveries—bikes, canoes, horses	

Community Centers and Playgrounds

These facilities deserve special mention because of their stabilizing effect on park and recreation programs throughout the country. While recreation centers and playgrounds have changed over the years, professionals are continually evolving and searching for their identity. When well-organized and operated with qualified leadership, recreation centers and playgrounds, whether developed on separate sites, in conjunction with parks and playfields, or as integral parts of a park-school complex, serve people's recreation needs.

Community centers take on a variety of forms. In some instances, YMCAs, YWCAs, Boys' Clubs, Girls Clubs, and settlement houses serve the indoor recreation needs of a neighborhood. Because these semipublic and private agencies have been discussed at length in other chapters, only community centers operated by municipalities are discussed here.

Community centers may serve as the common meeting place for all ages or may be restricted to youth, aged, handicapped, or some interest group (art, nature, garden). They should be designed to offer a wide variety of civic and recreation opportunities. Facilities normally found in multipurpose centers include:

Gymnasium—locker room and showers

Auditorium—assembly hall

Game rooms—table tennis, pool, games

Club and meeting rooms

Arts and crafts shops

Kitchen or snack bar

Swimming pool

Library or reading room

Lounge

Office, service, and storage rooms

A question often raised is: "How can a community justify a separate recreation building when school facilities are available?" This is not an either–or situation. When school buildings are planned, designed, or adapted for community use and school authorities approve the principle of total community use, it would seem unwise and uneconomical to duplicate school facilities. However, one or more separate recreation buildings are usually needed in most cities (see Figure 4.4) for the following reasons:

1. A separate recreation building can be used all hours of the day; schools are available only after school hours. Even then, facilities are reserved for school

groups engaged in co-curricular activities.

2. The joint use of any facility raises problems. Custodians, teachers, and principals who have not been convinced of the need for groups to use "their" buildings may cause conflicts.

3. Many schools, especially the older ones, are not designed for community use.

Most community centers, operated as functions of municipal park and recreation departments, are administered by a community-center director and staff. In larger cities, the directors are generally full-time professionals. In small communities, the superintendents of recreation might also serve as the directors of the centers. The community center staff is responsible to the superintendent of recreation and to the park and recreation board or commission.

In view of reduced workweeks, double shifts, and flexible work hours, centers will need continually to evaluate their operating hours in order to serve neighborhood needs. Advisory councils made up of representatives of the community or neighborhood leaders can provide a valuable service in interpreting the needs of the community to the staff. Quality leadership is the key to successful center operation. Leaders require the confidence and respect of the participants as they work toward mutually satisfying goals.

Organized activities can generally be classified under five major categories: drop-in activities, clubs, classes, leagues and tournaments, and special events.

Playground, as we use the term here, refers to the physical facility that traditionally is found in every city, town, and village throughout the country. These are the play lots and play areas that are always part of the three basic types of parks, mini, neighborhood, and community, described earlier.

Figure 4.4. A community center in Oakland, California.

Playgrounds serve children from tots to teens depending on the area's size, location, and equipment. The size varies from one-fourth acre to five acres or more, depending upon the availability of land and characteristics of the neighborhood. It is generally agreed that playgrounds should be located within easy walking distance, one-fourth to one-half mile, from every home. The features and development of playgrounds are dependent upon the needs and conditions of the neighborhood.

In the ghetto area, for example, sufficient land and adequate facilities may not be available. The clearing of a vacant lot and the development of a vest-pocket park may be the best or only solution. Blocking off a street and providing mobile recreation facilities often provides a temporary solution.

Well-designed playgrounds have the following features: tot-lots, apparatus areas, multiple-use areas, open spaces for informal play, areas for field games, areas for crafts and quiet games, and shelters. Furthermore, playgrounds should be properly lighted, appropriately landscaped, and creatively developed. The trend toward creative design in equipment and facility development merits encouragement. The physical features of playgrounds influence, in no small measure, the scope of opportunities and the effectiveness of the supervised playground program.

Popular for more than three decades in Europe, adventure playgrounds have been gaining prominence in the United States since the early 1970s. The words *adventure playground* have been interpreted to mean anything from a piece of painted sewer pipe to elaborate schemes of wood, metal, and dilapidated junk. We suggest the following definition taken from *What is an Adventure Playground?*, published by the National Playing Fields Association in London:

> An adventure playground is a place where children of all ages, under friendly supervision, are free to do many things they can no longer easily do in our crowded urban society: things like building huts, walks, forts, dens, treehouses; lighting fires and cooking; tree climbing; digging, camping; perhaps gardening and keeping animals; as well as playing team and group games, painting, dressing up, modelling, reading—or doing nothing. For it must also be a place where children just meet and talk in a free, relaxed atmosphere. They do not have to pay to enter, nor do they join as members. They just come to the playground whenever they feel like it.[5]

The emphasis in adventure playgrounds is on the human side; it's a people-to-people program of involvement, participation, and community effort. The physical structure is only a means to endless opportunities for creativity, fun, and adventure (see Figure 4.5). This phenomenon will be discussed further in Chapter 12.

Libraries

Libraries date back as far as the clay tablets of Babylonia in the twenty-first century B.C. Libraries in America are believed to have originated as early as 1653 in Boston. Today there are over 32,000 libraries in the United States, containing nearly a billion volumes.

A 1976 study by the Department of Health, Education, and Welfare indicated the following information about the percentage of the U.S. population served by libraries. Five to 9 years old, 8.7 percent of population served; 10–14 years, 9.9 percent; 15–19 years, 10.6 percent; 20–24 years, 9.9 percent; 25–64 years, 49.5 percent; and those 65 and over,

Figure 4.5. An adventure playground.

11.4 percent. The same study revealed that 32 percent of library users came from nonmetropolitan areas, while 29.2 percent of the 68 percent of metropolitan users came from the central cities and 38.8 came from outside the central city within metropolitan areas.

Today's library is inviting to the eye, cheerful, bright, and comfortably furnished. It carries on a public-relations program to keep the people informed of its new acquisitions and special activities, keeps its doors open at hours most convenient for the public, and offers visitors pleasant surprises in its changing and timely displays. The library is a gold mine of information on community recreation, with material on city planning, means of organizing recreation programs, and home recreation activities. Its supply of current magazines gives new information to public, private, and voluntary organizations.

Libraries maintain sections of records,

photographs, manuscripts, art reproductions, clippings, films, video cassette tapes for watch-a-book programs, radio shows on tape, and maps; story hours for children and story hour extravaganzas for preschoolers and their parents; reading clubs; book reviews; great-books courses; learn-to-write programs; discussion groups; lecture series; little theater; live arts lounge; listening rooms; meet-the-author programs; and courses in gardening, arts and crafts, music, and dramatics. Some libraries provide mail-a-book service; computer terminals and service; lend-a-pet programs; automated book retrieval; bookmobiles; language programs using games and rhythms; and a variety of services to handicapped children and parents needing special assistance. Libraries have helped schools develop and maintain all-purpose media centers and have provided darkroom services. One library organized book, toy, and game centers to entertain the children of parents visiting prison inmates; another library provided a twenty-four-hour telephone story program in Spanish. In some communities without museums, the libraries assume some of the functions of museums and display museum materials.

Since the library is one of the most important leisure resources of a community, its staff should be involved in any program planning for the use of leisure in the community. At least one state has enabling legislation that provides for a library board member to become a regular voting member of the local park and recreation board. Similarly, representatives of museums, nature centers, zoos, botanical gardens, and similar establishments that serve leisure needs should periodically be invited to exchange information with park and recreation board members and staffs.

Museums and Nature Centers

The old-fashioned museums were places for miscellaneous displays, study, research, and the storage of collections. They were learned institutions which had meaning for only those already knowledgeable in their subjects. They were not open to lay people and children were not welcome. Today, museums throughout the country are institutions for popular education and enjoyment. The modern museum, well lighted, artistically planned, and with highly selective displays, is a far cry from its predecessors. New techniques of display are used to give continuity and significance to the exhibits. There are unified themes that progress chronologically or in terms of complexity of thought from display to display. Exhibits include habitat groups, murals, models, restorations, diaramas, displays involving action, and self-testing devices. The museum has come to life.

Museums in America began in 1773, when the Library Society of Charlestown, South Carolina, began to collect materials in natural history. Throughout the nineteenth century many museums were founded by individuals and societies and financed chiefly by contributions, memberships, and endowments. Indiana, in 1914, was the first state to pass an enabling law for the use of tax money to support museums.

Today, there are over 6,000 museums in the United States and Canada supported by local, state, and national governments and by universities as well as by private groups. More than twenty percent of these museums have been established since 1950. About half of the museums are operated as nonprofit organizations, thirty percent by government agencies, and the rest by educational institutions, companies, businesses, individuals, and religious groups. Approximately half of the museums in the United States and Canada emphasize history, art, science, or combinations of these categories. The rest are specialized and cater to interests varying from agriculture to wood carving, including comedy, crime, money, and rocks.

Though differing widely in scope and interest, museums may be generally divided into the following kinds.

Large comprehensive museums. Museums such as the Smithsonian Institution in Washington, D.C., endeavor to include interests ranging from fine art and history through various branches of science. Such museums serve the public through numerous means, such as sponsorship of expeditions; research; publications and audiovisual materials; field trips; lecture programs; special-interest clubs; traveling displays; leadership training courses for teachers and youth leaders; libraries; kits and starters for hobbyists; programs for junior leaders and junior teachers; conducted tours of the museum; radio and television programs; and school services, such as visits to the schools, lectures to school groups, and the lending of movies and exhibits.

Special-interest museums. Many museums center on special interests, such as particular forms of art or science. There are museums of history, archeology, anthropology, astronomy (planetariums), oceanography, ethnology, applied science, and industry. Some of these museums are as large as some of the comprehensive museums and offer similar services within the limits of their specialties. Particularly outstanding in originating special services are the American Museum of Natural History in New York and the Chicago Natural History Museum.

There are many unique museums that are major tourist attractions: the Henry Ford Museum; the Baseball Hall of Fame; the George Eastman House of Photography; the Corning Glass Center; and historic structures, such as homes of famous persons, forts, battlefields, churches, and even whole communities, of which Williamsburg, Virginia, is an outstanding example.

Nature centers and children's museums. Children's departments are often part of the large museums, but special children's museums have also developed. The Brooklyn Children's Museum and the Boston Children's

Museum were among the first. In recent years a great many others have sprung up, some referred to as junior museums and others, in which the emphasis is on natural history, as nature centers. The National Audubon Society's Nature Centers Division and the Natural Science for Youth Foundation offer aid in planning such developments.

Children's museums, although they may contain extensive displays, are considered essentially activity centers. Children themselves may sometimes prepare the exhibits, which are changed often enough to encourage more participation in the preparations. The programs may consist of special-interest clubs, classes, field trips, demonstrations, lectures, and viewing movies and slides. Some children's museums are located in parks or other natural areas and make use of adjacent land for their programs. One of their most beneficial services is rendered to outdoor education groups from schools. School classes with teachers come regularly to the centers to participate in demonstrations in the center and field trips in adjoining areas.

Trailside museums. The term *trailside museum* is applied to the small museum, usually located in a natural area, which is intended primarily to interpret the local features. Its displays explain the environs and encourage the visitor to venture outdoors and observe the phenomena explained. Naturalist-guided field trips, lectures, demonstrations, and self-guiding nature trails are typical developments. National, state, and metropolitan parks contain many such museums.

Recreation and education values of museums. The uncomplicated phenomenon of education and recreation that takes place in the museums of the world is indeed a happy combination. Not only are the things one learns in a museum pleasurable at the time of learning, but the enjoyment is repeated again and again in the process of daily living beyond the museum walls. Knowing the *why* of unfamiliar things of science, nature, history, and arts vastly enriches the adventure of life.

Zoological Parks and Aquariums

Living animals are intensely interesting to both children and adults, as evidenced by the tremendous numbers of visitors to zoological gardens. Living animal collections are referred to as zoos, preserves, animal farms, ranches, nurseries, gardens, parks, and nature centers. If one uses a liberal definition of a zoological park, more than 280 have been identified in the United States. There are fifty separate aquariums in the United States; however, this figure is misleading, since most major zoological parks have aquarium collections.

Like the libraries and museums of today, zoos and aquariums have undergone a face-lifting and modernization. Today's zoo is apt to provide a "total atmosphere" with animals living in areas resembling their native habitats, in which the means of confinement are cleverly concealed. New commercially operated parks, such as Lion Country Safaris, simulate natural habitats by permitting wild animals to roam freely within extensive areas. Human visitors are "caged" in the cars in which they drive through the areas.

Urban children are fascinated with any kind of animal; a goat is as exciting as a llama to a child who has never seen, touched, or smelled one. Many cities have developed extensive children's zoos, combining domestic and exotic animals. Visitors are encouraged to feed and pet the animals in special walk-in corrals or petting areas.

Zoos and aquariums have recognized their potentials educationally and recreationally by providing livelier programs and better publications than in the past. Services include field trips and conducted tours; lectures; printed information on animal life; well-prepared labels, often bilingual; television shows; special children's programs, including clubs and classes;

performances of trained mammals; and research.

Although many people visit national and state parks primarily to see large animals, such as bears, the keeping of animals in captivity in these parks is extremely limited. Sometimes a paddock for deer, elk, or buffalo is maintained; and sometimes a few live specimens of small forms of life, such as snakes and turtles, are kept at nature centers. The trend in national parks is away from keeping any animal in captivity; instead, effort is made to protect animals so that the interested visitor may find them in their native habitats.

The keepers of zoological parks and aquariums have become more consumer-conscious. They realize how important it is for visitors to have a good experience at their facilities. These same people will indirectly determine, by their vote or contribution, whether zoos, aquariums, national parks, and wildlife areas remain for the protection and propagation of animal life.

Gardens, Conservatoriums, and Arboretums

From a simple window box to the magnificent splendor of the ancient Hanging Gardens of Babylon, humans have, over the millennia, taken great pleasure in growing things of beauty. Of all the recreation activities with universal appeal, gardening is certainly near the top of the list. The National Leisure Gardeners' Association encourages this universality in gardening by holding an international congress each year for the exchange of information and ideas and to focus attention on the positive aspects of gardening for pleasure.

Historically, gardens were very practical, providing their owners with herbs, fruits, flowers, and fragrances for medicinal and culinary purposes. During World War II, there was a rebirth of vegetable gardens (victory gardens) to help in the war effort. The reasons for the tremendous popularity of vegetable gardening today are a combination of avocational interest and a desire to economize on food bills. Practically every park and recreation department in the country has developed garden plots or garden centers for this purpose. Many are also holding how-to-do-it sessions on canning, preserving, and storing extra produce.

In America, many of the greatest formal gardens are the result of the dedication of one individual or of garden clubs and horticultural organizations. Such renowned show places as the Callaway Gardens in Pine Mountain, Georgia; the Huntington Botanical Gardens in San Marino, California; and Shaw's Missouri Botanical Gardens in St. Louis are striking examples of private gardens now open to the public. In addition, many of the fine municipal gardens such as the Tulsa, Oklahoma, Municipal Rose Garden; the Gage Park Rose and Rock Gardens in Topeka, Kansas; and the Mitchell Conservatory in Milwaukee were built because public park and recreation officials worked closely with thousands of garden enthusiasts, horticulturists, and civic-minded individuals interested in city beautification, parks, and public gardens.

While botanical gardens, conservatories, and arboretums were originally developed and used for the scientific propagation and study of plants, herbs, trees, and shrubs, their doors have been opened to accommodate millions of visitors interested in the recreation and education values of such facilities.

The botanical gardens, conservatories, and arboretums often contain libraries, herbariums, lecture halls, study rooms, research facilities, nature trails, formal gardens, and children's gardens. Frequently there are information centers, which provide information on lawn and flower care to community residents. By arousing an interest in plants and gardens and an awareness of their beauty, these centers contribute not only to the leisure life of a community but also to its attractiveness as a place to live.

Rural America—Focus on Change

The face of rural America today is vastly different from the past. While the total number of people still living in what we will refer to as rural America has not changed much in the last twenty-five years, vital changes in their makeup have taken place. For the purpose of discussion, the rural population will be defined as those who live either in the open country or in towns and villages of not more than 2,500 population.

There has been a dramatic decline in the number of farms over the past twenty-five years, down by one-half to 2.8 million in 1975; yet the rural population has remained steady at about fifty-four million people. The increase in the number of nonfarm persons moving to rural areas is the reason for this stability of the rural population. The nonfarm rural population has increased by more than one-third, thus raising its proportion of the rural population from sixty percent in 1950 to more than eighty percent in the 1970s.

No longer do we have a strict dichotomy, with the farm on one side and the highly industrialized city on the other. Today's concept of rural recreation must change to include not only the farmers, but also the increasing numbers who live in open country and small villages and towns. They share with the farmer some of the same opportunities and the same difficulties for leisure outlets.

Early Efforts in Building Rural Recreation

The medicine shows, tent chautauquas, circuses, and fairs provided the only real outside entertainment to reach rural America for many years. Of these former pillars of the entertainment industry, one can still find an occasional circus, usually in an urban area where a large crowd is assured, and the ever-popular county and state fairs.

The popularity of the circus peaked during the last quarter of the nineteenth century, about the time the Chautauqua Institution began presenting education, music, art, drama, and religious programs. Originating at Lake Chautauqua in western New York in 1874, the chautauqua programs took to the road in the early 1900s and were extremely popular throughout the early twentieth century. Such well-known personalities as James Whitcomb Riley, Horace Greeley, William Jennings Bryan, Mark Twain, and P. T. Barnum brought color, excitement, and fame to this once-popular form of entertainment.

The county and state fairs, expanded and even more popular today, came to America from Europe during the colonial period. Ronald M. Fisher, writing in *Life in Rural America,* indicates that the modern agriculture fairs sponsored by the Berkshire Agriculture Society were started early in the nineteenth century.[6] By 1868, more than 1,300 agriculture societies were formed, with most of them holding annual fairs. Today, more than 100 million Americans spend in excess of $200 million at 2,150 state and county fairs.

County school fairs originated in Campbell County, Virginia, in 1908, in an attempt on the part of rural schools to give youngsters a chance to display their work and play interests. Other efforts to organize children's play were found in the numerous corn-and-calf clubs that flourished in the first decade of the twentieth century, and the Playground and Recreation Association of America focused attention on the problems of rural recreation in its fifth annual meeting in 1911.

The Patrons of Husbandry, more commonly known as the Grange, which originated in 1867, made strides toward providing social gatherings as a part of their objective to provide a "more satisfactory rural life." In the second decade of the century, the schools in West Virginia led the way to acceptance of school responsibility for better recreation in rural areas when 1,000 rural teachers volunteered to organize their schools as social centers. Small inroads of success were being made as early as

1914 with the passage of laws that empowered counties to form county parks for better appreciation and enjoyment of natural surroundings. By the end of World War I, a number of community councils had been formed in rural areas to integrate existing agencies concerned with the development of services for country districts. Other organizations, such as the Farmers' Union, Farm Women's Clubs, and Agricultural Extension agents, also contributed to the early opportunities in recreation for rural youth or adults.

In 1919, following the first national conference on country life held at Baltimore, the American Country Life Association was formed. It included among its concerns the recreation and social life of the rural population. It was the first national attempt to form a channel of organization and communication among all agencies dealing with problems in rural districts.

Present Opportunities in Rural Recreation

The past half-century has seen a tremendous expansion of club activity in the rural districts. The county programs of YMCA and YWCA, the 4-H Clubs and Home Demonstration Clubs of the Cooperative Extension Service, the Farm Bureau, the Grange, the Farmers' Union, the Farm Women's Clubs, Boy Scouts, and Girl Scouts all attempt to service some of the recreation needs of country residents. Future Farmers of America and Future Homemakers of America carry on active programs of leadership training. The County Agent and Home Demonstration Agent foster training institutes, and the National 4-H Recreation and Rural Arts program is now functioning in every state in the union.

Educational systems and extension divisions are promoting better facilities and opportunities for learning recreation skills through use of itinerant special supervisors. Municipal recreation programs are helping by supplying professional recreation leadership for noon-hour, after-school, and evening leisure outlets. Rural churches are accepting greater responsibility for facilities and leadership in wholesome recreation. County parks are being constructed for fishing, hunting, picnicking, camping, and hiking. Libraries are becoming increasingly aware of their responsibility for whetting the reading appetites of the rural youngsters and adults. Bookmobiles have proved successful and popular for summer and winter service.

Industries in small towns and villages are easing some of the financial burden by contributing money for facilities and leadership for better recreation opportunities in the community. The American Music Conference has stimulated interest in and emphasis on music in rural areas. Interesting and successful experiments in family camping have been initiated.

Some of the early problems remain. Isolation, inaccessibility, lack of sufficient funds, and absence of community solidarity still prevail. But changing attitudes, greater mobility, greater literacy, and more leisure hours are brightening the picture. Significant progress is being made, if at a slower pace than in the more heavily populated, more prosperous urban areas.

Trends in Rural Recreation

What of the future? As the numbers of leisure hours have increased for rural residents, the demands for adequate and satisfying use of those hours have multiplied. Some communities have solved the problem by joining forces to hire professional leadership to train and supervise volunteers for their areas. Flourishing tax-supported programs have grown in such places as Jefferson County, Kentucky; Union County, New Jersey; Los Angeles County, California; and Davidson County, Tennessee. Although these communities are composed of a series of rural areas, in their organization they have extensive programs. In some rural areas, county conservation boards perform recreation functions. In

the 1960s and 1970s, federal aid, given on a county basis, increased local incentive to deal with rural recreation needs and brought about the development of more county park and recreation departments.

As the trend toward suburbia and small towns increases, visionary planners and subdividers are including land for community playgrounds within each division. The swimming pool and surrounding play area are most frequently operated on a membership basis for those who live in the area. Many farmers have found new use for untilled soil by offering their lands as vacation spots for city dwellers. The establishment of hunting preserves, fishing lakes, and commercial park and picnic areas has sometimes brought income that has resulted in greatly increased land values.

University extension departments are extending recreation services through consultation, training of volunteers, and publications. The inclusion of recreation courses in the education of the teacher who is to staff the rural school of the future may foster some changes in the philosophy of and opportunity for recreation within the school day.

National organizations are including education in recreation skills in almost every agency that deals with rural residents. The recreation needs of rural people have never been drastically different from those of their urban neighbors. People's needs are primarily the same, wherever they reside, and the few characteristics that did somewhat distinguish the rural resident are fast dissolving as the American city and country blend into an almost indistinguishable spectrum of rural-suburban-urban living.

A Creative Approach for the Future

One of the most encouraging trends in parks and recreation has been the resourceful-

Figure 4.6. Creative playground equipment supplements the standard swings and slides.

ness and imagination that European park and recreation planners have shown in developing areas and equipment that challenge the imagination of children of all ages. This movement should be expanded. Many schools and park and recreation departments are still designing areas and installing equipment along the traditional lines that can be traced back to our early playgrounds and parks.

As our society radically changes and automation takes many of the satisfactions and creative outlets from our daily tasks, unique and stimulating opportunities for leisure activities are of paramount importance. If cities are to meet successfully the challenges of today, school and community planners must continue to experiment with new and exciting approaches to tot-lots, playgrounds, playfields, and parks (see Figure 4.6). The transition that has taken place in Philadelphia, Oakland, and Boulder is worthy of high commendation. Park and recreation planners elsewhere must experiment with creative types of areas and facilities that are functional, yet add color, attractiveness, and adventure. In most instances, it has been the larger cities that have taken the lead; others must follow.

Selected References

Breeden, Robert L., ed. *Life in Rural America.* Washington, D.C.: National Geographic Society, 1974.

Butler, George D. *Introduction to Community Recreation.* 5th ed. New York: McGraw-Hill Book Co., 1976.

Doell, Charles E., and Twardzik, Louis F. *Elements of Park and Recreation Administration.* 3d ed. Minneapolis: Burgess Publishing Company, 1973.

Gold, Seymour M. *Urban Recreation Planning.* Philadelphia: Lea and Febiger, 1973.

Hjelte, George, and Shivers, Jay S. *Public Administration of Recreational Services.* Philadelphia: Lea and Febiger, 1972.

Kraus, Richard. *Recreation and Leisure in Modern Society.* New York: Appleton-Century-Crofts, 1971.

Kraus, Richard, and Curtis, J. E. *Creative Administration in Recreation and Parks.* 2d ed. St. Louis: C. V. Mosby Company, 1977.

Lutzin, Sidney G., and Storey, Edward H., eds. *Managing Municipal Leisure Services.* Washington, D.C.: International City Management Association, 1973.

Reynolds, Jesse A., and Hormachea, Marion N. *Public Recreation Administration.* Reston: Reston Publishing Company, Inc., 1976.

5
State Responsibility for Recreation

It is one of the happy incidents of the federal system that a single, courageous state may, if its citizens choose, serve as a laboratory, and try novel social economic experiments without risk to the rest of the country.

Louis D. Brandeis

At an ever-increasing tempo, states are expanding their leisure services. The concept that leisure services are a state responsibility on a par with services in education, welfare, health, police protection, and environmental control is relatively new. The present emphasis emerged in the 1960s and 1970s as the federal government gave the states more authority to dispense certain federal funds to their own agencies and to local communities, and the three levels of government began to cooperate more closely.

State governments are closer than the federal government to the people. They can gauge local needs and sentiments more accurately than the federal government can, and they often serve as a means whereby local units make their voices heard in Washington.

State governments were slow in entering the field of leisure services. The first state park was established in 1864, the first fish and game commission in 1878, and the first state forest in 1885. No provisions were made for recreation in these early years.

The depression of the 1930s brought many benefits to recreation programs. Federal funds poured into states and communities for facilities and services. Several state park systems originated as a result of the impetus of various emergency agencies of this period.

Slowed only by World War II, state services continued to grow. A great spurt came in 1965 with the Land and Water Conservation Fund, which motivated the states and their subdivisions to prepare recreation plans. With the establishment of the National Endowment on the Arts and the Humanities in the same year, state committees were formed to disperse funds and encourage creative activities in these areas. State agencies for planning and dissemination of federal money are one of the most important recent expansions of state services.

Diversity of State Structures

The states are extremely diverse in character and needs. Even the original thirteen states showed great differences in their traditions and concepts of government. As new states came into the Union, they brought their own patterns, altering them only to fit the general framework of the federal government. State structures for leisure services are almost as diverse as the states themselves. Some of the factors affecting these services are:

Topography—lakes, seashores, and rivers; mountains, deserts

Climate—arctic, temperate, or subtropic; even, variable; windy, calm; rainy, dry

Wildlife and forests

Population—density, wealth, mobility, education, traditions, age, political structure

Proximity to national parks, forests, reservoirs, and refuges

A sparsely settled state with abundant natural attractions needs different state recreation services than does a densely populated state dominated by urban populations. The following list of the numbers of state agencies responsible for outdoor recreation gives an idea of the variety of structures for recreation services:

Combined fish, game, forests, and parks	16
Combined fish, game, and parks	2
Combined fish, game, and forests	3
Combined fish and game	26
Special recreation agencies	21
Combined park and forest agencies	11
Separate park agencies	16
Separate forest agencies	17
Separate fish or game agencies	3

If to these are added the state agencies concerned primarily with water resources, pollution control, highways, tourism, health, and education—all of which are related to recreation, the total reaches more than 800.[1] Even this figure does not include the grant-in-aid structures related to recreation.

State Functions in Leisure and Recreation

No matter what agency or agencies are assigned the responsibilities, certain leisure and recreation functions should be performed. A brief description of these functions follows.

Enactment of Permissive Legislation

Every local government receives from the state the legal authority to operate recreation programs. Through enabling laws, state legislatures should specify local administrative structures, their functions, methods of financing, tax limitations, and the like, thereby establishing a base upon which local units of government may build.

Services to Local Subdivisions

State services in leisure and recreation should be offered to local areas by special state recreation offices, interagency commissions, and other state agencies or educational institutions. These services include: studying park and recreation needs and making recommendations for establishing or improving services; providing information on financing, administering, and conducting community programs; exchanging useful information and ideas; assisting in recruiting and selecting personnel; conducting in-service training courses and workshops for leaders; developing standards for conducting programs; allocating grants-in-aid for local programs; and coordinating and monitoring certain federally funded programs.

Provision of Areas, Facilities, and Services

About forty-two million acres of state-owned land are available for recreation. Although the acreage is less than ten percent the size of federal recreation holdings, state areas are frequently nearer to population centers and more heavily used per acre. Developments on state lands should include roads, trails, campgrounds, picnic grounds, shelters, museums, swimming pools, beaches, and bath houses. Important historical sites and buildings should be protected.

States should offer direct recreation services on their recreation lands. At first states merely provided land for recreation, but as time went on, they added facilities, with necessary lifeguards, wardens, and caretakers. Public demand required them to employ recreation specialists, lecturers, interpreters, and guides. Recreation programs should also be offered in state-maintained hospitals, prisons, detention homes, and homes for children and the aged.

Propagation and Distribution of Plants and Wildlife

The management and sometimes the propagation of fish and game, the provision of public hunting and fishing grounds, the setting aside of reserves, and the protection of endangered species are major state recreation responsibilities. With federal cooperation, the states should attempt to improve wildlife habitats on both public and private lands.

Unlike other resources on private land, wildlife belongs not to the landholders but to the state. Wildlife that crosses state and international boundaries becomes the concern of the federal government; and therefore migratory birds are under the joint control of the state and the nation.

Plants, too, should be state concerns. Stands of rare trees should be protected in parks or special reserves. Laws should prohibit the picking of many wildflowers; some western states forbid digging up cactus. State nurseries should encourage forests by distributing seedlings at little or no cost.

Research and Education

State agencies involved in economic development, land acquisition and management, wildlife, special populations, or special recreation programs must carry on research, be it analyzing the tourist business or the pheasant population. In states with separate state recreation commissions or boards, much planning and research should revolve around community recreation development.

Educational services related to recreation can be performed by many state agencies and should include slides and films, publications, radio and television programs, traveling exhibits, conservation workshops, conservation camps for children, lectures, and personal services to schools and camps. Several state agencies publish outdoor magazines that rival or surpass commercial publications. Outstanding is the beautiful *Arizona Highways* published by that state's Department of Transportation.

Lack of educated leaders has often hampered progress in recreation, but in recent years professional recreation curriculums in universities and colleges have proliferated. Many state agencies can improve professional leadership through conferences, conventions, workshops, and training institutes.

Promotion of Tourism

Departments of commerce, planning, highways, natural resources, tourism, and other state agencies often make special efforts to attract visitors, since they contribute materially to the well-being of a state.

Establishment and Enforcement of Standards and Regulations

Regulations affecting recreation are of two types: those protecting the users and those protecting the resources. Those protecting the users should include regulations for safety, cleanliness, and health in camps, resorts, swimming pools, restaurants, and the like. Regulations pertaining to resources should involve hunting and fishing, fire danger, vandalism, water pollution, and plant life. Many agencies, such as those concerned with health, conservation, and water resources, enforce these regulations with their own officers by means of licensing, granting permits, and inspecting.

Cooperation with Federal Agencies

Counterparts of national agencies have developed on state levels. We have the National Park Service and state park departments; the Fish and Wildlife Service and state departments of fish and wildlife; the Federal Extension Service and state cooperative extension services; the Forest Service and state forestry divisions; the Office of Education and state departments of education; and so on. The federal and state agencies should work closely with one another, and state agencies may often serve as channels for federal funds and services to local communities. The state-federal cooperation has enabled many states to expand their lands, facilities, and programs.

State Recreation Services

Numerous state agencies, described in the following pages, carry out the functions just discussed. It must not be assumed that all states carry out these functions successfully; some functions may not be carried out at all.

State Recreation Commissions and Boards

Many recreation authorities believe that only when recreation is recognized as a separate function of state government, along with health, welfare, and education, can recreation

services contribute fully to the well-being of citizens. At least thirty-four states have separate recreation commissions, departments, councils, or boards; and in each of the fifty states some agency serves as the liaison for recreation in the administration of the Land and Water Conservation Fund.[2]

North Carolina was the first state to establish a separate recreation agency when it created a state recreation commission in 1945. Vermont, California, and Washington took similar action in 1947.[3] Other states followed slowly until pressed into action by the availability of Land and Water Conservation Fund money in 1965. This state agency does not operate recreation programs itself. It advises local communities, sponsors training institutes, organizes conferences, makes surveys and long-range plans, and channels federal funds.

Outdoor Recreation Services

States have given their greatest recreation services in relation to outdoor programs. The availability of federal funds in recent years has spurred them to give more encouragement and authority to local governments.

State outdoor recreation plans. In order to become eligible for federal money from the Land and Water Conservation Fund Act of 1965, each state was required (1) to designate an agency to handle the funds, (2) to prepare a state outdoor recreation plan acceptable to the Bureau of Outdoor Recreation, and (3) to develop a procedure for granting matching funds to local communities.

Since many states required local units to submit comprehensive local plans in order to qualify for matching funds, local communities, counties, and districts reevaluated their programs and developed acceptable plans. Many of them that had never before established park and recreation boards or commissions did so. Citizens' advisory groups, both state and local, were enlarged in importance and in numbers. The matching funds made possible a great expansion of areas and facilities. Many states gave preference to plans that would serve the disadvantaged and provide lands and facilities near crowded urban centers.

The additional funds also benefited state parks, forests, and wildlife agencies and stimulated new recreation services. Among these were bicycle trails in abandoned canal routes, the study of water routes to secure their protection as scenic rivers and to make some of them available for public use, and the establishment and protection of canoe and boating routes.

The preparation of plans stimulated a study of hiking trails and wilderness backpacking routes and encouraged the states to assume more responsibility for managing the land around public reservoirs. In some cases states shared expenses of reservoir construction with the federal government. State studies of pollution-damaged water recreation areas were undertaken with the expectation that these areas might again meet recreation needs. States began to secure and protect natural areas needed for camping, boating, hiking, and other outdoor activities, and made special efforts to obtain more land near population centers where they are most needed.

Concern for the environment is by no means a recent state phenomenon. The National Conservation Conference of Governors, called by President Theodore Roosevelt in 1908, was responsible for the appointment of state conservation agencies in forty-one states. Today each state has one or more agencies devoted to conservation and natural resources.

State parks. State park authorities often extend their jurisdiction not only over state parks (including arboretums, reservations, reservoirs, and lakes) but also over state monuments, historical sites, recreation areas, park-

ways, and wayside parks. About one third of the state-owned areas have fewer than fifty acres each; others comprise thousands of acres.

State parks differ from local parks in that usually—not always—they are more remote from population centers, are of wider significance, attract visitors from greater distances, contain greater acreage, retain more natural characteristics, and carry on programs more suited to the natural environment.

Most states administer their parks in one of three ways: (1) in a department that includes all natural resources, (2) in a department that administers only parks and forests, or (3) in a separate department of parks. In a few states, authority rests with a highway department, state historical society, state publicity and parks commission, department of public lands, or department of public works.

Background of state parks. The first state park in the United States was the Yosemite Grant, comprising a spectacular glacier-cut valley and the nearby Mariposa Grove of Big Trees. It was created in 1864 from land committed to California by Congress. The concept of reserving superlative areas for public use was a new one. Yosemite was a forerunner of our vast system of national and state parks; it was transferred to the national park system in 1890 (see Figure 5.1). The second state park, established by Michigan at Mackinac Island in 1885, was outstanding for its historical background, having served French, English, and Americans in the dramatic days of the fur trade. A small piece of property was set aside by the state of New York at Niagara Falls in 1885. The first parks were administered individually; state park systems did not come into existence until 1917, when Illinois established the first agency to manage state parks.

Although several other states established parks, the movement lagged until 1921, when Stephen T. Mather, the dynamic first director of the National Park Service, brought together in Des Moines, Iowa, a meeting that resulted

Figure 5.1. Yosemite, the first state park, now a national park.

in the organization of the National Conference on State Parks, which has devoted itself to state park improvement. It is known today as the National Society for Park Resources, a branch of the National Recreation and Park Association.

The depression years of the 1930s encouraged the development of state parks. With help from the National Park Service, state parks grew from 484 areas and 2.7 million acres of land in 1928 to 1,335 areas and 4.4 million acres in 1941. Many camps, lodges, picnic areas, roads, trails, and shelters were constructed in state parks. World War II abruptly stopped this expansion; but following the war, park attendance increased sharply, from 92.5 million people in 1946 to 560 million in 1975. Acreage grew, but not proportionately, from 4.6 million acres in 1946 to 9.8 million in 1975; and the number of areas increased from 1,531

to 3,625. The economic recession of 1974–75 and inflation reduced park revenue and slowed park development. Strenuous efforts are now being made to prepare for anticipated demands.

Financing state parks. The states differ greatly in the ways in which they secure and develop parks. Some parks are gifts from private benefactors. States sometimes exchange land with the federal government or acquire federal property by transfer, such as Conservation Corps land and surplus military land. Increasingly, however, states find it necessary to buy their park lands and must finance the purchases through bond issues, income from offshore oil, and taxes, such as on cigarettes. The offer of federal matching funds through the Land and Water Conservation Fund has been a strong stimulus.

Many state park systems obtain income

Table 5.1. *Comparison of Selected State Park Statistics*

	1962	1967	1970	Est. 1975	Average Annual Percentage of Change		
					1962–67	1967–70	1970–75
Total expenditures (in millions)	$ 108.8	$ 279.3	$ 386.8	$ 670.0	% 31.3	% 12.8	% 14.6
Operations and maintenance (in millions)	61.1	114.0	186.8	295.0	17.3	21.2	11.6
Grants to others (in millions)	NA	15.6	16.1	53.0	NA	1.1	45.8
Total funds available (in millions)	144.6	472.4	619.1	1,411.0	45.3	10.3	25.6
Revenue from operations (in millions)	26.5	50.0	70.9	114.0	17.7	13.9	12.1
Attendance (in millions)	284.8	391.0	482.5	560.0	7.5	7.8	3.2
Total personnel (actual)	17,621	29,254	34,334	45,000	13.2	5.7	6.2
Total areas (actual)	2,479	3,202	3,425	3,625	5.8	2.3	1.2
Total acres (in millions)	5.7	7.3	8.5	9.8	5.6	5.5	3.0

NA—not available

Source: Parks & Recreation 11, no. 7 (July 1976): 35. Reprinted by permission.

from gate fees, seasonal fees admitting visitors to all parks in a given state, parking fees, fees for use of special facilities such as swimming pools, and returns from concessions. Some authorities feel that, although fees should be kept low, at least fifty percent of the cost of maintenance and improvements should be borne by park users.

Variety in state parks. Like the national parks, early state parks concentrated on scenic, scientific, or historical features. As the years passed, active recreation, such as swimming, hiking, and camping, became more important considerations.

States differ somewhat in their park purposes. Some states, such as Kentucky, emphasize their parks as tourist attractions and provide hotel and restaurant facilities with this in mind. Other states concentrate on the needs of nearby residents who use the parks chiefly on a day basis.

Some of the types of areas under state park jurisdiction are:

State parks—large areas emphasizing the natural environment and providing picnic sites and trails and sometimes boating, swimming, horseback riding, visitor centers, lodges, and campsites (see Figure 5.2)

State recreation areas—areas emphasizing active recreation, such as swimming, boating, and skiing

State historical sites and memorials—

Figure 5.2. State park systems preserve scenic areas, such as Devil's Lake, Wisconsin.

usually small areas commemorating historical events and personages

State natural areas or reserves—land undeveloped except for means of access

Numerous innovative programs in state areas include underwater exploration in Florida and California; winter sports, with special snowmobile areas, in northern states; historical pageants; seasonal celebrations; and special music, drama, and art events. Parks specifically for the use of all-terrain vehicles have been created in Delaware and Michigan. The numbers of trails of all types have increased; Missouri and Wisconsin especially have encouraged use of abandoned railroad rights-of-way as trails.

Many state parks, such as those in Michigan, California, and Indiana, conduct interpretive programs with nature hikes, campfire talks, and services in environmental education for schools and youth agencies. Interpretive

facilities include museums, visitor centers, displays-in-place, and nature trails, both labeled and self-guiding. The interpretive programs may explain not only the parks but also the broad environment.

More state parks are being developed near large centers of population to serve urban residents. This trend, encouraged by the Bureau of Outdoor Recreation, is well under way in California, Michigan, and New York.

Overcrowding in campgrounds led many states to introduce computerized reservation systems a few years ago. There were many problems with the systems, however, and some states dropped them.

State forests. State forests were originally reserved for timber production and watershed protection. In many cases states acquired cut-over, abused lands and abandoned farms, which, through planting and natural reproduction, eventually became valuable for timber and prevented further land erosion.

Just as state parks preceded national parks, state forests preceded national forests. As early as 1867, when Wyoming appointed a forestry inquiry commission, states showed interest in the preservation of trees. In 1885, six years before the national forest system was established, New York created the first state forest preserve in the Adirondacks. California, Colorado, and Ohio established forestry departments that same year; and during the next fifteen years, several other states followed suit.

State forests totaled nineteen million acres in 1972, not counting the forests in state parks. Most of this acreage was commercial timber-producing land. State forests are particularly extensive in Minnesota, Michigan, New York, Pennsylvania, and Washington.

Though less developed than state parks, state forests are in general much larger. They have always been used for recreation to some extent, and today most of the forests are open for recreation. Unlike state parks, they usually permit hunting. Fishing is also allowed, and provisions are often made for renting and launching boats.

Day-use areas for picnickers and casual visitors are increasing. Families may camp, and in some places resident youth camps may be leased. Much of the growth of family camping in recent years has taken place in state forests. Hiking, sight-seeing, horseback riding, sailing, swimming, canoeing, boating, and skiing are other activities accommodated in state forests.

State fish and wildlife agencies. California and New Hampshire were the first states to establish fish and game commissions in 1878, but other states soon followed. In some states, two or more agencies share the responsibility, although more commonly a department of fish and wildlife is the single authority.

Commercial fishing and trapping, which are regulated in all states, often compete with sports fishing, resulting in conflicts difficult to resolve. The state must consider the people who make a livelihood from these activities, while at the same time satisfying the demands of those who pursue them for sport.

With the numbers of sportsmen growing at the same time that industries, highways, homes, and farms are preempting natural habitats, many states are attempting to protect and improve these areas by enlarging public fishing and hunting areas in state forests and, more frequently, on state fish and wildlife reserves; leasing private lands and waters for public fishing and hunting; stocking fish and game; improving food and cover for wildlife; and maintaining hatcheries and game farms to provide seed stock for depleted species.

Financial support for these efforts comes largely from hunting and fishing license fees. The federal government assists in accordance with several acts of Congress, notably the Pittman-Robertson Act of 1937 and the Dingell-Johnson Act of 1950. The former provides for a tax on firearms and ammunition, the proceeds of which are distributed to the states on the basis of the number of hunting licenses issued in each state. The latter places a tax on fishing tackle, the funds from which are granted to the states to improve fishing.

All states establish laws governing seasons and bag limits for hunting and fishing. They require licenses for these sports, although specific provisions vary from state to state. An innovative California law requires new licensees to receive instruction in hunting. States employ conservation officers, with varying success, to enforce the laws.

Education and research are important in most state fish and wildlife agencies, which often enlist the support of both adults and children by organizing conservation clubs, promoting school conservation programs, publishing magazines and periodicals, assisting youth agencies, distributing news releases and motion pictures, and making staff members available for talks and consultation and for giving instruction in casting, use of firearms, and archery. Research programs are usually carried

Who May Use State Property?

Promoters of the annual field trials for hunting dogs were annoyed. The State Fish and Wildlife Division had drastically restricted the area in which they could run their dogs. How could they conduct successful field trials?

"We had to do it," explained the manager of the fish and game reserve. "There were only a few dog owners, but the galleries (spectators on horseback) following the dogs rode through the wildlife croplands, caused erosion problems, and disturbed the ducks and geese."

"But state lands belong to us as much as to anyone," argued a field trial representative, "and we cooperated with you. We held the trials when very little wildlife was around and when hunting was out of season."

Should the state authorities reconsider their stand? What is the state's major responsibility in administering a fish and game reserve? Since people who hunt and fish pay license fees and taxes on guns and ammunition and thus provide the chief financial support for such an area, should their interests receive priority?

Similar problems arise on state-owned lands when airplane owners request landing strips, when snowmobilers and motorcyclists want special trails, and when nonhunters ask to observe wildlife on hunting grounds. How far can a state go to accommodate special interests? Should only those who contribute financially be allowed to use state-owned areas?

on in cooperation with educational institutions.

It is only through the most strenuous efforts at propagation, habitat improvement, legal control, and public education that fish and wildlife can continue to survive on our overcrowded planet.

State water resource agencies. Although water resources are frequently administered by a separate state agency, the responsibility is sometimes assigned to a department of health, geology, or natural resources. Water resources are important to recreation in two ways: first, lakes, streams, and ocean shores are themselves major recreation attractions; and second, pure water for drinking, bathing, and other uses is necessary for the development of resorts, camps, and lodges.

Federal water standards and federal assistance in water pollution control are having an impact on recreation. Rivers and streams that a few years ago were too polluted for fishing, swimming, and boating are again becoming attractive and usable.

Educational Services

State departments of education, colleges and universities, museums, and libraries, though concerned primarily with education, render significant services in recreation.

Departments of education. In many states, departments of education employ special recreation consultants or include community recreation services in their divisions of physical education and health. They often encourage recreation through consultation, financial aid for community programs, and education for recreation leaders. These departments may promote the use of school facilities for recreation, may stimulate the inclusion of various types of recreation in school curriculums, and may help in developing school camping programs. The increase in environmental education is in part the result of state assistance.

Colleges and universities. Although state colleges and universities offer many important recreation services and programs, the education of professional leaders in recreation and park management is probably the most valuable of these. Such services are explored in Chapter 15. Under the Community Schools Act of 1974, 13 institutions of higher learning, along with 48 local school districts and 33 state departments of education, were allocated funds to assist community education programs in the first year.

Some colleges and universities, particularly the land-grant colleges through the Cooperative Extension Service, offer direct field consultant services to communities, with either part-time faculty or full-time field staffs. They organize in-service training courses, workshops, and conferences.

All institutions of higher learning foster sports, lectures, and musical and dramatic productions. The student unions alone conduct full programs of recreation. Most of these events are open to the public as well as to students and greatly enrich community recreation life.

State museums and libraries. While state museums and libraries are thought of as primarily educational, at their best they also become means of recreation. Small-town and rural residents who do not have ready access to city libraries especially value state libraries. A state museum usually emphasizes the history, art, folklore, archaeology, anthropology, geology, or biology of the state in which it is located. It may carry on fieldwork and supply audiovisual materials to schools.

Services Concerned with Health, Welfare, and Correction

Most states offer both direct and advisory services in health (physical and mental), wel-

fare, and correction, administering them separately or in combinations. The numbers of special commissions, such as those assigned to problems of juvenile delinquency or aging, have increased in recent years. The commissions may be appointed by state legislators, governors, or both.

Health. State health agencies affect recreation by maintaining standards of health and safety in camps, resorts, swimming pools, beaches, amusement parks, theaters, and other recreation facilities. The agencies usually recognize the importance of recreation in physical and mental fitness and encourage physical education programs in schools and communities. Where state health agencies operate hospitals, recreation is usually part of the therapeutic treatment. These programs are discussed in Chapter 13.

Welfare. With federal help, state welfare agencies provide financial assistance to the needy, the blind, dependent children, and the aged. Some states require recreation facilities and programs in licensed nursing homes and homes for the aged.

The growing numbers of old people are the province of many state commissions, which cooperate with the federal government in studying the problems of aging, including employability, income, education, health, housing, and use of leisure. Recreation is emphasized because it can help to make later life a blessing rather than a burden. More detailed consideration of programs for the aged and aging is given in Chapter 13.

Delinquency and correction. Although youth programs in some states are administered by public welfare agencies, rather than by special commissions, special youth commissions or councils exist in a number of states. In the effort to combat juvenile delinquency, many such commissions promote recreation. The New York Youth Commission, for example, has assisted local communities in establishing and improving recreation programs on the assumption that wholesome activities deter antisocial behavior.

Separate boards deal with correctional institutions in some states; other states combine these functions with public welfare boards. Recreation is regarded as a tool in rehabilitation in prisons and detention homes, a subject that is discussed further in Chapter 13. As a result of the 1974 Juvenile Justice and Delinquency Recreation Act, strenuous efforts are being made to keep juvenile offenders out of institutions through alternatives offered by community agencies.

Other State Services

Several other agencies, described in the paragraphs that follow, perform state recreation functions.

Cooperative extension services. The state cooperative extension services are directed through the state land-grant agricultural colleges as provided by the Smith-Lever Law of 1914. Financed jointly by the state, the federal government, and the counties, the extension services work in three main fields: agriculture for farmers, home economics for homemakers, and the 4-H program for boys and girls. Volunteer leaders are used on the local level.

Recreation permeates the entire program through folk games, dancing, drama, choral groups, community singing, handicrafts, sports, camping, nature study, outings, picnics, and family events. Vacation camps for women have been sponsored by home demonstration agents since the early 1920s. Today's programs include community planning, social issues, and self-discovery features.

Among the extension services are recreation leadership training institutes and conferences, fairs and festivals, loan libraries, and recreation publications such as bulletins, game and song books, and program materials for leaders. The extension staff helps small communities, counties, and organizations in analyzing their recreation needs and working out programs. The staff promotes recreation indirectly by assisting farmers in reforesting, building farm ponds, and making improvements for wildlife that increase the desirability of land for recreation use. (The 4-H program of the Cooperative Extension Services is considered in Chapter 8.)

Highway departments. In a broad sense, the highways are a major recreation resource. Not only are they means of travel to recreation areas, but they can also make recreation out of travel itself. Over half of the use of major highways is for recreation.

Scenic enjoyment should be considered in locating highways. Plantings can be used to hide construction scars, prevent erosion, and transform highways into passageways of beauty. Parkways and scenic turnouts add to enjoyment. Roadside parks equipped with drinking water, picnic tables, and fireplaces are boons to travelers, breaking the routine of a day at the wheel and giving needed relaxation.

Commerce agencies. State departments of commerce and tourist bureaus attempt to attract the money and business that visitors bring to a state. Many of them advertise, prepare booklets and maps describing the attractions of a state, and maintain information centers or visitor bureaus. (See Figure 5.3.) Private associations, such as chambers of commerce, may participate in such promotion.

State councils on the arts. Except for programs in state colleges and universities, encouraging the arts and humanities on a state basis is a new and as yet small part of state services. State committees or commissions are intermediaries between the National Foundation on the Arts and the Humanities and local communities. Federal money is matched by state and private sources and regranted within the states by these committees.

Figure 5.3. State parks provide recreation opportunities.

Coordination of State Services

With so many state agencies giving recreation services, coordination and cooperation are essential. These are provided in some cases by interagency committees or advisory committees. Michigan established its Inter-Agency Council for Recreation as early as 1949. Membership in interagency organizations may consist exclusively of state agencies or may also include private agencies. State recreation commissions and state agencies dealing with education, natural resources, and health are usually members. A successfully functioning committee can make the work of member agencies more effective by preventing overlapping of services and revealing areas in which further services are needed.

These committees exchange information and may conduct studies of recreation resources and needs, organize conferences and workshops, sponsor leadership-training institutes, provide information to the general public, encourage communities to establish recreation programs, and render field service to local communities.

Interstate Cooperation

Cooperation between the states is facilitated through the Council of State Governments, founded in 1933, which acts as a central agency for research and information among the states, between state and federal governments, and between states and their subdivisions. Numerous organizations and interstate commissions are associated with the council.

State officers who work with the federal government in administering the Land and Water Conservation Fund program are affiliated in the National Association of State Outdoor Recreation Liaison Officers.

Needs and Challenges

Although states have made great progress in recent years, important challenges remain. Population pressures and increasing recreation demands will multiply the problems of most states. Land prices are escalating, making it increasingly difficult for states to expand their park and recreation holdings, while at the same time the energy crunch makes it imperative to secure recreation land close to people's homes. The great increase in the numbers of bicyclists, canoeists, hikers, and campers makes it necessary to find new means of financing trails, waterways, and campgrounds for their use.

Even with the expansion and improvement of hunting and fishing habitats, the demand for these activities outruns the ability of the states to provide for them. Stricter regulations will be necessary to protect both the hunter and the hunted. States can encourage enjoyment of wildlife without its destruction through special developments such as trails, photography blinds, and observation platforms for those who hunt with field glasses and cameras instead of guns.

More effective use of state areas and personnel would improve programs in education for leisure, including school environmental education. Herein lies an opportunity for instilling an understanding of the proper use and conservation of state resources, developing a sense of pride in the state's heritage, and spreading knowledge of state history and ecological problems. Interpretive services, printed materials, and cooperation of the media must be expanded. Too many appointments for state park and recreation personnel are made on a political, rather than a merit, basis. The departments of state government related to recreation must work together to keep standards high.

Protection of the environment must continue to be a high priority. State budgets must assure clean air and water and must protect forests, wildlife, and scenic and historical resources. Sound planning and research are more essential than ever to secure maximum recreation opportunities at minimum cost.

Much of the progress in recreation in recent years is due to the vigor of many states in implementing federal programs. They have aroused an awareness of park and recreation needs and have encouraged sluggish communities to establish local councils and committees to prepare long-term plans. States have stimulated communities to find local funds so that they might benefit from matching federal aid. The response in terms of new opportunities for recreation and increased citizen planning has proven the importance of continued emphasis on cooperation among the three levels of government, with the states serving as interpreters both of local needs to the federal government and of federal programs to local governments.

Selected References

The Book of the States. Lexington, Ky.: The Council of State Governments, 1976–77.

Buechner, Robert D. "State Park Systems," Parks and Recreation 11, no. 7 (July 1976): 35–37.

Jensen, Clayne R. Outdoor Recreation in America. 3d ed. Minneapolis: Burgess Publishing Company, 1977.

Recreation and Park Yearbook, 1966. Washington, D.C.: National Recreation and Park Association, 1967.

The Recreation Imperative, A Draft of the Nationwide Outdoor Recreation Plan Prepared by the Department of the Interior. Washington, D.C.: U.S. Government Printing Office, 1974.

Statistical Abstract of the United States. Washington, D.C.: Bureau of the Census, U.S. Department of Commerce, published annually.

Tilden, Freeman. *State Parks, Their Meaning in American Life.* New York: Alfred A. Knopf, 1962.

Van Doren, Carlton S., and Hodges, Louis. *America's Park and Recreation Heritage, A Chronology.* Washington, D.C.: U.S. Department of the Interior, Bureau of Outdoor Recreation, 1975.

6
Federal Recreation Services

This will not be a good place for any of us to live until it is a good place for all of us to live.

Theodore Roosevelt

In the more than two hundred years of our history as a nation, the attitudes and services of the federal government regarding responsibility for leisure have undergone dramatic changes. In the early days of the republic, the official attitude was one of indifference, even though public lands were used for recreation, particularly fishing and hunting. Later, as public lands were reserved for parks and forests, recreation gained status as one of their important uses. Even though recreation was permitted, however, the federal government held—and still holds—these lands primarily for the protection of natural resources.

The federal government today participates in a broad field of leisure services in addition to those related to landholding. More than ninety federal agencies, commissions, committees, and councils are concerned with leisure services. Because of the number and diversity of agencies, there are continual changes in available funds and in federal activities related to leisure. Coordination and cooperation among the many agencies have been difficult.

In recognition of these problems, as far as they affected outdoor recreation, Congress in 1958 instituted a national study of outdoor recreation resources under the auspices of the Outdoor Recreation Resources Review Commission, headed by Laurance S. Rockefeller. The report, issued in 1962, contained the most complete information and analysis to that date regarding outdoor recreation interests, needs, and resources.[1] The Bureau of Outdoor Recreation, established as a result of these recommendations, spread the federal government's interest in leisure services to state and local levels.

Federal Functions in Recreation

Because of the many agencies concerned with leisure and recreation, no unified federal policies have evolved. Each agency has determined its own policies and has altered them as time and circumstances have dictated. Many of the major functions listed here overlap; others are by-products of activities that are not themselves recreation. For example, for economic reasons conservation efforts are directed toward soil, wildlife, forests, and water; yet the recreation value of the resources conserved may be as great as or greater than their economic value.

Ownership and management of land, water, and wildlife in the public interest. Approximately one third of the land in the fifty states is managed by federal agencies (see Figure 6.1). Recreation may be the primary land use, a coordinate use, or a minimal use. Government management for recreation includes the provision of access and facilities, protection, information, and leadership. No comprehensive national land-use policy for both public and private lands has yet been developed.

Grants to state and local governments.

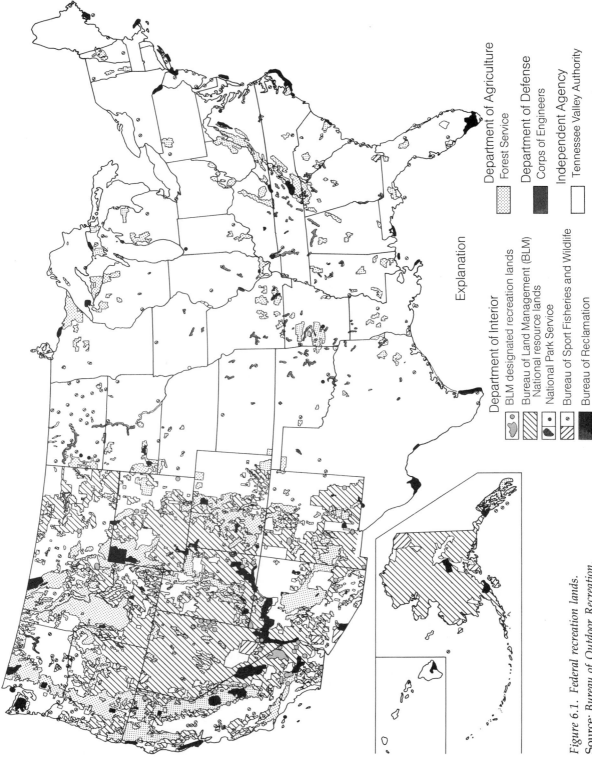

Figure 6.1. Federal recreation lands.
Source: Bureau of Outdoor Recreation.

Explanation

Department of Interior

BLM designated recreation lands

Bureau of Land Management (BLM)
National resource lands

National Park Service

Bureau of Sport Fisheries and Wildlife

Bureau of Reclamation

Department of Agriculture
Forest Service

Department of Defense
Corps of Engineers

Independent Agency
Tennessee Valley Authority

About twenty-nine federal agencies make financial grants to state and local governments for land and facility acquisition, planning, programs for special groups (such as the aged, the handicapped, and those with low incomes), wildlife protection, watershed development, research, and summer leadership.

Direct program operation. In national parks and forests, wildlife reserves, veterans' hospitals, military establishments, and federal institutions, the federal government itself operates the recreation program.

Research and education. Illustrative of the broad spectrum of federal research are studies of the use of and demand for leisure, wildlife problems, forest recreation, and the tourist and travel business. The federal government is a primary source of information on natural resources, travel opportunities, and historical resources of the nation.

Several federal agencies carry on education programs related to their own special concerns and may offer programs to prepare professional leaders, either directly or in cooperation with institutions of higher education.

Regulation. Federal regulations affecting recreation include standards for environmental quality and the impact of recreation activities on the environment. Regulation of hunting and fishing, boating safety, television and radio, and health contribute to a fairer distribution of recreation opportunities.

International agreements. Migrating birds, fish, and mammals that need international protection receive help through agreements between nations. Concern for water quality in recent years has resulted in international agreements about boundary waters and rivers.

Assistance and advisory services. Financial assistance at low interest rates is available to public and private borrowers, including recreation enterprises, through eighteen programs in ten federal agencies. More than thirty federal programs offer technical assistance in areas such as land use, facility development, management, preservation, and program development.

State and local groups may receive advisory services from federal agencies. In addition, private citizens act in advisory capacities for agencies concerned with historical preservation, environmental quality, soil and water conservation, and services to the handicapped and mentally retarded.

Coordination. Various agencies are concerned with coordination to reduce duplication, provide better use of resources, insure better distribution of opportunity, improve access to recreation lands, and provide for long-term needs of the people.

The Bureau of Outdoor Recreation and a National Plan

The establishment of the Bureau of Outdoor Recreation in the Department of the Interior in 1963 and the inauguration of the Land and Water Conservation Fund in 1965 have been called "landmark legislation" for recreation. Their impact has been felt at all levels of government, not only for outdoor recreation but also for many other recreation aspects. By presenting the nation's first outdoor recreation plan and offering financial support, the Bureau of Outdoor Recreation has provided so much incentive that all fifty states have now prepared initial outdoor recreation plans and numerous local communities have also qualified for funds. Using a broad interpretation of "outdoor recreation," the bureau has granted funds on a matching basis for swimming pools, playfields, and open space near crowded urban centers.

Mandate of the Bureau of Outdoor Recreation

When established, the Bureau of Outdoor Recreation (now the Heritage Conservation and Recreation Service) was given these broad responsibilities by Congress in Public Law 88–29:

1. Prepare and maintain a continuing inventory of the outdoor recreation resources and needs of the United States.

2. Prepare a system for classification of outdoor recreation resources.

3. Formulate and maintain a nationwide outdoor recreation plan.

4. Give technical assistance and cooperate with the states, their political subdivisions, and private interests.

5. Encourage interstate and regional cooperation in planning, acquisition, and development of outdoor recreation.

6. Sponsor, engage in, and assist research and education programs.

7. Encourage interdepartmental cooperation and promote coordination of federal plans and activities relating to outdoor recreation.

8. Accept and use donations for outdoor recreation purposes. [2]

(See the vignette on page 121 for an account of the changes made in the responsibilities of the bureau when it was changed into the Heritage Conservation and Recreation Service.)

To make it possible for the Bureau of Outdoor Recreation to carry out its responsibilities, Congress passed the Land and Water Conservation Fund Act in 1965. This act, which will remain in effect through 1989, provides funds from federal taxes on marine gasoline, the sale of federal real property, off-shore oil leases, and admission charges at federal recreation sites. Since the passage of the act, direct appropriations have been made to provide additional funds.

A National Outdoor Recreation Plan

In 1973 the Bureau of Outdoor Recreation submitted to the President the first Nationwide Outdoor Recreation Plan, the result of many years of study aided by suggestions from all levels of government, private citizens, and educational agencies. The significance of the plan lies in its comprehensive approach and its guidelines for the future. Its important considerations include:

A study of people's needs and recreation choices

An analysis of the recreation resources of America

Areas of critical concern—shorelines, beaches, and estuaries; flood plains; wetlands; unique and valuable natural areas; natural lakes; reservoirs; islands; rivers and streams; wilderness; historical properties; and arid and semiarid lands

Roles and responsibilities—federal programs and services, planning and cooperation

State program services

Local programs and services

The private sector

Certain national developments in outdoor recreation that cut across federal departmental and agency lines and also concern the states and the private sector are considered in the Nationwide Outdoor Recreation Plan. [3] Four such national systems are discussed here.

Wild and natural rivers. Stream and river protection has been a critical problem as pollution, dams, and shoreline abuse have reduced the aesthetic and recreational enjoyment of some of the finest water areas of America. In an attempt to save and restore certain rivers and streams, the National Wild and Scenic Rivers Act of 1968 began a system whereby seven rivers were designated for immediate protection and others were marked for study and possible future protection. By 1976, five more had been selected. The states also began a study of their rivers, designating many for protection and making their recreational resources known.

A national trails system. With the goal of eventually developing a national comprehensive trails system, Congress, in 1968, passed the National Trails System Act, providing for two categories of trails—national scenic trails and national recreation trails. The Appalachian Trail in the East and the Pacific Crest Trail in the West were designated as national scenic trails, and others were selected for study. By 1973, forty-two national recreation trails had been established, and many others were under consideration (see Figure 6.2).

It will take many years to develop a truly national trail system. Of present interest is the use of abandoned railroad rights-of-way as trails. Congress has authorized a study of such rights-of-way and their use for recreation. The practicality of the idea is shown by the success of the Illinois Prairie Path, west of Chicago, used by hikers and bicyclists.

Wilderness. Wilderness protection was the basis of the Wilderness Act of 1964. Wilderness had previously been set aside by the U.S. Forest Service and other agencies, but the growing population and economic development have increased pressures on wild lands so much that, without special protection, they would inevitably shrink. The act designated fifty-four units with more than nine million acres and required the Departments of Agriculture and Interior to study and report on other lands to include in the system. The report was made in 1974, and by 1977 about fifteen million acres were in the total wilderness system. Because most designated wilderness had been located in the western United States, Congress in 1975 authorized studies of eastern lands that might be added.

Very few lands in the East can qualify as "wilderness"—that is, land that has been relatively undisturbed by human beings. Nevertheless, many can qualify for a limited wilderness status and as such are sought for inclusion in the wilderness system. The study will proceed until a national comprehensive program of wilderness has been achieved.

The complications of wilderness preservation are illustrated by the establishment of Hell's Canyon National Recreation Area in Idaho. This wild gorge on the Salmon River, the deepest gorge in America, had been proposed as a reservoir site. Enraged conserva-

The Heritage Conservation and Recreation Service

On January 27, 1978, Congress established the Heritage Conservation and Recreation Service within the Department of the Interior. The new agency is a reconstitution of the Bureau of Outdoor Recreation. It retains the previous responsibilities and duties of the BOR, except those related to federal water project studies, wild and scenic river studies, and national trail systems studies. (These functions have been turned over to the National Park Service.) The HCRS has taken over the duties and responsibilities of the National Natural Landmarks Program and the Office of Archaeology and Historic Preservation, both of which were within the National Park Service.

What kinds of problems would you anticipate if you had to deal with a reorganization such as this? How would you minimize the problems? Do you think the changes an improvement?

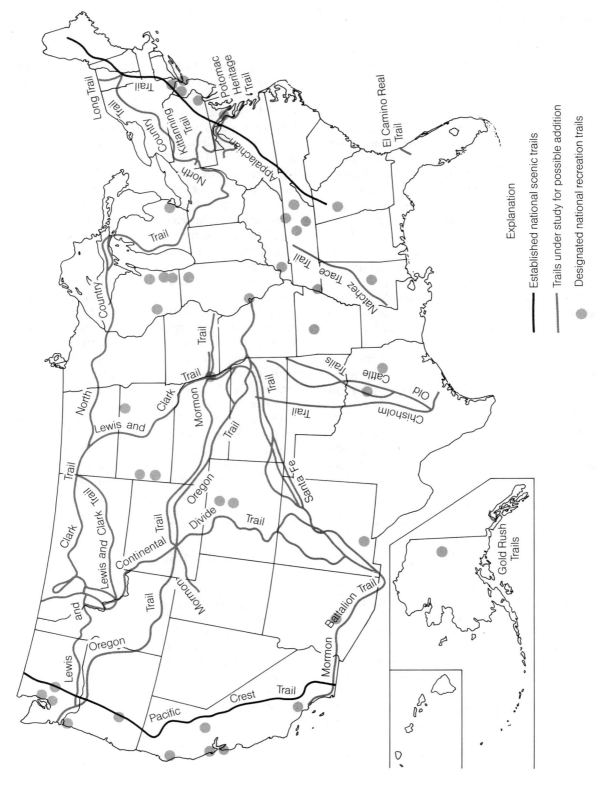

Figure 6.2. *National trails system.* Source: *Bureau of Outdoor Recreation.*

tionists began a struggle to save its natural character. Their efforts culminated in 1976 in the designation of a national recreation area of 670,000 acres, 200,000 of which were designated as wilderness and another 110,000 as a wilderness study area.

Historical and archeological resources. As the nation has grown older, it has regarded its history with growing respect. Congress has acted to preserve historical sites and archeological resources through the Antiquities Act of 1906, the Historic Sites Act of 1935, and the Historic Properties Preservation Act of 1966. Inventories of historical sites have been made, and a national register of historical sites has been developed. The Bicentennial celebrations of 1976 gave impetus to the designation and preservation of historical resources.

Land-Administering Agencies

Of the nearly two billion acres of land once in the public domain, more than one billion have been disposed of through the years by sales; homesteading; grants to states, railroads, schools, institutions, and veterans; and other means. Placing the land in private hands seemed to a young country to be the most effective way to hasten its development. However, about 760 million acres, or one third of the total U.S. acreage, are today in the hands of the federal government. Of these, about 270 million acres are used primarily for public outdoor recreation and include parks, monuments, historical sites, memorials, geological areas, archeological areas, forests, recreation areas, public hunting and shooting grounds, water access areas, fish hatcheries, and wildlife areas.

The agencies administering lands and waters used for recreation are the National Park Service, Forest Service, Fish and Wildlife Service, Bureau of Land Management, Bureau of Indian Affairs, U.S. Army Corps of En-

gineers, Bureau of Reclamation, Tennessee Valley Authority, and Department of Defense.

National Park Service (Department of the Interior)

As early as 1832, Congress showed an interest in holding lands for public use when it established Hot Springs Reservation in Arkansas, not as a park but as a health resort. Some historical sites and cemeteries had also been set aside for protection in these early years. In 1864 Congress granted the Yosemite Valley and the Mariposa Grove of Big Trees to the state of California. But it was not until 1872 that the first specific act recognizing parks and recreation as federal responsibilities was passed.

In 1870, a small group of explorers in the Washburn-Doane-Langford expedition discussed the wild and strangely beautiful land of geysers, mountains, waterfalls, and wild beasts in which they found themselves. Some of them suggested that they lay claim to the land, for, after all, couldn't they make a lot of money from visitors to these unique wonders? Then another idea arose and was accepted. Why not ask the nation, through Congress, to protect this land as a public trust, forbidding private ownership and exploitation, so that generations yet to come could still enjoy it? Spreading their enthusiasm to others in the months that followed, they mustered support that led in 1872 to the establishment of Yellowstone National Park as a "public park or pleasuring ground for the benefit and enjoyment of the people." The loftiness of this ideal and the unselfishness of its purpose remain the core of national park philosophy today.

Congress did not provide funds or an administrative structure for its first parks; so to give them protection, the U.S. Cavalry stepped in.[4] As more parks were created, it became evident that a definite system for their development and protection was necessary; in 1916 the National Park Service was established. Under the aggressive direction of Stephen T. Mather, the first director, the system was enlarged and strengthened. In 1933, all national parks, monuments, battlefield parks and sites, memorials, the national capital parks, and certain national cemeteries were consolidated under the administration of the National Park Service. Congress enlarged the scope of the service beyond federal lands in 1936 by authorizing it to aid states and their subdivisions in planning park and recreation areas.

The National Park Service today. By the late 1970s, the jurisdiction of the National Park Service covered nearly 300 areas and more than thirty-one million acres of federally owned land bearing a variety of designations. The term *national parks* is reserved for the superb treasures of America, mostly large primeval areas with outstanding or unique historical, scenic, or scientific features, such as the Grand Canyon (see Figure 6.3). A national park is established only by act of Congress. *National monuments*, on the other hand, may be created by presidential action. Usually, but not necessarily, they are smaller than national parks and protect some specific feature— archeological, historical, scientific, or scenic. *National historical parks* and *national historic sites* preserve objects, structures, and sites of historical or prehistorical value. Rather recent designations include *national seashores* and *national recreation areas*, where activities may be provided which are not always compatible with the protection of resources so important in other national park areas. New areas are continually under study. A proposed Alaskan addition could well double national park acreage in coming years.

Changing functions and problems. We have seen that the National Park Service, restricted in its early history to jurisdiction over lands of scenic, scientific, or historical significance, grew to include areas designated

Figure 6.3. The Grand Canyon attracts visitors from around the world.

primarily for outdoor recreation. Most recently the question of responsibility for urban areas has arisen. Gateway (near New York), Golden Gate (near San Francisco), and Cuyahoga (in Ohio), all established in the 1970s as national recreation areas, adjoin large metropolitan areas and serve quite different functions from early parks. Many argue that local park agencies should retain this responsibility for parks in urban areas and that federal participation should be limited to grants-in-aid. Expansion into the local sphere would mean a dramatic shift in the original concept of the National Park Service.

With the opening in 1971 of Wolf Trap Farm Park in Vienna, Virginia, the first national park for the performing arts, there was born the concept that the parks might encourage singing, dancing, and acting.

The act creating the National Park Service specified that the parks were to protect the scenic, natural, historical, and wildlife resources in the parks and "to provide for the enjoyment of the same in such manner and by such means and will leave them unimpaired for the enjoyment of future generations." Yet, protection and enjoyment are often at odds. The very popularity of the parks leads to overuse and deterioration of the resources that made them desirable in the first place. As Newton B. Drury wrote, "Many a great landscape carries in its beauty the seeds of its own destruction."[5]

From their inception the national parks attracted visitors, but at first their numbers were modest. The coming of the automobile and good roads brought an ever-swelling flood of visitors, slowed down through the years only by the two world wars and the Great Depression. The numbers of visitors reached more than 250 million by the mid-1970s, with no end in sight.

So the national parks continue to move from crisis to crisis. As visitors increase, the problems of protecting the resources mount; and accommodations and visitor services cannot keep pace with the growing numbers of people. Funds for maintenance, repair, and staff do not keep up with inflation and increasing demands.

Additional difficulties result from the varying points of view as to what kinds of developments are in harmony with park pur-

poses, particularly in the primeval parks. How many roads can be developed before wilderness dies? Do ski lifts destroy natural beauty? How many campers does it take to ruin a campsite? Are tennis courts, golf courses, and speedboats suitable in natural areas? If the major purpose of the national parks, monuments, and historical areas is to provide enjoyment and appreciation of their intrinsic features, shouldn't active recreation pursuits that could be carried on just as well elsewhere be forbidden in the parks? Questions such as these plague the National Park Service.

Steps to safeguard the parks. Even with its limited budget, the National Park Service has taken the following recent steps to alleviate some of its problems:

Accommodations. A movement is now under way to decrease and even eliminate overnight accommodations from national parks.

Campgrounds. There are efforts to move campgrounds either outside the park boundaries or at least to areas of the parks where usage will have the least effect on sensitive resources.

Stay limitations. No longer can families spend long summers in a national park. The

Overused Wilderness

"What happens when a hundred or more hikers converge at evening upon a shelter meant to accommodate eight or twelve persons? Fresh water and sanitation facilities are obviously overtaxed. The wilderness experience they sought evaporates into a supermarket parking lot with wall-to-wall bedrolls."*

Is the expansion of the wilderness system an answer to this problem? Should more wilderness experiences be encouraged in multiple-use areas? How can wilderness users be dispersed into less-frequented areas?

*Tom Wilson, in U.S. Department of the Interior, *Conservation Yearbook Series No. 9*, 1973, p. 17.

length of stay is limited in order to afford fairer use and to reduce congestion. Computerized information may help to equalize future use.

Transportation. To reduce the burden of heavy traffic, some of the most popular parks have instituted public transportation systems.

Back-country travel. Because even wilderness has been overused, the numbers of users must be limited in some areas, and visitors must obtain permits for back-country travel. Attempts are made to divert hikers to less-frequented areas.

Alternate areas. The establishment of the national recreation areas has brought the hope that nonconforming recreation activities might be moved from the national parks to these areas. The expansion of state and private outdoor recreation areas may also, in time, reduce pressures on national parks.

Encouragement of activities that do not impair resources. Visitor information and interpretive services have been expanded. Interpretation is carried out by staffs of naturalists, historians, and archaeologists and includes publications, visitor centers with museums or other exhibits, guided trips such as auto caravans and hikes, nature trails, exhibits-in-place, displays, lectures, campfire programs, libraries, traveling exhibits, slide shows, photographs, television, motion pictures, and research (see Figure 6.4). Through these means the visitor is led to enjoy, understand, and appreciate the parks.

Forest Service (Department of Agriculture)

About 187 million acres—one acre out of each twelve in the United States, or a little less than one acre for every person—including some of the finest recreation lands, are administered by the Forest Service on its 154 national forests and nineteen grasslands. Here one may find those types of recreation that require abundant space and offer escape from the bustle of metropolitan life.

Our national forests were founded not for

recreation but for economic reasons. Except for a few timber reserves established for naval purposes during the early nineteenth century, it was late in the century before the ruthless depredations, by which public forests were obtained, laid bare, and abandoned, were halted. Pressure from the American Forestry Association and its supporters led Congress in 1891 to authorize the President to place public lands in "forest reserves." President Harrison accordingly set aside more than thirteen million acres. In 1897 Congress passed legislation for administering them and opening them for use.

Under the vigorous leadership of Gifford Pinchot in the early 1900s, policies for forest protection, management, and development were formed. The reserves were transferred from the Department of Interior to the Department of Agriculture in 1905, and the resulting agency was called the Forest Service. President Theodore Roosevelt increased the forest holdings to over 148 million acres.

All the early forest reserves were in the West. Two significant acts of Congress, the Weeks Law of 1911 and the Clark-McNary Bill of 1924, made possible the purchase of some eastern land and provided for cooperative programs with the states for fire protection, tree propagation, and planting.

Recreation as a use of national forests. Although at first recreation was merely tolerated and even discouraged on forest reserves, the idea gradually emerged that forest recreation both served the public and won converts to conservation. Recreation thus became recognized as compatible with timber production and watershed protection. Enactment of the Multiple Use Bill in 1960 gave statutory recognition to the principle of multiple use, under which national forests may be used for water, wood, forage, wildlife, and recreation concurrently.

With over 200 million visitor-days spent in recreation use of the national forests annually, recreation is the fastest-growing activity on

Figure 6.4. Guides provide interpretation on many federal lands.

these lands. The Recreation Research Division of the Forest Service found that camping is the most common form of recreation, followed by automobile travel, fishing, hunting, recreation residence use, picnicking, winter sports, hiking and mountain climbing, organizational camp use, resort use, boating, swimming, scuba diving, horseback riding, and use of the visitor information service.

To clarify the frequent confusion of the National Park Service with the Forest Service in the public mind, remember that the former is dedicated to a single use—the preservation and enjoyment of natural areas. Mining, grazing, lumbering, hunting, and even picking flowers or removing rock specimens are for-

bidden. The Forest Service, on the other hand, holds to the multiple-use concept, although recreation may predominate in one place, timbering in another, watershed protection in a third, and so on.

Forest areas and facilities. Forest lands include sea coasts, mountain peaks, lakes, hiking trails, and most of America's big game. Some of the land may be commercially worthless yet have high recreation value. Except for restrictions because of fire danger, all forests are open to the public for recreation.

About thirteen million acres are set aside as wilderness, which is accessible only by horse, canoe, or foot, and from which timber is not harvested. The campsites here offer no amenities for comfort. On areas not designated as wilderness, however, about 8,000 developed camping and picnic sites furnish safe drinking water, sanitary latrines, fire grates, and tables. Campers must bring their own tents and other equipment. In heavily used areas, a time limit, usually of two weeks, is placed on visitors. Much of the explosive growth in family camping in recent years has focused on the national forests.

For people who require more comfort than the camps supply, there are privately owned facilities. The forests can accommodate over 350 thousand overnight visitors at one time in the campgrounds, hotels, and lodges.

How do visitors penetrate these wild lands? About 194 thousand miles of roads and numerous waterways, such as the spacious Boundary Waters Canoe Area of northern Minnesota, crisscross their terrain and waters; and 100 thousand miles of trails, including such famous systems as the Appalachian Trail from Maine to Georgia and the Pacific Crest Trail, which will eventually stretch from Canada to Mexico, ribbon its mountains and valleys.

About 81,000 miles of fishing streams and over three million acres of fishing lakes entice anglers, and hunters find lands on which game abounds. Streams and lakes are stocked with fish, and state fish and game laws are enforced. About 200 winter sports areas have been developed, some with toboggan slides and many with lifts and tows operated by commercial concessionaires.

Visitor information. The year 1960 witnessed the beginnings of the Visitor Information Service, a program somewhat similar to the interpretive services so well developed in the national parks. Guided walks, tours, nature trails, informative signs, talks, exhibits, demonstration areas, information centers, and campfire programs are included.

The Forest Service is actively concerned with the extension of its services to the disadvantaged. Its conservation education program provides school materials and services. Efforts are being made to establish visitor services, particularly for the benefit of low-income families, near large urban centers. The Forest Service has an excellent research system that includes the whole field of outdoor recreation.

For all the people. From time to time, the Forest Service has suffered from efforts to reduce its holdings or turn them over to the states or private individuals. In recent years, however, there has come a recognition of the importance to the national well-being of public land carefully managed for its timber, water, wildlife, grasslands, and recreation. These vast areas, open for recreation and inspiration, belong to all the people for the use of all the people. In the face of population pressures, it is more essential than ever to hold these reserves for public benefit.

Fish and Wildlife Service (Department of the Interior)

Many people consider fishing to be the favorite sport of Americans. Hunting also ranks high in popularity; it is estimated that about thirty percent of the population fish and ten percent hunt.[6] The existence of these activities hinges upon a continuing supply of fish and wildlife as well as waters and lands to support them. As in the case of national forests, the federal government's interest in conserving these resources originated from economic rather than recreation concerns.

The abundant fish and wildlife of our pioneer days suffered from the inroads of civilization. Widespread stream pollution and watershed destruction played havoc with the supply of fish, while indiscriminate shooting and the elimination of breeding grounds and habitats diminished the numbers of wildlife.

To protect and increase the fish and wildlife supply, the Bureau of Fisheries was established in 1871 in the Department of Commerce, and the Bureau of Biological Survey in 1885 in the Department of Agriculture. In 1940 these two bureaus were consolidated to form the Fish and Wildlife Service in the Department of the Interior. In 1956, two separate bureaus were set up in the service; the Bureau of Commercial Fisheries and the Bureau of Sport Fisheries and Wildlife. The former was transferred to the Department of Commerce in 1970; and the latter, which is concerned with recreation rather than economic activities, was renamed the Fish and Wildlife Service in 1974.

The chief objective of the service is to assure maximum opportunities for fishing and hunting. Briefly, it administers laws designed to increase and protect fish and wildlife; provides and maintains wildlife refuges; conducts research; furnishes advice and leadership to control destructive or injured animals, birds, and fish; enforces federal game laws; and cooperates with state fish and wildlife agencies.

Fish are propagated in the ninety or so national fish hatcheries, and with state cooperation, fishing waters are stocked and restocked annually with millions of fingerlings.

A program to acquire 4.5 million acres of wetlands to aid migratory waterfowl was authorized in 1961 by the Dingell Bill. This program and the stepped-up efforts at pollution control aid in the protection of America's fish and game. As population increases and the competition for land and water becomes more intense, stricter controls of fishing and hunting will become necessary and further efforts will be required to obtain homes for wildlife.

The Fish and Wildlife Service administers over 370 national wildlife refuges and ranges, aggregating about thirty-two million acres, some of which are on lands controlled by other federal agencies. The refuges shelter all forms of wildlife but are particularly significant in protecting migratory waterfowl and such animals as bison, antelope, mountain sheep, and others that need special consideration.

Interestingly, of the twenty million or so people who travel to the refuges annually, only about a third go to fish and a twentieth go to hunt. The great majority go to sight-see, photograph wildlife, hike, picnic, study nature, swim, boat, or enjoy the newly developed visitor centers, nature trails, observation towers, and interpretive services.

Liberal federal aid to state fish and game programs is given through laws administered by the Fish and Wildlife Service. Funds for this program are derived largely from the Migratory Bird Hunting Stamp Act of 1934, which requires hunters of migratory fowl to buy stamps that are affixed to their state licenses; from the Pittman-Robertson Act of 1937, which makes available to states the funds from a federal excise tax on sporting arms and ammunitions; and from the Dingell-Johnson Act of 1950, mentioned in Chapter 5.

The service cooperates with public and private agencies by making recommendations regarding marshlands, fences to control grazing and poaching, dams and waterways for fish that leave the ocean to spawn in fresh waters, and other aids to fish and wildlife.

Bureau of Land Management (Department of the Interior)

All the public domain that is not specifically reserved by other agencies—in other words, about two thirds of it—falls into the hands of the Bureau of Land Management (BLM). Its total jurisdiction extends over nearly 474 million acres.

Considered the least desirable of public lands, the BLM holdings were long neglected and ignored as recreation assets. But with passage of the Classification and Multiple Use Act of 1964, the BLM role in recreation began to enlarge. The bureau made its first recreation inventory and classified over six million acres as having primary value for recreation and millions of other acres as having limited value. By 1974 about 196 million acres, primarily in Alaska and the eleven western states, were classified as usable or suitable for recreation.[7]

About 150 sites receive BLM attention, with priority given to developments near western urban centers and overburdened national parks and forests. Recreation use of BLM lands in Alaska and in the western deserts has begun. Protection of natural areas, begun in 1968, is planned along with recreation use.

The bureau cooperates with state and local governments and private interests in developing recreation facilities on its land. It may lease or sell sites for museums, restaurants, cabins, and the like, while retaining and administering surrounding areas. To encourage public provision of recreation areas, the bureau may make land available to states and their political subdivisions at nominal cost. Tracts of five acres or less may be leased or sold for private recreation purposes such as weekend residences or camping.

Use of BLM lands has skyrocketed despite severely limited funds for development. Under multiple-use management, recreation takes its place along with grazing, wildlife management, forestry, and mineral development.

Bureau of Indian Affairs (Department of the Interior)

Indian reservations are administered for the benefit of the Indians and are not considered public lands. Many Indian tribes, however, have opened their lands to the public for recreation. Tourists travel to Indian reservations partly because of fascination with the ceremonies, architecture, and arts and crafts, and partly because of curiosity about the everyday life of the Indians. Scenic beauty, historical sites, and opportunities for swimming and hiking offer further enticements. Hunters and anglers use these lands only with

the permission of the Indian tribes, which sometimes require special reservation licenses. Over ten million visitor-days on Indian lands were reported for 1968.

The Bureau of Indian Affairs, created in 1824, was intended primarily to provide services in health, education, and land management. It has advisory jurisdiction over fifty million acres of Indian trust lands and directly administers five million acres of related federal land.

Since the establishment in 1968 of the National Council for Indian Opportunity, Indians have played more aggressive roles in their own development. Through their own tribal organizations, the tribes are developing tourist attractions. The Navajo tribe, for example, maintains Monument Valley in Arizona as a park, with roads, a visitor center, and camp sites. Elsewhere, tourist accommodations, picnic sites, campgrounds, hotels, motels, boating facilities, lakes, and ski resorts are being built or planned by Indians. Most ceremonies are held during the summer and early fall, when visitors are most numerous. Museums, maintained at several reservations, display modern Indian arts and crafts as well as historical materials.

U.S. Army Corps of Engineers (Department of Defense)

As old as the nation itself, the Corps of Engineers, which dates from 1775, is authorized to improve and maintain rivers and other waterways in the interest of navigation and flood control. In so doing, it has built reservoirs that have become major attractions for boating, swimming, fishing, picnicking, and camping (see Figure 6.5), even though priority is given to flood control, navigation, water for consumption, and power development.

The Flood Control Act of 1944 allowed the establishment and maintenance of public park and recreation facilities in the Corps of Engineer reservoir areas and provided that the waters be open without charge for recreation when such use was not contrary to the public interest. In 1965 the Federal Water Project Recreation Act made outdoor recreation coequal with other purposes for which federal water resource projects may be developed.

The corps protects and improves beaches and develops small harbors for recreation craft. It cooperates with other authorities in studying proposed projects in order to explore their recreation possibilities. Since benefits of reservoir recreation fall particularly to nearby residents, state and local governments are encouraged to develop public parks on reservoir shores. States, local governments, and private groups have invested many times more money than has the federal government for recreation on corps lands.

The corps gives priority in recreation development of reservoir areas in the following order: public day-use facilities, such as parking areas, observation points, picnic grounds, toilets, access roads, and trails; public boat launches and docks; public campgrounds; and nonprofit organized camps operated in the public interest.

Private exploitation is forbidden. The Department of the Army licenses state and federal agencies to manage fish and wildlife resources; grants commercial leases for docks and restaurants and for furnishing boats; and leases lots to private groups and individuals if such uses will not conflict with public needs.

On no other federal lands has recreation use skyrocketed as rapidly in recent years as on corps reservoir areas. Attendance exceeds

Figure 6.5. Army Corps of Engineers reservoirs draw millions of boaters.

that of any other federal lands, reaching 344 million visitor-days of recreation in 1973. About eleven million acres of land and water, with about 400 water areas of considerable variance in size, 2,700 recreation areas, and 40,000 miles of shoreline are under Corps of Engineers' control in forty-four different states.

Why has reservoir use become so popular? One explanation is ease of access. Many reservoirs are located near large centers of population or interstate highways in the eastern United States, where there are relatively few national parks and forests. Another reason lies in the burgeoning participation in camping and water-related sports.

The day of the big dams may be ending. Many projects have met with considerable opposition from environmentalists intent upon preserving the natural features of proposed reservoir sites. The potential damage must be weighed against the values in flood control, navigation, and water improvement that the reservoirs might bring. Further opposition comes from use of the corps as a "pork barrel" by members of Congress who bargain to secure reservoirs for their own districts without regard for the good of the nation as a whole. No doubt some projects have been inadvisable; but, from a purely recreation point of view, the vast water areas of the corps meet an important public demand.

Bureau of Reclamation (Department of the Interior)

Among the many agencies related to water resources is the Bureau of Reclamation, established in 1902, with a special responsibility for the development of water resources, primarily for irrigation and power, in the seventeen contiguous western states and Hawaii. As early as 1936, when the bureau agreed that the National Park Service should develop recreation facilities and administer land around Hoover Dam, recreation was one of its considerations. Since 1944, the bureau has incorporated recre-

ation in its planning. However, only in recent years has much money been allotted for the construction of recreation facilities.

In studying reservoir proposals, the bureau considers both the recreation potentials and the possible destruction of existing recreation resources by dam constructions. It cooperates with several other federal agencies, such as the new HCRS, the Forest Service, and the National Park Service, in investigating and appraising recreation potentials, preparing plans, and supervising facility construction. The Smithsonian Institution assists in archaeological surveys and salvage operations, whereas the Fish and Wildlife Service studies and prepares recommendations regarding sport fishing and hunting.

Wherever possible, the Bureau of Reclamation transfers its reservoir areas to other agencies. If the areas have national significance, they might be administered by the National Park Service as national recreation areas. The Forest Service develops and administers Bureau of Reclamation reservoir recreation areas located in national forests. State and local agencies assume responsibility for other recreation areas created by Bureau of Reclamation reservoirs.

Tennessee Valley Authority

With its many lakes within a two-day drive of more than half the people of the United States, the Tennessee Valley Authority (TVA), created in 1933, provides recreation in connection with its operation of the Tennessee River for navigation, flood control, and electric power. Its reservoirs in Alabama, Georgia, Kentucky, Mississippi, North Carolina, Tennessee, and Virginia attract residents not only of those states but of neighboring states as well.

At full-pool level there are about 700,000 acres of water and more than 10,000 miles of shoreline, most of which are available for recreation developments. About forty group camps have been built on TVA property. Over 6,000 summer cottages and many state, county, and municipal parks are strung along the shorelines.

Fishing, accompanied by boating, camping, and picnicking, is the outstanding activity on TVA lakes. Speedboat races, sailboat regattas, and other recreation events attract large numbers of people. The lakes have revolutionized the economy and the leisure patterns of many of the communities nearby. In the Land Between the Lakes project in western Kentucky and Tennessee, the TVA is demonstrating ways of restoring natural beauty to misused land and is creating opportunities for recreation and conservation education.

TVA lands are often transferred to other federal, state, and local government units, to quasipublic groups (such as Boy Scouts), or to private individuals.

Military Lands (Department of Defense)

Some of the lands held by the Department of Defense serve extensive recreation purposes, not only for the military but also for the general public. Many of these areas were acquired during World War II, but, with changing military needs, have become surplus properties. Several have been allocated to state and local government agencies; others are being held for possible future military emergencies.

Agencies Offering Advisory, Technical, and Financial Assistance

Although the federal government makes its greatest contribution to recreation through its land-resource management, other services to states and communities are constantly growing. Most of the land-administering agencies just described give consultant assistance and carry on extensive research. Some of the many additional agencies that perform recreation functions are listed below.

Heritage Conservation and Recreation Service
(Department of the Interior)

This bureau, considered in more detail early in this chapter, manages grants, conducts research, and gives advisory assistance to state and local outdoor recreation programs.

Extension Service (Department of Agriculture)

Cooperation is the keynote to the success of the Extension Service, an outstanding example of all levels of government working together. Its services are available in all fifty states and Puerto Rico. The federal government supplies about fifty percent of the funds, and the remainder comes from state and local sources. Federal services are strictly advisory and educational in nature. They are available on request. Various publications are issued from both the federal and the state offices. (Further discussion of the Extension Service is found in Chapters 4, 5, and 8.)

Soil Conservation Service (Department of Agriculture)

By its work with landowners and operators—private as well as public—the Soil Conservation Service encourages the improvement of recreation resources. It encourages farmers to build ponds for swimming, boating, and fishing as well as for the benefit of waterfowl. It offers suggestions for plantings to attract wildlife and improve wildlife habitats.

In existence since 1935, the Soil Conservation Service (SCS) carries out its activities principally through 3,000 locally organized and managed soil and water conservation districts formed under state laws. SCS specialists, upon request, make long-range plans and maps for using land for its best capabilities. The service helps camp operators as well as farmers in rehabilitating worn-out land, developing water resources, and restoring wildlife. In recent years, the SCS has become involved in urban land use planning and environmental education.

Through its Small Watershed Program, the SCS assists public and nonprofit projects for public recreation and for fish and wildlife protection.

Office of Education (Department of Health, Education, and Welfare)

The Office of Education was one of the first federal agencies interested in the use of leisure. Even in its earliest report in 1868 (the year following its establishment), it recognized the significance of recreation in the education of children. It has encouraged the teaching of the arts of leisure and the provision of recreation opportunities by schools for both students and communities. Recreation is seen not only as an end in itself but also as a method of teaching.

Coordinating its efforts with those of other units within the Department of HEW through the Departmental Committee on Recreation, the Office of Education works with various national organizations, state and local school systems, colleges and universities, and individuals. Through the Elementary and Secondary Education Act of 1965, it provides funds for supplementary education centers and assistance to camping, physical education, and outdoor education, as well as for programs for the ill and handicapped.

Public Health Service (Department of Health, Education, and Welfare)

Since health hazards can mount wherever large numbers of people congregate, the planning and education program of the Public Health Service is vital to parks, playgrounds, camps, bathing beaches, boating areas, trailer parks, and picnic sites. Federal, state, and local agencies call on it for advice on such matters as bathing sanitation, food handling, disposal of refuse and sewage, and even detection of smog damage to forest trees. The agency stimulates state and community action through financial grants.

The Bureau of Family Services supports a better family environment through various activities, some of which are recreational in nature. It provides grants-in-aid to the aged, blind, and disabled and is involved in a vocational rehabilitation program.

U.S. Travel Service (Department of Commerce)

Americans love to travel. The numbers of Americans traveling throughout the world far exceed the numbers of foreigners visiting the United States. The dollar value of tourism to the economy was acknowledged in 1961 with the establishment of a U.S. Travel Service in the Department of Commerce to encourage travel in the United States by residents of other countries and to promote hospitality to these visitors.

Federal Highway Administration (Department of Transportation)

The highway traveler who is refreshed or who picnics at a wayside rest park, pauses at an overlook to admire a spectacular scene, or simply enjoys a road unspoiled by billboards and harsh construction scars can give some credit to the Highway Administration. Known formerly as the Bureau of Public Roads, the agency merged with the Department of Transportation when the latter was created in 1966. The act creating the department directed it to make special efforts to preserve the natural beauty of recreation lands, wildlife refuges, and historical sites and to avoid using such lands for transportation unless there were no alternatives and unless all possible ways of minimizing harm were used.

The Federal Highway Administration administers the federal highway beautification program and the program of financial help to the states for constructing interstate defense highways and certain other roads. Revenues are derived from special taxes on highway users.

Federal Communications Commission

Since radios and televisions operate in millions of homes for several hours a day, they are major recreation resources. About seventy million homes in the United States have at least one radio, and about as many have television sets. Although the Federal Communications Commission does not censor radio and television programs, it authorizes stations of all types and makes periodic checkups to see that stations meet community needs and provide public service programs.

Department of Housing and Urban Development

HUD is the principal federal agency concerned with housing and community environments. In administering the Open Space Land Program and the Urban Beautification Program, HUD provides grants to local governments for recreation and related purposes. It may give assistance for developing or improving neighborhoods, waterfronts, downtown parks, and open spaces. HUD's biggest problem is providing open space in crowded low- and middle-cost housing developments.

National Foundation on the Arts and the Humanities

Created as an independent agency in 1965, the National Foundation on the Arts and the Humanities encourages national programs in the arts (music, dance, drama, folk art, creative writing, architecture, painting, sculpture, photography, design, motion pictures, and television) and the humanities (the study of language, literature, history, and philosophy) through its two major divisions, the National Endowment for the Arts and the National Endowment for the Humanities. A third division, the Federal Council on the Arts and Humanities, coordinates the activities of the two endowments. The foundation awards grants to individuals, groups, and institutions in furtherance of its goals to preserve our cultural heritage, advance the quality of life through the arts, and increase understanding and appreciation of the humanities.

Environmental Protection

Alarm over the deteriorating environment led in 1970 to the establishment of the Environmental Protection Agency as an independent agency to control and abate air and water pollution and to reduce hazards from noxious wastes, pesticides, herbicides, noise, and radiation. As the public's advocate for a livable environment, it strengthens the efforts of other federal agencies to improve the environment.

The Council on Environmental Quality in the executive office of the President, established by the National Environmental Policy Act of 1969, recommends policies to improve the environment. All requests for federally funded recreation developments must now be accompanied by environmental impact statements, a requirement that has helped in securing plans that cause minimal environmental damage.

The President's Council on Physical Fitness and Sports

Continuing the work of the President's Council on Physical Fitness formed in 1956, this council, established in 1968, attempts to improve physical fitness through community agencies of all kinds. It recommends programs to enhance the physical fitness of all Americans and to increase their opportunities for sports participation. Through widespread publicity and regional clinics, it encourages adults as well as children to become active participants. The Presidential Sports Award is granted to adults taking part regularly in any of thirty-eight different sports.

Agencies Serving Special Groups

In a huge government with hundreds of agencies, many offer services for special purposes or groups. Programs for the disadvantaged have been thrust into recent prominence. Other special groups are military personnel, veterans, federal employees, and the national capital itself.

Agencies Serving the Disadvantaged

While a major effort has been made to raise the economic level of the disadvantaged, the federal government has also acted to improve the quality of living through housing, education, and recreation. The extensive federal recreation services during the depression of the 1930s faded away as local and state programs took hold. In recent years, the growing interest in civil rights and poverty programs has revived federal participation in recreation for the disadvantaged.

ACTION, an independent agency created in 1971, coordinates and administers volunteer services under government auspices, both at home and abroad. Its programs include VISTA (Volunteers in Service to America); Special Volunteer Programs (SVP) which focus on services related to poverty, such as Foster Grandparent Program, Retired Senior Volunteer Program (RSVP), Senior Companion Program, National Student Volunteer Program (NSVP), and Youth Challenge Program (YCP); and the

Peace Corps, for service in foreign lands. Chapter 11 gives more details on these programs.

Among its programs to help low-income families and individuals, the Community Service Administration funds the Community Action Program (CAP), which supports local activities to meet a whole range of needs, including recreation, among the poor and elderly. Its National Summer Youth Sports Program gives disadvantaged youth a chance to participate in summer sports on college campuses.

The Job Corps, created in 1973 in the Department of Labor, offers two types of programs: one providing instruction in occupational skills and the other (Civilian Conservation Centers) conducted on public lands, such as the national forests.

The Youth Conservation Corps provides employment in more than 400 YCC camps, improving their recreation attractions while teaching environmental education and resource conservation. The Summer Program for the Education and Development of Youth (SPEDY) opens work opportunities, many of them in park and recreation agencies, for low-income youth. The Young Adult Conservation Corps (YACC) provides work in forest improvement for young people sixteen through twenty-three years of age.

Office of Human Development
(Department of Health, Education, and Welfare)

Thirteen agencies, six of which have authority for funding grants, are in the Office of Human Development, which directs its work toward children and youth, the aged, the disabled, native Americans (Indians), and persons living in rural areas. Among the agencies are the Administration on Aging, Office of Child Development, Office of Native American Programs, Office of Youth Development, Rehabilitation Services Administration, Office for Handicapped Individuals, and President's Committee on Mental Retardation.

The Office of Youth Development works with youth-serving organizations and youth groups. Its emphasis is on programs for runaway youth and their families.

Two major bureaus, the Child Development Services and the Children's Bureau, are in the Office of Child Development. There are five functions of the office: (1) to operate federally funded programs for children, such as Head Start; (2) to develop innovative programs for children and parents; (3) to coordinate federal programs for children and parents; (4) to administer the National Center of Child Abuse and Neglect; and (5) to act as the advocate for the children of the nation.

As the percentage of older people in the population has increased, the need for services for them has expanded. The Older Americans Act of 1965 and the 1973 amendments established the Administration of Aging and provided funds for local projects. Programs for the aging are described in Chapter 13.

The Armed Forces

Recreation has become accepted as a valuable contribution to the physical and mental well-being of men and women in the military forces, and the federal government supports free-time centers and activities.

Programs from World War I to Vietnam. In World War I, the burden of providing recreation rested primarily on the shoulders of voluntary agencies, including the YMCA, the Salvation Army, the Knights of Columbus, the Jewish Welfare Board, the American Library Association, the American Red Cross, and the War Camp Community Service.

It was not until 1919, after the close of World War I, that the government itself accepted responsibility. During World War II, recreation on military bases was handled by the military. The programs were organized hurriedly, and civilians were commissioned to direct the military recreation program. The Navy and the Marines offered extensive sports activities, and entertainment was stressed in all branches of the military. Off-base recreation for the armed forces during World War II was handled by many public agencies, the United Service Organizations, the American Red Cross, and the National Recreation Association.

With demobilization, the military recreation programs were reduced except in the armies of occupation. Peacetime needs differed from those of wartime. Those on active duty during war years wanted relaxation and nondemanding forms of amusement, such as movies, stage shows, and entertainment by big-name stars. When the war ended, the men and women in uniform discovered more value in active and creative participation.

In the Vietnam struggle, recreation accompanied the soldiers to war as never before. Recreation centers with clubs, stages, playing courts, and swimming pools were established in forward base camps; and showmobiles, crafts trailers, library trailers, and recreation kits were used. Recreation centers in Vietnam and ten cities outside the country provided rest and recuperation leaves for combat personnel.

Today's program. In the armed forces today, active participation is stressed and passive entertainment is minimized.

Service Clubs. A Service Club is "a facility on a military installation designed for use during off-duty time by enlisted personnel, their families, and friends."[8] The Service Club offers facilities and equipment not requiring leadership, as well as a directed program supervised by professional recreation leaders. Meeting rooms for hobby and special-interest groups, billiards and table tennis equipment, musical instruments, record libraries, small games, and reading and writing materials make self-directed activities possible. The directed recreation program includes instruction in crafts, dramatics, music, and dancing, as well as such scheduled activities as discussion groups, holiday observances, special parties, picnics, all-base events, tournaments, contests, exhibits, dances, and tours to places of interest.

Sports and outdoor recreation. Widespread participation is encouraged, and organized competitions are popular. Teams compete worldwide with teams from other services and from colleges, universities, and communities.

Outdoor recreation, including camping, water sports, horseback riding, bicycling, mountain climbing, kayacking, skiing, ice skating, curling, fishing, hiking, hunting, and skeet, is extremely popular. Military installations frequently contain areas suitable for outdoor recreation, such as lakes, streams, woods, and large open spaces; and family camps are often available.

Arts and crafts. Craft shops provide opportunities in ceramics, graphic arts, metal work, lapidary, woodwork, leather work, plastics, model building, painting, photography, and others. Classes and clubs are sparked with contests, exhibits, and demonstrations.

Entertainment. Dramatic and musical productions invite active participation. Contests are held, and winners sometimes organize touring troupes. Vocal and instrumental groups attract many of the musically inclined. Entertainment, such as movies, is offered at minimum fees.

Libraries. Libraries are considered integral parts of the recreation program. They offer recreation reading material and literature of a technical, reference, or general educational nature. The service includes discussion groups and audiovisual resources.

Leadership. More and more emphasis is being placed on the employment of professionally prepared civilians to direct recreation in the armed forces. Professional leadership is offered in arts and crafts, dramatics, music, radio and television, social activities, sports, and

general recreation. Since there are very large numbers of young people spending at least part of their lives in military service, the importance of sound recreation programs cannot be overestimated.

The following staff offices provide supervision of recreation:

Department of the Army—Education and Morale Support Directorate, the Adjutant General's Office

Department of the Air Force—Special Services Branch, Personnel Services Division, Directorate of Military Personnel

Department of the Navy—Recreation and Physical Fitness Branch, Office of Assistant Chief of Naval Personnel

Marine Corps—Special Services Branch, Office of Director of Personnel

The USO and the American Red Cross continue to serve the armed forces, and communities near military bases also assist.

Veterans Administration

The Veterans Administration, created in 1930, combines the functions of the Veterans Bureau, Pension Bureau, and National Home for Disabled Volunteer Soldiers. Its program includes medical care, insurance, and financial assistance for veterans of the armed forces.

It is in connection with operation of its 171 hospitals that recreation becomes an important aspect of Veterans Administration responsibility. Under professional leadership, the recreation program is considered part of the medical treatment. It includes sports, dramatic entertainment, social recreation, motion pictures, music, and arts and crafts.

The objectives of the recreation program are several: to facilitate patients' adjustment to hospital life, to give doctors opportunities to observe patients' behavior, to help patients ad-

Figure 6.6. A U.S. Forest Service interpretive visitor center at Lake Tahoe, California.

just to their limitations, to maintain the physical condition of patients while they are in the hospital, and to develop interests in activities that will continue after patients are discharged.

Programs in the National Capital

The federal government maintains many special services and facilities related to leisure in Washington, D.C. Its many monuments, buildings, and parks belong to the people of the country. The national capital parks in the District of Columbia, Maryland, and Virginia are administered by the National Park Service. The District of Columbia recreation department receives its funds from Congress.

The John F. Kennedy Center for the Performing Arts, opened in 1971, is the national cultural center.

The amazing Smithsonian Institution, founded in 1846, is the world's largest historical, cultural, and scientific museum-gallery complex. Although officially the national museum, it is not supported entirely by government funds. It receives about twenty million visitors annually, and its traveling exhibits reach many more throughout the country and Canada. The several branches include such prestigious institutions as the National Museum of Natural History, the National Collection of Fine Arts, the Freer Gallery of Art, the National Zoological Park, the National

Air and Space Museum, and the National Museum of History and Technology. The National Gallery of Art, though autonomous, is technically a part of the Smithsonian Institution.

The Commission on Fine Arts supplies expert advice and reviews plans regarding public buildings, parks, and private buildings of national interest in Washington.

Recreation for Federal Employees

In addition to providing recreation for military personnel and their families, the federal government offers programs for employees in many of the civilian departments of government. These are comparable to programs that industries provide for their employees.

Other Agencies, Boards, Committees, and Commissions

Among the ninety or so agencies having some relation to recreation, only the most active have been considered. Numerous other agencies within the various government departments as well as independent agencies, boards, commissions, and councils offer advice, financial assistance, technical assistance, and other valuable services. A small sampling of these government bodies, with a superficial summary of their functions, is given here.

The Agricultural Stabilization and Conservation Service (Department of Agriculture) helps fund timber stand improvements and the development of lands and waters for wildlife and recreation. The Farmers' Home Administration (Department of Agriculture) makes loans to farmers for converting farms to recreation enterprises.

The Coast Guard (Department of Transportation) attempts to control water pollution and establishes safety standards for recreational boats. The Small Business Adminis-

tration, by making loans, encourages small commercial recreation enterprises. The U.S. Information Agency seeks to promote a better understanding of the United States in other countries.

The several river basin commissions consider the recreational aspects of river basin developments, and, along with other agencies, help with environmental protection.

International Affiliations

The United States belongs to ninety-one international organizations that reach around the world. Through their efforts to improve the quality of life, many of them affect leisure and recreation. As a member of the United Nations, the United States participates in the work of its related agencies, such as the International Labor Organization (ILO), the United Nations Children's Fund (UNICEF), Food and Agriculture Organization (FAO), United Nations Educational, Scientific, and Cultural Organization (UNESCO), and World Health Organization (WHO), all of which have a bearing on recreation. UNESCO promotes cooperation in education, science, mass communication, and culture. It has held a number of international meetings concerned with youth services and recreation, and it fosters cultural exchanges in literature and the arts. Its International Environmental Education Program has promoted regional meetings on environmental education throughout the world. WHO seeks to obtain the highest possible level of health—physical, mental, and social, and recognizes the place of recreation in seeking this goal.

The U.S. Peace Corps volunteers have worked effectively in the developing nations, not only in industrial and agricultural areas, but also in education and recreation. They have organized a variety of recreation activities including youth programs, clubs, sports teams, camps, and crafts, with both children and adults to raise the standard of living.

Working closely with the United Nations is the World Leisure and Recreation Association which cooperates with national organizations in more than 100 countries. Its work is considered in Chapter 15.

Problems and Needs

Although the federal government has increasingly recognized its responsibility for recreation, certain problems and needs still demand action. Federal funds for many programs are channeled through state and local agencies. It has been suggested that the federal government become more directly involved in community programs; but many people feel that federal help can best be given through grants, consultation, and technical assistance rather than through performance of services usually in the province of local authorities. Questions raised are: Should the federal government build, maintain, and program park and recreation areas and facilities in cities? How can the federal government best serve the park and recreation needs of urban dwellers without destroying local initiative?

Attempts to equalize recreation opportunities for all people will continue to grow. Recent years have witnessed a continuing expansion of funds and programs for special populations. Attempts have also been made to obtain recreation lands closer to population centers.

In a government as enormous and complicated as ours, there is always a problem of overlapping services and wasted effort. Many attempts have been made to establish a national recreation agency to coordinate the efforts of the various units of government.

Chapter 10 considers ways in which the various provinces of recreation—government, voluntary, and private—work together.

Selected References

Bureau of Outdoor Recreation, U.S. Department of Interior. *Outdoor Recreation; A Legacy for America.* Washington, D.C.: U.S. Government Printing Office, 1973.

Conservation Report. Washington, D.C.: National Wildlife Federation, published periodically during congressional sessions.

Harrison, Jean. "The Corps' Stake in Recreation," *Parks & Recreation* 10, no. 3 (March 1975): 2b–8b.

Jensen, Clayne R. *Outdoor Recreation in America.* 3d ed. Minneapolis: Burgess Publishing Company, 1977.

Kyle, George M. "Federal Agencies," *Parks & Recreation* 11, no. 7 (July 1976):38 ff.

A Nationwide Outdoor Recreation Plan. Printed for the use of the Committee on Interior and Insular Affairs, 93d Congress, 2d Session. Washington, D.C.: U.S. Government Printing Office, June 1974.

The Recreation Imperative, A Draft of the Nationwide Outdoor Recreation Plan Prepared by the Department of the Interior. Washington, D.C.: U.S. Government Printing Office, 1974.

Statistical Abstract of the United States. Washington, D.C.: Bureau of the Census, Department of Commerce, published annually.

Tilden, Freeman. *The National Parks.* Rev. ed. New York: Alfred A. Knopf, Inc., 1968.

Tindall, Barry S. "Federal Legislation," *Parks & Recreation* 11, no. 7 (July 1976): 44 ff.

United States Government Manual. Washington, D.C.: U.S. Government Printing Office, revised May 1, 1976.

7
Public Education and Leisure

Education has no more serious responsibility than making adequate provision for the enjoyment of recreative leisure; not only for the sake of immediate health, but . . . for the sake of its lasting effect upon habits of mind.

John Dewey

The little red schoolhouse of the nineteenth century has come and gone or has been reborn, according to the differing perspectives of the viewer. The old-fashioned, one-room learning arena had one positive aspect to which education must return—involvement and interaction between community and public education in terms of goals, policies, programs, and facilities.

Human needs can be classified into two categories: those necessary for survival and those necessary for enrichment of life. The latter category has been divided by Maslow and others into hierarchies of social need, self-esteem needs, and self-realization needs, but each describes a state or stage of potential for individual growth and enrichment. Public schools should serve both as channels for meeting survival needs and as resources for life enrichment—as constructive influences upon society for individual and community betterment. No other organization has a more vital role, since, by law, public education touches every child.

At no time in civilization has the complexity of an age so challenged social and human values. Transitions in every phase of daily life have resulted in additional responsibilities for educational institutions. Traditionally, we have placed upon the schools the responsibility for teaching the basic fundamentals for learning. In recent years, the demands have centered on a much broader range of experiences. Educators have felt that children should develop desirable attitudes, make social adjustments, grow in personality, and learn to cope with the social and physical environments in which they live. This concept has resulted in an enlarged curriculum needing community interaction and support.

Education should reflect the culture, but it also has an obligation to direct and shape it. The emphasis has turned from a goal of preparing people to "make a living" to one of "making a life." Within the confines of the latter philosophy, education for use of our increased abundance of leisure must assume vital importance. Bobbitt forecast such implications for the school's role as early as 1918: "It is probable that in the newer schools of the oncoming humanistic age, education for leisure occupations will be recognized as one of the most serious educational tasks—if not the largest and the most vital of all."[1]

In 1918, educators accepted the "worthy use of leisure time" as one of the cardinal principles of education. The other principles included health, command of the fundamental processes, worthy home membership, vocation, citizenship, and ethical character. As education attempted to meet the new developments in society, educators redefined their goals. The Educational Policies Commission of the National Education Association, in 1946, published a new set of aims for education. The objectives of self-realization, human relationships, economic efficiency, and civic responsibility stressed the importance of the individual and relationships to society. There was an emphasis on leisure use as it affects self-realization.

The Society of Park and Recreation Educators (SPRE) wrote a position paper on *Education for Leisure* in 1972 and formed a special Leisure Education Committee in 1973, which initiated annual leisure education conferences. The SPRE Committee and an experimental Education in the Appropriate Use of Discretionary Time project, developed by the National Recreation and Park Association (NRPA) and the Department of Defense, provided the stimulation for the NRPA Leisure Education Advancement Project (LEAP), which is described later in this chapter.

The National Education Association Bicentennial Committee reevaluated the original cardinal principles in 1976 and found in general that although they needed some updating, the original foundations had been surprisingly intuitive about the future. As the Cardinal Principles Panel, chaired by Dr. Harold Shane, looked at the "worthy use of leisure" principle, they drew attention to the infiltration of the work ethic in the use of the term "worthy." They also commented on the need to help "young and old alike to prevent today's complexities from totally eroding their leisure time."[2]

In any perusal of educational objectives, the "preparation for life" theme runs strong. Since American people are having an ever-increasing amount of time for leisure activities, recreation and education must work together toward their very similar goals.

The School's Role

In terms of facilities, leadership, and knowledge, the schools have the potential to educate for satisfying leisure use, to conduct recreation programs, and to aid other recreation agencies in the interpretation or maintenance of their offerings.

Leisure Education

What do we mean by the term *leisure education?* In a survey of state superintendents of public instruction, the conclusion was that "it is apparent that there is much misunderstanding of leisure education both as a concept and as a process."[3]

Perhaps the best explanation of the term is found in the comments of Dr. Jean Mundy, chairwoman of the first SPRE Leisure Education Committee.[4] See the list on page 144.

Leisure education, then, is a process through which individuals acquire the appropriate attitudes, skills, knowledge, and behaviors that will allow them to benefit from their leisure choices. That process is not confined to the public school alone but may be a legitimate objective for many other community agencies. Because this chapter deals with the public education function, the details of the Leisure Education Advancement Project (LEAP) are pertinent here.

Leisure Education Advancement Project. In 1975, a two-year leisure education project was initiated by the National Recreation and Park Association with funding by the Lilly Endowment, Inc. Roger Lancaster, principal investigator, and Linda Odum, research associate, detailed the purposes of the venture in these terms:

Leisure education is *not*:	Leisure education *is*:
Attempting to replace one set of values with another set of values	A process to enable the individual to identify and clarify his or her own leisure values and goals
A new name for recreation or recreation services	An approach to enable an individual to enhance the quality of his or her life during leisure
A watered-down, simplified version of a recreational leisure professional preparation program	Deciding for oneself what place leisure has in life
A focus on the value of recreation or the recreation profession	Coming to know oneself in relation to leisure
A focus on getting people to participate more in recreational activities	A life-long continuous process
Imparting standards of what is "good" or "bad" use of leisure	Relating one's own needs, values, and capabilities to leisure and leisure experiences
Relating every school subject to leisure	Increasing the individual's options for satisfying quality experiences in leisure
A course or series of courses	
Restricted to the educational system	
Restricted to what educators should do but not what leisure service personnel do	
A program to undermine the work ethic	

Source: *Jean Mundy. Reprinted by permission.*

The immediate goal of this project is to develop and implement a change model that will effectively integrate leisure education into the ongoing instructional program in grades K through 12 in selected schools in the public school education system in Indiana.

The long range goal is to have the model program developed in Indiana serve as the basis for leisure education programs in the school systems throughout the nation.

The major purpose is to assist public schools in embarking upon a concentrated education program which will instill in students:

1. The use of leisure (discretionary) time as an avenue for personal satisfaction and enrichment
2. An understanding of the array of valuable opportunities available in leisure time
3. An understanding of the significant impact that leisure time has and will have on society
4. An appreciation of the natural resources and their relationships to discretionary time and the quality of life
5. An ability to make decisions regarding their own leisure behavior[5]

The first steps of the project included a literature search, a survey of what programs were already in existence, and the development of general learning objectives to be translated into behavioral objectives and desired competencies. The latter would serve as a base for preparation of resources and techniques that the teacher could use in the regular curriculum.

The general learning objectives, evolved through a workshop of park and recreation professionals, included twelve target areas.

1. The student will appreciate that the dimensions of leisure in a world with the potential for increased discretionary time may affect not only the quality of life, but its survival.

2. The student will recognize that discretionary time is inherently neither good nor bad, that the value assigned is a matter of personal and societal judgment.

3. The student will understand that any life experience can be a leisure experience, it is a matter of personal choice and attitude. It may be the result of social integration or private thoughts, can occur while one is physically active or passive, includes anticipation and reflection, may be structured or unstructured, planned or spontaneous.

4. The student will understand that effective leisure living and leisure choices will be dependent upon the development (acquisition) of skills, knowledges, and attitudes learned through study, experience, and practice.

5. The student will understand and appreciate the dynamic relationship which exists between and among environment, social institutions, and individual life-styles as they affect leisure behavior and opportunities, and to identify sources which influence leisure attitudes and choices.

6. The student will understand the potential of leisure for personal growth and personal satisfaction and the relationship among work, family, leisure, and other social roles in the evolution of a life plan.

7. The student will recognize that there is general understanding of the importance of work in American society, that the potential contribution of leisure is not well understood and that work and leisure are both possible sources of feelings of dignity and self-worth and can be mutually supportive.

8. The student will appreciate those intangible qualities of the leisure experience which transcend an individual's physical existence, but are experienced on the emotional and spiritual plane.

9. The student will recognize that the use of discretionary time has meaning which extends beyond the individual's satisfaction and has implications for the total environment (social, human, physical, and natural).

10. The student will understand and demonstrate that a leisure experience is self-motivated in response to personal perceptions of an appropriate pace, natural rhythms, interest, and opportunities (e.g., laws, peer pressure, etc.), and that the choice of leisure experience is often limited by social control.

11. The student will identify, understand, and evaluate leisure resources, choices, and environments available in the community, state, and nation, and develop appreciation of various modes that individuals may have of utilizing these resources.

12. The student will recognize and evaluate the consequences of leisure choices to oneself, to others, and to the environment; and to accept that both the individual and the community are ultimately responsible for one's leisure behavior and experiences.[6]

From these general goals, the LEAP staff produced and tested leisure education materials and published the *Kangaroo Kit: Leisure Education Curriculum*. The classroom teacher, using the kit materials as a base, can further the leisure education in five distinct ways:

1. By developing positive attitudes about the role of leisure in individual growth and development

2. By developing skills and appreciations needed to broaden leisure choices

3. By making available information about pertinent resources, both human and environmental, that will extend opportunities

146   The Public Sector

4. By encouraging evaluation of the results of leisure choices

5. By being an example of a person who values leisure and makes rewarding leisure decisions

Education for leisure is not, we repeat, adding a separate course to an already overloaded curriculum. It is a process related to subject matters already being taught. At times, teacher attitude alone will make the transition; at other times, a block of knowledge or development of skills or appreciations will be necessary. Two examples are pertinent: (1) Why is it that the child who was excited about learning to read becomes a freshman in high school and is less than ecstatic when his parents suggest that he read a book when he asks what he can do? (2) What has happened to the preschool child who spends half her time with a coloring book, paints, or drawing, yet rarely chooses art classes as electives in secondary school?

Could we educate toward a nation of amateurs in the true sense of the word—those who "love" what they are doing? Children need to be introduced to musical knowledge to allow them to choose instruments as recreation, but they must also be encouraged to examine what they get from the blare of the horn or the involvement with the combo in comparison with other choices in sports or drama.

Toward a national policy.   In the words of Tay Green, Florida educator, "The leisure education service professionals occupy the advocate position and are necessary in order to activate the system toward a national policy on leisure education."[7] Green suggested working through political channels to get permissive legislation passed in the U.S. Congress. The Society of Park and Recreation Educators Leisure Education Committee drafted a prototype for a Leisure Education Legislative Resolution, which ended with the words:

> Therefore, be it resolved that leisure education be incorporated into the educational process and curriculum to stimulate and enable the individual to develop an awareness of his own inner creative resources, the wide variety of leisure opportunities that are open to him, the concept that leisure experiences are a source of self-fulfillment and further to make it possible for an individual to seek leisure experiences and to choose those that will satisfy his search for self-fulfillment and lead to an enhanced life-style that is not destructive to himself, to others, or to the environment.[8]

Active political advocacy plus a sophisticated network of information for professions with similar goals will be necessary to accomplish such a national legislative thrust.

Leisure Counseling

The term *leisure counseling*, although often associated with the needs of atypical or special populations, has extended its focus to all segments of the population. A Milwaukee, Wisconsin, team developed a computerized model for use in counseling Milwaukee citizens.[9] In essence, the process consisted of interviewing a client to identify his or her life-style, leisure interests, needs, and capabilities; exploring locally available activities and resources; and counseling the individual to match leisure needs and desires with appropriate available recreation offerings. Interest-finders were developed for testing and counseling purposes; information on the availability of program and environmental resources was fed into a computer; and the individual's interests and the available resources for exploring them could be matched on a fairly quick yet sophisticated basis.

Leisure counseling, as they perceived it, encompasses the needs of three populations:

(1) mainstream or so-called normal persons who seek to increase their potential through available recreation outlets; (2) sheltered populations who have been temporarily removed from the mainstream and are institutionalized in prisons, hospitals, or halfway houses and need rehabilitation channels; and (3) special populations who because of infirmity need special assistance to attain satisfactions in leisure.[10]

The general focus on leisure counseling is simply to try to match a person's leisure interests and needs with those resources that are readily available in the community. The leisure counselor's role, regardless of the population with which he or she works, is to

Explore the client's value system with regard to leisure

Identify interests and capabilities through testing and interviews

Discover the available resources through which his designated interests or needs can be satisfied

Overcome the physical, psychological, or environmental barriers that stand between what the client wants to do and what resources are available

Evaluate the results of leisure choices and behaviors

The increased emphasis on leisure in the life-styles of Americans can be seen in the mounting interest in leisure counseling. Private leisure counseling firms have evolved in some parts of the country. Those who deal with special populations are doing more research to test the results of their efforts. They are increasing the sophistication of their techniques for identifying leisure behavioral problems and exploring the channels for ameliorating them.

Leisure counseling is a very important part of leisure education. In the future we may find that guidance counselors may be educated to focus as much attention on leisure opportunities and choices as on occupation or career decisions.

Career Education

In spite of nearly a third of the country's school districts now boasting formal career education programs, and an increase in the U.S. Office of Education expenditures on career education from $9 million in 1971 to nearly $61 million five years later, the concept of career education is still not clearly defined.

Although career education systems differ, Verhoven and Vinton indicate that the school-based Comprehensive Career Education model is the most fully developed.[11] It is divided into four stages: career awareness, career exploration, career orientation, and skill development.

An alternate concept that ties career education much more closely to leisure education was described by Casmer Heilman at the Third Leisure Education Conference:

The concept of career education that has been accepted in the state of Michigan . . . suggests that every individual is searching for a sense of identity and belonging, and they are also extremely concerned about developing a level of capability. We suggest that if we view career education as having a primary focus on attempting to help people to develop a sense of self-capacitation, that we must address four life roles . . . the occupational role, the family role, the citizen role, and the avocational or leisure role.[12]

In the latter description, leisure education is closely allied with career education, with the emphasis placed not only on jobs for earning a livelihood but also on other aspects of human involvement that affect life-styles, decision making, and life enrichment.

148

Figure 7.1. Soil examination is interesting and educational for young students.

Community Education

The growth of community education in the last decade has exceeded the expectations of even the most optimistic early leaders of the movement. Its perspective has expanded from the early community school ideal to a broad umbrella for diverse services, including health, recreation, and social welfare programs.

Community education, like career education, is a concept that is more readily acceptable in its philosophy than understandable in its practical implementation. "Community education's general objective is to make the schools the centers of neighborhoods by providing educational, recreational, cultural, and social programs and services to meet the interest and needs of all community members."[13] Such an umbrella, depending on the leadership, power structure, and systems for coordination, includes not only academic programs, but vocational, recreation, health, and adult education, and other social services as well.

From a few school districts that had emulated the Flint, Michigan, leadership in community use of school facilities, the community education movement has grown to the extent that there are now at least twenty states with some community education legislation, a state community education director for nearly every state, a thriving National Community Education Association, and an International Association of Community Education.

The Community Schools Act of 1974 created a Community Education Advisory Council in the Department of Health, Education, and Welfare and provided federal funding for community education programs beginning with fiscal year 1976.

Sample programs. To show the breadth and diversity of the types of programs undertaken by the community education structure, let's look at a sampling from one area. The St. Louis Park School District 1975 winter program brochure included a diverse array of opportunities for all ages. Here are samples at random in several categories:

Arts and crafts

Batik

Business and the consumer

Business finance

Cards and table games

Collective bargaining

Child care

Communication and discussion groups

Education—driver education, lip reading, typing

Hobbies and handy repairs

Ice skating

Income tax seminar

Office procedures

Oil painting

Swimming

Some of the experiences were offered in the school; others were in recreation and park facilities. It is obvious from the brochure that there has been cooperation between community educators and recreators. Such has not been the case in all communities.

Challenges for parks and recreation. The ideals of better coordination of finances and facilities, the maximizing of human energies, and the elimination of duplication in the community education objectives are commendable. The challenge to the leisure services professions came when community education legislation in some states sought to restrict program or funding to only community education personnel when similar programs and the financial resources for them had formerly been administered by health or recreation professionals.

In an effort to gain better understanding and coordination of resources on a national scale, the National Joint Steering Committee on Community Schools–Community Education was formed in 1974. The three organizations represented on the committee included the National Recreation and Park Association, the American Association for Leisure and Recreation, and the National Community Education Association. The common goal of the representatives was: "to mobilize total community resources to provide services that offer opportunities for education, recreation, and social services to citizens of all ages, in order to cultivate and enhance the human and environmental potential of our society."[14]

These are noble goals. The implementation of those aims, however, will take personnel with a variety of skills and expertise and a zeal for coordinating efforts without regard to vested interests.

Cocurricular Experiences

Limiting the school's role in recreation to recess or a meager noon-time program is now outmoded. Cocurricular experiences such as clubs, sports, drama, orchestras, choral groups, trips, science fairs, language clinics, student government activities, school newspaper development, and conservation advocacy are now meaningful contributors to the learning environments. Mini-courses, offered in many high schools and chosen voluntarily, offer the student an opportunity to extend or expand skills or appreciations in anything from lapidary and ceramics to debating techniques.

Planning School Centers and Their Surroundings

The extended use of the school plant beyond school hours and school needs provides for maximum use of facilities and supplements the existing park and recreation facilities in the community. In order that effective use of these

Signs of the Times

A 1977 judgment in a Maryland high school may portend a brighter future in the public education contribution to leisure use. After heavy criticisms of the "Johnny can't write" and "Sally can't add" variety, the secondary school imposed three tests as a condition for graduation. The first two pertained to basic communication competencies and mathematical principles. The third was a test on "leisure literacy." Thus public education has come of age in its attention to preparation for life.

Did your high school education help broaden your leisure choices? How?

facilities can be made by both school and community groups with a minimum of money and problems, cooperative planning must be undertaken. The use of school facilities by citizen groups or community agencies does not necessitate building expensive or elaborate additional facilities. It does mean that schools must be properly designed, zoned, and adapted, and that sufficient area must be acquired so that the school plant can be utilized to its maximum. With this type of action, duplicate facilities need not be developed in the same neighborhood at additional expense to the community.

Planning school buildings for community use. To facilitate cooperation between the school and the city, mutually accepted policies should be established. Policies should cover the purchase of land, the planning and designing of the building and playground area, and the joint use of the school plant. Many cities have benefited from joint school-city planning. In Peoria, Illinois, an indoor-outdoor swimming pool represents a significant milestone in cooperative planning and financing between the Peoria Park District and the Peoria Public

School District. Richmond, Virginia, is another example of a city whose schools and recreation department have a cooperative approach to school and recreation needs. The extent to which public schools incorporate ideas already in practice in the cities will determine whether schools can effectively serve as indoor recreation centers.

The park-school concept. Of momentous importance is the trend in many cities for land acquisition agreements between the park and recreation departments and the school districts. Under contractual agreements, each new school that is planned allows for sufficient acreage to develop an adjoining park area. Depending on the cooperative directive, the park department may help finance the purchase, develop, or maintain the park area. In light of the increased attention given to environmental concerns in the school curriculum, the park-school concept provides a natural laboratory as well as a recreation facility.

A fine example of park-school cooperation can be found in the agreement between the Peoria Park District and School District 150 in Peoria County, Illinois.

General Statement of Agreement

The Peoria Park District Board and School District 150 Board agree that:

1. Recreation is a basic human need. Full living cannot be achieved without the creative use of leisure time, which affords man the opportunity to release his energies and emotions, express his social and creative nature, and find outlets for his desire for adventure and competitive spirit.

2. The objectives of recreation involving the advancement of social, intellectual, physical, creative, and moral growth are consistent with education's general aim of developing the individual to his fullest. Recreation and education both seek enrichment of life for individuals. Further, education in the worthy use of leisure is an educational objective.

3. Like education, recreation benefits not only the individual but society itself. Therefore, like other functions essential to the general welfare, recreation is a proper concern of a democratic society. Public recreation makes possible participation on a democratic inclusive basis and insures wholesome recreation opportunities for all.

4. Public services should be provided at the lowest cost that is compatible with good service. A wise administrative principle to follow is that all facilities, activities, and services should yield as large an educational return as possible.

5. Since most school buildings and facilities are located near the center of the community they serve,

they are admirably situated to meet many of the recreation needs of their constituents. Further, schools lie idle much of the time when people are free to use them.

6. There is a great similarity in the kinds of areas and facilities required for the conduct of many educational and recreational programs. Cooperative planning and programming can eliminate much of the duplication of school and park facilities for recreation purposes.

7. Just as many educational facilities are well suited or can be adapted for recreational uses, so park and recreation facilities in many instances can admirably serve an educational function. Efforts should be made not only to use present park facilities for educational purposes, but to develop cooperatively new areas and facilities which can serve both recreation and education interests.

8. Through joint efforts, the boards of Peoria School District 150 and the Peoria Park District can contribute to greater public service without giving up their identities or any of their legitimate responsibilities. The respective boards will, therefore, endeavor to follow a policy for the reciprocal use of facilities and services at a mutually agreed basic minimum cost.

9. Liability insurance in adequate amounts shall be carried by both parties to this agreement as their interest requires.

10. The Board of School District 150 and the Peoria Park District Board recognize the necessity for collaboration and planning by all local governmental units. The Park-School-Recreation-Planning Committee, with membership representing School District 150, the Park District and its Recreation Committee, the City of Peoria, and Tri-County Planning Commission, meets monthly to discuss and consider ways and means of obtaining greater effectiveness in the coordinated use of all public agency facilities.[15]

The document continues with descriptions of specific policies for after-school recreation programs, theater education, dance, arts, summer centers, and others.

The contract in Irving, Texas, between the city and the school district is an example of the legal format used in such agreements.

Agreement

WHEREAS, the City of Irving, Texas, and the Irving Independent School District recognize the need to utilize all of their respectively owned facilities to their maximum capacity in order to provide needed services for the citizens living in the City and the District at the least expense; and

WHEREAS, the City and the School District desire to enter into a contractual agreement setting out the terms and requirements by which property of one entity may be leased to or utilized by the other entity; and

WHEREAS, the purpose and spirit of this agreement is to facilitate and encourage the leasing of available property by one entity to the other and provide the respective administrations a framework by which to accomplish this professed goal;

NOW, THEREFORE, ABOVE PREMISES CONSIDERED:

The City of Irving, Texas, a municipal corporation incorporated under Article XI, Section 5 of the Constitution of the State of Texas, hereinafter referred to as "CITY" and the Irving Independent School District, hereinafter referred to as "SCHOOL DISTRICT" hereby enter into a contract and agreement in accordance with the following terms:

I.
LEASE OF PROPERTY
LONG-TERM BASIS
(more than one week)

A. CONSIDERATION:
The following formula will be incorporated into all contracts for the lease of property on a long-term basis:

1. Tax Assessor for each entity appraises property with the average value inserted in the formula.
2. Market value capitalized on a "Fair Rate of Return" at 8% per annum.
3. Discount of 50% calculated.
4. Percentage that lessee has "right" to utilize property is then ascertained based on a 16-hour day, 5-day week.
5. Example of Formula
    (a) Appraisal of property $52,500
    (b) Fair rate of return

$$\begin{array}{r} \$52,500 \\ \times\ 0.08 \\ \hline \$\ 4,200 \end{array}$$

    (c) $4,200 × ½ (discount) × 100% (percentage lessee has right to utilize facility) = $2,100 per year

B. PRIORITY

Each entity will give the other entity priority in scheduling of events over other individual groups or entities. The respective administrations are directed to work out the scheduling of events as far in advance as possible.

C. EXPENSES—CLEAN-UP

Lessee shall pay utility expenses, assume normal clean-up and maintenance responsibilities and pay for all damages to property sustained while in use by lessee.

II.
LEASE OR UTILIZATION OF PROPERTY
SHORT-TERM BASIS
(one week or less)

A. CONSIDERATION.
   1. Gymnasium
      (a) High school—$20.00 per night
      (b) Junior High—$15.00 per night
City gymnasiums will be classified in accordance with comparability to school gymnasiums.
   2. Auditorium—$25.00 per night.
   3. Smaller Office Buildings

(a) Classrooms (day or night)	$ 6.00
(b) Study hall	7.50
(c) Elementary school lunchrooms (non-air-conditioned)	12.50
(d) Elementary school lunchrooms (air-conditioned)	20.00
(e) Junior high school cafeteria (non-air-conditioned)	12.50

Use of City facilities to be charged in accordance with comparability to School facilities.
   4. Fields/Football, etc.—no charge

B. EXPENSES—CLEAN-UP

Lessee or user pays no expenses, but is responsible for minimal maintenance and damages to property incurred while in use.

C. PROCEDURE.

City Manager and School Superintendent are directed to formulate a procedure for handling all uses of property under Paragraph II which shall be placed in effect and distributed to all necessary personnel.

III.
TENNIS COURTS

All future contracts relative to the construction and operation of joint tennis courts are to be on the same basis as contract between 'CITY' and 'DISTRICT' dated February 2, 1968, relating to Tennis Courts at Irving High School.

IV.
STREET SWEEPER AND FOGGING MACHINE

Use of Street Sweeper and Fogging Machine by City at request of School District shall be at following rates:

Street Sweeper—$5.00 per hour
Fogging Machine—10.00 per hour

V.
GENERAL PROVISIONS APPLICABLE TO ALL CONTRACTS

A. Each entity shall send the other a detailed monthly bill but payment shall be made only once each year for period of September 1 through August 31 in order to balance the books.

B. CONCESSION STANDS

Owner of property shall operate concession stands except to the extent this may be modified by agreement between the two administrations.

C. LIABILITY

The following paragraph shall be placed in each written contract or be considered part of every agreement:

> "City and School District each agree to hold the other respective entity harmless for any and all liability that may arise as a result of the other entity's negligence in carrying out the terms of contract."

VI.

This contract shall remain in force and effect until rescinded, modified, or repealed by one or both of the parties.[16]

Outdoor Environmental Education

In today's schools one finds a new sense of responsibility relative to education for understanding, protecting, and using the environment. Why? The United States has changed from an agricultural society to a society of 216 million people, two thirds of them urban dwellers, dependent on technology and huge sources of energy. Accompanying this change has been a decline in both the quality and quantity of natural resources. Educators have been alerted to their responsibility in helping young people become aware of the need to understand environmental problems and seek their solution.

What is outdoor environmental education? The roots of outdoor environmental education reach back many years. Colleges and universities have long been the sources of much of our understanding of the environment; and elementary and high schools almost from their beginnings in the United States have carried on programs related in some way to the outdoors.

These programs have had many names and have taken many forms. The term *nature study* was used in the nineteenth century to describe learning about outdoor phenomena. Cornell University led in the development of materials and the education of teachers in the nature study movement. Field trips on school grounds, in the woods, and on farms were integral parts of the program. School gardening, particularly for city children, also began in the nineteenth century. Many schools set aside land for their own garden plots or participated in community programs.

As the concern for conservation began to develop late in the nineteenth century, what became known as *conservation education* was introduced in many schools. Opinions differed as to whether this was a separate subject or whether its concepts and materials should be absorbed into established school subjects such as science and social studies.

The concept of using camps for educational purposes originated with the Gunnery School in 1861. Although organized camps were supported primarily by youth agencies and private groups, educators looked on them as important settings for learning about the outdoors, learning to live with others, and achieving outdoor-related skills. During the 1920s and 1930s, camping education was the subject of much discussion among educators. In 1940 the Kellogg Foundation, in cooperation with the Battle Creek, Michigan, schools, began an experiment in what was called *school camping,* in which all fifth graders in the school system spent one week in camp, and others, including high school students, also used the camp for learning purposes.

The first large school system to develop a citywide school camp program was San Diego. In the 1940s and 1950s many other school systems followed.

Largely through the efforts of Dr. Lloyd B. Sharp, who had in 1940 established a graduate leadership training program in cooperation with New York University, the term *outdoor education* began to be used. The term denoted the school programs taking place outdoors, whether in camps or elsewhere, using the environment for educational purposes. It was recognized that outdoor education was not a subject; rather, it was a method of using the outdoors in science, social studies, literature, arts and crafts, mathematics, physical education, and other subjects. This statement by Dr. Sharp expresses the viewpoint of outdoor education advocates: "That which can best be learned inside the classroom should be learned

there. That which can best be learned in the out-of-doors through direct experience, dealing with native materials and life situations, should there be learned."[17]

As time went on, the terms *school camping* and *school camps* came to be used less and less, giving way to *outdoor education, outdoor learning centers,* and *outdoor laboratories.* These terms were applied to many kinds of outdoor experiences carried on by schools.

In the 1970s, educators began to use a broader concept called *environmental education,* which placed emphasis on the study of community problems, such as air and water pollution, waste disposal, and energy use, but included all types of educational experiences concerned with the environment, whether inside or outside the classroom. The word *ecology* took on new meaning in recognizing our interrelationships with all aspects of the environment. Some federal funding encouraged schools to move rapidly in expanding and improving programs related to these new concerns.

Some principles of outdoor environmental education.   A few important principles of outdoor environmental education follow:

1. Some learning takes place best in direct relationship with the environment.

2. The techniques of discovery, encounter, and problem solving used in outdoor education are more effective and interesting methods of learning than are many traditional classroom methods.

3. Outdoor experiences can enrich and increase understanding of textbook learning.

4. Environmental education should include study of human dependence on the earth and responsibility for using it properly.

5. Outdoor recreation is greatly enhanced through knowledge and understanding of the natural world.

6. Outdoor environmental education should include concepts, attitudes, and skills that enhance the enjoyment of the environment without destroying it.

Implications of environmental education for the use of leisure. The enjoyment of the outdoors is an important leisure experience. The tremendous increase in the numbers of people pouring outdoors for recreation has accentuated the problems of misuse and has intensified the need for education in the proper use, enjoyment, and understanding of the natural environment. For these reasons outdoor environmental education deserves a place in the school program.

What schools can do to help young people understand and appreciate their natural heritage has a direct relationship to recreation; for not only do recreation activities affect the environment, but the environment also affects recreation activities. Forests provide more than lumber; they provide camping, hiking, fishing, hunting, and sheer enjoyment. Leisure values as well as economic considerations determine the wise use of land and the life it supports.

It is the schools' responsibility to teach skills that make it possible to enjoy the outdoors and at the same time protect it for the future. For the student, the learning itself, about both the environment and the skills needed to use it, can be a form of recreation, enhancing the satisfaction gained in the outdoors. Schools should encourage nonconsumptive forms of recreation that remove nothing from the environment, and activities that do not use scarce forms of energy. Since even these activities can be destructive in overcrowded areas, the schools should promote restrictions on the numbers of people using a given space.

Kindergarten through high school. Attitudes are developed early in life, and students in the years from kindergarten through elementary school are especially impressionable. This is the time to instill attitudes and understanding about the world and the need for protecting natural resources. The lively curiosity of children is an ally in this attempt.

Two segments of the environment are used in elementary schools. First are the neighborhood and community—parks, streets, school grounds, industries, shops, water and sewage systems, and how the city plans and zones them. Second, and not completely divorced from the first, are the wilder aspects—forests, waters, and wildlife, particularly in relation to humans.

In the high school, specialized courses deal with conservation, ecology, agriculture, and various sciences, often with a vocational emphasis. Outdoor-related skills are often included in physical education classes; sometimes these resemble the challenge programs of the Outward Bound schools, in which students pit their skills for survival against a hostile environment. Many extracurricular programs in secondary schools include outdoor recreation and conservation activities.

Some special provisions by schools. Direct experiences with the outdoors are offered through field trips, outdoor projects, camps, and outdoor laboratories. School grounds and their environs are the handiest settings for environmental education. Many school grounds offer opportunities not only for outdoor studies but also for landscaping and work projects.

Camps and residence centers are operated by many schools. The most common practice is to take fifth or sixth graders for a five-day program to a camp, although some schools also operate programs for middle school and high school students.

Nature centers are generally buildings, located in natural areas, that function as focal points for displays, meetings, and work projects that interpret the immediate environment.

Nature trails are often constructed on the grounds around the center. While schools often operate nature centers, the centers may also be operated by park and recreation departments or private organizations primarily for school use.

Outdoor laboratories take many forms. Commonly a piece of natural land is set aside for study and use by various age groups for trips, explorations, and skill learning.

School garden programs, including garden plots and instructions for planting, cultivating, and harvesting, are offered in many places, sometimes in cooperation with public agencies, and private associations, such as garden clubs. Inflationary food costs give the gardens an economic as well as an educational importance. Less common are school farms, where children may become acquainted with a variety of domestic animals and plants and may perform farm chores.

School and community cooperation in outdoor education. The schools call upon many community resources in their outdoor education programs. There should be a close working relationship between schools and community agencies, both public and private, to attain more effective and economical programs. The schools need not set up separate programs if the same results can be obtained through community cooperation.

Federal, state, and local agencies all have resources of land, facilities, and personnel that are primarily for the benefit of the general public and can effectively serve school purposes. Many park agencies, for example, have naturalists on their staffs who will lead field trips for school classes. The National Park Service National Environmental Education Program has a distinctive approach that many schools have adopted. Some local agencies analyze local resources, offer suggestions to schools for their use, and even provide leadership.

Community parks, natural reserves, ponds, lakes, farms, camps, water works,

sewage systems, and solid waste disposal plants are but a few of the study areas available for environmental education in almost all communities. Museums of science and industry, museums of natural history, zoos, botanical gardens, arboretums, aquariums, and historical sites enrich the program where they are available. Some schools use areas set aside by communities for teaching and practicing skills in outdoor living, rock climbing, canoeing, fishing, and shooting safety.

Conducting the Community Recreation Program

In some instances, the public schools have proved to be the logical agency to organize and conduct the recreation program for the entire community. This situation is particularly true in smaller communities that cannot afford to operate a separate recreation agency. Under such circumstances, civic leaders normally look to the school to conduct the program. In many smaller cities, schools administer a part-time or summer recreation program utilizing school facilities and leadership.

Schools can be successful in this function if school authorities fully accept recreation as a significant aspect of community life and have a broad concept of recreation. With the provision of qualified leaders, adequate financing, and full executive support, public schools can be of real service to the community in conducting the recreation program. See Chapter 4 for additional information on this topic.

The Recreation Role in Colleges and Universities

Institutions of higher learning have varied responsibilities related to park and recreation services. Their role is primarily concerned with: fulfillment of the leisure needs of students, preparation of leaders for the profession, research, interpretation, continuing education, consultant services, instructional resources, and publications and other assistance to communities.

Campus Recreation and Recreation Sports

The college or university must take the place of the home and community in providing leisure activities for students. College unions offer varied recreation opportunities, including theaters, outdoor areas, snack bars, lounges and reading areas, game rooms, and many others, depending on the size of the union and the university. Sororities, fraternities, and housing units normally have social or recreation committees that plan for the needs of their residents. Ample choices are offered on most campuses in the form of convocations, operas, concerts, plays, lectures, and other cultural activities for students. Many departments offer outdoor skills, such as canoeing and rappelling. Athletic contests and recreation sports are conducted to satisfy active physical needs or spectator interests, and dance performances and art exhibits add to the spectator opportunities not only for the campus population but also for the general community.

Professional Preparation

The kinds of park and recreation personnel are described in Chapter 15. Institutions that professionally prepare those who administer park and recreation programs and facilities in hospitals, environmental centers, parks, community centers, wildlife reserves, resorts, and colleges and universities should possess adequate personnel, facilities, and community resources to meet established standards as described in the national accreditation documents.

It is also important in teacher-education institutions that future teachers be exposed to courses that explore the meaning of leisure choices as they relate to psychological, physical, sociological, economic, and environmental welfare. Since these individuals will be direct examples for leisure education because of their interaction with students, they must develop a philosophy of life that includes leisure as a significant factor. Many colleges are introducing courses in general education, which explore the impact of leisure on individual and societal welfare.

Continuing Education and Community Service

The numbers of continuing education and extension services offered by colleges and universities have increased exponentially. The Great Lakes Park Training Institute held each year in Indiana has explored supervisory and managerial roles in both human and natural resources for well over a quarter of a century. The Executive Development Program, developed by the Department of Recreation and Park Administration at Indiana University for the continuing professional growth of top managers, has proved extremely beneficial. The Revenue Resources Management School, held under the auspices of North Carolina State University, has been equally popular.

These are but a few examples of service to the profession. Pre-retirement counseling, workshops for the area agency directors in the older Americans service network, leadership institutes, and camping experiences for teachers represent the diversity of the potential for updating skills, appreciations, and attitudes.

The National 4-H Leisure Education Project. A committee of extension staff members from several universities in 1976 developed a comprehensive leisure education program for use in their communities. Objectives included leisure awareness, self-awareness, decision making, social interaction, and leisure skills. Specific programs and rationale were derived from the objectives for both adult and youth leaders. In addition to these efforts, other innovations are being made to interpret leisure education information through leisure lifestyle games as developed at the University of Missouri.

Research

The responsibility for instigating quality research frequently falls to the colleges and universities. Because the organized recreation movement is still relatively new and broad in scope, much of the progress in this movement has been based on research in related disciplines. With the advent of federal funding and the proliferation of graduate professional preparation programs, a renewed thrust toward research initiatives has emerged. There is still a need to bridge the gap between theory and practice in park and recreation efforts with sound, supportive documentation.

The Ultimate Challenge

Someone once said that the greatest failure we can experience as human beings is the margin of difference between what we are *capable of becoming* and what we actually *become.* In the foreseeable future, in our judgment, education for leisure will have a significant role in cutting down the size of that failure span.

Educating for leisure is not solely the responsibility of public education. The church, the home, and the park and recreation agencies must accept their considerable obligations. Education for the arts of leisure is, in essence, everybody's business. Unfortunately, what is everybody's business often becomes nobody's business. The school is in an excellent position to condition future attitudes toward leisure, stimulate action, and cooperate with other community agencies concerned with leisure.

The year-round school, the summer enrichment programs, the adult education offerings, and the supportive federal programs place more emphasis on the public education system as a focal point for enlarging leisure opportunities.

On the other hand, school responsibilities have increased in many areas. With restrictions on finance, personnel, and facilities, it is understandable if school personnel do not always meet their obligations in leisure education. The ultimate responsibility rests with park and recreation personnel to stimulate, instigate, interpret, and inveigle so that every agency that has the potential for serving individual and community leisure needs will rise to its task.

The school of the future will undoubtedly be less formal, nonterminal, community-based, and unrestricted by its walls or architectural barriers. It will stretch over into the parks beside it, the recreation centers, the museums, the libraries, and the art centers. Cooperation and coordination will be the keys to improving the quality of the school's objectives that relate to education for the worthy use of leisure.

Selected References

Clayre, Alasdair. *Work and Play: Ideas and Experience of Work and Leisure.* New York: Harper & Row, 1975.

Decker, Larry E. *Foundations of Community Education.* Midland, Michigan: Pendell Publishing Co., 1972.

Donaldson, George W., and Goering, Oswald. *Perspectives in Outdoor Education.* Dubuque, Iowa: William C. Brown Company, 1972.

Educational Facilities Laboratories, Inc. *Community/School, Sharing the Space and Action.* New York: Educational Facilities Laboratories, Inc., 1973.

Environmental Education in the Public Schools. Washington, D.C.: Research Division of the National Education Association, 1970.

Epperson, Arlin; Witt, Peter A.; and Hitzhuzen, Gerald. *Leisure Counseling: An Aspect of Leisure Education.* Springfield, Ill.: Charles C. Thomas, Publisher, 1977.

Fairchild, Effie, and Neal, Larry. *Common-Unity in the Community.* Eugene: University of Oregon Center of Leisure Studies, 1975.

Grabowski, Stanley M., and Mason, W. Dean, eds. *Learning for Aging.* Washington, D.C.: Adult Education Association of the U.S.A., 1975.

Green, Thomas F. *Work, Leisure, and the American Schools.* New York: Random House, 1968.

Hammerman, Donald R., and Hammerman, William M. *Outdoor Education: A Book of Readings.* Minneapolis: Burgess Publishing Company, 1968.

Hostrop, Richard W., ed. *Education . . . Beyond Tomorrow.* Homewood, Ill.: ETC Publications, 1975.

Jubenville, Alan. *Outdoor Recreation Management.* Laramie: University of Wyoming, 1978.

Leonard, George B. *Education and Ecstasy.* New York: Dell Publishing Company, Inc., 1968.

MacLean, Janet R., ed. *Third National Leisure Education Conference: Accent on Coordination.* Arlington, Virginia: National Recreation and Park Association, 1977.

McClellan, Robert W., and Pellett, Lane. "Leisure Counseling—the First Step," *Therapeutic Recreation Journal* 60, no. 4 (1975).

McInnis, Noel, and Albrecht, Don, eds. *What Makes Education Environmental?* Washington, D.C.: Environmental Educators, Inc., 1975; and Louisville, Ky.: Data Courier, Inc., 1975.

Mundy, Jean. *Leisure Education.* New York: John Wiley & Sons, Inc., 1978.

Mundy, Jean, and Cannon, Frances, eds. *Leisure Education and the Quality of Life, First National Conference on Leisure Education.* Tallahassee: Florida State University, 1975.

Seay, Maurice F. *Community Education, A Developing Concept.* Midland, Michigan: Pendell Publishing Co., 1974.

Smith, Julian W.; Carlson, Reynold E.; Donaldson, George W.; and Masters, Hugh B. *Outdoor Education.* Englewood Cliffs, N.J.: Prentice-Hall, Inc., 1972.

The following national organizations have excellent materials available:

National Recreation and Park Association

Odum, Linda, and Lancaster, Roger
Kangaroo Kit, vol. I. Kindergarten–Grade 6, 1977

Kangaroo Kit, vol. II, Grades 7–12, 1977

Leisure Education Curriculum Bibliography, 1977

Leisure Education Curriculum Guidelines, 1977

American Alliance for Leisure and Recreation *Leisure Today* series, particularly,

Leisure Counseling, March 1977

Education for Leisure, March 1976

Community Education, April 1974

Part Three
The Voluntary and Private Sector

We certainly can't create conditions of peace through recreation alone, but we can contribute considerably to establishing the value of human life and the decision of every person as to whether it is worth saving.

Margaret Mead

If, in viewing society's provisions for recreation, we regard government services as the warp, the weft comprises the nongovernment organizations and individuals who strengthen the fabric, fill in the design, and complete the patterns. Without them, recreation in many communities would be reduced to bare threads. These organizations include an overwhelming number of religious, political, social, civic, fraternal, labor, conservation, and veterans organizations as well as special-interest groups in art, music, drama, nature sports, and other areas.

Chapters 8, 9, and 10 examine this weft, categorizing the services for the sake of discussion, even though many of them cross our arbitrary lines of division. Chapter 8 considers the voluntary, tax-exempt, nonprofit services—such as the youth-serving agencies,

religious groups, and settlement houses—that are open in membership, offer some recreation services, and depend essentially upon public contributions. Chapter 9 covers the recreation and leisure aspects of loosely structured home and family groups and also nonprofit civic organizations, lodges, special-interest clubs, and employee organizations that are financed primarily by their own members. Chapter 10, viewing the entire pattern of recreation, public and nonpublic, considers efforts to order the design so as to meet human needs more effectively.

Almost everyone has been served by one or more of these associations, for they touch the entire range of human leisure interests.

8
Semipublic and Religious Organizations

The future of our civilization does not depend upon what we do on the job, but what we do in our life off the job.

Herbert Hoover

Those quasi-public agencies that include recreation among the basic human needs with which they are concerned are the subject of this chapter. Most of these would describe themselves as health, education, social service, or welfare agencies rather than as recreation agencies. None is self-sustaining; all depend upon contributions for most of their programs.

Tax-exempt yet not tax-supported, independent yet in varying degrees related to government, these organizations evolved to meet needs that were not met by government. Those that have continued over the years have responded to the changing demands of society, experimenting, offering new approaches, and revising their goals.

Goals for Human Services

In order to help agencies clarify their individual goals, the United Way of America has classified human needs into eight categories:

It can be said that all organized human endeavors . . . can be traced to one ultimate purpose or goal overriding all others, and that is, to enable individuals to live a well-adjusted and satisfying existence and to enable them to realize their full potential. In order to achieve that ideal, individuals living in a modern, industrialized society must:

1. Have adequate money income
2. Enjoy good health
3. Have their basic material needs (food, clothing, shelter, and transportation) met
4. Be able to obtain the necessary education
5. Be able to live in a healthy and pleasing natural environment
6. Be safe and secure in person and property
7. Be able to function well in a complex society and develop themselves to their potential
8. Have organized institutions and systems to assure that the above-mentioned services are effectively provided[1]

Many agencies today are broadening their services to achieve more of these goals. Recreation can play an important part in reaching the goals, especially the second, fifth, and seventh.

Throughout their history, the voluntary agencies have attempted to reach the neglected, the poor, the handicapped, and the culturally deprived. Indeed, the settlement houses, the Salvation Army, the Boys' Clubs, the Girls Clubs, and many others were founded specifically for such purposes. But because of today's focus on social equality and the availability of federal funds for specific projects to achieve it, the agencies now cover a wider range of human services than ever before and attract a cross section of the population.

A number of agencies are actively involved in juvenile justice. With a $1.5 million grant from the U.S. Department of Justice, a collaboration of several major organizations is trying to develop alternatives to the juvenile justice system in treating young offenders (truants, runaways, incorrigibles). In this and other ways, the agencies, with government aid, are reaching into new areas for solving social problems and, in so doing, put their recreation functions in a new perspective. Recreation is used as a channel to achieve agency goals; yet, to the participants, recreation remains a goal in itself.

Background of Voluntary Agencies

The first large national voluntary agencies appeared in the United States about a century ago. Several more developed around 1910 and grew rapidly in the next few decades. Many a community owes its recreation program to a voluntary agency that successfully pioneered in a service that was later taken over by a tax-supported agency. Today, in most communities, tax-supported agencies and voluntary agencies work side by side.

Functions and Problems of Voluntary Agencies

There are several functions that voluntary agencies can perform more readily than can public agencies.

1. A voluntary organization is free to focus upon specific segments of society and to maintain certain types of programs—religious, for example—that a public agency is legally unable to conduct.

2. It can respond to emerging needs more quickly than can a government agency, which may have to wait for legislative approval.

3. It is free to explore, to experiment, and to act as a proving ground for new ideas and innovative activities.

4. It offers a channel for voluntary initiative and service whereby individuals may help to see their particular ideas carried out.

These advantages are counterbalanced, however, by certain limitations.

1. Being dependent upon public contributions, the voluntary agencies may have to dissipate much of their energy in fund raising, even though the United Way has assumed this responsibility for many agencies.

2. Their income may fluctuate markedly according to the whims of individual contributors, whereas the cost of tax-supported programs, being distributed among all taxpayers, is apt to remain more stable.

3. The difficulty of recruiting, training, and holding volunteers is a major handicap.

4. The lack of adequate land and facilities presents difficulties. Most volunteer agencies that engage in recreation use public parks, forests, and play areas. When public use conflicts, the voluntary agency program must adapt.

Another serious situation—unfortunately shared by government recreation agencies—is the overlapping of services and the competition for funds, a problem that Chapter 10 considers.

What Is a Voluntary Organization?

The terms *volunteer* and *voluntary* must not be confused. The voluntary organization is voluntary in a fourfold sense: origin, membership, finance, and, to a very large extent, leadership. However, a tax-supported agency may use volunteer leaders as well as paid professionals; and a voluntary agency uses paid professionals as well as volunteers. Moreover, tax-supported agencies may be assisted by donations, and voluntary agencies may accept government grants. The lines between the two types of services are not always sharply drawn.

Youth Organizations

Youth organizations grew rapidly throughout the first half of the twentieth century and boomed in membership after World War II. Despite a loss in membership in some cases in the 1970s, the voluntary youth organizations remain an accepted part of American life. Children in almost every part of America have the opportunity to belong. In many homes, membership is considered an essential part of growing up, like going to school or church.

The youth organizations have many features in common. Most of them aspire:

1. To contribute toward the personality development of the young people they serve

2. To help them integrate socially and learn to accept civic responsibility

3. To teach them new skills and interests, including those that have vocational value

Tax Funds for a Voluntary Organization?

The city council was discussing the struggle of the small new Girls Club to raise enough money to get on its feet. No help was available from the United Fund, although the club might be included in the next fund drive if its program is firmly established.

City Councilman O'Toole was deeply concerned. "Here we are in a city of nearly 40,000 people, with plenty of recreation programs for boys. But what are we doing for the girls? They've been neglected year after year. The least we can do is to give the Girls Club a hand. The city can well afford to give them enough to carry on through this year."

Ann Smith interrupted. "We have a big public park and recreation program to support, and it's hard enough to pay for it with the amount of tax money we have. Voluntary agencies should raise their own money. If we give money to one organization, every other organization will feel it has an equal right to some support. How can we say yes to one and no to another?"

"But this program is just getting started," O'Toole urged. "All we need to do is to give enough to keep it going through the next few months. The United Fund will place it under its wing once it has proven itself."

To what extent should municipalities support voluntary agencies? To what extent should voluntary agencies accept such support? What disadvantages or advantages does an agency have in accepting support? What disadvantages or advantages does it have in being free of such support?

4. To show them how to use leisure constructively

5. To promote their health and spiritual growth

All of the major youth organizations are open to young people regardless of race or religion, and fees are generally low so that any child can afford to join. The programs appeal to the needs of youth for adventure, companionship, security, social participation, social acceptance, and self-expression. They are based on the belief that personal and social development can take place through participating, under adult leaders, in activities with peer groups.

In some foreign countries the youth programs are established, financed, and dominated by government; but in the United States the programs have developed voluntarily. Because financial support and leadership are largely voluntary, these organizations are close to the pulse and thinking of the people they serve.

The opportunity for these organizations to obtain federal financing for specific projects has influenced many of them in recent years to shape their programs according to federal guidelines in order to qualify for funds. Yet few can deny that the danger of losing their own initiative lurks in the acceptance of federal funds.

The Programs

Broadly conceived, a *program* includes everything that happens in a group, even casual and unscheduled activities, through which the agencies attempt to meet their goals. Programs are carried out in three principal ways:

Small-group activities.   The most common program method in youth organizations is the use of small democratic groups in which teamwork and democratic procedures are stressed. Learning takes place through doing and becomes a form of play. The small groups may be subdivided into interest or hobby groups that meet simultaneously.

Large-group activities.   Building-centered organizations may carry on large-group activities in gymnasiums, swimming pools, and auditoriums while carrying on small-group activities in clubrooms and craft shops. Organizations without buildings usually operate in small groups, limiting their mass activities to such events as exhibits, banquets, parades, jamborees, and conventions.

Individual activities.   Much of the badge work in scouting, the project work in 4-H, and the honor work in Camp Fire Girls is carried on by members working alone outside of club meetings. Individual guidance is a feature of all the major youth organizations.

Nationally established programs.   Programs of several of the large youth agencies, such as the Boy Scouts, Girl Scouts, and Camp Fire Girls, are set up on a national basis, although the trend today is toward more local flexibility, especially with older groups. The national programs are based on studies of the interests and needs of young people and long years of experience. Handbooks for members and leaders give detailed guidance. In general, home-centered programs for the youngest children progress through gradual steps to community-centered programs in which older children find opportunities for wide service, vocational exploration, social experience, and specialized interests.

Members in these programs receive awards and badges or rise in rank by completing projects and passing tests of knowledge or skill. Critics of the award system believe that children may work for awards themselves rather than for the sake of the learning. Yet we must realize that many a lifetime career was born in the enthusiasms aroused by the prospect of awards.

Locally determined programs.   In such agencies as Boys' Clubs and Girls Clubs, local interests and needs, restricted, of course, by available facilities, leadership, and money, determine the program. Since these organizations maintain drop-in centers, many of the services revolve around these facilities. Because their basic structure is so different from that of organizations using prescribed programs, they do not necessarily compete; so a Boy Scout troop may meet in the building of a Boys' Club.

Leadership, Administration, and Finance

Each of the major youth organizations is administered nationally by a lay council that charters local councils and gives them resource materials and guidance through the aid of a professional staff and state or regional offices. Local units are under the jurisdiction of local lay councils or, as in 4-H, are advised by local committees.

Volunteers at both local and national levels are the backbone of the programs, especially in the agencies with nationally outlined programs. Training courses, with the aid of manuals or handbooks, make it possible for volunteers to proceed easily and confidently with little additional help, leaving the professionals to concentrate on supervisory or administrative work. In this way large numbers of children can be served with a minimal paid staff. The Girl Scouts express the feeling toward volunteers in this sentence from the Preamble of their Constitution: "We hold that ultimate responsibility for the Girl Scout movement rests with volunteers."[2]

In agencies in which programs are determined locally, there are more likely to be professional leaders for the children's groups, although volunteers are used extensively as assistants, specialists, and board or committee members.

With the exception of 4-H, which receives partial tax support, the local youth organizations depend for funds upon annual drives, usually part of the United Way drives. Membership fees, cookie sales, gifts, special fund-raising drives, and, more recently, government grants supplement their income. National headquarters are financed by fees from individual members or member clubs, gifts, grants, the sale of literature and equipment, and other sources.

Despite their voluntary nature, many of the national organizations maintain loose government relationships and are chartered by Congress.

Where Are the Youth Organizations Headed?

The twentieth century has witnessed more changes than any other period in history. It is impressive that the youth organizations have been able to adapt and survive, even though at times they have had to retrench and reorganize. What, then, caused several of them suddenly to lose membership in the 1970s?

Among the explanations offered were changing life-styles; competing youth programs, such as athletic teams and even television; decreasing numbers of children in the age bracket to which the agencies appeal; mobility of modern families; difficulty in securing and holding volunteers, especially with more women in the labor market; increased costs of living; and rising costs of operation, which forced a reduction in professional personnel.

Looking internally, the organizations have agonizingly reappraised some of their restrictive policies and have become more responsive to community needs. Camp Fire Girls, for example, opened membership in its Horizon Clubs to boys and authorized additional services, such as teen centers, to supplement its traditional program. Boys' Clubs started enrolling girls; and Boy Scouts admitted girls to its Explorer Posts.

The youth organizations have attempted with increased vigor to help solve social problems through work with juvenile delinquents, the poor, the handicapped, and racial minorities. They have tackled problems of interracial and intercultural relationships and encouraged friendships between those of different ethnic and national backgrounds. They have entered the field of vocational guidance for older youth. Their recreation programs have been augmented by attention to community needs. In the process, there has arisen consideration of the merging of certain agencies to achieve mutual goals.

Boy Scouts of America

The Boy Scouts of America, the nation's largest organization for boys, has five million members, about a fourth of whom are adult leaders. From the inception of the Boy Scouts to the end of 1976, total membership has numbered about 60 million persons.

Background of scouting. Scouting can claim both English and American origins. There were several forerunners of the Boy Scouts in the United States. Among them was the Woodcraft Indians, the first boys' organization to emphasize woodcraft and camping skills, founded in 1902 by Ernest Thompson Seton. When the Boy Scout movement began, Seton disbanded the Woodcraft Indians.

The Boy Scouts were organized in England in 1908 by Sir Robert Baden-Powell (later Lord Baden-Powell). During the Boer War, he had seen how much the English soldiers were in need of outdoor skills; after the war, he set about to help boys secure this essential training. When William D. Boyce, a Chicago publisher, visited England in 1909, he was deeply impressed by the new movement. With his help and that of other enthusiastic supporters, the Boy Scouts of America was founded in 1910.

The movement has spread throughout the world. The international structure represents about 110 countries and maintains headquarters in Switzerland. Representatives from each nation form the council.

Organization and programs. Scouting is open to boys of all religions and races. Though nondenominational, it encourages members to do their "duty to God"; and about half of its 150,000 units are sponsored by religious institutions. Another third are sponsored by civic groups and about a fifth by schools and parent-teacher organizations.

The program offers opportunities for vocational exploration and endeavors to develop character, health, mental alertness, manual skills, self-reliance, and leadership ability. It operates through three main divisions:

Cub Scouts (ages 8–10) are more numerous than Boy Scouts. The program began in 1930. In the home-centered program, mothers and fathers help the boys progress from Bobcat to Wolf and Bear. Small neighborhood groups meet weekly in dens. Several dens join for monthly pack meetings.

Scout (ages 11–14) troops consist of several smaller units called patrols. A boy progresses from Scout to Tenderfoot to Second Class to First Class and can earn merit badges to advance through Star, Life, and Eagle awards.

Exploring (ages 15–21) offers an advanced program for both boys and girls in vocational explorations, outdoor adventure, service, social activities, personal fitness, and citizenship, with attention given to special-interest groups.

Scouting/USA is attempting to meet the needs of contemporary youth. Among recent innovations are twelve "skill award" areas, with specially written pamphlets to aid the slow reader; modified requirements for mentally and physically retarded youngsters; a new name (Scouting/USA) that includes both sexes; increased high-adventure opportunities in the outdoors, athletics, good citizenship, and career exploration; and the opening of virtually all leadership roles to women.

Boys' Clubs of America

The plight of boys in crowded and crime-ridden slums of New England, with no place to play but the streets, spurred concerned citizens more than a century ago into organizing several independent boys' clubs. The first club opened in 1860 in Hartford, Massachusetts. In 1906 the clubs combined into what is now known as the national Boys' Clubs of America.

The clients. Urban boys, aged seven to fifteen, from low-income families, inadequate homes, and poor neighborhoods are the special concern of the 1,000 Boys' Clubs. The clubs often extend services, however, to older and younger boys, girls, and even the elderly. In small communities the Boys' Clubs reach all classes of society, providing a "home away from home" and sometimes the only available recreation for boys. Boys of all races and religions are welcome.

The Boys' Clubs of America is one of the fastest-growing youth guidance movements in the United States. There are more than a million members in over 700 cities. Ten thousand full- and part-time career persons and several thousand volunteers are involved.

Mission and program of the Boys' Clubs. Today the primary mission of the Boys' Clubs of America is "to assure and enhance the quality of life for boys as participating members of a richly diverse urban society." There is no national prearranged program; the national office offers guidance, but each club determines its own program on the basis of local needs and interests. Individual counseling is considered a valuable tool.

A building is necessary to a Boys' Club, and some large communities maintain both a central building and small neighborhood branches. The game rooms, libraries, gymnasiums, locker rooms, shops, classrooms, space for dramatics and music, and club meeting rooms invite diversified activities. Swimming pools, playgrounds, athletic fields, kitchens, craft rooms, quiet rooms for studying and reading, and auditoriums are desirable features of many of the buildings.

Day and overnight camps are conducted and about a fifth of the Boys' Clubs run summer camps.

A recent survey showed that the most popular activities in the Boys' Clubs were, in order of attendance: general recreation and game rooms, organized team sports, arts and crafts, and gym and physical fitness.[3]

Boys' Clubs serve an ever-widening range of human needs. Many of the services relate to health and nutrition; and medical and dental examinations are given. Prevocational training and youth employment are major concerns. Attention is given to special populations. .

Projects such as education for parenthood, physical fitness programs, and the new alcohol-abuse prevention program, Project TEAM (Teens Explore Alcohol Moderation), are receiving emphasis. The Boys' Clubs have joined forces with other agencies to find better ways of treating young offenders than putting them in jails and detention homes; many member clubs are providing residential care for these boys, with help from federal funds.

Camp Fire Girls

The Camp Fire Girls was the first national nonsectarian organization for girls, established in 1910. Dr. and Mrs. Luther Halsey Gulick, the founders, had tested their theories at home with their own children, in schools, and at their summer camp. Incorporated in 1912, Camp Fire Girls now has a half million members in about 350 units throughout the country.

The purpose of the Camp Fire Girls, Inc., is: ". . . to provide, through a program of informal education, opportunities for youth to realize their potential and to function effectively as caring, self-directed individuals, responsible to themselves and to others. It seeks also to improve those conditions in society which affect youth."[4] A not-for-profit, national agency for youth to twenty-one years of age, Camp Fire is open to all without regard to race, creed, ethnic origin, sex, or income level.

New program. Over the years Camp Fire has often experimented with new approaches to working with youth, and there is change in the organization today. A design for the future, called "It's a New Day," was adopted in 1975, expanding the traditional program by providing more variety and flexibility, such as drop-in and day-care programs; co-ed activities; adult enrichment and career development seminars; storefront recreation programs; activities for young people with special needs and interests; and special programs for young status offenders, parolees, the retarded, and the handicapped. The new structure gave Camp Fire councils more freedom in developing local programs, although they still had to comply with the broad objectives, policies, and standards of the corporation.

Traditional program. The Camp Fire traditional program is also still in effect, focusing on the development of the individual and the attainment of skills in leadership, citizenship, interpersonal relations, the creative arts, and other programs in small peer groups with trained adult leaders.

Blue Birds (ages 6–8) have fun as they learn about the world, play games, tell stories, and make pictures and puppets. They picnic and visit factories, museums, parks, zoos, and other places near their homes

Adventurers (ages 9–11) learn and play in the areas of business, citizenship, the creative arts, games and sports, home, outdoors, and science. For each skill mastered, an honor bead is earned, with which an Adventurer may decorate her ceremonial vest.

Discovery Clubs encourage twelve- and thirteen-year-olds to learn about their own feelings and ideas as they participate in camping, sports, cooking, music, the arts, and volunteer community work.

Horizon Clubs help high school boys and girls recognize their desires, abilities, and limitations and begin to make decisions about their careers and ways they can improve the world. They give service at hospitals, tutor children, engage in community conservation projects, and help in other ways.

Adult volunteers serve as club leaders. Each club has from one to five adult sponsors, who help the group leaders and find meeting places, such as churches, synagogues, schools, and buildings owned by civic clubs.

4-H Program

At about the turn of the century, a few corn-raising clubs for boys and canning clubs for girls began a rural program that led to the founding of 4-H. Today 4-H has over 5.5 million members in more than 3,000 U.S. counties, with 130,000 clubs and special-interest groups guided by 550,000 adult and teenage leaders. By 1975, only twenty-three percent of its members lived on farms; forty percent lived in towns with less than 10,000 population and in open country; and the remainder lived in larger towns, suburbs, and cities.

4-H is the youth educational system of the Cooperative Extension Service, with national headquarters at the U.S. Department of Agriculture, state headquarters at state land-grant universities, and local headquarters at the offices of the county extension agents. Its program is offered to all boys and girls nine through nineteen years of age, of all racial, cultural, economic, and social backgrounds.

The Smith-Lever Act of 1914, which provided for cooperative extension work in agriculture and home economics, included what was then known as "boys' and girls' club work," and set up a system of support through federal funds matched by the states and counties. By the 1920s, the 4-H name, standing for Head, Heart, Hands, and Health, had been generally adopted. Today about two-thirds of 4-H funds come from taxes and the remainder from private sources. A nongovernment agency, the National 4-H Council, channels private support at the national level.

The 4-H idea, with adaptations, has spread to more than eighty countries. Through the International Four-H Youth Exchange

Figure 8.1. Members of 4-H demonstrating canning techniques. Source: *U.S. Cooperative Extension Service.*

(IFYE), young Americans may visit other countries and young foreigners may live and work with American farm families for months at a time. Relatively new international programs include travel seminars, agricultural training, work exchange, and rural youth leaders exchange.

The number of volunteer leaders has tripled in the past twenty years. In some areas, paraprofessional program assistants and aides are employed as intermediaries between professionals and volunteer adult leaders. Program aides, for the most part, work with low-income disadvantaged youth.

Young people carry out their own diversified programs under guidance in accordance with their own needs and interests. Commu-

nity service is encouraged. Members may select from more than 100 projects, including such wide-ranging interests as aerospace, conservation, livestock and poultry, personal development, and photography. Typical projects are exhibited and judged at local, county, and state fairs.

A variety of work methods enhances the flexibility of 4-H: the traditional 4-H clubs; the special-interest groups; special projects presented on television, which thousands of children watch and duplicate; and the 4-H Expanded Food and Nutrition Education Programs (EFNEP), for low-income city youth, and 4-H urban and community development programs.

The years since the inception of 4-H have produced more than thirty-six million "alumni" who have gained not only practical skills but also the more enduring benefits of wide friendships, broad cultural horizons, adaptability, and willingness to assume citizenship responsibilities.

Girl Scouts of the United States of America

With more than three million members, the Girl Scouts is by far the largest girls' organization in the United States today. Girl Scouting followed closely upon the success of Boy Scouting. In 1909, in England, Agnes Baden-Powell, sister of the Boy Scout founder, became the first president of the Girl Guides. Her friend, Juliette Gordon Low, on a visit to her native city of Savannah, Georgia, organized the first U.S. Girl Guide group in 1912. The name in the United States was changed to Girl Scouts in 1913.

Girl Scouting has spread to ninety-four countries. National groups are joined in the World Association of Girl Guides and Girl Scouts, which promotes the world movement and encourages international friendships.

Girl Scouts include girls from six years of age through high school. The program has four emphases: deepening self-awareness, developing values, contributing to community, and relating to others. Program materials are organized under five "worlds": world of people; world of well-being; world of arts; natural world; and world of science, business, and technology. Planning by the girls themselves is important. Even the Brownies, sitting on the floor in a "Brownie ring," vote to decide plans for their troop.

Brownie Scouts (ages 6–8) are encouraged to emulate the good-natured goblins for whom they are named by helping unobtrusively around the house. Meeting weekly with their leaders in homes, schools, or churches, they accomplish the Brownie "B's" (Be Discoverers, Be Ready Helpers, and Be Friend-makers) (see Figure 8.2).

Junior Girl Scouts (ages 9–11) meet weekly in troops of twenty to thirty-two girls, divided into patrols of six to eight members. The elected officers and the adult leader form a Court of Honor, which makes plans for the troop based on suggestions from girls in the patrols. Juniors earn recognition through work on proficiency badges and "signs."

Cadette Girl Scouts (ages 12–14) grow in independence, facing twelve challenges that test their know-how in real-life situations. Cadettes may do extensive work on proficiency badges.

Senior Girl Scouts (ages 14–17) have a program much less structured than that of any other level. Service to others and vocational exploration are highlighted by their Aide programs.

Other areas of Girl Scouting include Campus Girl Scouts, through which college students serve the community; and Troops on Foreign Soil (TOFS), comprising daughters of U.S. military and civilian families living in fifty-three foreign countries. International friendships are emphasized.

Although it is difficult for a large democratic organization to change, the Girl Scouts have tried to keep pace with the changing needs of girls through frequent reexamination and revision of their structure and program. More effort is being made to reach disadvantaged and minority groups. Career awareness is being fostered in girls at earlier ages. A 1976 grant from the Department of Health, Education, and Welfare provided for a career exploration project for twelve- to seventeen-year-old Girl Scouts.

While they try to eliminate stereotyped sex roles, the Girl Scouts remain an all-girl organization as a result of a 1975 decision not to admit boys as members. The Girl Scout program is today more flexible across age lines, so that girls may find their own level in a wide range of activities. Today's program shows more concern for the elderly, family relationships, minorities, and migrants, and reemphasizes the long-time interest in environmental improvement.

Girls Clubs of America, Inc.

Girls Clubs of America is a nationwide federation of centers that provides girls with opportunities to recognize their worth as human beings, develop their talents and abilities, explore the changing role of women

Figure 8.2. Brownies' activities build friendships.
Source: *Girl Scouts of the U.S.A.*

in today's society, and prepare for the responsibilities they will have as adults, in the labor force as well as in the home.

Concern for disadvantaged girls led to the formation of the Girls Clubs of America in 1945 in Worcester, Massachusetts, by nineteen local clubs. The Girls Clubs stated that their purpose was to promote "the health, social, cultural, vocational, and character development of girls six years of age through high school age regardless of race, creed, or national origin."

The factors that make a Girls Club unique are: Girls Clubs are open every day—after school, in the evening, on Saturday, and during the summer; the services at these building-centered clubs are designed for the girls in that particular community; and girls pay a minimal membership fee—an average of $4 per year—so that girls from low-income urban families can participate. At present, approximately sixty-eight percent of the members are in this category.

Girls Clubs of America play a key role as an advocate for the rights of girls. They concentrate on helping girls to get their fair share of attention, funding, services, and educational and employment opportunities. They are active in programs for nonsexist career planning and job training, health and sex education, sports and recreation, youth leadership development opportunities, tutorial services, individual and group counseling, arts and crafts, and family life education.[5]

With crime among girls increasing more than twice as fast as crime among boys, the Girls Clubs try to provide satisfying programs to counteract the destructive forces leading to delinquency. The Girls Clubs are especially concerned with runaways, truants, and incorrigibles, of whom seventy percent are girls and young women, and feel that they should not be placed in detention or correctional facilities.

Obtaining financing has long been easier for boys' programs than for girls', a fact that has hampered the development of Girls Clubs.

Recently, however, funds for girls' programs have become more available, probably because of the aggressiveness fostered by the women's movement and the increase in female delinquency, which points up the need for better services to girls.

Organizations Serving Family Recreation Needs

While work with youth is very important in the organizations that follow, all ages are served by their programs. Leisure activities in some of them are a means to an end rather than an end in themselves.

Religious Groups

The inclusion of churches as voluntary agencies may seem unusual; but, in a free society, they are voluntary in every sense of the word. In theory, at least, the church is separate from government. Nonetheless, churches receive the blessing of government in the form of exemption from taxation; and gifts to churches, like gifts to certain charitable and educational organizations, are deductible from the donor's income tax. Many church-supported social services today receive financial aid from the government.

The place of recreation in the church. There has been considerable discussion in recent years as to the place of organized religion in American life. Yet, recreation and religion have been linked from the beginnings of human existence. Dance, music, and drama evolved in primitive societies in the religious ceremonies and festivals through which people expressed their beliefs, prayed for rains and good harvests, or tried to appease angry gods.

In colonial New England, the church, under Calvinistic influence, took a dim view of amusement and ruled against the theater and many other types of entertainment, although the church remained a place in which the young and old could socialize. It was not until the end of the nineteenth century that most religious leaders recognized the need for recreation in the church and began to sponsor games, bazaars, church suppers, lectures, concerts, sports, and discussion groups. As the workweek shortened and leisure increased, churches responded by offering more leisure activities and were openly aggressive in advocating better recreation opportunities.

Courses in recreation are now promoted in theological seminaries so that religious leaders may better understand the meaning and methods of recreation. National directors of recreation are hired by several religious groups, and many local churches and synagogues engaged professionally trained recreation leaders to minister to the needs of their members.

Types of church recreation activities. In general, churches and synagogues regard their responsibilities toward recreation as, first, to provide recreation for their own members in order to answer their needs and create a friendly atmosphere; and second, to support community recreation programs acceptable to their religious concepts. Churches and synagogues frequently sponsor or conduct the following services:

1. Outdoor activities, such as picnics, camps for young people and families, conferences, and retreats

2. Social gatherings, including family nights, potluck suppers, game nights, and dances, held in the church social parlors, gymnasiums, or activity rooms

3. Vacation schools, which run the gamut of recreation activities along with religious instruction

4. Workshops stressing arts, crafts, and music, especially in preparation for special events and holidays

5. Fellowship groups and clubs for youth and young adults, scout programs, and adult interest clubs

6. Sports, including bowling, basketball, and baseball, often using church-owned facilities

7. Study and discussion groups, including discussions of current social issues

8. Support, alone or in cooperation with other religious groups and agencies, for such enterprises as social centers for high school students, special ministries for college campuses, day-care centers, day camps, and community centers for the underprivileged, some of which qualify for federal funds.

9. Innovative worship programs, including dance and folk music

In addition, many churches and synagogues open their doors for use by community groups for nursery schools, meetings, sports, and entertainments.

Catholic recreation services. Local parishes offer recreation to both adults and young people. Most of their local youth groups are affiliated with the Catholic Youth Organizations (CYOs), one of the largest youth organizations in the country. The individual CYOs have a great deal of autonomy, with no strong national program, although most of them are related to the Youth Department of the U.S. Catholic Conference. The programs vary greatly and are strongest in large cities, where community centers, summer camps, and swimming are offered. Special projects for delinquency prevention have been developed.

Recreation in other Christian churches. All the major denominations offer recreation through individual churches, especially in the fellowship groups for young people and adults and in the women's associations. Encouragement at the national level is given in some denominations by hiring national recreation directors, publishing program suggestions, sponsoring workshops and conferences, and presenting training courses for recreation leaders.

The highly organized national youth clubs, such as the Girls' Friendly Society (Episcopal), the Methodist Youth Fellowship, and the Luther League, were disbanded in the 1960s. Their place has been taken by informal youth groups, often with no particular church affiliation, in which new forms of worship are tried. Discussions in these groups may revolve around self-realization and a searching for values.

Among the first of the religious faiths to affirm the value of recreation in modern times was the Church of Jesus Christ of Latter-Day Saints (Mormons). The Mutual Improvement Association (MIA), initiated for young women in 1869 and for young men in 1875, gives leadership to Mormons over twelve years of age. In addition to religious instruction, programs in sports, dance, music, public speaking, and drama are included. Family recreation is strongly emphasized.

The Salvation Army, which is a church although it is thought of more as an institution to help the poor and downtrodden, carries on a diversified recreation program for its congregation, often using programs of other agencies, such as the Boy Scouts, in its club work. Its Red Shield drop-in youth centers contain gymnasiums, auditoriums, and rooms for games and crafts. Sunbeams, Girl Guards, and Senior Guards are programs for girls and are similar to Girl Scouts, but with a religious emphasis. About 30,000 children a year are served through Salvation Army resident camps, day camps, music camps, family camps (for young children and mothers), Bible study camps, camps for handicapped, and others. A total of

450,000 young people share its youth activities, which are open to everyone.

Several national organizations use recreation as a device for interesting and holding youth in religious programs. Among them are Young Life, Youth for Christ, United Boys' Brigade, Christian Service Brigade, Pioneer Girls, and the Junior Missionary Volunteer Pathfinders Club (Seventh-Day Adventist). Other programs, such as the Fellowship of Christian Athletes, appeal to young adults.

Jewish involvement in recreation. Three dominant recreation programs are under the auspices of the National Jewish Welfare Board: the Jewish Community Centers, the Young Men's Hebrew Association, and the Young Women's Hebrew Association. The board, founded in 1971, has been active in promoting mergers of the YMHAs and the YWHAs with each other and with the Jewish Community Centers.

The Jewish Community Center is an outstanding influence in education and recreation and a unifying force in Jewish life in its attempts to mold character and educate leaders for citizenship responsibilities. The buildings offer space for clubs, games, crafts, classes, gymnastics, swimming, lectures, dances, concerts, and other activities. Membership is based on the family unit. Programs for boys and girls may include summer activities and camps.

Most of the centers are open to non-Jews, but membership and focus remain strongly Jewish. It is estimated that the services of the Jewish Welfare Board reach a million people.

The YMHA and Jewish Community Center idea has spread elsewhere in North and South America as well as to Europe, Israel, Japan, India, and Australia.

The B'nai B'rith Youth Organization offers social, athletic, and cultural activities for teenagers and young adults. Jewish youth are also served by the three main branches of Judaism in the United States (Reform, Conservative, and Orthodox), each sponsoring its own youth movement through loosely structured groups in local synagogues.

Current problems and criticisms. Programs with the best of intentions are often misinterpreted. Some critics object that religious organizations are using recreation to make their faiths attractive to nonmembers or even to keep their organizations alive. Others feel that if recreation attracts those who would otherwise not be enticed into a religious program, then this is an accomplishment of which to be proud, not ashamed.

Although many religious groups open their doors to people of all faiths, some are criticized for restricting activities to members only or for banning particular activities such as dancing or card playing. Others are accused of duplicating and competing with programs already offered successfully by other agencies in the community.

Some people feel strongly that religious organizations—which too often have inadequate facilities or untrained leaders—should not offer recreation but should, instead, strengthen community recreation programs with their support. Many believe that spiritual needs suffer if leadership energies are siphoned to recreation.

Despite these problems, the values of recreation in enriching life, improving physical and mental health, and promoting good fellowship are so apparent that its place in religious organizations seems secure. The ways in which religious organizations can cooperate with schools, homes, and private and public agencies to minister to community recreation needs are discussed in Chapter 10.

Young Men's Christian Association

During the late 1960s and the 1970s, when many volunteer agencies were forced to retrench, the Young Men's Christian Association expanded in both membership and services.

Today there are nine million regular constituents, a third of whom are women and girls, in about 1,840 local associations in the United States.

The YMCA, which views itself as a social service conglomerate delivering a wide spectrum of services, is the oldest of the large voluntary organizations. It was begun in London in 1844 by twelve young clerks headed by George Williams, a farm boy who, on coming to London to work, was appalled by the city's moral conditions. The first YMCAs were primarily religious discussion groups. In 1851, Thomas V. Sullivan, a retired sea captain, gathered together in Boston the group that became the first American YMCA. In seven years, YMCAs dotted the country from coast to coast. The national organization was formed in 1866.

"The Young Men's Christian Association we regard as being, in its essential genius, a world-wide fellowship united by a common loyalty to Jesus Christ for the purpose of developing Christian personality and building a Christian society."[6] This is the official purpose of the YMCA. Despite its Christian affirmation, boys, girls, men, and women of every age, race, and creed are welcome in the YMCA.

Programs. In large cities, the YMCA typically operates a building or buildings, many of them equipped with residence accommodations, dining facilities, gymnasiums, swimming pools, lecture halls, craft shops, and meeting rooms. A large part of the YMCA program is carried on in neighborhoods without central buildings; and meetings are held in schools, houses, or other places. In recent years the large downtown buildings have tended to be replaced by smaller satellite centers.

Health, physical fitness, and camping. The YMCA is a leader in developing standards and methods of physical activities. It annually teaches thousands to swim, and it is a pioneer in scuba training and research. Its cardiovascular programs, launched in 1975, contribute to the health and well-being of thousands of Americans. (See Figure 8.3.)

A pioneer in camping, the YMCA operates more than 400 residence camps and 1,200 day camps for all age groups. It early demonstrated the potential of YMCA-school collaboration in school camping and continues to develop new programs, such as sports camps, travel trip camps, and therapeutic camps.

Classes and juvenile justice programs. Since its early years, the YMCA has conducted informal classes on subjects varying from social and recreation skills to marriage, business, religion, and public affairs.

The YMCA regards as one of its major goals the elimination of social forces that result in youthful crime and alienation. To help achieve this goal, it has developed a growing core of youth outreach workers, programs for children of working parents, emergency counseling centers, youth homes, and other programs.

Clubs. Most YMCA programs are conducted in groups, even though many opportunities are provided for individual participation.

Family development clubs. The YMCA helps to strengthen family relationships through its rapidly growing parent-child clubs and activities. Over half a million parents and children are involved in four kinds of

Figure 8.3. A YMCA family fun run. Source: *Larry Crewell.*

groups: Y-Indian Guides (six- to nine-year-old boys and their fathers); Y-Indian Princesses (six- to nine-year-old girls and their fathers); Y-Indian Maidens (six- to nine-year-old girls and their mothers); and Y-Trailblazers (boys over nine years of age and their fathers). A YMCA Family Communication Skills Center supports the growth and development of family programs.

Youth clubs. The YMCA provides several purpose-based clubs with adult advisors. Gra-Y (boys) and Tri-Gra-Y (girls) include youngsters from nine through twelve years of age. Jr. Hi-Y and Jr. Tri-Y are clubs for boys and girls (respectively) in seventh through ninth grades. Hi-Y, Tri-Hi-Y, and Co-Ed-Hi-Y are for high school youth who engage in a wide range of activities in which service is an important element. Highlights for this group are state youth and government programs, Model United Nations assemblies, and youth conferences.

Adult clubs. Chief among the adult clubs are the Y's Men, which are service clubs. International Management Clubs for supervisors and managers in business, clubs for older adults and young married couples, and clubs for single parents are also sponsored.

Specialized Y services. The YMCA has carried on student YMCAs on college campuses, Armed Services YMCAs, and Railroad YMCAs. Associations for blacks began in 1853; for Indians in 1879.

Two colleges, now general liberal arts colleges, were established primarily for the training of YMCA workers: Springfield College, in Springfield, Massachusetts; and George Williams College, in Downers Grove, Illinois.

National and international affiliations. Each local YMCA is a self-governing unit affiliated with other YMCAs through the National Council. The World Alliance of YMCAs, founded in 1855, is a federation of national YMCA movements.

The Y as a pioneer. The YMCA has pioneered in many successful programs that have spread to other agencies. Among them are health and fitness programs, development of the games of basketball and volleyball, learn-to-swim campaigns, camping for boys, and night-school education. The Boy Scouts and the Camp Fire Girls were aided in their beginning days by YMCA leaders. The YMCA thus offers an outstanding example of the contributions that a voluntary organization can render in experimental programs.

Young Women's Christian Association

The emblem of the Blue Triangle, familiar in cities from coast to coast, marks a "home away from home" for many young women, a recreation center for many more, and a social action movement that is at work for peace, justice, freedom, and dignity for all persons. Any girl over twelve years of age who pays dues, regardless of her race, creed, or national origin, is a member of the YWCA. Most members are between fifteen and thirty-five years old. Over two million members and program participants avail themselves of the services of the YWCA in over 6,700 locations in the United States. More than 310,000 boys and men are associates of the YWCA.

Origins. The YWCA emerged in 1885 in London to meet the needs of young women going to work in the cities. Similar migrations of women workers were occurring in the United States, and the movement found an early footing in industrial centers. The earliest association in the United States was the Ladies Christian Union in New York, founded in 1858; and in 1866, the first organization bearing the name of the Young Women's Christian Association was formed in Boston. In 1906, the present national organization was created. A World YWCA was formed in 1894. Eighty-three countries are represented in its membership.

Goals and programs. The YWCA's Statement of Purpose, revised in the twenty-fourth national convention in 1967, is as follows: "The Young Women's Christian Association of the United States of America, a movement rooted in the Christian faith as known in Jesus and nourished by the resources of that faith, seeks to respond to the barrier-breaking love of God in this day. The Association draws together into responsible membership women and girls of diverse experiences and faiths, that their lives may be open to new understanding and deeper relationships and that together they may join in the struggle for peace and justice, freedom and dignity for all people."

The YWCA, the world's oldest multi-racial, autonomous women's movement, has as its major goal the empowerment of women and the elimination of institutional racism. It attempts to advance economic opportunities, optimal environment for human existence, good health, and quality education. It helps women and girls to develop as persons, to acquire skills, and to accept their citizenship responsibilities. The YWCA takes action—alone or in cooperation with other groups—on social issues.

Both large and small cities as well as campuses are served by the YWCA. Community associations usually are building-centered and may include dormitories, restaurants, classrooms, lecture rooms, gymnasiums, swimming pools, and social rooms.

Various cultural, social, and recreation programs are offered. There are groups for providing new personal contacts, sharing ideas, discovering and rediscovering values, acquiring employment and leisure skills, and giving community services. Classes range from homemaking to consciousness-raising ses-

sions, job discrimination courses, and day-care centers. Recreation includes music, arts and crafts, dramatics, tennis, swimming, archery, badminton, volleyball, bowling, camping, and outdoor activities. Many of the leaders are volunteer, although the top leadership is professional.

Y-Teens are twelve- to seventeen-year-old members. Work with younger girls began in Oakland, California, where in 1881 the Little Girls' Christian Association originated. The girls' clubs, which united under the name of Girls Reserves in 1918, changed their name to Y-Teens in 1946. Y-Teens participate through interest groups, clubs, classes, co-ed recreation centers, health activities, and camping. They work in partnership with adults on YWCA boards, committees, and councils; on community action and public affairs programs; and for special events.

Some sixty college and university campuses have student members who take active roles in projects aimed at achieving YWCA goals. The first association for college girls was organized at Normal University in Illinois in 1874.

YWCA as a social force. The YWCA can look back upon years of effort and achievement in many welfare fields. Although primarily concerned with girls and women, it exerts its influence in wide spheres, as the following examples show:

1. Health education for women has been a part of YWCA work since the 1870s.

2. Low-cost vacation camps, day camps, and child-care centers are maintained.

3. Classes in various subjects are offered to enrich the intellectual, physical, and cultural lives of its members.

4. The principle of full equality for all races and nationalities is stressed. The achievement of justice for third-world

persons takes priority in today's program.

5. Standards for the improvement of working conditions for women have been promulgated.

6. World cooperation through international organizations, especially the United Nations, is vigorously supported.

Settlement Houses

Like many other social movements, the settlement house movement originated on a voluntary basis in England. The first settlement was Toynbee Hall, founded in 1884 in east London. Samuel Barrett, its founder, described the settlement as a place where individuals in a neighborhood could discuss common problems, attempt to improve conditions, and foster a better way of life for all people in the neighborhood.

The original settlement in the United States was the Neighborhood Guild, founded in 1886 in the lower east side of New York City. Leaders in the movement joined in 1911 to form the National Federation of Settlements and Neighborhood Centers, which serves today to help existing settlements and promote new ones. Federations throughout the world are united in the International Federation of Settlements.

The settlements are governed by boards of directors representing the contributing public, sponsoring agencies, and sometimes the neighborhood served. Their operations are financed through community drives, such as United Way, gifts, and, increasingly today, public funds. The staffs are composed mainly of social group workers. Volunteer workers are considered important in most settlements.

Settlements are found most often in poverty-ridden areas of large cities and serve everyone in the neighborhood, not just those who come to the settlement for advice, assistance, or planned activities. The objectives of the settlements are generally broader in scope than those of most community recreation agencies, since they are concerned with all aspects of neighborhood and family living, with recreation as only one of their functions.

The programs follow no single pattern. The group-work method, based upon the principle of individual development by means of group participation in various activities under trained leadership, is used; but individual counseling on personal problems is also an important service.

Whatever the leisure needs of people in the neighborhood are, the settlement attempts to meet them. Building-centered activities depend upon the facilities and might include playground programs, camping, hobby or interest clubs, athletics, arts and crafts, games, shop work, swimming, and cultural activities. Programs are not necessarily building-centered, and many activities take place in homes and in the neighborhood.

United Service Organizations

The USO, organized in 1941 as a cooperative venture of six national agencies (Jewish Welfare Board, Salvation Army, Catholic Community Service, YMCA, YWCA, and the National Travelers' Aid), operates clubs for men and women in the armed forces. During World War II and in Korea and Vietnam, the USO sponsored big-name entertainment for the overseas fighting forces, with the cooperation of famous Hollywood stars, notably Bob Hope. The clubs, mobile units, and centers in the United States offered lonesome or bored service personnel dancing, a good book, or simply some friendly conversation.

Peacetime programs include not only recreation but also help in housing and counseling, family programs, and local community organization.

American Red Cross

The nation's outstanding disaster-relief organization also serves recreation. Not only in war but also in peace, the American Red Cross has provided recreation to the U.S. armed forces wherever they are stationed in the world and has conducted extensive hospital recreation programs. As a quasi-public agency, it has worked closely with the federal government.

Water sports, especially swimming and boating, are safer and more enjoyable because of the courses in lifesaving, water safety, and first aid offered by the American Red Cross and the certification of those who meet its requirements.

Functioning through the schools and local communities, the Red Cross Youth programs, for children from elementary grades through high school, encourage international friendships, community service, and health and safety programs. Children become members by participating in programs or contributing to the Red Cross Youth Service Programs Fund.

Participants in Red Cross programs, including both children and adults, were estimated at nearly thirty-one million in 1976.

Summary

Since a majority of U.S. children and adults are related in some degree to the groups discussed in this chapter, these organizations have considerable influence in shaping behavior patterns. There is every reason to believe that they will continue to be forces in American life, for their philosophy of operation is in harmony with the traditional American values.

The following list summarizes both the strengths and problems of the volunteer organizations:

1. Their direction, support, and management are based on the assumption that groups may organize for the benefit of themselves and society in general.

2. Freedom of choice—to be a member or not, to help finance or not—is available to everyone.

3. They provide an important outlet for altruistic service.

4. Although they must continually change to meet emerging needs, they also act as stabilizing forces in a world of shifting values.

5. Because these organizations are voluntary, they face continual problems of recruiting leadership, financing, and maintaining community understanding and support.

6. All organizations must become viable influences in solving problems of racial and social justice, environment and energy, delinquency and crime.

Selected References

Galloway, Howard P., ed. *New Dimensions in Youth Work.* North Plainfield, N.J.: Galloway Publications, 1973. Also vol. 2, 1974.

Hanson, Robert F., and Carlson, Reynold E. *Organizations for Children and Youth.* Englewood Cliffs, N.J.: Prentice-Hall, Inc., 1972.

Konopka, Gisela. *Social Group Work—A Helping Process.* 2d ed. Englewood Cliffs, N.J.: Prentice-Hall, Inc., 1972.

Lurie, Harry L., ed. *Encyclopedia of Social Work.* New York: National Association of Social Workers, 1965.

Mobley, Tony A., ed. *An Integrative Review of Research in Church Recreation and Related Areas.* Penn State HPER Series No. 8. State College: The Pennsylvania State University, 1975.

Trecker, Harleigh B. *Social Group Work.* Rev. ed. New York: Association Press, 1972.

Handbooks, annual reports, and other literature published by individual organizations, including the following:

Boy Scouts of America, North Brunswick, N.J. 08902

Boys' Clubs of America, 771 First Avenue, New York, N.Y. 10017

Camp Fire Girls, Inc., 4601 Madison Avenue, Kansas City, Mo. 64112

4-H Programs, Federal Extension Service, U.S. Department of Agriculture, Washington, D.C. 20250

Girl Scouts of the United States of America, 830 Third Avenue, New York, N.Y. 10022

Young Men's Christian Association, 291 Broadway, New York, N.Y. 10007

Young Women's Christian Association of the U.S.A., 600 Lexington Avenue, New York, N.Y. 10022

9
Other Settings for Recreation

Leisure will be treasured only by those who use it wisely.

Unknown author

Recreation—always a matter of free choice—must remain primarily self-motivated. The individual must decide whether to sleep an extra hour, watch television, ask friends for a game of tennis, try out for a baseball team, or go to a party. Yet behind these decisions often lies dependence upon the work of other people. Watching television requires very little initiative, but bringing television to the screen is complex; television watchers do *not* provide their own recreation. If you ask a friend to play tennis, you are an organizer of recreation, although you probably use facilities that are planned and paid for by public funds. In short, even individually planned recreation depends heavily upon the facilities and leadership of others.

Previous chapters describe public and semipublic agencies that serve leisure needs. The place of home and family, clubs, civic organizations, industry, and commercial enterprise forms the substance of the pages that follow.

Leisure Provisions for Home and Family

In these days of increased leisure the home, the oldest of our social institutions, must be alert to the challenge for creative use of that leisure. Families can be fun; families should be fun; and—stronger still—families must be fun if they are to uphold their place in the present social order.

The early American pioneers banded together for protection from their enemies. In a rural setting, life was a cooperative family affair. When work was done, the leisure hours were spent in singing, backyard games, quilting bees, Bible reading, or parlor games with the same closely knit circle, sometimes including other relatives or neighbors. There were few alternatives; the children's recreation was of their own improvisation, an open field was their playground, and the home was the original community center. Economic necessity put all family members on the same team, pushing shoulder to shoulder, with a keen sense of unity and belonging.

The Changing Household

Today's complex and mobile society has eliminated many of the earlier reasons for the existence of the family group. Not only have family ties been weakened but also the traditional extended family of parents, grandparents, and grandchildren has been supplemented or supplanted by several alternative life-styles.

One-parent families. With nearly half as many divorces as marriages today and with the rise in the numbers of unmarried mothers

183

(roughly four out of ten births are illegitimate today as compared with 1.5 out of ten in 1950), many children are being reared by one parent. The proportion of children in one-parent households climbed from nine percent in 1948 to eighteen percent in 1975.

In response to the void left in the child's life by the missing parent, there has been a spectacular growth in the Big Brothers-Big Sisters, a volunteer organization whose purpose is to match a man with a fatherless boy or a woman with a motherless girl so that the adult can be a companion, friend, and guide. Emotional support and social programs for the one-parent family are also offered by voluntary organizations such as Parents Without Partners.

Singles households.   The number of Americans living alone or with unmarried roommates rose more than forty percent from 1970 to 1977. Wider social acceptance has made life for the single person more pleasant today than it was in the past. Including singles raising children, statistics show that one out of every three households is now made up of singles.

Detached grandparents.   More older people are in better health than their grandparents were at the same age, and these healthy and active people are choosing, after retirement, to keep their homes, travel, or enter retirement communities rather than live with their children (see Figure 9.1). If their health fails, they are more apt to seek care in nursing homes than in their children's homes. Government authorities are giving more and more attention to the housing, health, and recreation of this growing segment of the population. The federally promoted Foster Grandparents program serves to relate older people to young children in a one-to-one relationship.

Working mothers.   The character of the nuclear family—consisting of both parents and

their children—has changed as more and more mothers have chosen to work outside the home. In 1960 both parents worked in twenty-nine percent of husband-wife households. By 1977 the percentage had increased to forty-two percent.[1] It is predicted that the percentage will continue to increase. Small children may be reared by close relatives, baby sitters, and nurseries. Through certification of nurseries and courses for baby sitters, attempts are being made to upgrade the care of small children of working parents.

Communes.   Although communal living is nothing new in American life, as the Oneida, Amana, and New Harmony communities demonstrate, considerable fresh interest in this mode of life arose in the 1960s and continues to some extent today. In such situations children may be the responsibility of the entire commune rather than only the parents.

Some authorities predict further weakening of the nuclear family, but others believe that it will continue to be the basic organization of society. However, we must recognize alternative life-styles and make provisions for the leisure needs created by them.

Importance of the Home as a Leisure Center

Despite influences on all sides that weaken family ties, the home remains the basic foundation of society. Whether children are reared by their parents, relatives, or baby sitters, it is usually in the home that they receive their first and most lasting set of values and first learn how to play. In a day when juvenile crime is on the upsurge, adults may shake their heads and place the blame on television, comic books, movies, automobiles, drugs, or current political tensions. Some of the blame, however, must be directed at the home. The home may help stem the tide of discontent and delinquency by giving time and space for recreation. Mom and Dad as recreation leaders still

Figure 9.1. Retirement center in Sun City, Florida.

outnumber any other category of recreation leadership.

A generation or two ago, new parents were advised to follow strict schedules that allowed neither the stimulation of baby's gurglings nor the bliss of the rocking chair. Modern adults are encouraged to enjoy their youngsters at any age. Life is lived not just as preparation for the child's future but as a healthful, meaningful experience. Community recreation leaders must help those responsible for child rearing to acquire skills and wisdom in regard to filling leisure hours in the home.

Family recreation does not necessarily imply that the entire family must participate in each activity. Recreation should be chosen because

it is attractive rather than because of a sense of obligation. The interests of the home are best served when there are times for doing things together and times for doing things individually or in small groups.

For childless couples and for those whose children have grown and gone, the home can still be the center of leisure interest. Couples should see in their home a place in which to find self-expression and development rather than merely a place in which to get ready to go out.

Settings for family fun. Houses, apartments, and even whole communities today are planned with an eye to recreation. New single-family dwellings often include family rooms, furnished with television sets, electronic games, stereos, pianos, and game equipment, as well as backyards with basketball backboards, playing courts, play apparatus and patios for cooking, eating, and lounging. There are more than 700,000 residential swimming pools in the United States, many in middle-income homes. Apartments, condominiums, and mobile home parks often provide swimming pools, game and party rooms, exercise rooms, hobby workshops, and sometimes outdoor play areas and even golf courses.

Hobbies of all kinds are generally carried on at home, some requiring only a few tools, and others needing elaborately equipped workshops. Although space reserved for rec-

reation is highly desirable, it is not necessary. The kitchen table can serve as an excellent game table; and many hobbies, such as cooking, sewing, and some collections, require little extra space.

There is a new interest in home gardening. Indoor plants are once more fashionable, and outdoor flower gardens often become family projects. The revitalized interest in vegetable gardens provides a venture that may include all members of the family. Even apartment dwellers may have plots in community tract gardens.

Many families maintain second homes for summer recreation and vacation use, ranging from simple cabins to expensive homes by the seashore or in the mountains. Travel trailers, motor homes, and campers serve as second

Figure 9.2. A golf course in a private leisure-oriented community.

homes for a growing proportion of the population.

Leisure-oriented communities, such as Leisure World in California and Sun City in Arizona and Florida, provide a full range of recreation facilities and programs. Rossmoor Leisure World in Laguna Hills, California, for example, is a complete city with shopping centers, service stations, banks, medical facilities, and churches, open to adults fifty-two years of age and older. The schedule is heavy with club meetings, lectures, entertainment, excursions, hobby activities, and sports.

While many of these leisure centers cater to retired people, some, such as the Marina del Rey in Los Angeles and Carl Sandburg Village in Chicago, appeal primarily to single adults. Other developments entice couples with children who enjoy the vacation-like atmosphere after working hours and on weekends. Such a place is Rancho Bernardo, near San Diego, where clubhouses with multiple facilities for all age groups are strategically located in residential areas.

Community emphasis on family recreation. Churches, municipal agencies, youth-serving organizations, clubs, schools, and even commercial ventures are realizing that each has a responsibility toward uniting the family in recreation. At the same time, clubs, centers, and other programs for people with special needs are increasing in number.

Community centers sponsor family fun nights; churches find success with family dinners and workshops; and PTAs encourage family potluck and carnival nights. Other evidences of family support are found in the backyard play kits and picnic kits lent to families on a sign-out basis by recreation agencies; how-to-do-it bulletins and television shows with ideas for fun at home; fun-en-route pamphlets suggesting travel games, furnished by insurance companies, oil companies, or recreation departments; newspaper columns that explore ideas for family recreation; and low-cost family memberships in swimming and boating activities. The tremendous surge in the numbers of family camping clubs and camping facilities attests to the popularity of family activities.

Clubs, Societies, and Civic Organizations

We do not need organized programs in order to enjoy our leisure. Nevertheless, the urge to organize is strong, as evidenced by the countless clubs, lodges, leagues, societies, and other associations that flourish worldwide, particularly in the United States. "Get three Americans together," it is said, "and they'll elect a president, vice-president, and secretary."

Organizations spring up to fill every need and desire or to find ways of getting government agencies to fill them. Individuals who feel helpless alone make their efforts count and their voices heard through organized group action. There is pressure upon all organizations today to open their membership without discrimination as to race, sex, and religion; and a growing number have done so. The League of Women Voters, for example, is now open to men. Increasingly, public officials find it necessary to drop membership in clubs that bar blacks. Organizations wishing to receive federal grants must abide by nondiscriminatory rulings.

Community Service Organizations

Desire for community improvement, as well as for personal growth and social relationships, has spurred the formation of numerous service groups. The special events and regular meetings are important in the leisure life of the members.

Public and voluntary agencies concerned with leisure should cooperate with community service organizations. The members generally have the civic mindedness, motivation, influence, and resources to bring about community recreation improvements. Some of their recreation services are: sponsoring recreation groups and programs, working for better community recreation facilities and programs, and financing special recreation projects.

Many services provided by local organizations are spearheaded by their national headquarters, which show their chapters how to assist local recreation projects. The following paragraphs suggest the scope of the recreational activities of these organizations; the list is not intended to be all-inclusive.

Men's service clubs. Men's service clubs, composed of community business and professional men, include Kiwanis, Rotary, Lions, Jaycees, Optimists, Y's Men's Clubs, Civitan, 20/30 Active Club, and Exchange. Their purposes are both good fellowship and community service.

Numbered among the recreation projects undertaken by service clubs are: promoting the establishment of public and voluntary recreation programs; financing park, camp, and playground equipment; sponsoring scout troops, 4-H, and athletic teams; and paying camp fees, youth-center fees, and club memberships for underprivileged youth. Kiwanis sponsors the Key Club, its own program for high school boys, and stresses service to youth and old age. The Optimists, whose slogan is "friend of the boy," sponsor the Junior Optimist Clubs and youth recognition programs.

Veterans' organizations. Of the many veterans' groups in the nation, two of the most prominent are the American Legion and the Veterans of Foreign Wars (VFW). Both have long been concerned with recreation not only for themselves but also for the youth who will some day lead the country.

For years the American Legion has sponsored nationwide programs of Junior Baseball and the Sons of the American Legion. The Veterans of Foreign Wars, through its national Youth Activities Department, prepares ideas for youth programs for local post directors and urges local VFW posts to assist city officials and other organizations in their community recreation programs.

Women's service organizations. Great numbers of women's organizations serve much the same purposes as the men's groups, offering recreation to their own members and aiding community efforts. They usually mix social, philanthropic, and civic activities. Among the organizations are the Association of Junior Leagues, Altrusa, General Federation of Women's Clubs, League of Women Voters, and Business and Professional Women's Clubs, all with long histories of community service. In relation to recreation, their emphasis has varied from organization to organization but has included efforts to establish and enlarge park and recreation facilities, conserve recreation lands, and establish programs in music, drama, and fine arts.

Other service organizations. The Parent-Teacher Associations, federated into the National Congress of Parents and Teachers, have 7.6 million members. With other parent-teacher associations, they are primarily concerned with the welfare of school children. Generally strong supporters of recreation agencies, they often sponsor scout troops or other clubs, purchase equipment and supplies for school-related recreation programs, and serve as important channels for interpretation of leisure needs and services to the community.

The Police Athletic Leagues is a voluntary attempt by police officers to provide play programs for children in slum areas, particularly those in large cities.

Lodges and Fraternal Groups

Organizations such as the Elks, Eagles, Moose, Masons, Odd Fellows, and Knights of Columbus can be classified as charitable fraternal organizations. Though concerned with the welfare of their own members, many of them give generously to community programs. Membership is exclusive, and meetings may be secret and ritualistic. Facilities might include clubhouses with bowling alleys, billiard rooms, and card rooms. Bowling leagues, golf tournaments, bingo parties, dances, and picnics are sponsored by some of the organizations.

Related organizations have sprung up around many of these groups. The Masonic umbrella covers Eastern Star for women, De-Molay for boys, and Job's Daughters and Rainbow Girls for girls; the Knights of Columbus sponsor the Columbian Squires for Catholic boys.

Among fraternal organizations, college fraternities and sororities should be mentioned. Languishing during the tumultuous 1960s but thriving again in the 1970s, these groups provide a home and fill a leisure need in the lives of their members. Many of them also perform community services and sponsor philanthropic work on chapter and national levels. Social sororities, both local and national, commonly carry on money-raising projects for the benefit of community recreation.

Conservation Organizations

Open in membership and devoted to conservation, there are about 15,000 conservation societies with some forty million members.[2] They exert considerable influence on legislation to preserve the natural environment. Many of these organizations restrict their efforts to specific areas, such as the California redwoods or the Indiana dunes. Others are national in scope. A few outstanding examples of large national organizations follow.

The National Wildlife Federation is active in the conservation of all natural resources. It sponsors the annual National Wildlife Week, distributes over a million pieces of educational literature annually, conducts tours, and keeps its eye on public agencies and environmental legislation. The venerable National Audubon Society operates nature centers, four leadership training camps, and more than forty wildlife sanctuaries; works to save unique areas; organizes Audubon Wildlife Films; conducts international tours and workshops; issues teaching aids and classroom bulletins; and conducts research. About 300 chapters promote local conservation efforts.

Founded by Stephen Mather, first director of the National Park Service, as a citizen watchdog for the national parks, the National Park and Conservation Association is the one conservation organization focusing upon the great national parks. The Izaak Walton League, named for the seventeenth-century author of *The Compleat Angler*, fights pollution and spurs legislative action to protect the natural environment.

The Nature Conservancy is unique in directing its efforts to preserve land. With money raised by public subscription, the Nature Conservancy buys endangered natural areas and usually turns them over to other agencies that can guarantee adequate protection. Wilderness preservation is the chief concern of the Wilderness Society, which intervenes directly with government officials and goes to court when necessary to halt projects that threaten wilderness or pollute air and water. The society sponsors annual wilderness trips afoot, by horseback, by raft, and by canoe.

Heavily criticized in recent years because it is financed primarily by industries whose products are packaged in potential litter (such as beer cans and bottles), Keep America Beautiful has nonetheless performed a great public service in fighting vandalism and encouraging community clean-ups. The American Forestry Association, concerned with both forest protection and forest productivity, sponsors trips to wild and scenic areas.

Most of these organizations are classified by the federal government as educational and therefore enjoy tax-free status. The Sierra Club, however, lost its tax-exempt status as it entered the controversial political arena to fight more aggressively than most organizations for conservation legislation. However, it gained freedom to act boldly, a feature that attracts a large active membership. The Sierra Club chapters sponsor a large number of outings, such as hikes, canoe trips, mountain trips, bicycle tours, and underwater exploration.

Many international organizations approach conservation problems on a global scale, establishing wildlife sanctuaries, conducting educational programs, and promoting international agreements to protect endangered species. Prominent among these are the World Wildlife Fund and the International Union for the Conservation of Nature and Natural Resources.

Sports and Outdoor Organizations

Privately organized not-for-profit amateur sports and outdoor organizations exist for practically every sport, indoors and out, on both local and national levels. Some are open in membership, others admit members only by invitation. For major sports such as baseball and football, the organizations may include informal teams and leagues for both children and adults, special camps, and national organizations to encourage and regulate the activities.

Outdoor-oriented clubs include those interested in hiking, cycling, motorcycling, mountaineering, skiing, motoring, boating, sailing, flying, swimming, camping, fishing, hunting, riflery, trailer travel, international travel, and others ad infinitum. Some own lands and facilities. Many publish news bulletins, information literature, or magazines; offer advice and services; and sponsor exhibits and outings ranging from weekend trips to worldwide tours. Their membership mounts into the millions.

A unique organization is American Youth Hostels, Inc., which maintains low-cost hostels, where hikers and bicyclists can cook meals and stay overnight. Through its affiliation with the International Youth Hostel Federation, hostels in thirty-four countries are open to American youth, permitting them to make friends, exchange experiences, and learn about the countries they visit (see Figure 9.3).

Promoting sports for children are Little League Baseball, which enrolls 2.5 million children worldwide; Babe Ruth Baseball; Boys Baseball, Inc.; Pop Warner Junior League Football; Biddy Basketball; and many others, sometimes sponsored privately and sometimes included in municipal recreation programs.

Adult sports clubs, both professional and amateur, cover every kind of sport interest. Many are promoted by municipal park and recreation agencies and are open in membership. Others are exclusive in membership and maintain their own facilities, such as golf courses, swimming pools, and tennis courts. Country clubs usually provide a variety of facilities for outdoor sports with indoor game rooms and dance floors to round out the recreational offerings.

With the slogan, "Tennis is for everyone,"

Figure 9.3. A sailing ship becomes a unique youth hostel in Stockholm, Sweden.

the U.S. Lawn Tennis Association caters to the expanding interest in tennis by promoting instruction and strengthening suburban and inner-city tennis programs. It helps groups raise money by sending instructional materials and showing how to organize programs. There is also a National Junior Tennis League.

Societies Fostering Cultural Activities

The private organizations fostering cultural activities include music, drama, literary, historical, and art associations both for performers and for those who help them through raising money, awarding scholarships, and supporting performances.

Among the earliest musical organizations of the United States were the psalm-singing schools of the eighteenth century, followed by choral societies. Orchestral societies soon emerged; the oldest one still in existence is the New York Philharmonic Society, organized in 1842. The number of civic orchestras grew rapidly after World War II, and by the 1970s there were 232 such orchestras, heavily subsidized by public gifts.

Several large cities, including San Francisco, Chicago, Boston, St. Louis, Cincinnati, and Philadelphia, maintain opera associations, the outstanding one being the Metropolitan Opera Association of New York, founded in 1883.

The National Federation of Music Clubs, founded in 1898, claiming a membership of half a million, fosters Junior Festivals to promote the interest of young people. Singing groups such as the Society for the Preservation and Encouragement of Barber Shop Quartet Singing in America and the Sweet Adelines foster enjoyment of popular music.

Support for ballet is found throughout the world. The American Ballet in the United States and civic ballet groups in many American cities support this form of art.

Drama clubs and little theater groups flourish at the local level, along with art associations that maintain galleries and museums on a nonprofit basis. Literary societies, such as the National League of American Pen Women, local book study clubs, and poetry groups encourage both creativity and appreciation.

Historical societies not only study history but also maintain museums, encourage the preservation of historical sites and buildings of architectural and historical interest, publish historical documents, engage in genealogical research, and stimulate interest in history through pageants, tours, and celebrations.

Other Special-Interest Clubs

The tremendous numbers of garden clubs are to a large extent represented in such organizations as the National Council of State Garden Clubs, the Garden Club of America, and the Men's Garden Club of America. They encourage gardening both for their own members and for youth groups, often sponsoring children's gardens, flower shows, and park and city beautification projects.

Spanning the alphabet from archeology to zoology, numerous science clubs promote their special interests for both adults and children. The American Association of Museums, the Natural Science for Youth Foundation, and the Science Clubs of America are a few of the national groups that encourage recreation-related scientific pursuits.

Largely local in character but often nationally affiliated, hobby clubs in confusing array, from collecting clubs to chess clubs, book review groups, gourmet cooking clubs, wine-tasting societies, genealogical groups, and bridge clubs, augment the recreational life of a community.

Employee Recreation

The industrial development of the nineteenth century was accompanied by poor working conditions and labor problems. As time went on, both management and organized labor felt an obligation to alleviate these situations, and recreation for employees was part of the solution.

The first provision of recreation by industry has been attributed to the Peacedale Manufacturing Company of Peacedale, Rhode Island, which offered library resources and singing classes to employees as early as 1854. During the next fifty years, the Pullman Company, the Conant Thread Company, Ludlow Manufacturing Associates, Johnson and Johnson, the Metropolitan Life Insurance Company, the National Cash Register Company, and others sponsored outings, picnics, and athletics, and provided recreation buildings and golf courses.

In 1868 the YMCA stepped in to become the first private agency to work with industry in serving the needs of workers. Its cooperation with the Union Pacific Railroad Company was the first of a series of YMCA projects to help industrial workers during off-the-job hours. The YMCA organized the YMCA Industrial Department in 1902. Centers were established in lumber camps, mining towns, steel industry locations, and textile villages to provide something besides taverns and saloons for a worker's leisure. The Playground and Recreation Association of America (now the National Recreation and Park Association) also assisted companies in establishing programs.

A 1913 survey by the U.S. Bureau of Labor Statistics showed that more than half of the fifty-one firms polled offered some form of employee recreation. A more inclusive study by the bureau in 1916 disclosed recreation facilities and services in 431 companies in thirty-one states. By 1918 San Francisco had established the first citywide industrial recreation association. New Haven, Connecticut, and Oakland, California, soon followed.

After World War I, the number and variety of industries offering recreation to employees increased slowly and steadily as a means of improving employee-employer relations. The depression years of the 1930s saw the pro-

grams curtailed, but the value of recreation to industry had been recognized.

In the late 1930s, a comprehensive study of 639 firms in thirty-eight states indicated a significant increase in the numbers and kinds of programs. However, the leaders had no specific training for this particular responsibility. Only a third of the leaders had been trained even in related fields, such as physical education or personnel management. Spurred by this discovery, Purdue University, under the direction of Floyd R. Eastwood, who had participated in the study, set up the first program for a degree for professional industrial recreation workers. Another step forward occurred in 1941 with the formation of the Recreation Association for American Industry (later renamed the National Industrial Recreation Association).

The establishment in 1937 of the international recreation department of the United Auto Workers spearheaded union-sponsored recreation. At present the union recreation budget in any large factory may well exceed the recreation budget for some small communities. During and after World War II, recreation programs in industry expanded; and they continue to grow.

Structure and Organization

There is no set pattern for organizing an employee recreation program. The choice of structure and administration seems to depend somewhat on the size of the industry. The forms of organization include the following:

1. The management takes complete responsibility.

2. An independent employee association takes complete responsibility.

3. The employer provides facilities and areas; the employees administer the program.

4. The management provides facilities and areas; the employees and

employer take joint responsibility for administration.

5. The company union organizes the program without help from the management.

6. The industry provides a committee and funds to cooperate with an existing community program that includes opportunities for industrial workers.

Methods of financing employee recreation programs vary from company to company. They may include one of a combination of the following: contributions from management, voluntary dues from employees, receipts from vending machines, receipts from other money-making projects, admission charges for entertainment, appropriations from the union, and fees for activities. The program is usually more successful if the employees have some financial as well as operational responsibility. Arguments favoring an independent employee association are that it allows acquisition of facilities, freedom from company authority in programming, and absolvement of management responsibility in accidents.

Recent years have brought a definite increase in the number of companies who employ full-time recreation professionals. Recreation directors employed by management are frequently responsible to the personnel director, although other channels of authority may exist.

Many of the program planning factors that apply to public recreation apply also to employee recreation. The money available, the leadership, the size of the factory, the needs and interests of the workers and their families, and the facilities all influence the program. Employees must feel free to participate or not as they wish, especially if the program is run entirely by management. Morale wanes if employees feel that they must take part in order to maintain good relations with management.

Some companies use community facilities rather than setting up their own in order to economize or to seek closer relationships with the community. Other companies, because of the absence of adequate or conveniently located community facilities, build and operate their own, which may range from simple game rooms and open areas for sports to golf courses, country clubs, camps, swimming pools, and parks.

Activities

Lunch-hour activities, such as ping-pong, cards, and board games, are popular. Social recreation, including picnics, parties, family outings, award banquets, and dances, are usually important parts of the program. Other program items include: libraries offering noon-hour and take-home reading; sports with league play in everything from bowling to softball; hikes and local excursions; tours to concerts, plays, or art centers; group travel, sometimes overseas at special economy rates; and participation in hobby clubs.

To see how one employee recreation program works, let us look at Texins Association, a nonprofit corporation for employees of Texas Instruments Incorporated, in Dallas, Texas. The company gives a large annual contribution, but the association is owned by the employees and run by a board of directors employed by them. Members pay fees, and all employees and their families are eligible. Within the association are many individual clubs catering to specialized interests. Activities include amateur radio, bass fishing, basketball, billiards, bowling, camera, camping, chess, divers, flag football, gems and minerals, group travel, handball, instructional classes, physical fitness, sailing, softball, tennis, and volleyball.

Community Cooperation

A new industry may be attracted to a community because of a satisfying recreation program. Areas of cooperation between an industry and the community include joint use of facilities by industrial and community groups; joint leadership training institutes and the provision of volunteer leaders by industry for community service; cooperative ventures in special programs for industrial workers; cooperation on pre-retirement or retirement programs; provision of meeting places in plant facilities for youth groups; use of city parks for social outings for employees; and representation of industrial personnel on recreation advisory boards. Some industries sponsor special programs in cooperation with public agencies. An example is the ten-week summer Mobile Tennis program of the Pepsi-Cola Company.

An industry may add to the value of a community as a tourist attraction by opening its doors to visitors for tours at specified hours. More than 1,500 businesses and factories in all fifty states and three territories help to fill the demand for this increasingly popular activity. Among them are mines, shipyards, wineries, bakeries, stock exchanges, aircraft factories, and sugar refineries.[3]

Commercial Recreation

In an affluent society people are willing or even eager to pay for their recreation; public and voluntary agencies have found that charging for certain programs has increased, not reduced, participation. Some people will not accept free programs but will spend money for programs of similar or even lower quality offered commercially, perhaps feeling that paying one's own way bestows a certain status.

Commercial recreation is recreation for which the participant pays and from which the supplier intends to make a profit. It is one of the most important and fastest growing aspects of American culture today. Expenditures for commercial recreation far exceed those for programs offered by public and voluntary agencies.

Too often students of recreation and leaders of public and voluntary recreation programs have ignored the impact of commercial recreation. It is encouraging, however, that serious college preparation for leadership in commercial recreation enterprises is taking place, including both business and recreation courses, to prepare young people for careers in this promising field.[4]

Types of Commercial Recreation

Certain types of recreation have come to be regarded as the responsibilities of public or voluntary agencies. Parks, playgrounds, playfields, and community centers are for the most part operated by public or quasi-public agencies with the assumption that these programs have social value and should be available to all of the population on an equal basis. Programs concerned with particular segments of society are generally the responsibility of nonprofit private organizations.

This is not to say that commercial operators do not also offer these forms of recreation. Many activities, such as organized camping, golf, tennis, swimming, bowling, ice skating, and team sports, may be provided by public, voluntary, or commercial operators. Increasingly, forms of recreation that had been restricted to nonprofit agencies are being offered commercially. For example, hunting, fishing, picnicking, and camping have in the past been provided primarily by state and federal governments. Today, a growing number of farmers, ranchers, and private forest owners are opening their lands to the public for these activities; commercial campgrounds number in the thousands. The ski industry is one of the more rapidly growing fields of commercial recreation (see Figure 9.4).

Commercial recreation in its broadest sense also includes the media—television, radio, newspapers, magazines, and books. It also includes spectator sports, such as professional horse racing, automobile racing, football, baseball, and hockey; passive enter-

Figure 9.4. The ski industry is one field of commercial recreation.

tainments such as movies, stage shows, nightclubs; and participation activities such as bowling, horseback riding, billiards, skating, gambling, and dancing. Ski resorts, spas, other private resorts, and commercially led tours are extensive commercial enterprises. To the extent to which eating is recreation, restaurants should also be included. So should massage parlors.

Many commercial enterprises can be grouped as part of the tourist industry, which employs more than four million Americans, one out of every twenty in the civilian labor force.[5]

An isolated recreation facility is often far less successful commercially than one that is part of a complex. A resort with swimming, golf, fishing, archery, horseback riding, boat-ing, hiking, sight-seeing, and evening activities such as bowling, movies, dancing, and bridge attracts people and money more successfully than if the activities were scattered. Amusement parks illustrate successful recreation complexes. For example, Disney World in Florida combines certain aspects of parks, playgrounds, campgrounds, fairs, resorts, and museums into an imaginative compound that is an inspiration to park and recreation planners.

A growing development has been the use of the shopping mall as a recreation resource. In cold or hot weather, the enclosed malls provide large, comfortable indoor areas that include movie theaters, game rooms, eating establishments, bars, game courts, resting spots, and children's play areas, along with shops supplying recreation necessities. In cooperation with community agencies, both public and voluntary, the malls may, throughout the year, sponsor special events such as musicals, seasonal festivals, charitable balls, handcraft exhibits, antique displays, recreation vehicle shows, and garden shows.

Contributions to Community Recreation

Some of the values of commercial recreation to the community are listed here.

Enlargement of recreation opportunities. It would be a crushing and unfair burden upon the taxpayer and the philanthropist to offer all recreation through public and quasi-public means. Types of recreation that are unduly expensive, that cater to only a limited clientele, or that may be only passing whims or fancies are better left in commercial hands.

Introduction of new ideas. Public money is seldom available for new and untried facilities or programs. Commercial recreation can introduce new recreational programs that might later be accepted by public agencies.

Stimulation of public programs. Commercial enterprise can serve as a goad to lethargic nonprofit agencies. Because commercial operators must make a profit, they are under constant pressure to improve efficiency and make their enterprise attractive. Many lively and imaginative ideas from commercial recre-

ation can be adopted by public authorities. Being highly competitive, commercial recreation dares not be dull; public recreation should be equally alert to the needs, interests, and comforts of the public.

Cooperation with public recreation. In state and national parks, private concessionaires frequently operate restaurants and lodges, thereby freeing park personnel for administration of the park property, maintenance, and interpretive programs.

Criticisms of Commercial Recreation

There are those who criticize commercial recreation because its primary purpose is profit, not the welfare of people. Some purveyors of commercial recreation disregard the effect of their activities and justify their programs on the basis that they are merely meeting public demands. This contention is true only in part; through advertising and glamorization, sellers can create demands where none existed previously.

Another charge hurled against commercial recreation is that it encourages "spectatoritis." Many enterprises thrive on the theory that people want their recreation spoon-fed to them. It takes little effort to attend a movie or turn on the television. However, it must be remembered that some programs stimulate

Television on Trial

Television violence became involved in a court case in late 1977 when Ronny Zamora was arrested in Miami, Florida, for murdering an eighty-five-year-old woman. His lawyer volunteered in defense that the fifteen-year-old boy had been intoxicated by viewing television violence and committed the act under its spell.

The court exonerated television, ruling the boy guilty.

Was this a fair verdict? Do you believe that television viewing affects behavior? If so, how? Specifically, what effects has television had on leisure? How can television be used constructively in furthering leisure skills and interests?

serious thought, creative action, and self-improvement.

One of the strongest attacks is against television sex and violence, a matter of special importance because of the long hours—more than six per day—that a television set is on in the average home. Although some experts claim that there is little or no harmful effect and that the portrayal of sex and violence may even act as a healthy emotional cathartic, others find a close connection between the increase in crime and the attention given to violence on television. Such prestigious groups as the American Medical Association, national PTA, Southern Baptists, Roman Catholics, United Methodist Church, Church of the Brethren, and the National Council of Churches have opposed such use of the air channels; and many young criminals themselves have admitted receiving ideas for their crimes from television.

Perhaps it would be fair to say that television both shapes and is shaped by our culture and that it can be an influence for the best as well as for the worst. The same statement applies to all types of commercial operations. Many commercial operators are aware of their social influence and attempt to contribute to the well-being of participants.

Regulation

The following types of restrictions are placed upon operators of taverns, nightclubs, dance halls, gambling houses, theaters, bookstores, and other vendors of commercial recreation.

Legal and trade control. State, county, and municipal laws limit commercial operations. These laws differ from state to state and community to community but usually include health and safety practices, zoning, hours of operation, and other concerns. Some practices, such as gambling and liquor sales, are illegal in some places but are a major form of income in others. Licensing accompanied by inspection is a common method of control, and licenses may be revoked for failure to comply with regulations. Censorship, a controversial form of control, is difficult to apply and sometimes defeats its purpose by publicizing the forbidden item.

In trade control, standards are set by an industry, which exerts pressure on individual operators to conform.

Competition. A positive approach is for socially acceptable recreation to compete with the undesirable. A tawdry or shady operation may have to close its doors when a responsible competitor sets up business. The competitor may often be a public agency, such as a teen center designed to give young people an attractive and safe meeting place.

Public opinion. In the last analysis, control lies in the hands of the public. Commercial ventures can operate only with public support. Action from civic groups, parent-teacher associations, religious organizations, schools, youth agencies, public recreation agencies, and particularly the home, can make or break commercial undertakings.

Attempts to regulate the motion picture industry illustrate all control methods. In 1930, efforts to place legal restrictions on the movies led the industry itself, through the Motion Picture Association of America, which is composed of the major producing and distributing companies, to set up its own production code. The code was not well enforced, however, until outside pressures, particularly from the Legion of Decency (now known as the National Catholic Office for Motion Pictures), were applied to the industry. For many years, city and state censorship boards attempted to cut or ban morally offensive movies, but legal decisions reaching up to the Supreme Court generally favored freedom of expression. As a result, these boards have practically disappeared.

After several revisions through the years, the production code today is extremely liberal. Movies are rated (G, PG, R, and X) according to their suitability for viewing by children and families, with the practical result that everyone except children can view almost anything, despite obscenity trials, arrests, fines, and seizure of films by police.

Several cities have laws that ban people under eighteen years of age from violent movies. The strongest weapons for control, however, are public opinion, personal taste, and attractive competition. An example of the force of public opinion is Beverly Theater, in Brooklyn, which was forced by community pressure to offer family-type films.

Ironically, the very movies that stir up the most opposition, such as *The Godfather* and *The Exorcist,* are often the greatest box-office hits. Movie ratings from consumer guides, *Film and Broadcasting Review* (published by the U.S. Catholic Conference), and other magazines help movie-goers to make enlightened choices.

Some Principles of Commercial Recreation

A few basic principles of commercial recreation follow:

1. Commercial recreation should be recognized as a large and important part of a community recreation program.

2. Where commercial entrepreneurs can supply programs at a reasonable cost, they should be encouraged. Well-conducted commercial bowling alleys, swimming pools, skating rinks, golf courses, tennis courts, and organized camps enrich the community program at no cost to the taxpayer. (See Figure 9.5.)

3. Commercial operators should be made fully aware of their social responsibility.

Figure 9.5. *Theme parks are popular commercial recreation ventures.*

4. Citizens interested in community improvement should support and patronize commercial recreation that contributes toward this end.

5. Operators of acceptable commercial recreation ventures should be represented on community recreation committees or boards concerned with planning for recreation.

6. Communities should develop procedures to control or eliminate commercial practices that affect the community adversely, bearing in mind that elimination is not enough. It must be accompanied by substitution of the desirable.

The Whole Picture

The life-style of a human being is colored not only by biological needs but also by educational and cultural background, social and economic status, and physical environment. Recreation gives a channel for achievement, a place for belonging, a chance to express personal interests and creative urges, and an opportunity for close relationships with other human beings.

Selected References

Directory of Social and Health Agencies of New York City, 1973–74. New York: Columbia University Press, 1973.

Epperson, Arlin. *Private and Commercial Recreation: A Text and Reference.* New York: John Wiley & Sons, Inc., 1977.

Fisk, Margaret, and Pair, Mary W. *Encyclopedia of Associations.* 11th ed. Detroit: Gale Research Co., 1977.

Hanson, Robert F., and Carlson, Reynold E. *Organizations for Children and Youth.* Englewood Cliffs, N.J.: Prentice-Hall, Inc., 1972.

Langman, Robert R., and Rockwood, Linn R. "Be Prepared . . . For a Career in Commercial Recreation," *Parks & Recreation* 10, no. 7 (July 1975): 30–31.

"Leisure Today, The Concept of Life Style," *Journal of Physical Education and Recreation* (November–December 1974).

"Leisure Today, The Leisure Industries: Investigations of Commercial Recreation and Tourism." *Journal of Physical Education and Recreation* 46, no. 9 (November–December 1975).

Munn, Louise N., ed. *Service Directory of National Organizations.* 10th ed. New York: The National Assembly for Social Policy and Development, Inc., 1969.

National Association of Social Workers. *Encyclopedia of Social Work.* New York: National Association of Social Workers, 1971.

Rapoport, Rhona, and Rapoport, Robert N. *Leisure and the Family Life Cycle.* London and Boston: Routledge and Kegan, 1975.

10
Cooperation, Coordination, and Citizen Involvement

In this country the whole system works best when the public and private sectors both work well. Private organizations can and do effectively cooperate with and strengthen the work of public agencies. They also can and do act as watchdogs, as keepers of the social conscience, as critics, as goads.

Elvis J. Stahr

"The highest and best form of efficiency is the spontaneous cooperation of a free people." Bernard Baruch wrote these words in a 1921 report about American industry during World War I. Our goal in the recreation field is to make these same words of efficient and spontaneous cooperation applicable to the various park and recreation disciplines and citizen groups in communities throughout the land.

Working Together

There is growing evidence that such cooperation and coordination are on the rise. This idea was expressed by the editors of *California Parks and Recreation* magazine, when they stated:

Cooperation and coordination among public and private agencies, citizens, and government officials, different agencies within the same community, and local-state-federal agencies have been the cornerstone for successful recreation programs and park projects throughout the history of the recreation and park movement. . . . By "working together" recreation and park agencies are able to avoid duplication of services and facilities, produce superior and more varied facilities and programs, and insure that the citizens of their communities get more for their money.

Whether your goal is the development of a regional park, a neighborhood park, a community center, a senior citizens complex, or innovative programs to take place in these facilities, it is almost impossible, and certainly not desirable, to proceed without cooperating and coordinating with citizen groups, other community agencies, private agencies, and in many cases the state and federal government.[1]

This belief was strongly supported by Hjelte and Shivers when they reported reasons why no single existing department is capable of fulfilling the recreation need of the various populations within a community: "Increasing population, sophistication of demands on the public system, the increasing complexity of community organizations, and the variety of public, quasi-public, and private sector agencies require correlation for the satisfaction of public recreational needs."[2]

In view of new and mounting evidence, our position on the subject of community cooperation and coordination is one of exciting optimism. We do not mean that suddenly everyone is cooperating with everyone else; we mean that a greater number of professionals are realizing that more can be accomplished by cooperating and coordinating and they are trying to do something about it. This idea was aptly expressed by Dunn and Phillips as they applied the principle of synergism to recreation programming.[3] The concept of synergy, simply stated, means that a greater total result can be expected from combined efforts in a cooperative situation than from the same individuals working independently. As our community development colleagues say, "None of us is as smart as all of us!" Management Professor John F. Mee indicated: "Organizational

systems that employ the synergistic effect for realizing the highest and best use of human talents can enable managers to make a greater contribution to economic growth, social progress, human satisfactions, and the profitability of an enterprise. The concept is presently in use for research teams, production work groups, marketing personnel, and other groups with assignments that require innovation and creativity."[4]

There is an impressive number of organizations offering recreation services in most communities. These include public, private, semipublic, and commercial agencies. Most leisure agencies have the same major goal— individual and community betterment. However, agencies do differ as to the scope of their organizational efforts and the way they achieve their goals. As each agency limits itself to its specific responsibility, it is essential that there be an understanding among organizations of how each contributes to the community effort.

Even within each agency there are several

A Beginning Relationship

I was ready to resign. "I came to the Health and Welfare Council two years ago," I said, "expecting to develop working relationships among our youth-serving groups. But I'm completely frustrated. They are jealous of one another; they compete for the same money, some of the same leaders, and even for some of the same members."

My chief, who headed the council, tried to soothe me. "Well, some competition can be healthy. Keeps everybody alert. But why don't you try a new tack? Our youth services reach only a small percentage of young people. There's plenty of work for all the agencies. No need for so much competition. Get them together."

Later I persuaded representatives from schools, youth agencies, and the park and recreation department to meet as the chief had suggested. The schools agreed to survey the children to learn how many were involved in youth programs and what their interests were. Many weeks later, the completed study proved just what we suspected. As a result, the agencies began to develop a cooperative program to reach children from all sectors of the city.

I'll stick around and work with them.

Why are agencies often jealous of each other? Can a person be loyal to one organization and still respect other organizations with different programs and goals? How may board members help develop better cooperation?

levels of cooperative action required if the job is to be done well. First, where administrative and advisory boards or commissions exist, it is important to have their official sanction or policy direction regarding the agency's overall philosophy toward working with other agencies. Second, executive sanction and participation are absolutely vital if a favorable attitude is to prevail and ultimately permeate the entire agency. Third, it is not enough to have the boards and executives agree. The supervisory, specialist, and leadership staffs are a vital link in the process. Unless the entire staff is imbued with a sense of the importance and an understanding of what can be accomplished through coordinated efforts, it is not likely that much progress will be made.

Cooperation is a two-way process. The manner in which the various agencies pool their resources will largely determine the degree to which the total community needs are met. Not only does each organization benefit from this cooperative process, but also it contributes to a more unified total community effort.

Whatever methods of cooperation are used, they must be accompanied by a real desire on the part of the lay and professional leaders of each agency to gain a full knowledge and understanding of how other agencies operate and how their agency can best share its resources for the benefits of the community. Machinery must be provided as a framework for organized cooperative action.

Methods of Coordination

Cooperation among organizations and agencies takes place at many levels. The simplest form is informal cooperation, in which one agency director might meet with one or more directors to coordinate schedules, offer use of one another's facilities, and the like. A more organized form is a temporary or-

ganization to achieve a particular purpose, such as planning a citywide parade, a cooperative leadership training program, or joint use of a camp. Continued coordination and cooperation are achieved through permanent community councils, clearinghouses, fund-raising organizations, and special committees.

Coordinating through Community Councils

Historically, community councils have been used as a means for elected or appointed individuals representing organizations to assemble for deliberating, consulting, advising, and coordinating. It is important to acknowledge the primary function, leadership, available facilities, and local commitments of each organization represented.

Some of the more common names given to such bodies are: Councils of Social Agencies, Coordinating Councils, Health and Welfare Councils, Neighborhood Councils, and Interagency Councils, Regional Councils, Advisory Councils, Community Service Councils, and Community Councils. Such bodies may be instituted to survey, plan, and investigate action to improve community life. Local community councils give attention to problems relating to health, welfare, schools, government, economic improvement, and recreation.

In order to be most successful, the community council should represent all community groups, such as government agencies, churches, youth-serving agencies, health organizations, conservation organizations, women's groups, luncheon clubs, lodges, business organizations, recreation clubs, and interest groups. Recreation needs are often approached through a "youth and recreation" or a "group-work and recreation" committee. Both lay and professional leaders of representative recreation agencies should actively participate in these activities if a coordinated recreation effort is to be achieved.

The types of organizations with coordinating functions include:

1. Organizations representing all agencies participating in the united finance drives, such as United Way.

2. Citizen planning organizations open in membership to any interested volunteer.

3. Organizations with wide representation from public and private agencies, service clubs, civic organizations, schools, and any other group interested in community health, welfare, and recreation.

4. Organizations consisting of small numbers of individuals, each of whom represents multiple community interests.

5. Volunteer service bureaus that act as clearinghouses and aid in securing volunteers for member agencies for volunteer projects. These bureaus may be part of other coordinating organizations.

6. Councils or committees set up to coordinate particular functions in an area, such as services for youth, the aging, or health, in order to facilitate fair distribution of federal grants.

7. Organizations representing only government agencies.

No one type of council merits recommendation over another. The council, its type, and its organization are dependent upon local needs, conditions, and community organization.

Coordination of Fund-Raising Activities

Voluntary organizations that attempt to raise their own budgets often find that much of the time and energy of their staffs and the money for services are dissipated in fund-raising drives. Moreover, the burden of soliciting funds too often falls on a small group of public-spirited citizens. For these reasons, in most communities, voluntary agencies band together to conduct one annual drive to raise enough money to meet their combined budgets. In order to establish fair budget requests and conduct such drives, organizations are set up, variously called "United Way," "United Fund," "Community Chest," or similar designations. The United Way of America (formerly the United Community Fund and Councils of America) is the national clearinghouse for these fund-raising organizations.

Through its UWASIS program (United Way of America Services Identification System) the United Way is helping voluntary agencies to analyze and clarify their goals and the ways in which the goals are achieved and, thereby, to discover how to improve their services.

The United Way offers more than relief from fund raising for its member organizations. By setting up standards of performance, planning, budgeting, maintaining public relations, and helping agencies with everyday problems, it gives stability to its members and assurance to contributors that, when they give, they aren't being "taken." Because of the United Way, the high fund-raising costs of many charities (over seventy-five cents on every dollar raised in some terrible examples) are cut to a bare minimum, contributors are beseiged for funds less often, volunteer fund raisers are called upon to help less often, and professional leaders can turn their money management problems over to experts.

Local Government Cooperation

A community large enough to provide public recreation services for its residents is large enough to require cooperative efforts among the public agencies concerned with leisure use, if the best interests of the taxpayers are to be served and the widest possible recreation opportunities are to be provided. These agencies include schools, park and/or recreation departments, libraries, museums, and housing authorities, as well as divisions of government such as purchasing, planning, personnel, and finance. Close coordination is required between park and recreation personnel and elected officials, as well as the departments of police, fire, public works, welfare, and health.

City-School Relationships

The cooperative relationships between school resources and other community and recreation agencies presented in Chapter 7 are reemphasized here to maximize their importance. Each agency has much to gain, administratively and professionally. From the citizen-user point of view, it can be the best of several worlds.

In our opinion, each new school facility should be carefully analyzed by administrators and school boards, in cooperation with community agencies, for possible joint use by those agencies that have a stake in the education and recreation aspects of the community. The cooperative planning of areas and facilities, joint use of facilities, coordination of program ventures, and provision of leadership are but a few ways in which schools can establish better cooperative relationships. The school and city administrations in Austin, Texas, to mention only one example, have developed a comprehensive list of policies to facilitate better school-city relationships. Detailed policies have been written for each of the following concerns: purchase of sites, planning of new construction, use of building and grounds, and the programs to be conducted. Columbia, Missouri; Madison and Milwaukee,

Wisconsin; Denver, Colorado; Minneapolis, Minnesota; Edinburg, Indiana; and Pasadena, California, are other cities that have successfully established good city-school relationships.

The C. S. Mott Foundation, a philanthropic organization supporting the community education concept, reported in 1977 that more than five percent of the schools in America are community schools. There are more than 3,000 trained community school coordinators working at least half time in 5,083 community schools located in about 1,200 districts nationwide. Nearly five million people enroll as participants, and it is estimated that expenditures for community education activities exceed $100 million a year.

Favorable legislation, public opinion, and understanding municipal and school authorities provide climates for coordinated action. Cities have used various methods to secure cooperation, including: school board representation on park and recreation boards; joint employment of recreation personnel; and cooperative planning committees with membership from city government, planning department, park and recreation department, teachers, PTA, school administration, school board, and voluntary agencies.

Local-State-Federal Responsibilities

Each level of government—city, county, state, and federal—has a fairly well-defined role to play in providing park and recreation services. In order to insure adequate facilities and programs in each state, it is essential to identify the parameters of these respective roles.

Local governments (cities, towns, villages) should provide for intensive use areas. Facilities should include golf courses, ball diamonds, tennis courts, playgrounds, recreation centers, and swimming pools. Programs should be offered in arts and crafts, music, drama, athletics, social recreation, and community-wide events.

County governments have a special role to play in serving the needs of rural and small-town residents as well as urbanites who need facilities greater in size and diversity than the city can manage but less than what the state or federal government can provide. Many counties are providing recreation services to small units of local government where no local agency exists.

State government has traditionally acquired, developed, and maintained outstanding scenic and historical sites which serve the needs of an entire state. Normally these facilities provide unusual natural areas, camping, bike trails, and water recreation facilities. The state has a distinct role to play in providing enabling legislation, technical assistance, propagation of plant and animal life, transportation, and higher education opportunities, to name a few.

The federal role is to acquire, develop, and maintain areas of significant national scenic, historical, and scientific value. In addition, the federal government provides technical assistance, financial incentives, research grants, and wilderness areas. (See Chapters 4, 5, and 6 for greater details on local, state, and federal responsibilities.)

Sometimes the roles of government are not clearly defined and disagreement arises. There is a variety of inter- and intra-agency councils and committees at all government levels to avoid as much duplication as possible. Many states, such as Pennsylvania, have a general cooperation law giving any municipality, city of the third class, borough, township, or school district, in or out of state, the opportunity to jointly exercise and perform any functions, including park and recreation services, which each of them could have undertaken alone.

The federal government, in instances such as the Land and Water Conservation Fund Act of 1965 and the Older Americans Act network, is requiring states to cooperate by developing state master plans for recreation before becoming eligible for funds.

Interstate and regional committees, such as the various river basin authorities, promote cooperation on a broad scale. Such organizations as the Council of State Governments, the National Governors' Conference, and the United States Conference of Mayors help states and cities explore mutual problems.

Other Cooperative Ventures

In the field of leisure services there is no hard and fast line between the functions of government and nongovernment agencies. Both serve human needs. Nongovernment agencies have pioneered in many programs later adopted by public agencies. In general, nongovernment agencies may be more selective in membership and more restrictive in the groups served. Their dependence on voluntary funding, volunteer leadership, and direction by carefully selected board members gives them a special kind of community support.

As important users of public facilities, nongovernment agencies often support public ventures that may be mutually beneficial. Both government and nongovernment organizations should function in a complementary and mutually helpful manner and should not be competitive.

Roadblocks to Cooperation

Although there is almost universal recognition of the need and value of cooperation, there are difficulties to overcome. Generally the leaders of an organization are convinced that their organization has a unique contribution to make to society and view with a jaundiced eye any projects that might seem to threaten their position.

Some intrinsic problems lead to competitive feelings between agencies and hinder cooperation. Competition is keen for membership, for scarce volunteer leaders, and for funds. Since each agency must make a good showing before the community, there is competition for space in newspapers and on radio and television. Status must be maintained, and therefore vying for the support of community leaders is prevalent.

Securing Interagency Cooperation

Cooperation is most effective when it involves a specific project of vital concern for all participants. A few of the kinds of community efforts that tend to enlist cooperation are: community studies of human needs (youth, underprivileged, elderly), a unified approach to delinquency problems, joint training courses, community celebrations, clean-up campaigns, development of camps or other facilities for joint use, special projects for low-income groups, and environmental problems.

Cooperation at the National Level

Organizations at the national level also serve functions in coordinating and cooperating. Prominent among these organizations is the National Assembly for Social Policy and Development, a voluntary association concerned with planning and coordination in social work. The National Association of Social Workers and the many other national organizations concerned with either social problems or special recreation interests act as coordinators in their respective areas of interest.

Voluntary organizations actively cooperate with federal agencies not only through grants for government-approved projects but also by serving on a national level in helping to determine policies and recommend legislation. The success of such federal services as the Department of Health, Education, and Welfare, the Heritage Conservation and Recreation Service, and ACTION depends heavily upon the cooperation of national voluntary organizations.

A trend is developing toward increased cooperative ventures between and among such national organizations as the National Park and Recreation Association, the National Community Education Association, the National Park Service, and the World Leisure and Recreation Association.

Case Studies

There are countless examples of cooperation, coordination and citizen involvement throughout the country. The following example was selected for its diverse approach to cooperative action.

Irvine, California's Heritage Park: A Product of Cooperation[5]

In Irvine, California, government agencies have pooled tax revenues and ventured into the spirited cooperative effort that resulted in Heritage Park. Officials for the city of Irvine, the Irvine Unified School District, and Orange County had the foresight to "stretch their tax dollars" when the expressed need for a major park in the northern sector of the city was revealed.

After overcoming their greatest obstacle, diverse objectives, the implementation was under way. The citizens showed support by passing a $6.5 million bond issue for the development of Heritage Park. Seventy percent of the voters were in favor of this project.

Irvine residents now enjoy the picnic areas, Youth Services Center, arts and crafts center, historical center, and fishing lagoon. Also lighted tennis and handball courts, an aquatic complex, and general activity areas are strategically located in Heritage Park. Hikers and bicyclists enjoy the numerous trails. (See Figure 10.1.)

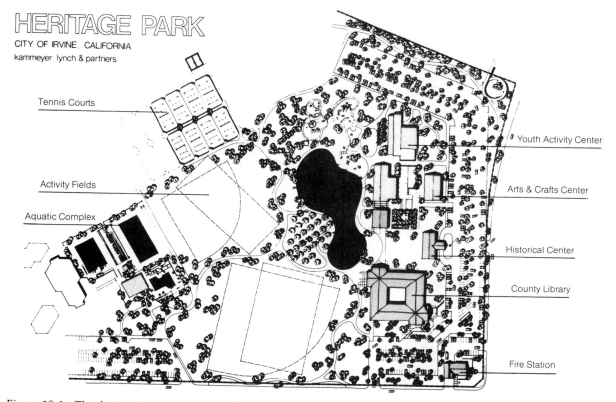

HERITAGE PARK
CITY OF IRVINE, CALIFORNIA
kammeyer lynch & partners

Tennis Courts

Activity Fields

Aquatic Complex

Youth Activity Center

Arts & Crafts Center

Historical Center

County Library

Fire Station

Figure 10.1. The design of Heritage Park, reflecting the co-operative efforts of government agencies.

The City Manager's Office provided the major coordination, and extensive public input was generated by sports groups, the Community Services Commission, and the City Council. Orange County provided funds for a library and fire station facilities in the park. Constructed on school district lands, the creative aquatic center will be used by the general public and the schools.

Recognizing the need for proper operation and maintenance of Heritage Park, public groups approved a cooperative agreement for this purpose. One unique feature of the agreement is the inclusion of a city water conservation policy—irrigating the park vegetation with reclaimed wastewater from the Irvine Ranch Water District.

Interagency Cooperation at the Regional Park Level

Richard C. Trudeau indicated that interagency cooperation is difficult and complex,[6] but the General Manager of the East Bay Regional Park District in Oakland, California, feels that such regional systems are connected to and dependent on local city and county governments. Trudeau explained a variety of ways their regional park system has found to fund new parks jointly. These ways are listed here.

Together with the Alameda County Water District, the park system purchased an abandoned quarry, each making use of that quarry for their own special purposes. The park, of course, uses it for recreation such as swimming and boating, and the Water District uses it as part of its ground water replenishment program.

A joint regional-city park along a four-mile shoreline area of some 308 acres has been planned thanks to the cooperation of the city of Martinez, a group of interested citizens, and some state legislators. It was a complex effort involving state legislation to clear up title to the lands, the division of the land into segments by city and regional agencies, and private grants.

To accelerate the district's master plan, several cities have provided the Regional Park Authority with part of the proceeds from their share of a State Park Bond measure so that projects in their area could proceed. Plans call for the development of a trail, which will connect three regional parks, plus funds to help in the development of two other water-oriented regional parks.

The park system pooled resources to hire consultants to develop a master plan and an open space study with the Association of Bay Area Governments (ABAG).

The park system supplied the basic funds to ABAG, which enabled it to get 701 planning funds from HUD to match all its allocations. It applied the same technique in a joint study with the Bay Area Rapid Transit (BART) on a proposed trails program going from BART stations to regional parks, with BART matching seed funds with a Department of Transportation grant.

The park system joined forces with the Alameda Contra Costa Transit District to jointly fund bus service during the summer months to a number of regional parks.

The park system persuaded the Board of Supervisors in one county to provide it with revenue sharing funds to help in the acquisition of new park lands in one area of that county.

The park system initiated a study of the Ridgeland area of several thousand acres.

Three counties, the Heritage Conservation and Recreation Service, and ABAG have joined in putting up $15,000 cash or services to fund the study, which will examine potential uses of the land, such as farming, cattle grazing, housing, mining, and open space.

Citizen Involvement—A Unique Partnership

Among local government services, the park and recreation department offerings are uniquely different from the "no choice" type of regulatory services offered by the departments of police, fire, health, planning, public works, and public utilities. What sets the park and recreation department aside from the other vital services is that participation in its programs is a matter of choice. It is this uniqueness that calls for an unusual amount of citizen involvement when it comes to the development of a broad-based system of park and recreation services.

Robert M. Artz, formerly a member of the staff of NRPA, says that there is a new awareness throughout the country concerning the need for citizens' participation and leadership in the priority-setting and decision-making process of government agencies. The citizen is continuing to demand a much greater voice in the use of his or her tax dollars. This demand represents the greatest opportunity park and recreation professionals have ever had to finally make park and recreation programs, facilities, and services a top priority at all levels, particularly at the community level.

The idea of a community of partners was expressed by Sterling S. Winans in *Managing Municipal Leisure Services*, when he identified four "communities" in which thought and action must function together as a musical ensemble if a truly coordinated effort is to prevail. First, there is the "community" of the agency itself, composed of a board or commission, administrators, supervisors, secretaries, custodians, and volunteers, who must act together in order to be effective. Second, there are the other official municipal departments that support one another by working together on land acquisition, legal matters, personnel, finance, and planning. A third element in this community of partners is made up of all public, voluntary, private, and commercial groups identified earlier, who parallel the public agency in providing maximum services. The final partner is the citizen-consumer of recreation services, who ultimately accepts or rejects the community efforts.[7]

Active, interested, articulate citizens are absolutely essential in order to capture and preserve the resources necessary for improving the quality of life through recreation. The provision of leisure services is a unique public trust which must be shared with professionals and citizens alike.

We believe that this public trust, and subsequently the public image of park and recreation departments, could be improved if communities would follow the lead of private agencies and recruit more outstanding community leaders for service on park and recreation boards. Any leisure delivery system will require the combined efforts of citizen leaders and professionals if it is to reach its potential for humanizing people's lives.

Selected References

Artz, Robert M. *School-Community Recreation and Park Cooperation*, Management Aids Bulletin No. 82. Arlington, Virginia: National Recreation and Park Association, 1970.

Cwik, Peter J.; King, Marilyn J.; and Van Voorhees, Curtis. *Community Education and Recreation in 1975.* Community Education Research Monograph: Vol. II. Ann Arbor, Michigan: Office of Community Education Research in cooperation with the National Community Education Association, 1975.

Hjelte, George, and Shivers, Jay S. *Public Administration of Recreational Services.* Philadelphia: Lea & Febiger, 1972.

"Interagency Cooperation." National Recreation and Park Association Special Newsletter. Special Edition. September 1977.

Lutzin, Sidney G., and Storey, Edward H., eds. *Managing Municipal Leisure Services.* Washington, D.C.: International City Management Association, 1973.

"Working Together." *California Parks and Recreation* 32, no. 5 (1976–77): 11–21.

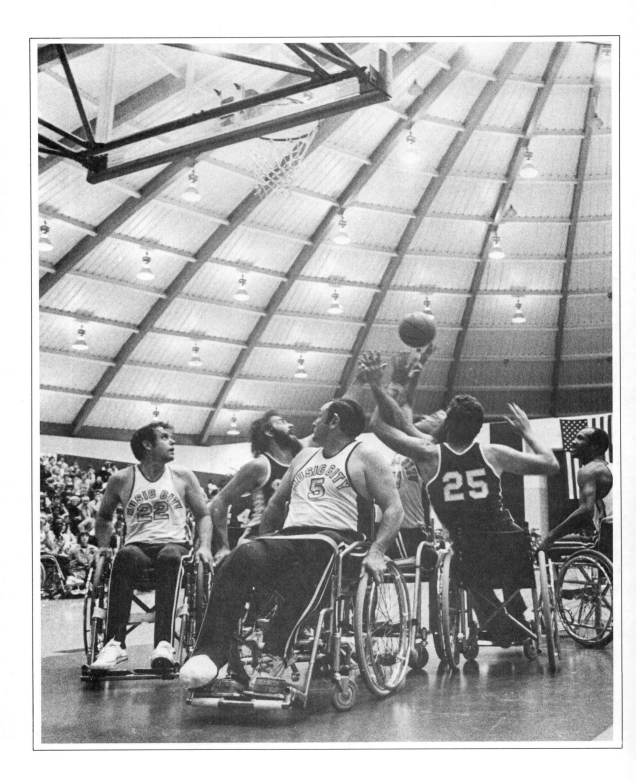

Part Four
Leisure Choices—What and Where?

It is far more important that a man should play something himself, even if he plays it badly, than that he should go to see someone else play it well.

Theodore Roosevelt

People are different; they think differently, work differently, and play differently. Meeting these individual needs is the essence of the challenge of recreation programming.

The most exciting and challenging goal for the park and recreation profession is to make available a broad spectrum of leisure experiences for all those who live in our communities. If such a goal is to be achieved, we must provide attractive and stimulating programs at a variety of times; in a variety of settings; within the framework of differing physical, mental, and social capabilities; and spanning a broad spectrum and continuum within each of the designated program categories.

Successful programs do not just happen; they evolve from careful planning, dynamic supervision, and concerned evaluation. This section deals with the what, the where, and the with whom aspects of recreation programming.

11
Recreation Smorgasbord

Variety is the mother of enjoyment.

Benjamin Disraeli

The horizons of recreation are limitless, ranging from the simple to the complex, from the organized to the laissez faire, from individual enjoyment to group fun, and from the mental and aesthetic to the physical. Many authors have attempted classification of recreation experiences, with a variety of results. Any approach to program categorization is arbitrary and will meet with conflicting reactions. The activities in this book have been classified into nine categories: arts and crafts; dance; drama; mental, linguistic, and literary activities; music; outdoor recreation; social recreation; sports and games; and service activities.

The many agencies that have responsibility for providing recreation in the community have been described in the preceding chapters. The following pages introduce the recreation experiences through which the organizations function.

Activities in themselves are meaningless unless they satisfy the creative, cultural, social, and physical needs and desires of people. Recreation leaders must place primary emphasis not on the activity but on what happens to individuals. Since recreation is voluntary, participants will not return to programs, and sponsoring agencies will not fulfill their objectives, unless basic recreation needs are served.

Arts and Crafts

The first stories of our cultural heritage, including dance, music, and drama, were depicted by prehistoric artists on their cave walls and on their everyday utensils and weapons which were decorated in times of leisure. Down through the ages, arts and crafts objects have told the story of the discovery of fire, metal, glass, and cloth, not only for their utilitarian value, but as conveyors of great personal satisfaction and enjoyment.

All of the cultural arts are deeply ingrained in the lives and heritage of the American people. Artists, in particular, played an important role in the development of parks, recreation, and conservation in the United States. Pioneer American artists who traveled with wilderness explorers and trappers into the uncharted West recorded on paper and canvas a magnificence beyond imagination.

> In recreating these visions in painting, which became brilliant images of a fresh and sweeping New World, the artists played an important role. Their work was instrumental in the great migration westward. Paintings became proclamations displayed before great audiences in tents and halls in every eastern town.
>
> It was the artists, then, who offered Americans a chance to see and accept the majesty of their chosen country; and they struck an enormously responsive chord. At no time in the country's history have the public and the artist shared so common a vision, founded on mutually accepted beliefs and morals.[1]

Scope

Many names have been given to the rise in popularity of arts and crafts programs. The movement has been called an explosion, a quiet revolution, or the revival of our innate instincts to express ourselves creatively. Others say it is not a rebirth or renaissance at all, that it has been here all the time, and that we are just now beginning to see the tip of the iceberg that lies below.

Because arts and crafts appeal to people of all ages, backgrounds, interests, and abilities, there must be a wide variety of opportunities within each craft area. At any time, in any season, there are literally hundreds of arts and crafts programs going on. Fads come and go. The following list serves only to indicate the diversity:

Batiking

Bead craft

Cartooning

Crewel embroidery

Decoupage

Doll making

Folk toys and homemade games

Macrame

Multigraphics

Needlecraft

Painting and drawing—pencil, water, oil, chalk

Papercraft

Sand casting

Sand painting

Sculpting—clay, ice, sand, wood, plastic, metal

Spinning and weaving

Stained glass art

Tie dyeing

Tole painting

Wheat weaving

Woodwork

In addition to instructional programs in specific skill areas, many communities offer art appreciation classes, seminars, workshops, and trips to art centers and museums here and abroad.

Organizational Patterns and Settings

There are probably as many ways to organize a community arts and crafts program as there are courses to offer and instructors to teach them. We suggest that there is no best way. What works well in Bellingham, Washington, may not be accepted in Bangor, Maine. In some communities, the park and recreation department plays a lead role in providing facilities, instructors, equipment, and supplies; in others, the department plays a supportive role and assists arts and crafts clubs and associations, museums, and others to bring these services to the community.

Ray Forsberg, Recreation Director in Waterloo, Iowa, which has an outstanding arts program, says:

> Recreation departments will never make much of a dent within the community arts picture by trying to go it alone. The best approach lies in developing community-wide cooperation among tax-supported departments and voluntary, nonprofit arts and hobby groups. . . .
>
> Especially when it comes to the arts, recreation departments should "stay in the wings" as much as possible and endeavor to serve the multiple role of catalyst, innovator, facilitator, and coordinator. This concept can lead to one of the most productive investments of the tax dollar.[2]

Similar things can be said about the settings in which arts and crafts instructional programs, shows, workshops, and exhibits take place. There is a growing feeling among arts and crafts proponents that quality programs cannot be developed within the traditional settings, such as public playgrounds, camps, and neighborhood centers. These programs play a key role in an introductory and supportive way and may be the only exposure many people will ever have to arts and crafts. However, limitations on department budgets, staff, facilities, storage, and time preclude in-depth activities on a community-wide basis. What is developing are specialized centers, commonly referred to as leisure art centers or art activity centers, strategically located throughout the community. Some of these centers house all of the performing arts; and others, depending on size, staff, and budget, accommodate one or two specialties. For convenience, we list a variety of settings, categorized by permanent and temporary places in which one or all of the programs associated with the arts and crafts movement may take place:

Permanent Places	Temporary Places
Leisure art centers	Playgrounds
Community centers	Camps
Barns	Parks
Abandoned schools	Streets
Railroad stations	Malls—indoor and outdoor
Bath houses	
Riverboats	Fairs
Old jails	Schools
Movie theaters	Libraries
Fire stations	Sidewalks
Warehouses	Gardens
Churches	Museums
Old houses	Open fields
Museums	Vacant lots
Libraries	Monuments
	Show wagons
	Mobile vans

Bernice Reed reminds us that the important thing to remember in offering arts and crafts programs is to be mobile and flexible in presentation and adaptation to the environment.[3]

Integration with Other Program Areas

It is very important to coordinate and integrate arts and crafts with ongoing dance, music, and drama programs. The possibilities are many. Artisans can make puppets, marionettes, and costumes; actors and writers can bring them to life. Artisans can produce musical instruments; musicians can interpret these instruments to a waiting audience. The creators of poster art can tell the community all about that next performance.

National Foundation on the Arts and the Humanities

In recent years, the federal government has become actively involved in promoting the arts through the National Foundation on the Arts and the Humanities. This wide-ranging program offers project grants for the promotion of the arts in dance, education, literature, music, public media, theater, visual arts, expansion arts, and museums.

The National Foundation has brought diverse and specialized interest groups, such as colleges and universities, libraries, park and recreation departments, nonprofit institutions, museums, and others, together by forming arts councils and advisory groups to oversee funding programs for research, program development, professional education, and public awareness programs.

One of the most exciting activities to develop out of the program has been the featured artist-in-residence programs. Artists and craftsmen in the parks, performing, demonstrating, and conducting workshops, have brought a new perspective to the movement.

Trends

It seems that artists and craftsmen have regained old world respect and have emerged from their ivory towers and attics to share their skills with amateurs and to become a visible part of community life. The idea of making arts and crafts a participatory experience has come of age. Classes run the gamut from beginner to intermediate to advanced. Fees are common in order to cover the cost of instruction and supplies.

The specialized leisure art center is gaining strength and will probably continue. The Arts in the Parks program sponsored jointly by the National Park Service and the National Recreation and Park Association will undoubtedly expand. The close cooperation developing between park and recreation departments, state and local art councils, hobby clubs, libraries, universities, museums, and others will continue to aid in the advancement of the arts.

Some problems still exist. There will be territorial rights; there always will be financial problems; it will be difficult to convince public officials raised on a diet of sports and athletics that cultural arts are just as important if we are to provide a balanced community recreation program.

Dance

The word *dance* has a wide variety of meanings, depending upon an individual's past associations with the term. Some kind of rhythmic expression has always been a part of human activity. Early primitive dances had practical as well as aesthetic values. People danced to worship their gods, to stimulate an emotional pitch that would catapult them into battle, to celebrate a victory, to ward off evil spirits, or simply to release their energies. Dance has always been closely related to the folk patterns of the people, so knowledge of the kinds of dance for a given period is often quite revealing in characterizing the life and spirit of the era.

Through the years, dance has gained both favor and disfavor as acceptable recreation; yet no social or religious organization has been powerful enough to eliminate dancing. The need to blend physical, mental, and emotional expression in rhythmic patterns is, indeed, universal.

Scope

If dance is to gain its fullest potential as a program area in recreation, then a variety of offerings must be provided. The kinds of rhythmic movement must be varied so that:

1. The novice as well as the more accomplished dancer may enjoy opportunities that will be challenging without being discouraging.

2. There will be chances to explore simple rhythms and highly stylized dances.

3. Chances to perform, to communicate through dance to an audience, will motivate participation and enhance enjoyment.

4. The handicapped may experience this exhilaration of dance as a recreative outlet.

5. All age groups will have an opportunity to perform without embarrassment.

6. Social judgments will not restrict the freedom of expression in movement.

Many classifications of rhythmics and dance have been proposed. The types most frequently found in recreation programs are listed here.

Creative rhythms. In recent years, the emphasis in all education and, indeed, in recreation has been on those experiences that allow freedom of expression for the participant. Rhythmic movement, under guidance that stimulates a person to create patterns from familiar experiences, helps to develop one socially, mentally, and emotionally, as well as physically.

Alert leaders can do much to spark interest in creative activity by recognizing those moments when the group or an individual is ready to explore the fun of interpretation and communication through movement. Any child or adult has the basic urge and the physical equipment for this kind of activity. The leader must provide the environment in which the participants will feel free to express their ideas.

Mixers.   Dance activities in which couples change partners frequently have a dual purpose: the joy of moving in patterns to music and the opportunity to socialize. The dance mixer provides an excellent social recreation tool for large groups. Almost any kind of dance can be adjusted to provide change of partners and an opportunity to meet people. The creative leader learns to organize the program so that a few such experiences will be mingled with other kinds of dance.

But leaders should not get carried away. The overzealous leader, in trying to allow socialization for the group, must avoid two common mistakes: the inclusion of so many mixers that a couple who comes to the dance together may never get a chance to be together again during the evening, and a program so jammed with activity that people who meet in a mixer will not be allowed time to get better acquainted. These two errors have given the mixer a poor reputation, which all too frequently decreases participation.

Folk dance.   Folk and square dances have gained considerable popularity in the last twenty years. Festivals, television exhibitions, state dance competitions, and church approval have helped to stimulate a revival of interest in dance patterns that have been handed down from the American pioneer or borrowed from other nations.

Unlike many forms of art, such as drama and literature, folk dance was for a long time neglected. It was easy to hand down from one generation to another the beauty of a painting or the pleasure of the written word, but until the motion picture made visual recording of movement possible, the folk dance lived in the hearts of the humble folk and had to be passed on through actually doing the dance. The folk dances of a different country are as diverse as the language—and just as distinctive. The dance patterns of peoples in other lands and in other times depict the environment in which they lived, the occupations they performed, the important events of their lives, the restrictions of their faith, and their relationship with other forms of the performing arts.

The folk dances, national dances, or character dances differ from creative dance in that they are composed of specific basic patterns that must be learned. They run the gamut from the simple chain dances of the Greek Kritikos, which is reminiscent of the pastoral features of the rolling terrain; to the Irish lilts with their vertical movement and swift footwork; to the Lithuanian occupational Kalvelis dance, which depicts the smithy; to the more intricate Swedish Hambo. The beauty of the typical folk music stimulates participation if intelligent leadership emphasizes the spirit of the dance.

Square dance.   Although it has its origins in the European quadrille, the square dance is the only truly American folk dance, if one discounts the fads that have come and gone since the pioneer days. It evolved from the restrictions placed upon dance by the church in the early days of the nation and grew from the singing games and play-party patterns sanctioned by religious groups.

The popularity of square dancing has been increased by its inclusion in school physical education programs. Square dance clubs for all ages have been promoted in agency, private, and municipal recreation programs. The format for the square dance remains fairly constant: introduction, basic dance sequence, break, and ending. Although the dance patterns are similar, there is opportunity for creative changes in the introductions, endings, and breaks. The music is lively, and the dance moves at a rapid pace. Styles of dance patterns, calls, music, and costuming vary in different sections of the nation. Dance calls are sometimes as distinctively revealing as provincial dialects.

Couple dances or round dances. Lloyd Shaw and his Colorado enthusiasts renewed the popularity of the old-time couple dances—the waltz, schottische, polka, or mazurka steps inspired by music of yesterday. Some of the basic steps have been and are still popular in the so-called social dance area, but the term *couple dance* here relates to the progression of specific patterns such as the Varsouvianna, the Rye Waltz, the Boston Two-Step, or the Texas Schottische. The couple dances have waned in popularity except for special dance club interest.

Social dance. The social dance has had a long period of struggle for approval and recognition. Although dances that allowed physical contact between the sexes were frowned upon by some religious groups, such stigma has been slowly removed by all but a very few church groups.

The social dance, perhaps more than any of the other types, reveals the spirit of the times. Colonial restrictions and severity were evident in the stately minuet for the aristocracy; the barn dance offered an expression of the exuberance of the frontier. The eighteenth century saw the polka, the lancers, the military march, the quadrille, and finally the two-step in a revealing fluctuation between formalism and freedom of expression. The uncertainties of the wars and the depression brought such fads as the Charleston, the Conga, the Black Bottom, the Susie Q, the Mambo, the Stroll, the Hokey Pokey, and in 1961, the Twist, executed, according to one graphic description,

"by simulating the action of rubbing your lower back with a towel while trying to put out a cigarette with your right foot." The 1960s and 1970s saw a new form of mass participation in social dance; it separated the partners, made dance a physically energetic activity, and provided new freedom of expression with total body movement.

Dance classes for adults flourished in the 1970s. The Arthur Murray dance studio offerings led to commercial ventures by other dance teachers in every geographic area. Private dance clubs, sometimes combined with a travel interest, are still popular choices, particularly for the middle-aged. Dancing on a boat as you wend your way down the Mississippi River is just one of the current opportunities.

Modern dance. In the early years of this century, Ruth St. Denis and Ted Shawn emerged as leading proponents of a new American contribution to dance. Other creative artists like Charles Weidman, Martha Graham, Doris Humphrey, and Martha Hill continued to popularize the new dance form, which allowed freer expression, fewer restrictions in technique, and a real challenge to explore and make use of the capabilities of the body. Many community agencies now include modern dance classes for children and teenagers. Others promote attendance at dance presentations as spectator recreation. Modern dance, like modern art, must be understood to be appreciated. Education in the art of communication through freely expressed body movements will increase the numbers who can enjoy active or spectator participation in modern dance.

Ballet. The rigid technique of ballet requires long hours of practice. Many dance teachers who support freer modes of expression in movement criticize the ballet as too formal, too restricted, and too disciplined. As a recreation offering, ballet is still popular among eight- to twelve-year-olds, who endure hours of practice for one glorious performance behind the footlights.

Acrobatic, tap, and clog dancing. Although the popularity of these types of dances has waned in the last twenty years, they are often combined with other activities, such as baton twirling. The 1930s and 1940s spurred the desire for tap dancing in particular, as Gene Kelly, Fred Astaire, and Ginger Rogers tapped their way into the hearts of the people through the motion picture screen. Small communities that indulge in frequent home-town talent shows often provide a stimulus for classes and clubs in such activities. Tap dancing has recently emerged as a physical fitness fad for adults in some parts of the nation.

Belly dancing. The return of belly dancing, not as a ritual or as an aid to childbirth, but as a form of healthful exercise, has made headlines in recent years, especially as older Americans have embraced it. Municipal recreation programs were first criticized and then applauded as the newspapers circulated pictures of people of all ages performing gyrations of the Egyptian belly dance.

Organizational Patterns in the Community Program

The methods of organization and the extent of the dance offerings in the park and recreation program vary with the felt need, the leadership available, and the facilities at hand. Commercial ventures in several of the areas have been most successful. We list here the most common types:

Classes. Instructional classes in tap, modern, social, square, and creative dance are found in most communities. Classes are usually arranged by age groupings or by level of proficiency.

Drop-in centers with dancing area provided. The nightclubs, discotheques, teen hangouts, and older-American centers offer dancing on a laissez faire basis. The space and the music are provided, and the participants proceed from there.

Clubs. Folk, square, and modern dance clubs, square dance calling clubs, and family dance clubs offer consistent progression for those who would like to learn more challenging dances. Clubs also offer sustained interest opportunities in industrial and hospital settings.

Special events. Street dances, fund-raising balls in the local mall, cake walks, festivals, or disc jockey nights in the teen centers all offer "specials" for the dance enthusiast.

Dance theater. Some larger communities have been successful with dance theater for both adults and children. The Salt Lake City Dance Theater has gained national acclaim. Dance theater demands a high degree of achievement for a few performers and provides fringe-area involvement for many more. It offers the chance to delight hundreds of spectators or to whet their appetites for active participation.

Dance for special groups. The handicapped are eager for dance experiences. Much progress has been made in the last few years in wheelchair dancing and other modifications of rhythmic activities. Also ethnic minority groups have clustered to explore and interpret their cultural heritage through the study and performance of pertinent dance rituals.

Integration with Other Program Areas

The possibility of combining dance with drama, arts and crafts, and music is obvious. Productions such as any of the Broadway musicals, when transferred to the local stage, involve craftsmanship for stage settings and interaction of dance specialties with music and drama.

The ethnic festivals sponsored in many communities (Polish days, Yugoslavian festivals, Indian powwows) include dance, music, food booths, and special arts and crafts.

Talent shows on playgrounds or in community centers give opportunities for solo, dual, or group performances. Even certain sports have resorted to dance, particularly ballet, to develop and discipline the movement and control of the body.

The Future

The television and film bombardment with all kinds of dances gives the average child a greater exposure to this program area than was previously possible. The increased numbers of schools that include dance in physical education classes, beginning in the elementary schools, cultivate a taste for further experiences in rhythmic expression.

The initiation of more dance curriculums at the college level will provide more and better leaders as specialists. National emphasis on all the performing arts will stimulate more and better opportunities at the local level. The language of dance is a universal one that knows no boundaries. Intelligent and inspired leadership is needed to promote its use as a truly recreative outlet.

Drama

The world of make-believe holds an eternal magic for young and old. From the primitive story-telling efforts through the ancient Greek dramatic classics to the ceremonial religious rites of the American Indian, drama has brought pleasure to people. From the cobbled innyards of Elizabethan England through the Mississippi showboats to the modern-day Broadway stage, television, and movie houses, the world of the theater has remained an enchanted realm.

The human need to communicate, to share thoughts, emotions, and problems, has been a constant motivation for expression. Drama for recreative outlets should offer broad horizons for the talented or for the uninspired, since all who explore the area find it one of the most challenging and rewarding of the performing arts.

Scope

Community recreation programs should give attention to adequate areas, facilities, and leadership for the gamut of dramatic opportunities. They should extend from improvisation of imaginative story telling to polished performances of the written word in full-scale theatrical productions; from the "imagination stirrers" in the playgrounds, centers, camps, and parks to the simplest or the most elaborate community theater; from play reading to play going. The recreation program should include any and all activities in which there is opportunity for individuals to project themselves in vocal and motor self-expression.

The emphasis in recreation drama is on the individual, not on the vehicle. The important thing is not what the child or adult does to drama, but what drama does for the performer. Such a philosophy does not necessarily deny the value of performances that present a challenge and require polish. Community recreation agencies are broadening opportunities for better quality as well as for more varied programs in drama.

The scope, organization, and types of dramatic programs depend on the sponsoring agency's philosophy and objectives and on its available leadership, facilities, and budget. It is reasonable to suppose that camps, playgrounds, community centers, youth-serving agencies, churches, hospitals, and industries might offer some, if not all, of the following activities.

Informal dramatics. This term is applied most frequently to those experiences in which ideas, events, or stories are improvised with action and/or dialogue without formal scripts, without rehearsal, and with or without the guidance of a leader. The following are examples of some program possibilities:

Creative dramatics. Scenes and stories that are developed through uninhibited expression of individual ideas and feelings form the realm of creative dramatics. Scenery and costumes are rarely used, and audiences are either nonexistent or incidental. The inherent sense of make-believe and the freedom of expression of children provide a fertile field for educational and recreation growth through creative dramatics.

But creative dramatics is not confined to youngsters. All ages enjoy this outlet as senior citizens role-play frustrations or teenagers create improvisations to interpret political and social issues.

Story telling. Vivid unfolding of a story is a dramatic activity at any age. Reading or telling stories of fact or fiction to elicit an emotional response from the audience is effective. Songs in which the group uses music and lyrics to express dramatic dialogue are popular. Story plays, in which the listeners react with action or dialogue on cue from the story teller, intrigue both young and old. Imitative audience participation, in which the group imitates words and actions of the leader, makes stunts like the "Lion Hunt" perennial favorites.

Dramatic games. Many dramatic games have evolved from folk customs, ceremonial rituals, or political satires of former years. Active and quiet games are illustrated by such activities as "New Orleans" or "Charades." Singing games such as "Farmer in the Dell" combine song and drama through action directed by lyrics sung by the participants.

Skits and stunts. Skits and stunts can vary from the simple to the complex. All involve an informal portrayal of some situation. Pantomimes, the comic or serious expression of ideas through movement without words, form the basis of games, stunts, skits, or full-scale artistic productions. Shadow plays, playing out scenes behind a back-lighted sheet in dark areas, are popular for parties and campfires. Creating a skit in a group, using a bag of objects as props, makes for exciting and often hilarious nosebag drama.

Facility- or equipment-centered activities. The mere availability of the proper tools and environment will often inspire dramatic creativity. Imagination stirrers such as a trunk of old clothes and shoes or an old fire truck may instigate much impromptu dramatic play. The sandbox offers scenes for a battleground or a cave dwelling. Finger puppets can inspire hours of social and dramatic activity.

Formal activities. More highly organized vehicles for displaying histrionic ability or for pleasing an audience are also within the responsibility of the recreation program. Such offerings present opportunities for development of talent, continuity of productions, rigor of rehearsal schedules, and a diverse choice of means for making an impact on the audience. Community programs throughout the country often offer one or more of the following types of production.

Talent shows. One of the most enchanting audience attractors is the show in which each child or adult displays talent in music, dance, or drama with forceful showmanship.

Puppet and marionette shows. Often the person who is reluctant to perform on stage will be lost in the character of the puppet or marionette into whose personality he or she projects without the necessity of facing an audience.

Musicals and operettas. The combination of dance and music is popular and versatile in its offering for performer or audience.

Carnivals, circuses, and pageants. The color and fanfare of the barker at the carnival booth, the portrayal of animal or trainer, and the special zest of the spirited pageant are dramatic special events.

Radio and television shows. Radio and television give challenges for creating and performing dramatic and informative productions for the listening and viewing public. Local public service stations are quite generous with their time.

One-act or three-act dramas. The formal production on a stage of carefully prepared plots gives excellent experience in dramatic communication to those who have large or small parts.

Play tournaments. Although drama is most frequently considered noncompetitive, some communities have stimulated interest in dramatic activity on regional or state levels by sponsoring play contests to determine excellence in acting, staging, and directing.

Play-reading and play-going clubs. Popular response has been great to many programs in which individuals gather to read plays or to attend plays and discuss them afterwards.

Instructional classes. Cities that have offered classes in acting, makeup, or stage design have found an increasing interest from people of all ages.

Film making. Creative productions of original plays have provided excellent outlets for all age groups.

Settings and Emphases

Drama in one form or another has proved popular in communities both large and small.

On the playground or in the park. Story telling by the playground leader or by a specialist who travels from playground to playground is the most common dramatic activity in this setting. Weekly themes around which activities are centered promote playground dramatics. An Early Settlers' Week may include outlets for costuming, building, and staging a town meeting, whereas a Pirate Week may produce puppet shows and a pageant.

The sandbox provides inspiration for much creative and imaginative play. The tree-stump throne or the horizontal telephone pole in which a succession of seats has been gouged may inspire characterizations from fairy princesses to the posse after the latest television villain. Other more elaborate equipment to stimulate dramatic play is found in the new creative playground equipment. The Oakland, California, seahorse swing or the Jamison moon-rocket climbing apparatus prove enchanting bases for imaginative activity. Even the playground slide takes a new dramatic dimension when the child emerges through the wide-open mouth of a friendly whale. Scrappy, the playground finger puppet, may give directions for clean-up or may become part of a puppet theater made from shoebox staging. It takes only mild stimulation to produce results in daily dramatic games or to finish the season with a culminating pageant.

In the community center. An indoor center can stimulate winter activity through play-reading clubs, play-going clubs, creative dramatic classes, radio and television productions, talent shows, classes in stage design, instruction in dramatic technique, experience in makeup application, or one-act play tournaments with professional critiques. Often, indoor centers provide an extension of the school dramatic program.

At camp. Camps provide excellent settings for drama. A flickering campfire or a grove of trees at the foot of a hill sets the mood for inspirational performances never dreamed of on a wooden stage. Shadow stunts, ceremonials, and simple pageants are popular.

In the therapeutic setting. Role playing and psycho- or sociodrama have long been effective techniques for investigation and problem solving in sociology and psychology. The cathartic effect of "playing out" stresses is useful for the healthy as well as for the mentally ill. Whole-hearted surrender to characterization may provide better understandings of others. Certainly, involvement in dramatic outlets can allow the individual the luxury of being lost in another's "shoes" for a few moments.

Show wagons. The traveling theater on wheels, gaining in popularity in many cities, is reminiscent of the old English guild carts from which the fifteenth-century mystery and morality plays were shown to audiences on street corners. Inexpensive, versatile show wagons can be formed on the flatbeds of trucks. There are also permanent wagons with dressing rooms and more ornate lighting and stage sets. The stagemobiles move with ease to all parts of the city for one-night stands. The Boston Children's Theater stagemobile is available for individuals or groups during the summer months.

Children's theater. Many communities sponsor children's theater with a threefold purpose: giving the opportunity for children to learn through performance, offering the educational and emotional experience of watching a story on stage, and fostering the children's interest in artistic entertainment of all kinds. Others provide facilities for teenagers to test their own creative dramatic efforts.

With dinner. A popular trend in many cities is the "theater in the round" produced by local amateur groups and presented in cooperating restaurants. The idea first started on college campuses and has spread to several communities and resorts.

Facilities, Equipment, and Supplies

The necessary tools for drama in its simplest form are a place, some potential participants, and an inspired leader. For productions, formal or informal, the major concern is obtaining an area free from distraction, in which atmosphere can be created. Experiments have proved that even a shopping mall or a rooftop may provide an effective stage setting. Summer theater in tents and street theater are popular and less expensive to maintain.

Equipment and supplies may vary from the meager to the elegant. The minimum requirements for production are some kind of lighting, intelligently used; some interchangeable flats for set design; a curtain; and a makeup kit.

Integration with Other Program Areas

Almost every phase of programming can carry a dramatic overtone, if the leader capitalizes on the emotional possibilities of the moment. There are also many ways in which drama can be integrated with other areas in planned programs. Some examples of integration are shown in Figure 11.1.

Literary, Mental, and Linguistic Activities

Few recreation experiences make no demands upon mental perception or linguistic ability. Just as there is rhythm in almost every recreation outlet, so there is also a thought or language process. In music, drama, social recreation, and hobbies, for example, there may be many opportunities for mental activites. Puzzles are tried at a picnic, skits are written for dramatic production, mathematical hobbies are pursued, or musical memory quizzes are attempted. There are recreation activities that cannot be categorized elsewhere, however, which emphasize mental, linguistic, or literary efforts. These activities comprise this special category.

A child who has learned to love reading may travel to the ends of the earth without leaving the fireside. The teenager who spends leisure composing short stories enjoys the thrill and achievement of creative experience. The adult who masters a foreign language through individual study finds stimulating

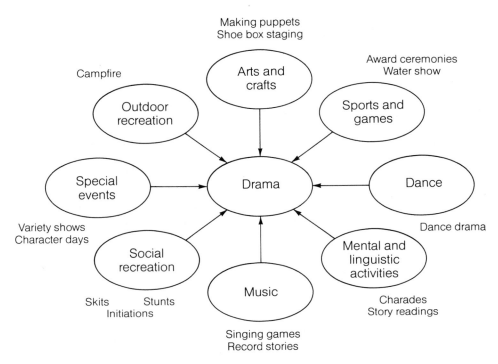

Figure 11.1. Integration of drama with other program areas.

mental exercise. Many of these activities demand no audience or no cohort. Study, research, creative writing, and reflective contemplation can best be enjoyed in solitude. Other mental and literary activities may involve several persons as the need arises to communicate, to display new skills or knowledge, or to compete against other minds. Recreation agencies have found success in offering the following opportunities, which tax mental, literary, or linguistic abilities for individual or group enjoyment.

Reading

Libraries are ever more keenly aware of their challenge and obligation to the leisure of all age groups. From the children's storytelling hours in the library or on the play-ground to the reading clubs and contests for vacation months to the adult book review clubs, reading is an inspiring and rewarding program for recreation agencies to encourage. Bookmobiles are now a popular program item for rural and municipal recreation offerings. Viscount Grey aptly describes the joys of reading in the following: "Books are the greatest and most satisfactory of recreations. I mean the use of books for pleasure. Without books, without having acquired the power of reading for pleasure, none of us can be independent, but if we can read we have a sure defence against boredom in solitude. If we have not that defence, we are dependent upon the charity of family, friends, or even strangers to save us from boredom; but if we can find delight in reading, even a long railway journey alone ceases to be tedious, and long winter evenings to ourselves are an inexhaustible opportunity for pleasure."[4]

Group Discussions and Classes

Gathering in small groups to discuss music, philosophy, current events, religion, or innumerable other topics has always been a popular leisure pastime and a rewarding recreation. In modern society, the art of conversation has too often been overshadowed by radio, television, or other spectator activities. Clubs that meet regularly for discussion purposes may be organized, or special meetings to explore particular subjects may be scheduled. Although there is a thin line between adult education and recreation in such program undertakings, those who participate in stimulating discussions do so with as much thought of the joy of exhilarating mental exercise as of the incidental learning that will take place.

Learning foreign languages by records or tapes and practicing in small groups affords opportunity for fun, challenge, and achievement.

Puzzles and Games

Crossword puzzles, acrostics, and other word games may be used as social recreation tools and to fill travel hours. There is exciting challenge in completing crossword puzzles or magazine quizzes.

Chess, with more than ten million regular players, plus checkers, Go, Parcheesi, Scrabble, or their many variations, provide mental exercise as well as competitive outlets. The national and international chess games that are played by correspondence often continue for long periods of time before a winner finally emerges.

Bridge boasts ten million regular players, and card games like pinochle and canasta are popular recreation choices for individual or group activity. The many kinds of solitaire provide fun for those who are alone; other card games provide social as well as mental rewards.

Clubs

Many letter-writing clubs exist today. Groups or individuals use many leisure hours in writing to friends, known and unknown. For example, a New England recreation department sets up correspondence with teenagers in South African communities. The exchange of letters leads to many hours of study and discussion of a foreign land. Club groups likewise often have "pen pals."

The desire to communicate intelligently and effectively brings many participants to groups studying and practicing the art of public speaking. Many Toastmasters' Clubs are formed from a few adults in the Civic Center, Women's Club, church, or service club who are searching for worthwhile, challenging, and rewarding uses for leisure hours. Debating clubs provide additional stimulation for those who enjoy competitive argument.

Personal Study

The exploration of any given topic by an individual is rarely the concern of the recreation program director, yet such continued diligence toward a goal is one of the most rewarding recreative experiences. Stimulation for individual endeavors can be provided by the recreation leader to participants of any age. Discovering and exploring through research cannot be minimized as a wholesome recreation opportunity. Genealogy with ten million researchers, stamp collection with sixteen million devotees, and coin collection with over a million enthusiasts attest to the popularity of these activities.

Creative Writing

Creative writing, whether the end result is a poem, short story, dramatic episode, or simply a brief message to a friend, is a recreative area that has been too long ignored. The beam on the face of a child who has just rhymed two lines for the first time and the pride in the voice of the eighty-year-old reading a description of the late fall colors exemplify the real worth of creative writing. Many a person whose creative urge may have been stifled by the assigned autobiographies in the school English class may soar to creative heights in exploring the joys of communicating during a creative expression session at a camp or community center.

To explore all the ways in which lives might be enhanced through stimulation of mental abilities would be an impossible task. Suffice it to say that the area of literary, mental, and linguistic activities cannot be ignored if our programs are to achieve the broad scope of satisfactions necessary in a challenging world.

Music

"I'd like to teach the world to sing in perfect harmony"—vibrant voices from faces of many colors persuade you from the television screen that music is integrative. Disneyland's "It's a Small World After All" molds the people of all lands into rhythmic unity. Music is often called the most universal of the arts. The broad appeal of music in its many forms has been recognized in every culture from the beginning of time. From the pagan rhythmic chants to the latest popular tune, music has dynamically demonstrated its ability to blend human beings in the participation at hand.

In spite of the repeated contentions that the American colonists, because of their preoccupation with life's hardships, had neither time nor inclination to cultivate the arts of music, the facts speak for themselves; the first book to be printed in America was a hymnal (the *Bay Psalm Book* in 1641); singing schools

were instituted in the early eighteenth century, and the Philharmonic Society of New York had been founded in 1842. Even the Puritan and the Quaker, who frowned upon music in religious environments, were not completely immune to the joys of whistling or the rhythms of the spinning top although they might have been reluctant to accept Jesus Christ Superstar.

Scope

Because tastes and appreciations in music must be cultivated and because there is a wide spectrum of native talent, which might influence ability and satisfaction in music experiences, we need to offer diverse programs to whet the musical appetite of the novice and to challenge the intellect or the emotions of the more accomplished musician.

The scope of programs varies from simple rhythms on the playground to sophisticated choral work or orchestrations; from spontaneous singing around the campfire to carefully planned gospel songs, music festivals, or opera; from talent shows to instructional instrument classes; from the mere provision of a facility for the wild jam session or the record listening exchange to the careful selection of shows by the latest rock or country music star.

Types

Music has appeal for people of every age and every capability. The types, organization, and extent of opportunities for music in recreation again depend upon the availability of competent and innovative leadership, the interests of the participants, and the philosophy of the sponsoring agency. The literature describes several categories of activities, which usually include singing, playing instruments, rhythmic movements or rhythm games, creating music with or without instruments, listening, spectator experiences, and combinations of all of these.

For the most part, two general categories emerge: those experiences that occur somewhat spontaneously or with little formal scheduling or direct leadership; and those that, because of the numbers involved or the challenge of the musical medium, need more expertise or more highly organized scheduling or leadership. We'll take a short look at programs in each division.

Informal activities with little organization. Because music is a satisfying means of self-expression, individuals or small groups often turn to music with little or no need for stimulation from any leader.

Informal singing. Experimenting with voice tones starts long before a child can walk. As a means of personal expression or group integration, lifting the voice in song has few equals in recreative experience. The teenager whistling or singing on the way home from school, the youngster humming a tune with intermittent words while castle building in the playground sandpile, and the adults gathered around the piano are all indulging in informal music making.

Musical games. Many simple games with a musical background afford pleasure for Sunday-school groups, picnickers, scout troops, or playground participants. Singing games such as Looby Loo, in which the instructions for the game are sung by the participants, are popular among the very young. Mental competition activities that include songs guessed from rhythmic clapping, rhythm games with tapping feet, vibrating rhythm sticks, and flashcard picture contests to which the group reacts with a song are popular for young or old.

Musical instruments. The child fingering the piano keys in an attempt to compose a melody is lost in a pleasureful world. The professional harpist may turn to the harp for recreation after practice hours are over. Musical instruments from the simplest wooden whistle to the most expensive pieces afford creative and recreative activity to an increasing number of individuals.

Listening activities. The flip of the dial on the television set or the turning of the switch on the record player may bring informal music activity to many. The size of the record industry increases each year, with thousands of dollars being expended, particularly by the teenage group. The gamut of preference runs from country and western to Debussy, but the satisfactions come in listening to music in informal situations, in the home, in the YWCA, or in the church social room.

Rhythm bands. An assortment of homemade or commercial bells, castanets, sandblocks, drums, cymbals, or sticks may form hours of enjoyment in rhythm bands. The arts and crafts program often provides handmade inner-tube or tin-can drums, castanets of wooden spoons, decorated wooden rulers, metal lamp-top cymbals, corn-filled paper plates, sleighbell bracelets, or a variety of paper-plate or bottle-cap tambourines.

Musical activities that require more organization. Singing or playing an instrument alone provides one kind of enchantment and meets certain needs for self-expression. Playing an instrument or singing in cooperation with others who have similar interests affords the additional pleasures of communication and coordination for achievement. The following kinds of activities need some measure of organization.

Musical opportunities for small groups. The barber shop quartet, which flourished in the Gay Nineties, has gained popularity in modern times. The Society for the Preservation and Encouragement of Barber Shop Quartet Singing in America, Inc., a national fraternity of male vocalists, was formed to promote barber shop singing. The female counterpart is the Sweet Adelines.

Small groups of instrumentalists find relaxation and achievement in their concerted efforts. Stringed ensembles and brass quartets are becoming more numerous in community recreation programs. Harmonica bands provide musical outlets for youngsters or senior citizens. Teenagers have flooded the market with guitar, drum, and vocal combos, as well as singing groups.

Some municipal departments give instruction in instruments during the summer months. Free instruction on the playground or in the center is so popular that administrators find that the demand far exceeds the ability of most communities to afford the opportunities. Policy usually dictates that no individual instruction will be given, but the class sessions provide incentive for many individuals to explore greater accomplishment in private lessons. Song-writing classes are well attended.

Informally organized listening hours have been initiated on playgrounds, in club activities, and on college campuses. The listening hour on playgrounds becomes an informal avenue to appreciations that lead to better listening habits. If listening to music is to have real value, the individual must learn how to listen.

Activities with large groups. Possibly the most popular of the musical offerings with large groups are community sings and rock concerts. Community sings are organized for particular interest groups and may be scheduled as continuing programs throughout the year. For many years, the community sing was synonymous with the less sophisticated, but with the impact of television singing programs and the early inclusion of group singing in elementary school programs, even the most aloof of sophisticates have come to know the joy of raising voices together in the sheer exuberance of melody.

More highly organized singing groups, with restricted participation because of talent requirements, are found in the a cappella choirs, glee clubs, and choruses of settlement houses, church fellowship groups, senior citizen clubs, agriculture extension clubs, and municipal recreation groups.

Rock concerts in the parks, the stadiums, or privately owned meadows have caused concern because of their seeming attraction for the drug culture, but thousands of enthusiasts still travel for miles to get near the brightly lighted, electronically amplified stage setting with the current favorite group. Concord Pavilion's 15,000-seat amphitheater draws record crowds in California.

Many an ardent high school band member has welcomed the opportunity for using the trumpet or saxophone after high school. Municipal recreation programs and other community groups are finding a real enthusiasm for municipal bands, community orchestras, state symphonies, scout fife and drum corps, American Legion bands, and similar organizations. Recreation agencies are in an excellent position to aid in the organization and coordination of such units and to make facilities available.

Special events that bring enjoyment to consumers and performers include talent shows, festivals, song-writing contests, concert tours, concert attendance, or special pageants. The Pittsfield, Massachusetts, Senior Citizens' Club combines travel and musical fun with a trip to Tanglewood, a famous music area, each year. All kinds of professional concerts for children are opening new recreation outlooks for future generations. Symphonic music is more available than ever before. Many radio stations fight the competition of television by offering long hours of the best in music, whether rock, country, classical, or "middle of the road" sound.

Some Problems in Music Programming

Too many music programs for recreation never progress past the very elementary stages of rhythm or jug-and-bottle bands, community singing, listening hours, and singing games. Budgets for programming in small communities are still not adequate to provide a broad cafeteria of opportunities for playing, listening, singing, or creating. Through better cooperation between the educational institutions and the recreation agencies, a progression of outlets must be offered in leisure for those who have explored music education in the school programs and would enjoy demanding musical opportunities.

Emphasis on and recognition for participation in instrumental or singing groups would help to stimulate the interest of many who could profit by musical recreation. Social conditioning should create a somewhat different public image of the musician, so that joining the chorus will be just as attractive as going out for basketball.

Basic to the expansion of musical activity in community programs is the acceptance of the idea that tastes for musical activities differ radically but that those tastes may be cultivated. *Good* music may connote classical masterpieces to one individual and the latest popular tunes to another. Musical tastes have too often become a mark of class or social distinction. In a recreation situation, the leader must find those musical activities that will prove enjoyable, give pleasure, and provide satisfaction for those participating. Too much emphasis on form and technique may make a tedious chore out of what could have been an emotional communication through music; on the other hand, complete lack of information may deny enjoyment for those who cannot interpret or participate successfully without such education. As in any of the arts, the leader must be sensitive to the needs of the group in order to select intelligently, introduce enthusiastically, and lead sensitively in the musical medium.

Integration with Other Program Areas

The possibilities for interweaving music with other program areas are so obvious and so numerous that little time will be spent on their enumeration. Music enhances or complements game activities, swimming, skating, and dancing; it combines with drama in the opera, pageant, and festival; it joins with the nature program in the hiking songs or the concert under the stars; it shares in social gatherings, in hobbies, and in special events of all kinds. Music knows no boundaries in setting; it adapts readily to its setting or to its participants with a universal appeal upon which the recreation leader should capitalize.

Trends

We have come a long way from the pre–Industrial Revolution days when it was necessary to travel to New York to hear Beethoven's Fifth Symphony. The New York Philharmonic performed in a half-dozen concerts in 1875. Today, local or state symphonies offer programs closer at hand. Literally millions are enrolled in the "society of music appreciators" through recordings. Thousands more are experiencing the pleasure of listening to talented stars on television, on radio, or in person in community concert series.

Hospitals, industries, and penal institutions are increasing their opportunities for musical outlets in leisure. Schools are placing more emphasis on music in the elementary grades. There has been an increasing number of bandshells, auditoriums, and listening rooms in the plans of new recreation facilities. Music from simple rhythms to the complexities of the opera will continue to entice the American public in their leisure hours. In the words of V. K. Brown, former Director of Recreation for the Chicago Park District, "When music dies, recreation dies with it."

Outdoor Recreation

We are still children of nature. For periods of time humans may wall themselves up in a cubbyhole, breathe noxious air, walk on a straight cement path in a canyon of steel and concrete, and work and play by artificial light. But sooner or later we break loose and seek the land—to bask in the sun, to plunge our hands into rich black soil, to cast a line after an elusive trout, or to test our skill against a mountain's height.

Outdoor recreation deals with the manifold leisure pursuits related to the use, enjoyment, and understanding of the outdoors. It encompasses interests as different as fishing, contemplating a sunset, and gathering shells on an ocean beach. The desires for adventure, for learning about the natural world, and for finding the beautiful are universal, and it is these desires that outdoor recreation seeks to satisfy.

The last few decades have seen a phenomenal turning to the outdoors during leisure. It would be difficult to find anyone beyond the first years of childhood who does not participate in some way in outdoor-related activities. See Figure 11.3 for a breakdown of the number of participants in various outdoor activities.

Although the vast landholdings of the federal and state governments constitute the major outdoor recreation land and water resources, local resources, both public and private, add considerably to the wealth of opportunities for outdoor enjoyment. They include playgrounds, community centers, outdoor skills areas, natural areas restricted to environmental studies, day and resident camps, nature centers, zoos, botanical gardens, garden centers, tract gardens, home gardens, vacant lots, parks, forest preserves, lakes, beaches, and many other areas.

The private sector, which controls two thirds of American land, provides a large share of outdoor recreation land. Enterprises such as the following suggest the diversity offered privately, either for profit or not for profit: recreation parks; family and children's camps; hunting and fishing on private property; hotels,

Figure 11.2. Interest in hot-air ballooning has grown in recent years.

resorts, and guest ranches; marinas and boat rentals; ski slopes and lifts; and horseback rentals and riding areas. Nonprofit groups such as yacht clubs, hunting and fishing clubs, saddle clubs, hiking clubs, outdoor hobby groups, and outdoor craft groups are further contributions of the private sector.

Varieties of Outdoor Recreation

How recreation offers something for everybody is evident in the following paragraphs.

Hunting and fishing. Perhaps the urge to hunt and fish is inborn, dating back to primitive days when survival depended upon skills in securing food. Large numbers of Americans today hunt or fish or do both (see

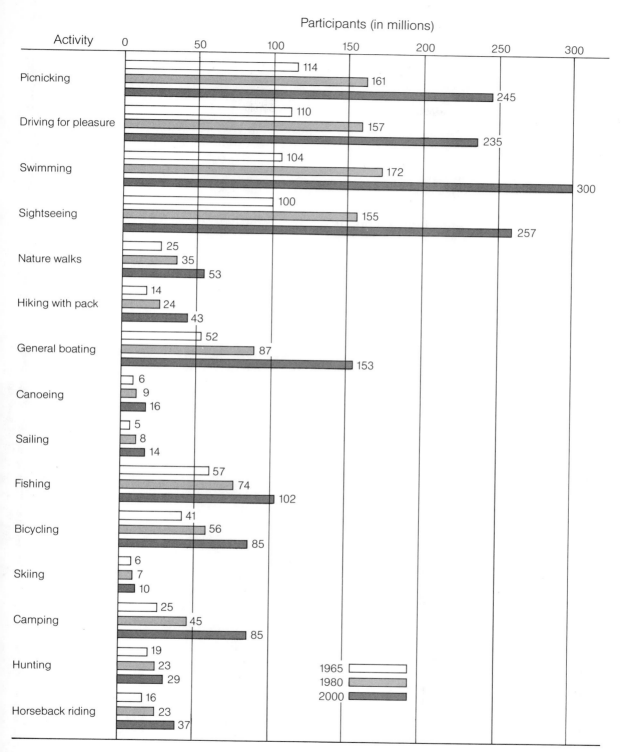

Figure 11.3. The number of outdoor participants projected to the year 2000.

232   Leisure Choices—What and Where?

Figure 11.4). The efforts of large national and state agencies are required to sustain these sports, which are financed primarily by license fees.

Hunting with guns and with bows and arrows, trapping, fishing in both fresh and salt waters, and collecting clams, abalone, and other shell fish occupy much leisure; however, hunting poses many problems for the future. Because of our large population, the places in which wildlife can live and reproduce have diminished hazardously at the same time as the numbers of hunters have increased. Hope for the continued existence of wild birds and animals lies in (1) the evidence that there are far more people than ever before interested in *observing* rather than *shooting* wildlife, (2) the continued investment of money from hunting and fishing licenses in wildlife habitats, and (3) stringent enforcement of hunting and fishing laws. Reconciling the hunters' interests with environmental concerns will nonetheless continue for some time to trouble administrators of natural resources.

High-risk adventure. Sedentary and prosaic living demands an outlet for some people in the form of dangerous adventure. Rock climbing, plane and kite sailing, parachute jumping, white-water canoeing, wilderness skiing, and similar activities involving high risks are such outlets. Instruction in these skills reduces the danger that might otherwise accompany them.

Figure 11.4. The promise of a catch lures millions of fishermen.

Figure 11.5. A college class backpacks into the Sierras.

Informal camping. Camping has been one of the most rapidly growing activities in recent years. It has numerous forms: camping in tents, trailers, and motor homes; or wilderness camping on sites reached by foot, canoe, horseback, snowmobiles, or all-terrain vehicle.

Trips by backpackers and canoeists have shown such phenomenal growth that they create problems for managers of wilderness areas. How many people can a wilderness support and still endure as wilderness? Since many of the wilderness adventurers are unskilled, they endanger their own safety and make more difficult the task of administrators who must protect both the visitor and the environment. Because of these difficulties, permits for back-country camping are now required in most national parks.

Over five million American families now own one or more recreation vehicles. A whole host of camping and trailer clubs, many with national affiliations, offer weekend outings, regional and national get-togethers, and travel by trailer throughout the world. Among these clubs are the Wally Byam Club, the Good Sams, and the National Campers and Hikers Association.

Family campgrounds, both public and private, have grown to accommodate the campers. Campgrounds on public lands tend to be simple. Some private campgrounds have elaborate recreation facilities, including swimming pools, play apparatus, game courts, boat docks, craft rooms, and club houses. These differ from established resorts only in that the patrons bring their own lodgings with them.

Instruction in outdoor living skills, campcraft, health and safety, and survival skills are offered in some communities to prepare individuals for camping experiences.

Organized camps are discussed later in this chapter.

Winter sports. When cold weather comes, some vacationers go south for sunshine, but an ever-increasing number turn to ski slopes and frozen waters and the exhilaration of winter sports. Here they engage in ski-ing, sledding, tobogganing, snow shoeing, snow tracking, snowmobiling, ice skating, ice fishing, and racing on ice.

Water-related recreation. More than half of all outdoor recreation is related to water. Such recreation ranges from sheer aesthetic appreciation to speedboat racing and includes activities in the water and along the shore, such as boating (rowing, sailing, canoeing, kayaking, float trips, scenic river trips), water skiing, swimming, diving, snorkeling, surfing, scuba diving, fishing, hunting, studying water birds and aquatic life, sunbathing, camping on the shore, and collecting shells, driftwood, and rocks.

Outdoor-related literary and artistic activities. From lake, forest, desert, and

Wilderness Disturbed

Three days of steady paddling and four hard portages brought us to this isolated Canadian lake. We pitch camp on a remote point of land, put up the tents, fix a light lunch, and stow away our duffel. We have seen only slight traces of people passing along the portage routes, and undisturbed isolation seems to surround us. We feel that we have left the world of civilization well behind. Now we get the canoes ready, put in the fishing tackle, and set out to try our fishing skills on the wilderness lake.

From far to the south we hear the noise of a plane. Our hearts sink as we watch it come into view, circle once, and come to rest on "our" lake. Four men pile out, unlash a canoe, quickly get out their tackle, and make ready to fish.

"This just isn't fair," says Hank. "They've taken the wilderness away," adds Otto. "Let's move on."

Should some places be reserved for those who want solitude and are willing to undergo hardships to get it?

Although airplanes are not allowed in designated wilderness areas in the United States, there are millions of wilderness acres not so designated on which planes may land. Many people have neither the time nor the physical energy for a strenuous canoe trip, backpack trip, or horseback trip. Should they have the right to visit wilderness areas?

What are the objections to motors in the wilderness?

seashore comes inspiration for creative expression through writing poetry and prose, painting, sketching, molding, weaving, photography, and carving. In the outdoors also are harvested materials used in arts and crafts—seeds, nuts, shells, clay, cones, pine needles, cattails, rushes, honeysuckle, native woods, driftwood, fibers, and dyes.

Interest in natural science provides incentive for much craft work, such as making terrariums and aquariums; weather stations; birdhouses and feeding tables; and insect nets, killing jars, and mounting boards. The desire to understand, identify, and display natural objects leads to collecting and arranging leaves, flowers, rocks, insects, and fossils, and to making prints and casts.

Horseback riding. Surprisingly, there are more horses in the United States today than there were a hundred years ago. The work animal has become a recreation animal. Saddle clubs, riding stables, bridle trails in forests and parks, horse shows, and horse racing are evidences of the high interest in this favored animal.

Horseback trips in mountain wilderness attract great numbers of people. In many places special campgrounds and resorts are operated for riders, their mounts, and their pack animals.

Bicycling. Despite traffic hazards, the scarcity of special trails, and the use of automobiles even for short trips, the old-fashioned sport of bicycling has revived. Next to walking and swimming, it is probably the favorite form of outdoor exercise.

In recent years some money has been available for constructing trails for cyclists. Many cities have designated lightly used roads as bicycle routes and have marked bicycle lanes on some streets. Abandoned railroad tracks and old canal banks are being converted

for use by cyclists. Cycling clubs, cross-country bicycle tours, and provisions for cyclists in campgrounds are increasing. Motorized bicycles (mopeds) are increasingly popular.

Experiences in natural science. In this category we place activities that are directly related to the understanding, appreciation, and enjoyment of nature. Although home yards, vacant lots, farms, cemeteries, or almost any open space can be a setting for nature experiences, special lands and developments invite participation. These include: parks, ponds, lakes, streams, zoos, wildlife reserves, nature centers, museums, planetariums, aquariums, botanical gardens, camps, and natural areas.

Practically all of the natural sciences are involved, notably botany, zoology, geology, and astronomy, not as separate subjects but as part of the total outdoor experience. A brief list of typical activities includes field trips, outdoor explorations, bird watching, star study, outdoor photography, raising pets, gardening, nature games, and maintaining aquariums and terrariums.

Interpretive services attract many visitors to forests, parks, camps, reserves, historical sites, and resorts, both public and commercial. The programs are generally directed toward aspects of the environment that pertain especially well at a given site—for example, archeology at Mesa Verde National Park, volcanic action at Hawaii National Park, coastal redwoods at California's Big Sur State Park, and so on.

Interpretive programs are relatively recent developments. The first employed naturalist staff dates back to the 1920s. Today's services often include naturalists, historians, and archeologists and such facilities as visitor centers, nature centers, labeled trails, trailside displays, conducted walks, campfire talks, and tours. More emphasis is placed on ecology and appreciation and less on identification of plants and animals than in earlier years. Because of the large crowds, more self-guiding techniques are used.

Outings and explorations. Many of our outdoor satisfactions depend upon movement and change of scenery. Pleasure driving and sight-seeing are among the most popular forms of outdoor activities.

Automobiles and airplanes have multiplied our capacity and hunger for movement and have made "impossible dreams" of adventure come true. At the same time they have created problems of misuse of our scenic treasures and have contributed to the energy problem. The all-terrain vehicle in particular has caused serious environmental havoc.

Farms, gardens, and forests. Both vegetable and flower gardening have always been important leisure activities for home owners, but interest in gardening has boomed with the rise in food costs. It was estimated that there were thirty-two million home gardens in 1976. While the economic benefits are uppermost in the minds of many gardeners, there is no doubt that the joy of planting and harvesting is reward enough for others.

It is more difficult for apartment dwellers, especially in crowded sections of cities, to have gardens; but even they have found it practical to put tomato plants among their flower pots on sunny balconies. Many park and recreation departments offer both instruction and space in tract gardens, usually at a small cost, especially for those who have no space for gardens at home.

Community forests have made it possible for both children and adults to plant and to care for forest trees and to develop an understanding of the principles of conservation.

Socializing out-of-doors. An informal outdoor get-together with good friends, good weather, and good food—in other words, the ever-popular picnic—is among the most widespread forms of outdoor recreation. Similar and also popular are cookouts, holiday celebrations, outdoor parties, and campfire programs.

Trends and Needs

Participation in outdoor recreation has increased at a much more rapid rate than has the population, and this trend is expected to continue. Growth has been most rapid in visits to parks and forests, water activities, camping, cycling, sight-seeing, and picnicking.

Serious environmental problems have accompanied this increase. Conflicts have arisen over such matters as wilderness protection; the use of all-terrain vehicles in deserts and forests; conflicting and incompatible recreation uses of a given area; and overuse of outstanding scenic, scientific, and historic sites. Various methods of solving these problems include enlarging recreation landholdings, restricting the numbers of people and vehicles allowed in overcrowded areas, encouraging visits to seldom-used parks and forests, developing special sites for active recreation in order to relieve the strain on much-loved but sensitive natural areas, and educating the population in the care of natural resources. Vandalism, theft, litter, and destructive play have made shambles of many a beautiful spot. Education in resource use and enjoyment has become a vital necessity and may be the best route to permanent protection.

Most of the federal recreation lands are in the western states, and the large eastern population has little access to public land. In order to distribute opportunities more fairly, efforts are under way to acquire semi-wilderness lands and lands for intensive recreation use in the eastern states.

Energy shortages will probably force a redirection of outdoor recreation toward non–energy-using activities such as cycling, hiking, sailing, environmental studies, and simple outdoor enjoyment and appreciation, using nearby areas rather than those far from home.

Organized Camping

Camping is simple outdoor living, with the camper assuming some responsibility for food and shelter and pursuing activities related to his or her surroundings. Whether camping involves large groups or small, its distinctive aspect is its close contact with the natural environment.

The term *organized camping* is applied to a program, usually for young people, that includes leadership, educational objectives, outdoor living in a group, and a program related to the outdoors. To the child it must spell fun and adventure; to the parent it must imply a safe and satisfying vacation for the child; and to the camp director it means the opportunity to contribute to the child's physical, intellectual, and emotional growth. All three viewpoints are integrated in the program of the superior camp.

Basic Organization

In terms of basic organization, the following types of organized camps are recognized.

Resident camp. In a resident or established camp, children stay usually from five days to eight weeks. The camp has a permanent base, usually with permanent buildings and other developments.

Group camp. A group or troop camp consists of a preexisting group, such as a scout troop, which attends camps as a unit, usually under the direction of its regular leaders. There is a bare minimum of facilities; groups bring their own camping equipment and plan their own programs.

Travel camp. Organized groups traveling by foot, car, bus, covered wagon, horseback, ship, float boat, bicycle, or canoe constitute travel camps, which generally have no permanent bases. Campers carry their own equipment and use public or private lands for overnight or longer stays.

Day camp. A day camp operates only during the day; campers sleep at home at night. Because many kinds of programs are labeled "day camps," even though they may have no relationship to camping, it is desirable to limit the name to programs that take place in natural and varied outdoor areas and in which at least part of the program is related to the outdoors. The day camp should accommodate small groups under leadership and should last at least six hours daily for five or more days.

Sponsorship

In terms of sponsorship, camps fall into four major categories.

Camps conducted by voluntary agencies. This category, which comprises the largest number of camps, includes camps operated by all the major youth-serving agencies. Generally these camps last only one or two weeks. Their price is reasonable, since part of the cost is usually borne by the sponsoring agency.

Private camps. These camps are operated by individuals or groups for profit. Camp periods are commonly four to eight weeks in length. There are about 3,000 private camps in the United States.

Camps operated by religious organizations. The three major faith groups—Catholic, Protestant, and Jewish—all carry on camping programs, usually not longer than one week in duration and moderate in price. The sponsors commonly assume part of the expense, and counselors are seldom paid. Religious instruction or observances are usually part of the program. A recent trend is to provide for family camping.

Camps operated by public agencies. Schools, park and recreation departments, and, less frequently, other public agencies sometimes operate camps. Most of these are day camps, but a number of resident camps are also operated, particularly in the West.

Program Emphasis

Most camps appeal to the normal child, and their programs cover a wide range of activities, geared neither to special interests nor to special problems. Some camps emphasize particular fields, such as music, arts and crafts, woodcraft, natural science, dramatics, athletics, riding, folk dancing, language, and even work projects. These special-interest camps usually include some general program activities to give variety. Older boys or girls often find these camps appealing, since they give them opportunities to develop skill and competence in a field of their choice.

Special-Purpose Camps

One of the most interesting developments in recent years is the emergence of the special-purpose camp to serve children with unusual problems or needs. There are camps today for diabetic, orthopedically handicapped, blind, cerebral palsied, and mentally retarded children, as well as those with other disabilities. Intended to give handicapped children experiences often denied them because of their physical ailments, the camps are not planned primarily as means of treatment, although living with other children and participating in the camp programs under good leadership are themselves forms of therapy. If a handicap is not so severe as to keep a child from adjusting in a camp with normal children, it is usually preferable to place the child there rather than in a special-purpose camp.

Children are not the only ones to benefit from special-purpose camps. Camps for the aged, particularly day camps, are popular. Camps for delinquents, for younger adults with physical and mental problems, and camps that integrate different age groups (aged and children) are now available.

Organized Camping Today

Organized camping expanded slowly before 1900, but the growth gained speed in the following years. Today about eight million children attend resident summer camps. There are at least 11,000 organized camps in the United States, about 8,000 of which are resident camps; the rest are day camps, troop camps, and other types. Organized camping has spread to all parts of the world. Now that it has become a major education-recreation movement, its place in the accepted pattern of youth services seems secure.

Goals of Camping

At its best, organized camping blends education and recreation. The camp has certain characteristics that make it effective in influencing behavior, teaching skills, and developing new interests.

1. The strong appeal of the outdoors makes the child eager to learn.

2. The fact that the child lives day in and day out with a small group of companions of similar age and interests on a friendly basis with a counselor offers numerous informal educational opportunities.

3. The camp program is one of doing; it consists of firsthand experiences.

This combination makes the camp a powerful educational setting and at the same time places on it the responsibility of seeing that its influence is constructive.

The following goals of camping are widely accepted:

1. Learning to live outdoors and become acquainted with the outdoor environment

2. Experiencing individual growth and development

3. Learning to live and work together

4. Practicing health and safety

5. Developing new skills and interests and perfecting old ones

6. Developing spiritual meanings and values

7. Enjoying a recreation experience

Notice that these objectives, except for the first, are held in common with youth-serving groups and, in part, with schools. Camp programs must be planned with these objectives in mind. A camp is not merely a place in which to keep children entertained; it is a place in which they may achieve, assume responsibility, learn to live with others, and find satisfaction in the world of nature.

What Happens in Camp

The camp program consists of everything that happens to the camper, including planned and unplanned activities. It is through the program that the purposes of the camp are attained.

How the program is determined. Even camps with general programs differ a great deal in their emphases. Some of the factors that determine the program are:

1. The philosophy of those who conduct the camp

2. The location, topography, and climate

3. The interests, skills, and understanding of the leaders

4. The background, age, physical characteristics, and interests of the clientele

5. Available facilities and equipment

6. The length of the camp period

7. Expectations of the campers' parents

Ideally the leadership, location, facilities, equipment, and even the length of stay at the camp should be determined by the program; but in practical application the reverse is true.

Unique program possibilities. The camp situation, in which children live together outdoors and use the natural environment, offers program possibilities unavailable in other situations. By concentrating on these possibilities rather than repeating activities that can be carried on in the school, playground, club, or community center, camps can fulfill a unique function.

How the program is carried out. Those conducting the camp usually determine how the program is organized, but the day-to-day planning should involve both the staff and the campers. The staff must be prepared with program ideas, but the campers should have opportunities to plan and choose among the program possibilities. There are four groupings in which the program may take place.

1. The small group of campers that live together—In some camps, most of the program revolves around this basic unit; in other camps, unit activities are minimal.

2. The interest group, such as a group concerned with arts and crafts, swimming, sailing, or innumerable other activities—Campers who live in the same unit may be in completely separate interest groups. Interest groups offer both the advantage of free choice and the opportunity to develop proficiency in particular skills.

3. The entire camp—All campers participate together in such activities as campfire programs, meals, and special celebrations.

4. The individual—Campers need some free time in which to read, relax, write letters, and attend to personal matters.

Most camps offer programs in all four categories.

Flexible and balanced scheduling. Recently camps have turned away from scheduled class periods to flexible scheduling, with long blocks of time available for various programs. Certain aspects of camp living must of course be scheduled; time must be clearly allotted for sleep, rest, meals, and camp chores. Apart from this basic scheduling, considerable freedom may be allowed.

A balance of strenuous and quiet activities and of small group and mass programs should be maintained. Good programming affords diversity. Programs must be inviting and challenging; but overstimulation must be avoided, as it produces a tired and irritable camper.

Program areas. Programs especially suited to the camp include: water activities; campcraft and woodcraft, including constructing shelters and fire building; arts and crafts; nature, ecology, and conservation; Indian life; sports and games; dramatics; music; social activities and dancing; and high-challenge activities, such as wilderness living and self-reliance programs for older campers as in the Outward Bound schools.

Camp Sites and Facilities

A site with varied natural resources and suitable facilities helps to create a good camp program. In resident and troop camps, there should be at least one acre per camper, most of it in a natural condition. Day camps may operate on smaller sites, but the land should be somewhat isolated and provide assorted program opportunities. Water for swimming and boating is desirable for the day camp and essential for the resident camp.

Camp facilities range from the rugged to the luxurious. All camps must provide for access, parking, safe water, sanitary food handling, refrigeration, sanitary waste disposal,

and fire protection. State boards of health generally inspect camps to insure safe and sanitary operations.

Group or troop camps, to which campers bring their own equipment, require little beyond basic necessities. Many of them maintain trading posts where campers may purchase supplies, as well as rainy-day shelters, cooking areas, and tent sites. Day camp facilities may be even simpler, since overnight shelters and trading posts are unnecessary. Some day camps maintain dining halls and kitchens; but generally children bring their own lunches or cook outdoors.

Resident camps require the most elaborate facilities—dining halls, well-equipped kitchens with electricity and refrigeration, tents or cabins, central lodges, infirmaries, campfire circles, central wash houses, laundries, docks, and beaches. To these, some camps add stables, craft shops, museums, chapels, game courts and diamonds, garages, and recreation halls.

Since most modern camps are decentralized, the living quarters, instead of being in a formal, close arrangement, are grouped into separated units or small camps. Such seclusion permits programs in small groups without prohibiting total-camp programs.

The Staff

More than 200,000 leaders staff U.S. camps. Most of them are teachers or college students employed in camp only in the summer. The American Camping Association has developed standards for camp staff that describe the age, education, experience, and personal qualifications necessary for various staff members, including the director, counselors, and program specialists. Qualified personnel are also required by the business, health, and food services and for camp maintenance.

The basic organization of personnel in a resident camp is indicated in Figure 11.6.

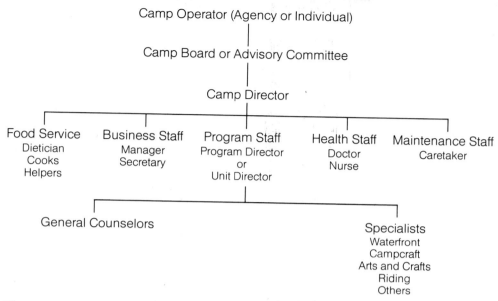

Figure 11.6. The administrative structure of a resident camp.

Trends and Problems

Although about forty percent of American children have at least one experience in camp, organized camping has not expanded at the rate once anticipated. Several reasons may be suggested. First, the population of camp-age children has not grown and in some places has actually decreased. Second, the cost of camping has increased; while wealthy children or poor children with camperships may find it possible to get to camp, children from middle-income families may not be able to afford the expense. Third, more summer recreation activities than ever before compete for children's time. Family camping has grown tremendously, and many parents consider it a substitute for organized camping.

Camps now reach out for the disadvantaged and minority groups. The American Camping Association, as a matter of policy, accepts membership only from camps that are open to campers of all races. With financial help from camperships and federal funds,

children from these groups have been able to attend camp.

More camps are being winterized as year-round use increases. Camps remain open for weekends and vacations during the off-season and for school programs during the school year.

The national standards program of the American Camping Association has improved adherence to desirable practices in camp operation. In most states, legislation regulating camp practices, particularly in health and safety, has expanded. Federal legislation to establish more uniform camp regulations and to make federal funds available has been under consideration.

Since camps are operated by diverse agencies and individuals with their own ideas and ideals, no single pattern of camping is possible. It is hoped that efforts to improve camping will not standardize the camps to such an extent that the unique and imaginative practices of innovative camp operators will be eliminated.

Social Recreation

There is nothing new about social recreation. Whenever two or more individuals come together, there is potential social recreation. On the streets of ancient Greece, social recreation was found in the leisurely, pleasant or bombastic, persuasive discussions of those who met for social conversation. In early London, the coffeehouses, like the grand ballrooms, afforded a chance for fun and fellowship with others. The earliest social recreation in America was found perhaps in the clandestine taverns of the seventeenth century or in the kissing games and card parties of the eighteenth century. The hardy pioneers combined their work and play to engage in wrestling contests or country dancing after a day of husking or barn-raising had brought neighbors together. In essence, social recreation can, and does, involve almost any activity, any age group, and any setting. One has only to look at the objectives of those involved in participation to determine what activities lie within the confines of this area.

Definition and Scope

Social recreation may best be defined as any recreation activity in which the stimulating or motivating force for participation is the basic social drive, the need to interrelate with people. Within such a definition, the scope of social recreation is limited only by the imagination and the ingenuity of the leadership available. The media through which social recreation can take place may range from mere conversation to games, or from dance to arts and crafts. Regardless of the medium, the underlying objective is the same. The participants are seeking *fun through fellowship*, the camaraderie that takes place when persons come together to know each other better in a relaxed atmosphere conducive to the building of cooperation rather than competition.

Although many activities may be simultaneously within the categories of social recreation and other types of recreation, depending upon the objectives involved, the following traits usually characterize the purely social event:

1. The emphasis in social recreation is on the interrelationships of people. The participants attend or are involved primarily because they want to meet others.

2. Social recreation demands little or no advance preparation on the part of the participant.

3. The emphasis on degree of skill for performers is minimized.

4. The emphasis is on cooperation, not competition.

5. The approach to the activity is usually informal.

6. The event can take place anytime, anywhere, and with any number.

7. No special equipment is needed by the participant. Many items may be needed for the leader, however; the tools of social recreation are varied.

8. The event should be an *integrating* activity, if it is truly in the social recreation realm. It should give repeated opportunities for the participants to meet or mingle.

Types

Although music, drama, art, or any other kind of recreation that involves more than one person may be used as a tool for social recreation, certain activities are noted for their primary emphasis on social objectives. They may involve one or more activity media. The following list is selective rather than inclusive:

1. Conversation, sometimes known as "the lost art," allows for better understanding of the feelings and ideas of others.

2. Teas and coffee hours may range from the informal college coffee-break to the very formal reception.

3. Parties centered around anything from a televised sport event to a holiday get-together are basic socializers.

4. Banquets, dinners, and picnics involve a meal, before, during, and after which groups find fellowship.

5. Game rooms and drop-in centers provide facilities in which people get acquainted or renew friendships.

6. Corecreation sports nights allow "boy-meets-girl" opportunities.

7. Outings that allow groups to travel together afford social recreation experiences.

8. Special events such as festivals, fairs, carnivals, and campfires provide the atmosphere and media for social participation.

Into these social events, characterized by a particular method of organization or by a special environment, the leader may weave arts and crafts, sports and games of both active and quiet nature, dance, dramatic outlets, music, nature lore, or mental and linguistic activities.

Leadership

The social recreation specialist is a social engineer, and, as such, must be personable, dynamic enough to move the larger groups, and sensitive enough to involve the smaller gatherings. At times, leadership must assume proportions of showmanship adequate to call a dance for 100 square dancers; at times, the best leadership technique is inconspicuous prodding done as a functioning member of a group in a songfest around a campfire. The wise leader learns to study the situation, feel the pulse of those involved, and recognize when to assert direct and forceful stimulation or control and when to allow the sequence of events seemingly to evolve from the participants. A leader must have enough social poise to disguise any feelings of insecurity before a group and enough humility and good sense to share the spotlight with others when the opportunity arises.

Services to the Community

In social recreation the municipal recreation department's responsibility does not and must not stop with the provision of a staff member reasonably versed in the arts of planning and executing social recreation gatherings, although provision of a social recreation specialist might help motivate the following types of services.

Consultant services for individuals or organizations. The specialist should be available for ideas or guidance in planning with committees from organizations who will sponsor and conduct their own programs but need help in planning.

Organization. The municipal agency is in an excellent position to stimulate coordination of social recreation events that involve large segments of the population. Publishing a calendar of events or acting as a clearinghouse when dates for socials are being considered greatly increases the chances for successful programs in the community. Some cities have found that the organization of a council to handle coordination and other social recreation needs has been a worthwhile innovation.

Resources. Some recreation departments lend backyard and picnic kits on a sign-out basis and have found that the demand far exceeds the supply. Other recreation departments offer the use of books, films, and public-address systems for social recreation events. Providing a card file of social recreation ideas at the department office and publishing monthly idea bulletins for parties have proved popular services. Establishing a name file of volunteers able to help with social recreation gatherings gives service opportunities to persons with special capabilities and, at the same time, enlarges the amount of social recreation leadership, otherwise financially impossible.

Training. The recreation department is often in the best position to organize social recreation institutes, which may involve the training of volunteers, subprofessionals, or professionals from churches, schools, youth-serving agencies, 4-H clubs, and industry.

Special Problems

As in most program areas, social recreation finds itself with special problems, which are listed here.

False impressions. Probably the greatest problem that arises in the social recreation area is the tardiness of the profession as a whole to recognize the social recreationist as a specialist, instead of a personable "Jack-of-all-trades," who is expected to pull something exciting out of a hat if a lull is experienced in any group setting.

Lack of careful planning. Too often, the inexperienced group relies on the false philosophy that if you get people together, they will naturally have fun. A careful, if inconspicuous, plan for making the first arrivals feel welcome and for sending off the group before enthusiasm wanes is social insurance. Inflexible leaders who stick to a plan that is not working create havoc.

Failure to involve people in the planning. Plans must be made *with,* not *for,* the people who are going to be involved. The social recreation leader who forces a plan without consultation or guidance from representative committees may expect difficulties. Social recreation is a "we" proposition.

The overenthusiastic leader. In social recreation, the novice leader all too frequently keeps the party going at such a fast pace of activity that participants have no time in which to explore further the interesting new friends whom they met in the last mixer. Overplanning activities without breaks and overemphasis on constant participation defeat the very purpose of the event and lend a somewhat odious reputation to the social recreation specialty. Intelligent planning and controlled zeal remedy such situations.

Absence of petty cash funds. The amount of money spent by most social recreation specialists during any given year would add up to cash totals that could not be called "petty." In spite of the reluctance of most departments to establish petty cash funds, social recreation frequently necessitates unexpected expenditures of small amounts. Items such as balloons, string, and crepe paper can be estimated and provided for in yearly budget plans, but the need for candies, potatoes, oranges, or a variety of other perishables that enhance an otherwise ordinary relay or provide prizes for a party may not be so easily predictable. Petty cash funds are a necessity for the social recreation leader.

Lack of evaluation. All too frequently, the important evaluation of what happened and why it happened at the social event is minimized with the statement, "Well, I guess they all had fun together." Until the social recreation leader looks objectively at each experience and explores with the committees the reasons for the successful or the unsuccessful moments, the quality of the experiences cannot hope to improve.

The Future

Social recreation touches every other program area. In a people-oriented profession, it is a very significant area, but it has yet to emerge as a distinctive program category in the minds of many professionals. The ability to use the media of sport, drama, dance, or any other program area for the purpose of channeling meaningful social interaction takes special skills in human relations. Perhaps, in the curriculums of the future, every professional will move through experiences which will make him or her a social recreation specialist in addition to acquiring other needed skills.

Sports and Games

For the first ten years of life, education shall be predominantly physical; every school is to have a playground; play and sport are to be the entire curriculum and in this decade such health will be stored up as will make all medicine unnecessary. —Plato

The growth of sports and games in the United States has been phenomenal. Sports appeal to all ages, in the form of either actual participation or spectator interest. A casual drive through the average community reveals the drawing power that sports and games have in our leisure hours. A pick-up softball game on the vacant lot, children playing hopscotch on the sidewalk, and the basketball hoops above the garage doors are but a few indications of the widespread participation in sports and games.

Cities, through their park and recreation departments, are confronted with increased demands for tennis courts, swimming pools, ballfields, skating rinks, marinas, golf courses, driving ranges, and other facilities normally found in our playgrounds, playfields, and parks. Our present facilities are jammed to capacity.

The tremendous numbers of commercial recreation activities indicate that the American public is willing to pay for its recreation. Some of the new "bowling palaces" are actually extensive recreation centers and are a far cry from the smoke-filled bowling alleys and pool halls of the past. See Chapter 3 for details of the economic impact of sports.

Each year new highs are reached in the attendance at amateur and professional sports events. Additional teams and leagues in professional baseball and football have been necessitated by the increased demands for more baseball and football games in cities throughout the country.

In the ten-year span from 1966 to 1976, the number of spectators attending the eighteen most popular sporting events increased from 216 million to 314 million, an increase of forty-five percent. Leading the list of all spectator sports was thoroughbred racing with 51.2 million spectators; auto racing was second with 50 million spectators attending each year. See Table 11.1 for additional details.

Sports and games are not strictly a city phenomenon, nor are they participated in exclusively by youth. These activities appeal to all ages, both sexes, the physically strong as well as the handicapped, and people in all environs. Children are introduced to sports at an early age in our schools, community centers, playgrounds, camps, youth-serving agencies, churches, and homes. Because of these backgrounds, sports are perhaps the easiest of all recreation activities to promote.

Table 11.2 shows that swimming remains the most popular participant sport in the United States, followed by bicycling and fishing. Tennis and snow skiing are the fastest-growing sports.

Types of Activities

Sports and games, as a part of a community's total recreation program, should be organized to meet the needs and interests of the many, not the few; of the novice as well as the

Table 11.1. Numbers of Spectators at Sporting Events

| | Attendance | | |
	1966 (in millions)	1976 (in millions)	Percentage increase
1. Thoroughbred racing	40.9	51.2	25%
2. Auto racing	39.0	50.0	28
3. Major-league baseball	25.2	32.6	29
4. College football	25.3	32.0	26
5. Harness racing	23.2	30.7	32
6. College basketball	17.0	25.5	50
7. Greyhound racing	11.1	19.0	71
8. Professional football	7.7	15.0	95
9. Major-league hockey	3.1	14.4	365
10. Minor-league baseball	10.1	11.3	12
11. Professional basketball	2.3	8.5	270
12. Professional wrestling	4.8	5.0	4
13. Minor-league hockey	2.9	4.9	69
14. College hockey	0.8	3.4	325
15. Professional boxing	1.7	3.2	88
16. Professional soccer	Negligible	2.8	—
17. Professional golf	1.5	2.3	53
18. Professional tennis	Negligible	2.2	—
Total	216.6	314.0	45

Note: Attendance figures are for seasons ending in 1966 and 1976, including professional teams in Canada.

Source: Reprinted from *U.S. News & World Report,* May 23, 1977. Copyright 1977 *U.S. News & World Report.*

highly skilled; of the young and the old; of the physically strong and the handicapped; and of the women and girls along with men and boys. They can be classified under the following major groupings.

Low organized games and contests. Activities of this type have value and interest especially to younger children. They are in-

formal in nature and do not require a high degree of organization. Few rules are needed, and usually a variable number of players can participate. The skills needed are simple but they are most important in that they provide experience for more complex and highly organized games. Games of this type can be participated in by individuals of various ages and therefore must be adapted to the physical

Table 11.2. Twenty-five Sports with the Most Participants

	Participants in 1976 (in millions)
1. Swimming	103.5
2. Bicycling	75.0
3. Fishing	63.9
4. Camping	58.1
5. Bowling	44.4
6. Pool/billiards	35.8
7. Boating	35.2
8. Table tennis	32.2
9. Tennis	29.2
10. Softball	27.3
11. Basketball	25.8
12. Ice skating	25.8
13. Hunting	20.5
14. Golf	16.6
15. Baseball	15.7
16. Football	14.9
17. Water skiing	14.7
18. Snow skiing	11.0
19. Motorbiking/ motorcycling	9.7
20. Snowmobiling	9.2
21. Jogging	8.5
22. Sailing	7.3
23. Archery	5.5
24. Handball	5.3
25. Racquetball	2.7

Source: Reprinted from *U.S. News & World Report,* May 23, 1977. Copyright 1977 *U.S. News & World Report.*

The Ten Fastest-Growing Sports

	Increase in participants 1973–76
Tennis	45%
Snow skiing	42
Jogging	31
Snowmobiling	19
Basketball	17
Bowling	16
Bicycling	14
Pool/billiards	9
Boating	8
Camping	7

skills, mental abilities, and interests of each age group. Low organized games are of fundamental importance to camp, playground, and other such programs. Examples include: tag, hide-and-seek, dodge ball, relays, club snatch, and three deep.

Individual sports. Although people actually are sociable creatures, many enjoy solitary activities. When friends are not available, lone participation in an activity may be a necessity. Activities that can be engaged in on an individual basis include hunting, fishing, skiing, riding, hiking, backpacking, golf, skating, archery, swimming, bicycling, boating, jogging, walking, and frisbee golf.

Dual sports. The previously mentioned examples of individual sports can be engaged in by two or more people. In fact, most people prefer the sociability of other persons while playing golf, hiking, or bowling. Friendly competition offers added incentive and enjoyment to many sports. Some activities require a minimum of at least two persons for successful participation. Examples include

Figure 11.7. For some, competition may heighten the enjoyment of swimming.

tennis, badminton, table tennis, horseshoes, fencing, wrestling, racquetball, squash, and handball.

Team sports. "Making the team" is an important goal of almost every youngster. It is in team play that the development of cooperative efforts toward common goals is achieved. Competitive play among teams requires a higher degree of organization than do most other kinds of sports activities. More rules and regulations are necessary in conducting team sports. Today, team sports have gained tremendous support in our school, college, and recreation agency programs, with millions of participants in such team activities as basketball, baseball, softball, volleyball, football, and soccer.

Creativity through New Games

The New Games movement (one of the most creative ideas in physical recreation to surface in a generation) offers unique addition and direction to traditional sports programs. In New Games, the goal is for everyone to have fun playing together. It is a people-centered program in which there are no second stringers. Attention is focused on the participants and what is happening to and among them, rather than on rules, regulations, and keeping score. The New Games philosophy teaches group sharing and togetherness. In the "everybody plays, no one gets hurt" philosophy, people have more than a good time. They develop a sense of freedom, creativity, and cooperation with others that sometimes is not found in the more traditional sports programs. Television coverage of the ideas plus leadership seminars and workshops have stimulated increased interest. Research studies in Canada are focusing attention on the results of such approaches to sports and games.

Values

Many values accrue from a well-organized sports and games program.

Fun. People who engage in sports and games do so primarily for fun. These activities, therefore, should be conducted in an atmosphere of fun and adventure. The actual enjoyment, satisfaction, and sense of accomplishment received by the participants are perhaps the richest rewards.

Fitness. Those who participate regularly in vigorous sports and games, including exercise, will enjoy the following benefits:

Better, trimmer physical appearance

More energy with less tendency to fatigue

Lower body weight

Less chance of developing diseases of the heart and arteries

A general slowing of the aging process

Freedom from the necessity for heavy dieting

Less nervous tension

Improved self-discipline

A feeling of well-being

Increased possibility of long life

Competition. The desire to compete with oneself, with another individual or team, or against a standard motivates many to participate in sports activities. This urge starts at an early age when small children "choose sides" to play capture the flag or alley basketball. Competition continues throughout life, and it is in the area of sports and games that competition in leisure activities is most dominant.

Catharsis. Sports and games offer unlimited opportunities for the release of pent-up emotions and stresses of daily living for both spectators and participants. Sports provide opportunity for success, for participants to see themselves as belongers and doers, and for creating a good self-image.

Competition—A Growing Controversy

Many professionals in education, health, medicine, and recreation view with growing alarm the emphasis placed on highly competitive sports at the junior high school level and below. Much has been said and written concerning such nationally sponsored sport programs as Biddy Basketball, Little League, and Pop Warner football. These programs have been charged with overemphasis on winning, exploitation of youth for commercial advertising, parental vanity, and approaches to competition that affect the child's physical and emotional health. Programs of this nature also tend to favor the few highly skilled players instead of the majority. Many communities are taking a critical look at athletic programs provided for boys and girls of this age and are attempting to modify many of the undesirable features.

Gelfand and Hartman suggest that children's involvement in organized competitive sports, particularly the Little League versions of major sports, may produce detrimental effects ranging from cognitive deficits to interpersonal deficiencies.[5] The Committee on the Medical Aspects of Sports of the American Medical Association indicated:

> The undue concern for immediate goals (winning) of the team has contributed in recent years to the depersonalization of the young athlete at all levels of amateur competition. Drug abuse, harsh conditioning methods, inordinate emotional pressures on very young athletes, and aggressive and unsportsmanlike acts are a few of the more common illustrations of the phenomenon.
>
> To prevent the depersonalization of the athlete and improve the humanistic emphasis of amateur sports programs, a number of measures are critical: A governing board needs to be devised, consisting of the coach, athletic trainer or nurse, officials, the team physician, the parents, and, of course, the players themselves. There must be constant attention to prevent abuses. The sports program must evaluate its goals (immediate and long-range) periodically with the needs of the participating youngsters in mind.[6]

Formula for Success

The Board of Directors of the California Park and Recreation Society recently adopted the following statement on competition in sports.[7] Its far-reaching tenets should be studied by all park and recreation agencies.

1. Recreation and park agencies shall evaluate and review their existing sports programs and

policies and adopt the necessary changes in order to insure that their program curriculum offers a full range of sports opportunities for the total community, and that it is not monopolized by the traditional team sport programming concept.

2. Recreation and park agencies shall set behavior objectives in their youth sports programs designed to de-emphasize the importance of winning, and establish participation and fun as the major programming goal. The program objectives shall include youth development, leadership experiences, a de-emphasis of the "all star" concept, and alternatives to traditional award systems.

3. Recreation and park agencies shall provide meaningful involvement of adults who participate in team sports programs. Agencies should organize sports associations' boards of directors and take similar action to insure that the participants will have a strong voice in the administration of the programs. Recreation staff's role should be one of guidance, assistance, and coordination.

4. Recreation and park agencies shall establish and follow an organized plan to maintain a strong balance of time, facility use, funds, and staff for both competitive sport and alternative forms of physical activity, such as individual sports, lifetime sports such as tennis, golf, swimming, etc.

5. Recreation and park agencies shall provide regular and in-depth training to leadership staff in diversified physical activities.

6. Recreation and park agencies shall establish a goal of equal distribution of funds, based on interest, to men's and women's sports programs. Agencies will actively promote women's programs and set an implementation date for equal distribution of funds.

7. Recreation and park agencies shall improve existing programs so as to attract a greater number of women and girls.

8. Recreation and park agencies shall establish the policy that all present and future athletic facilities shall be available to men and women at equally convenient hours.

9. CPRS shall encourage California Park and Recreation Commissioners and Board Members to adopt the principles of these goal statements.

10. CPRS shall use this goals statement to develop dialogue and interaction with related organizations such as California Teachers Association, State Department of Education, CAHPER, and colleges and universities offering degrees in recreation, park and environmental studies.

11. Recreation and park agencies shall assume an advocacy position in regard to local school districts' expenditure of public funds for athletic, recreation, and physical education programs. Special emphasis must be placed on lifetime leisure sports, equal opportunity for women and girls, special programs for the handicapped, and public use of school facilities.

12. Recreation and park agencies shall place a priority on providing sports experiences which are designed to improve self-concept for special populations such as handicapped, juvenile delinquents, older Americans, and disadvantaged young people.

13. The CPRS Competition Committee shall work in close cooperation with the Environmental and Legislative Committee in sponsoring and supporting legislation dealing with sports issues.

14. Recreation and park agencies shall develop agreements (or contracts) which define the behavior of recreation leaders and volunteers who serve as coaches in a youth sports program. This agreement would include a statement of goals of the program, standards of treatment to participants, standards of treatment to officials, and a statement of responsibility for policies and rules pertaining to the program.

15. Recreation and park agencies shall develop a system which will guarantee that youth sports organizations who utilize public facilities meet the requirements of Title IX of the Education Amendments of 1972 with regard to Section 86.41(c) as it relates to recreation programs.

Girls and Women in Sports

No longer can sports and games be considered the special privilege of boys and men. Even before Title IX of the Education Amendment Act of 1972, activities for girls and women were gaining prominence. Factors

Figure 11.8. Sailing.

influencing this emphasis on girls' and women's roles in sports include increased television coverage of major events for women, such as professional tennis, golf, and Olympic events such as gymnastics, track, swimming, diving, ice skating, and skiing. The equal rights movement was still another factor that contributed to the idea that it would be unreasonable and unfair not to allow their participation. There is medical evidence available that participation in athletics is as beneficial for women as it is for men. All of the fitness values listed earlier apply to both sexes. In fact, most medical authorities agree that steady exercise and participation in athletics are helpful in improving the effects of menstrual cycle, and assisting in complication-free pregnancies and ease of delivery. With all this emphasis, Title IX came along and, in essence, said to everybody that it would indeed be unlawful to exclude girls and women from their fair share of the facilities and programs for sports and games.

Use It or Lose It

The evidence is overwhelming; unless the human body is used physically and mentally, it tends to break down. It is one machine that performs better the more it is used. One of the major responsibilities of park and recreation agencies is to provide opportunities for all to pursue whatever form of game, sport, or exercise fits their personal and family life-style.

Service

Voluntary services and citizenship participation represent a traditional American ideal
in community living. In America alone, there
are a reported forty million volunteers working
in charitable, church, community, and other
worthwhile services. To be of service to others
is a most satisfying choice of leisure activity at
any age. Many park and recreation agencies
augment their own program offerings as they
create opportunities for individuals to give
service to others. The desire to be needed and
wanted is basic; service activities help to satisfy
this elemental urge.

Most agencies that offer recreation programs have ample opportunity for stimulating
service activities. Not all agencies have been
wise enough to make use of this challenge. The
youth-serving organizations that depend
largely on volunteers for their face-to-face
leaders capitalize on this approach. The result
provides not only needed services but also rewarding leisure outlets for those who choose
to be of service.

We often forget the strong service urge of
teenagers. Services to others give them a feeling of worth and dignity as well as recognition.
Retirees also find in community services opportunities to keep in contact with people and
substitutes for the busy demands, social role,
or sense of contribution often lost in withdrawal from the labor force, loss of immediate
family, or decreased participation in political,
religious, or school affairs.

Types of Service

The horizons of service possibilities
through which one may aid the community or
other individuals would make an endless list.
They depend upon the needs of the community and the talents of those who serve. The
following ideas are representative of some that
give benefit both to the giver and to the receiver

of the service. Other examples can be found in
Chapter 14.

Clean-up projects. Cleaning up that
river bed, lake shore, roadside, or city lot can
be very rewarding for teens, adults, family
groups, and clubs.

Membership on boards and commissions.
Voluntary service on a park and recreation
board, library board, school board, YMCA
board, or any one of hundreds of others is one
of the highest types of service-oriented activities.

Fund raising. Car washes by teenagers;
soliciting for special projects such as the
mental-health fund; aid in promotion of community bond drives through articles, mass
media interviews, or personal contacts; ticket
selling for special attractions; or duty at the
concession stand are just a few of the money-
raising services performed by all ages.

Professional services. Representatives
of most professions give their talents and
energies to community concerns. Guiding the
planning and layout of facilities, conducting
physical examinations for youngsters who are
to participate in sport or camp activities, directing discussions or lectures, writing or drawing
promotional materials, and instructing special
classes are examples of free services by professionals whose talents augment the programs
serviced.

Transportation and communication.
Many would not be able to participate in activities such as concerts, tournament play,
and camping trips if it were not for those who
give service by chauffeuring the young, the elderly, the handicapped, or others who are
without transportation. The homebound, who
are unable to participate in other activities, find
a real opportunity to help community organizations by providing telephone contacting ser-

vices for special events. Such contact makes the handicapped feel less isolated.

Visiting the ill and handicapped. Individuals and groups find visiting the homebound or institutionalized, in person or by letter, a rewarding service. The "forgotten patient" programs in mental hospitals give patients and visitors satisfactions and lasting rewards.

Officiating at athletic events. Whether the sport activity is a seasonal special or a weekly affair, good officiating is necessary. Extra services are always needed for official timing, scoring, refereeing, and umpiring, if the event is to be beneficial for the participants. Many adults find pleasure in coaching athletic teams in community leagues.

One-time specials. Special events give wide opportunity for service activities. The garden club holds a "planting day" to give the playground or park a much-needed landscape face-lifting; the older person who no longer has a family for whom to cook prepares the pre-performance meal for the high school drama club; many prominent citizens judge costume parades or pet shows in recreation programs. Such specials lend variety to the service and do not commit the volunteer to extended obligations.

Continuing leadership roles. Accepting responsibility for a scout troop, instructing a class, serving Grey Lady or Candy Striper duty at the hospital, and sponsoring a church young people's group all provide opportunities for continuing service. Frequently, the rewards for service in such jobs are greater, though more time-consuming, because the individual can watch the progress, growth, and development of the project.

Service clubs. The programs of service clubs are dealt with in Chapter 9. Suffice it to say here that the organizations are initiated and developed with a service motive.

Federal government services. Under the authority of the Domestic Volunteer Service Act of 1971, an umbrella program called ACTION was initiated. The following programs came under its jurisdiction:

The Foster Grandparents Program. This program provides part-time volunteer opportunities for low-income persons aged sixty and over and renders supportive person-to-person services in health, education, welfare, and related residential settings to children having special or exceptional needs.

Retired Senior Volunteer Program (RSVP). A recognized role in the community and a meaningful life in retirement are established by developing a wide variety of community volunteer service opportunities for persons sixty years of age and older.

Volunteers in Service to America (VISTA). This program supplements efforts of community organizations to eliminate poverty and poverty-related human, social, and environmental problems by enabling persons from all walks of life and all age groups to perform meaningful and constructive service as volunteers. The service applies in situations where the application of human talent and dedication may help the poor to overcome the handicaps of poverty-related problems and secure opportunities for self-advancement.

University Year for Action (UYA). The goal here is to expand the use of full-time university undergraduate and graduate volunteers, faculty assistance, and other university resources in problem-solving projects in low-income communities.

National Student Volunteer Program. This program provides technical assistance, materials, on-site consultation, and training for an estimated 422,000 students serving as part-time volunteers through some 1,900 local, independent college volunteer programs, and

and for newly emerging high school-sponsored student volunteer programs.

The Senior Companion Program. To provide part-time service opportunities for low-income persons aged sixty and over and to provide supportive person-to-person services to people (other than children) with special or exceptional needs are the aims of this program.

The Youth Challenge Program. Volunteer service delivery models are developed by a variety of community groups and organizations, which will give youth in the fourteen to twenty-one age category opportunities to serve poverty communities.

Mini-Grant Program. This program attempts to provide small amounts of money to local, private, and nonprofit organizations for mobilizing relatively large numbers of part-time volunteers to work on human, social, and environmental needs.

Rewards for Service

And so it goes; the opportunities for service are great. So are the rewards. No talent is too small when a helping hand is needed. The entire area of service to others is perhaps the most rewarding use of leisure. The warm friendliness in the face of the crippled child who has enjoyed the puppet show you made possible; the firm handshake of the aged gentleman as you return him to his home after the tour of autumn scenery; the contented faces of those who have just eaten the meal you prepared for the needy; the heartening development of the camp for underprivileged that your service club sponsored are but a few satisfactions received from the time and energies expended.

Selected References

Allen, Dorothy J. *Being Human in Sport.* Philadelphia: Lea & Febiger, 1977.

American Association for Health, Physical Education, and Recreation. *Physical Education and Recreation for Impaired, Disabled and Handicapped Persons.* Washington, D.C., 1977.

Arnold, Arnold. *The Complete Book of Arts and Crafts: An Encyclopedic Sourcebook of Techniques, Tools, Ideas and Instruction.* New York: New American Library, 1977.

Arnold, Nellie E. *The Interrelated Arts in Leisure, Perceiving and Creating.* St. Louis: C. V. Mosby Company, 1976.

Auburn, Mark, and Burkman, Katherine. *Drama Through Performance.* Boston: Houghton Mifflin Co., 1977.

Bodkin, Cora. *Crafts for Your Leisure Years.* Boston: Houghton Mifflin Co., 1976.

Camp Standards with Interpretations for the Accreditation of Organized Camps. Martinsville, Indiana: American Camping Association, 1975.

Carlson, Reynold E. "The Values of Camping." *Camping Magazine* 48, no. 3 (November–December 1975): 11–18.

Casey, Betty. *The Complete Book of Square Dancing and Round Dancing.* Garden City, N.Y.: Doubleday and Co., Inc., 1976.

Ellfeldt, Lois. *Dance, from Magic to Art.* Dubuque, Iowa: Wm. C. Brown Company Publishers, 1976.

Fast, Julius. *The Pleasure Book.* New York: Stein and Day, 1977.

Fleming, Gladys Andrews. *Creative Rhythmic Movement.* Englewood Cliffs, N.J.: Prentice-Hall, 1976.

Fluegelman, Andrew, ed. *The New Games Book.* New York: Doubleday and Co., Inc., 1976.

Gallahue, David L. *Motor Development and Movement Experiences.* New York: John Wiley & Sons, 1976.

Hall, Tillman. *The Program Book for Recreation Professionals.* Palo Alto, Cal.: National Press Books, 1973.

Jensen, Clayne R. *Outdoor Recreation in America: Trends, Problems and Opportunities.* Minneapolis: Burgess Publishing Co., 1977.

Jensen, Clayne R., and Thorstenson, Clark T. *Issues in Outdoor Recreation.* 2nd ed. Minneapolis: Burgess Publishing Company, 1977.

Jubenville, Alan. *Outdoor Recreation Planning.* Philadelphia: W. B. Saunders Co., 1976.

Keith, Harold. *Sports and Games.* New York: Thomas Y. Crowell Co., 1976.

Kraus, Richard G. *Recreation Today: Program Planning and Leadership.* Santa Monica, Cal.: Goodyear Publishers, 1977.

Laurie, Roma. *Festivals and Adjudications: The Organization of Music and Drama Festivals.* Brooklyn Heights, N.Y.: Beekman Publishers, Inc., 1975.

Linsley, Leslie. *Wildcrafts: Contemporary Designs for Over 100 Craft Projects Made From Natural Materials.* Garden City, N.Y.: Doubleday and Co., Inc., 1977.

McCall, Joseph R. *Outdoor Recreation: Forest, Park, and Wilderness.* Beverly Hills: Bruce Publishing Co., 1977.

Michener, James. *Sports in America.* New York: Random House, 1976.

Mitchell, Viola; Robertson, Julia D.; and Obley, June W. *Camp Counseling.* 5th ed. Philadelphia: W.B. Saunders Co., 1977.

Orlick, Terry, and Botterhill, Cal. *Every Kid Can Win.* Chicago: Nelson-Hall, 1975.

The Recreation Imperative, A Draft of the Nationwide Outdoor Recreation Plan Prepared by the Department of the Interior. Washington, D.C.: U.S. Government Printing Office, June 1974.

Rodney, Lynn S., and Ford, Phyllis M. *Camp Administration.* New York: Ronald Press Co., 1971.

Shears, Loyda M., and Bower, Eli M. *Games in Education and Development.* Springfield, Ill.: Charles C. Thomas Publishers, 1974.

Stone, Gregory P., ed. *Games, Sports, and Power.* New Brunswick, N.J.: Transaction Books, 1972. Distributed by E. P. Dutton and Co.

Tolman, Beth. *The Country Dance Book.* Brattleboro, Vermont: Greene Press, 1976.

Van Matre, Steve. *Acclimatization.* Martinsville, Indiana: American Camping Association, 1974.

Vannier, Maryhelen. *Recreation Leadership.* 3d ed. Philadelphia: Lea & Febiger, 1977.

Vickery, Florence E. *Creative Programming for Older Adults.* New York: Association Press, 1972.

Wasserman, Paul, and Herman, Esther, eds. *Festivals Sourcebook: A Reference Guide to Fairs, Festivals, and Celebrations.* Detroit: Gale Research Co., 1977.

12
Program Planning

It's a bad plan that admits of no modification.

Publius Syrus

Planning is essential in almost any phase of human endeavor. Builders use an architect's careful blueprint to guide them as they construct new homes or schools. Schools develop a curriculum to direct the education of the young. Park and recreation professionals have an equal need for intelligent, continuous planning if they are to bring efficient, successful, stimulating programs to the public.

The community recreation program involves many levels of activity; it can serve individuals or groups; be formal or informal; organized or unstructured; or offered by individuals, agencies, or organizations. Thus, cooperation and coordination are necessary if a program is to be cohesive. The ultimate goal of any program should be to satisfy the basic needs and desires of the participants and of society. An active three-year-old may not be satisfied with a story-telling session; an adventure-seeking teenager may find the center club program too confining; and a spirited seventy-year-old is likely to find traditional bingo and checkers less than absorbing. Unless recreation professionals design programs to meet needs and desires, all ages will go elsewhere for their leisure experience or possibly may not pursue it at all.

Some people measure a recreation program by the availability of vast areas, expensive equipment, showy facilities, adequate financing, or quality leadership. While such characteristics certainly add to a program, the ultimate keys to a good program are thoughtful planning, systematic coordination, and efficient execution so that competent leaders can present a broad range of acceptable recreation choices to the public. Part of this planning involves using the available facilities creatively and obtaining and administering funds.

Pitfalls

The following traditional approaches to program planning no longer meet the needs and varied interests of recreation clientele and should be discouraged:

1. The customary approach—Program directors merely repeat the same programs year after year.

2. The copy-cat planner—By observing other communities, program directors copy their programs on the assumption that what is good for someone else will also be good in their community.

3. Expressed desires—Recreation planners ask participants for ideas and design their program accordingly.

4. Best-guess approach—Planners use their best judgment about what program elements will be successful.

Effective program planning may contain some elements of each of these approaches, but none is particularly trustworthy if used in isolation. A program that is successful one year may not meet the needs of the following year's participants. Similarly, the same programs will not work in all communities. Professional workshops and conferences can be useful places to exchange ideas with other professionals, and a checklist to isolate a community's recreation interests could help in planning. However, the latter approach will be apt to uncover only those desires conditioned in individuals by what they have already experienced; it will not necessarily show new directions. Ultimately, directors must use their own best judgment in program selection, but only after they have weighed all the facts and carefully analyzed the particular needs of their community and specific groups within their community. Once a program is under way, planners must continue to evaluate its success and be willing to make adjustments necessary to better serve the participants.

The Planning Process

Joseph Bannon succinctly describes planning as follows: "In simple terms, planning is the recognition of an existing or anticipated need and the devising of specific steps for fulfilling that need. The primary motivation for planning, or for problem solving generally, is sensitivity to and awareness of a particular problem, dissatisfaction with conditions as they presently are, and a desire to change them. Planning should be initiated because of a real need for action in a given situation."[1]

The procedural model developed by Bannon is one approach to planning (see Figure 12.1). As he suggests, it is not inclusive, but concentrates on the critical initial stages essential for formulating a work plan to determine a leisure services package for a community.

Guiding Principles and Influencing Factors in Program Planning

Recreation leaders have evolved certain guiding principles and have become aware of key influences in program planning.

The Needs and Desires of the People Served

Basic psychological needs are universal, and the recreation program should attempt to meet them. Each individual seeks new experi-

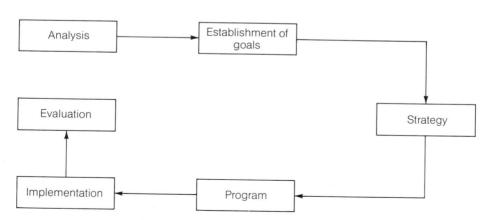

Figure 12.1. Comprehensive planning flow. Source: Joseph J. Bannon, Leisure Resources: Its Comprehensive Planning, © 1976, p. 3. Reprinted by permission of Prentice-Hall, Inc. Englewood Cliffs, N.J.

ence, recognition, security, response, a feeling of belonging, and a search for aesthetic rewards. People satisfy these universal desires in a variety of ways. An older person may play a game of chess as a means of relating to others, whereas a teenager may fill this need by attending a rock concert. Prosaic programs, such as card playing, may not satisfy the restless, the spirited, and those hungry for action, as would activities like learning to cross-country ski or attending a belly dancing class. In a world in which it becomes increasingly difficult to find satisfactions in the workday, people often turn to the recreation program to gratify their needs, stimulate new interests, and develop their skills.

Services for All People

Programs must allow all people in the community an equal opportunity for participation and involvement. This guideline is not meant to suggest that planning should aim for the greatest good for the greatest number. Such an approach may seem most expedient but seldom allows for individual differences. Thus, community leaders need to consider individual characteristics and how they affect program needs.

Age. Some programs should be geared especially to children, teenagers, adults, or the aged; other programs should attract mixed age groups by crosscutting the interests of entire families or other social units. Programs too frequently ignore young adults and adults in attempting to meet the needs of children and teenagers.

Although all persons do not mature physically and mentally at the same rate, chronological age is still a good guideline in planning. Programmers need to be aware of the psychological, social, mental, and physical attributes that characterize each age group and plan accordingly. Children, who are willingly enticed into a wide variety of recreation activities for short periods of time, grow into teenagers,

who must be involved with the planning if the program is to function successfully. Once involved, they may maintain their interests for long periods of time.

Age differences play a lesser role in planning for adults, although physical activity usually declines with advanced years.

Recreation planners must also be aware of the dominant age groups living in their communities. Sophisticated teen programs will inevitably go astray in a neighborhood of young families in which the majority of the children are age six or younger. By the same token, there will be a meager response to the tot-lot program in a neighborhood that has predominantly older adults.

Sex. Recreation programs should offer satisfying activities for both sexes. Some programs may still meet traditional sex-linked interests; others should offer wholesome outlets for coeducational recreation at many ages.

Social conditioning has done much to create definite differences in interests between the sexes. Thus, program planning must take into consideration whether the group will be all male, all female, or mixed. Nonetheless, changes in how we view sex roles have placed a new challenge on the recreation profession, encouraging the blending of sex roles in leisure. Almost all recreation offerings can be enjoyed equally by male or female. To insist upon steering boys toward heightened sports roles and girls toward more cultural activities is to deny both sexes recreation outlets they could enjoy.

Socioeconomic or educational status. The broadening of recreation horizons to include all social, economic, and educational groups is a challenge for the director. All too frequently, programs are directed toward the middle social or economic brackets, and the extremes in each category are ignored. City authorities may feel that upper-income groups can afford to use the facilities and offerings of private or commercial recreation ventures, but total community offerings should include opportunities for all groups. In many cases, minorities or low-income groups will seek different activities from those offered in standard programs.

Any program organized on democratic principles will avoid prejudices for or against racial or religious groups. Racial discrimination is one of the basic issues faced by recreation administrators, as well as other community leaders. Too often, program planning ignores the particular needs of ethnic groups in special neighborhoods.

Mores and prejudices. Programs should be planned with full knowledge of the customs and folkways of the community. Too many leaders have deprived themselves of goodwill and confidence by introducing programs that are in disrepute because of local mores. In some areas, for instance, social dancing is considered taboo, while folk dancing is encouraged; in other areas card playing is boycotted. Careful investigation of the community code is mandatory for good planning.

Needs. The needs of participants, expressed or unexpressed, affect choices in programming. Some groups need social outlets, a chance to get acquainted; others need opportunities for physical activities. Some need outlets for creative desires; others need opportunities to be of service. A broad program creates offerings to satisfy basic physical and psychological yearnings in a variety of media.

Interests and skills. A recreation planner must start with a program geared to the interests and skills of the participants, and then build new skills and stimulate new interests.

Special-interest groups will be found in every community and are a vital element of the total recreation program. Although leadership and facilities are sometimes hard to find in the daily program for those who would like to indulge in sculpture, sailing, rappelling, or batik-

ing, the skillful program planner will make every attempt to create outlets through specialists, hobby groups, classes, or volunteer leaders.

Mental and physical capacity. The physical and mental health of the expected participants conditions recreation offerings. For example, the aged and arthritic are often absent because an activity is not readily accessible. Communities are increasing their awareness of their responsibility to provide programs for special populations. The mentally retarded, the physically handicapped, and the homebound are getting a fairer share of consideration in the program, but there is need for greater concentration in these areas.

Numbers. The size of the community and the numbers of participants expected affect the planning and promotion of activities. In large cities, decentralization of the program on a neighborhood basis is sometimes more efficient than an attempt to interest the whole population at any one time or in any one activity. Although serving large numbers of people is important, a director should not play the numbers game as the only criterion for evaluating the success or failure of the program. Those outlets that attract only a few enthusiasts still have their place in the total program. Most new popular activities started with a handful of interested persons who spread their zeal to others.

Diversified Program

All too often, recreation connotes only sports and games. Programs should also include arts and crafts; dramatic activities; music; dance; literary, mental, and linguistic outlets; service to others; a chance for involvement in social concerns; social recreation; camping and outdoor recreation; hobbies; and special events.

A program should be in careful balance to include opportunities for active and passive recreation; physical, social, cultural, and creative activities; programs that allow individuals with varying degrees of skill to participate; programs that allow progress in proficiency within the activity; indoor and outdoor interests; activities for individual and group participation; and interests that involve long-range as well as short-term participation.

A Wide Variety of Times

Timing is important to the success of any program. Activities must be available during the times when people are free to participate. Too frequently, the morning hours, the weekends, and the winter months are overlooked, as program emphasis is geared too strongly to school children or working adults. Although there is a creditable tendency to avoid interference with church services on Sunday, many agencies also close their doors on Saturday, a day when families might best avail themselves of community offerings.

A center operating in only the afternoon and evening may not serve the early-rising aged, who often do not care to travel at night or have no public transportation after the evening rush hour.

In some communities a director will need to consider companies working two or three shifts; in others, those on three- or four-day workweeks as well as those on flexible time schemes may require special treatment.

Knowing when to initiate a special event, what hours are most apt to attract program participants, how frequently to offer different programs, and how long activities may run without loss of enthusiasm are all factors that allow the planner to balance the schedule successfully.

Location and Weather

Heat, cold, humidity, and topography are key factors in program planning and should be considered. Modern technology has made it possible to play tennis and handball indoors, and it is possible to ski downhill all year long on nylon slopes. However, it will be a long time before such activities are commonplace for the majority of people. Special trips involving teens, adults, or seniors for rock climbing, skiing, canoeing, or visiting historical sites are well within the scope of park and recreation departments. Directors will need to plan such trips with care because of the hazards involved, and the amount of staff time required for such trips may also be a limiting factor.

The Best Use of Community Facilities and Personnel

No one organization in the community is capable of satisfying all the leisure needs and interests of the people. Cooperative planning and coordination among individuals or agencies that offer recreation programs are important so that intelligent use can be made of existing facilities, leadership, and finance. For example, youth agencies frequently use churches, schools, and city recreation facilities for their programs. In-service training institutes should use capable leaders from all community agencies.

Quality Leadership

The capabilities of leaders will make or break programs. Activities cannot be initiated or executed successfully unless there are sufficient leaders capable of carrying on the activities. The organization without a leader to engender enthusiasm for drama finds a minimum of emphasis on dramatic activity. The secret of good planning is to employ professional staff members educated in a sound curriculum of recreation education and steeped in a knowledge of the breadth and scope of recreation opportunities. Such leaders will capitalize on their own skills and seek out volunteers to expand program areas in which they feel less competent. Indigenous leadership is especially important with minority groups.

Adequate Financial Backing

Intelligent program planning gives the best possible variety of opportunity for the money available. Few organizations have budgets that they feel are adequate.

Many activities must be free of charge to the participants in order to provide equal access. Other activities may be properly financed by fees and charges. Creative planning, careful coordination, and intelligent evaluation will produce the maximum in recreation benefits for the number of dollars expended.

Objectives of the Managing Authority

Churches, schools, industries, youth-serving organizations, commercial ventures, or tax-supported agencies that offer portions of the total community recreation program operate under certain policies with predetermined goals and objectives. The policies, scope, program, and methods of organization of many youth agencies are at least partially dictated by the parent organization. The agency that is trying to serve youth is not primarily interested in stimulating activity among the adult popula-tion; the church that has strong feelings against the advisability of dance as a social program cannot be expected to further the dance interests of other members of the community. Success comes from learning your agency.

The Safety and Health of the Participants

There is an ever-increasing emphasis on the responsibility of the sponsoring organization for insuring safe and healthful conditions for those who are participating in recreation. We cannot eliminate the risk from all recreation activities, because in risk there is recreation. What we must do is take every precaution to eliminate unnecessary risk by assuring that facilities and equipment are in good condition and that instructions meet the highest standards of excellence. Leaders must be instantly alerted to unhealthful or unsanitary practices, such as participant fatigue, unsanitary facilities, debris on playground, unsafe apparatus, or easy accessibility to acids in the craft center.

National Standards

Many agencies and organizations have developed standards for facilities, leadership, or

---

"There's Nothing To Do!"

"Mom," whined Tom on a hot summer afternoon, "there's nothing to do!"

Most communities—crowded cities and small towns alike—offer many choices of things to do alone, with small groups, or with crowds. Why, then, do some people say they have nothing to do?

Do they need more knowledge about the possibilities in their communities? Do they need motivation to become involved? Are there so many choices that they are confused? Have they had so much that they are satiated? Do the programs fail to meet their basic needs?

How can we stimulate and encourage participation?

programs. Conscientious program planners will utilize the standards put forth by such organizations as the American Camping Association; the National Recreation and Park Association; the American Red Cross; the Division of Girls' and Women's Sports of the American Alliance for Health, Physical Education, and Recreation; and the American Institute of Architects.

Constant Reevaluation

Surveys to investigate and promote recreation activities, continuous evaluation of existing programs, and planned observations of response to new offerings should guide program efforts. Constant awareness of changes in interest and needs will avoid wasting budget money on activities that have outlived their appeal.

Planning in Action

The concept that well-made plans usually bring satisfactory results is especially true in recreation. Just as the planner has an important role to play in administering a program, so the leader, who is responsible for putting the plans into action, has an equally important responsibility. The diversity of the recreation program and the many approaches to conducting programs make it imperative that the recreation leader have the proper training, resourcefulness, and management ability to accomplish the job.

Agencies that have somewhat the same goals often differ as to how these goals are achieved. For instance, the Boy Scouts, Girl Scouts, and Campfire Girls have nationally prescribed programs that determine not only the program content but also the methods that should be followed in carrying out the plans, whereas many other youth organizations have locally determined programs. Social workers seek to guide groups in a way that will meet

the needs of the individuals within the group or will help the group democratically bring about social change in the community.

The approach for carrying out the programs sponsored by park and recreation departments varies according to the type of program and the setting. In operating certain facilities, such as scenic parks, picnic areas, and beaches, the department is concerned mainly with the establishment of policies, maintenance, and supervision. When a recreation department sponsors an organized camp, tennis lessons, or an arts and crafts festival, the amount and complexity of organization are much greater. Within each of these operations, varied methods might be used in fulfilling the objectives.

Programs can become too highly organized; when this happens, activities often become regimented and stereotyped. A program that is made up primarily of drop-in or instructional activities also leaves much to be desired. Often, an overemphasis on special events tends to shortchange the basic program. Organizations should strive for balance in the different types of recreation activities offered. Such balance does not mean that equal portions of arts and crafts, sports and games, or other program areas should take place in every setting. Not all activities are of equal importance for given circumstances, nor do they require the same degree of supervision or the same type of organization.

Methods of Organization

Methods of organizing and conducting recreation can be generally classified as either informal or organized.

Informal Activities

There are many people who desire to pursue their recreation interests on their own initiative, at their own speed, and with a minimum of interference. They wish only for a place to play, fish, hike, or read, in which they may enjoy their leisure pursuit by themselves or with friends of their own choosing. Even in an organized camp program, time is needed for a child to seek relaxation or to individually explore the wonders of nature.

Informal or self-directed activities always will have an important place in recreation. They need little direct guidance and satisfy large numbers of the recreation public at a minimum of expense. The organization's responsibility with regard to informal activities may involve the following:

Provision of environment. Access to or availability of an attractive, safe, well-maintained facility in which recreation can take place may well be all that is needed for some pursuits. Examples include hiking and walking trails, picnic areas, and quiet places away from the noise of the city.

Supervision and stimulation. Drop-in activities, such as ping-pong, service projects, and open gym play in the community center need only general supervision to assure wholesome participation and equal opportunity. A leader has a challenge and responsibility, even in informal play, to whet the appetite of individuals for broader recreation horizons at home or in other settings.

Personal guidance and counseling. Informal activities allow time and atmosphere for guidance and more personal attention to the problems of single individuals or small groups.

Organized Activities

The main types of organized activities include clubs, classes, contests and tournaments, leagues, and special events.

Clubs. Clubs are considered one of the basic elements of community recreation programs. They normally consist of persons who

seek to associate with each other to promote some common interest or object. Club members elect their own officers, adopt a constitution, and establish qualifications for membership. There are basically two types of clubs: special-interest and general-interest.

Special-interest clubs are composed of persons who are concerned with a particular interest such as rock or coin collecting, gardening, photography, or sailing. General-interest clubs are composed of persons who seek social interaction. The reason that the members keep together is not so much the program as the chance to meet with others. Clubs of this nature may be established for most age levels.

Clubs can be established on a community-wide, nonsponsorship basis, or they may be sponsored by recreation departments, schools, settlement houses, or youth-serving agencies. When an agency sponsors a club, there may be several degrees of sponsorship, including complete sponsorship, provision of leadership and facilities, or provision of a meeting place or leadership.

Classes. Another method of conducting recreation in communities is to provide instructional classes. Agencies can offer classes in an almost unlimited number of subjects. Programs should supplement the classes sponsored by the public schools in their regular school curriculums or in the adult or community education programs. When needs and interests are evident, classes should be planned, scheduled, and conducted.

Leagues. Leagues are established to facilitate competition in various sports. They range from the informal intraplayground type to the highly organized and efficiently run citywide sport leagues. Most team sports, such as basketball, baseball, softball, volleyball, ice hockey, and soccer, are conducted on a league basis.

League play may be organized in a round-robin method of competition, which provides for each team to play the other teams in the league. The amount of organization needed in league play is largely determined by the formality desired and the number of teams taking part.

Community recreation departments usually guide and direct the operation of leagues in the city. In large cities, a supervisor of sports and athletics has this responsibility. Some cities organize sport associations, which are usually formed for the promotion of particular sports and are composed of sports enthusiasts and team representatives. In some cases, community-wide sport associations promote all sports events. Sports leagues are prevalent for youths, adults, churches, and industries. In many communities, Little League, Babe Ruth, and American Legion baseball leagues are operated separately from the municipal programs. Other cities find it beneficial for the recreation department to sponsor those leagues, so that the various leagues can be better coordinated and kept in proper perspective. Wherever possible, community park and recreation professionals should be represented on the boards of such leagues.

Contests and tournaments. Tournaments are series of contests conducted to determine winners in various activities. Most playgrounds and community centers sponsor tournaments as one of the main features of the weekly program.

Tournaments can be conducted on an informal or formal basis. They can be organized either to determine the winner of a weekly event that leads to a citywide playoff or to stimulate continuous competition over a longer period of time. The type of tournament method used will depend upon the purposes for which the activity is conducted. Recreation leaders should be familiar with the different kinds of tournament methods and the specific advantages and disadvantages of each. They will need to have a basic knowledge of the different kinds of tournaments and contests, including round-robin, single- and double-elim-

ination contests, and challenge tournaments of the ladder and pyramid type. Knowledge of seeding and handicapping is essential, as well as familiarity with management problems such as scheduling, assigning officials, handling protests, crowd control, and others.

Special events. Since special events can range from a simple, spontaneous talent show around the campfire to a week-long, citywide winter carnival, a description of organization methods that would be pertinent to all special events would be an endless task. Suffice it to say that the larger the spectacle, the more organization and coordination will be necessary. Special events are media attractions and serve to introduce other recreation offerings to the public. They are generally goodwill programs and can develop community unity. *Involvement* is a key word in organizing special events.

Changing Concepts

The recreation agency that continues to operate within the program scope deemed sufficient for the last twenty years is now giving way to the agency with a more visionary outlook. Certain heartening evidences have been observed in the following areas:

1. The concept of management by objectives (MBO) is rapidly becoming a useful tool for program planners. This system allows program leaders to establish measurable goals and objectives on a short- and long-term basis. When MBO is tied to such systems as Planning-Programming-Budgeting Systems (PPBS), the Performance Evaluation Review Technique (PERT), and the Critical Path Method (CPM) of management, leaders and administra-

tors have definable and measurable goals on which to base their requests for budgetary support.

Farrell and Lundegren support the use of performance budgeting when they say:

In the performance approach to budgeting, it is generally assumed that inputs and outputs will be given major emphasis. Expenditure data are utilized as they relate to anticipated program services for the dollars being sought. In this discovery process, one expects administrative efficiency to sharpen and budgets to reflect a clear interpretation of program goals and objectives. The programmer is interested in using a solid analytical process to measure the effectiveness of the programs which are being designed. In order to be able to know this a solid budget process must be followed. The authors recommend the following:

(1) Begin with well-defined objectives for the overall program. Work toward developing performance objectives for each individual program. If this step is neglected, the final measurement of effectiveness is impossible, regardless of how fancy we may be with counting participants or having strong feelings of success.

(2) If there has not been an element of measurement included in the statement of objectives it should be established as the next step. Measures of performance can be one of three types: program size, efficiency, and effectiveness.

(a) Program size is the traditional way of measuring performance. This measures the number of people attending an activity as a pure quantitative process.

(b) Efficiency is a ratio computation. In this measure we would look at amount of cost of a program per number of people served.

(c) Effectiveness is the qualification measure which is directed toward how well a program satisfied the participant.[2]

2. Evaluative techniques to assess the worth of program offerings have come a long way since the days when departments relied strictly on the numbers game, survey forms, and staff reviews. Added to today's mix are computer-based reporting systems. Recreation personnel have characteristically shied away from quantitative reporting as being impersonal and dehumanizing. The secret to unfolding this mystery is, as Strobell points out, to abandon our biases and improve research design in order to take advantage of computer technology.[3] (Refer to the selected references at the end of the chapter for details.)

3. There is an increasing awareness that agencies cannot operate as isolated units. More concepts of cooperative planning with similar agencies are being explored, resulting in better programming.

4. The cliché "What was good enough for us is good enough for our children" is being replaced by a new interest in creative ideas in facilities and programs for both adults and children.

5. More emphasis is being placed on activities that allow individual expression and quality and less on those that accent regimentation.

6. There is increasing interest in the effect of master plans upon programming. Such master plans do not discourage the initiative of the individual leaders but rather insure core programs of varied scope. More attention is given to long-range program plan-

ning in overall master plans for facilities.

7. There is a new recognition of the need for interpretation of the recreation program and profession to give an honest and positive picture of the value of recreation to the individual and to the community.

8. There is increased recognition of the value of allowing citizens from all walks of life to be involved in the planning and execution of their own programs.

Program planning will achieve its objectives only if we have the vision to expand with the fluctuating needs and interests of those who move in a constantly changing world. As amounts of leisure increase for greater numbers of people, program opportunities must keep pace by means of more and better leadership, wider varieties of challenging program ideas, and extended budgets for facilities and staff. Long-range and short-term planning are essential if the creative, physical, cultural, and social recreation needs of individuals and groups are to be met in the modern community. We cannot be content with the status quo. Alert, professionally educated leaders must, through quality research, continuously evaluate present offerings, explore new horizons, and plan creatively from factual data, if the recreation profession is to meet its mounting responsibilities.

Selected References

Bannon, Joseph J. *Leisure Resources: Its Comprehensive Planning.* Englewood Cliffs, N.J.: Prentice-Hall, Inc., 1976.

Corbin, H. Dan. *Recreation Leadership.* 2d ed. Englewood Cliffs, N.J.: Prentice-Hall, Inc., 1970.

Farrell, Patricia, and Lundegren, Herberta M. *The Process of Recreation Programming.* New York: John Wiley & Sons Inc., 1977.

Kraus, Richard G. *Recreation Today—Program Planning and Leadership.* 2d ed. Santa Monica, Cal.: Goodyear Publishing Co., Inc., 1977.

Wallach, Fran, ed. "Recreation Programming." *Parks & Recreation* 12, no. 6 (June 1977).

13
Recreation for Special Populations

A difference is a difference only when it makes a difference.

Anonymous author

The basic democratic principle of the right to life, liberty, and the pursuit of happiness demands an increasing awareness of our obligations to special populations. The term *special populations* refers to those individuals who differ from the so-called normal because of physical, emotional, intellectual, or social circumstances. Statistics concerning their numbers vary, but conservative estimates show that there are more than thirty-five million persons who are either socially or economically disadvantaged, physiologically or emotionally impaired to some degree, or socially deviant within the eyes of present laws.

We have more than twenty-two million aged, although not all are ill or disabled. We have another six million retardates with varying degrees of capacity to meet daily obligations. Although there is a trend to keep the mentally ill in community accommodations, there are still nearly 400,000 in state mental hospitals. Add to these figures those who are economically disadvantaged or imprisoned because of social deviancy, and we have a large clientele whose recreation wants must be met with special considerations. If the park and recreation profession is to attain the ideal of recreation opportunity for all, then the needs of these special populations must be a top priority. To serve those needs, therapeutic recreation has emerged as a specialty in the general field of recreation and parks.

By definition, "Therapeutic recreation refers to those recreation services that are pro-vided in relation to recovery from or adjustment to illness, disability, or a specific social problem. Although therapeutic recreation service is frequently recognized as an adjunctive component of treatment modalities, it primarily endeavors to promote the positive health and functional aspects of the ill, disabled, and disadvantaged."[1]

The Ill and the Disabled

Who are these individuals? Why should society be concerned? Regardless of the designation—the ill, the disabled, the medically disadvantaged, the impaired, the handicapped—we are talking about those individuals who cannot participate in our program offerings unless we make special considerations because of their physiological, emotional, or intellectual capabilities. The degree of the handicap is conditioned not so much by the degree of the disability itself, but by a person's power to compensate for the deficiency. All too often we make exciting programs unavailable to the handicapped because of false stereotypes (the blind can't ski); uncomplimentary identifications of persons *as* handicaps, rather than as human beings (the paraplegic in room 12); and inaccessibility of facilities (doors too narrow for wheelchairs).

A disability is an impairment of structure or function. It becomes a handicap when it is perceived by the individual or by others as a barrier to potential involvement in desired recreation experiences. For example, the amputee who still frequents the ski slopes is disabled but has not allowed the impairment to be a handicap.

Reasons for Increased Concern

New attention is being placed on these segments of our population for the following reasons:

1. Medical technology now succeeds in keeping alive many who would have died from their difficulties even a few years ago. They continue to exist with permanent disabilities.

2. Increases in the tempo of twentieth-century living with the attendant stresses result in accidents, emotional disturbances, or the painful effects of too many drugs or too much alcohol.

3. The wars of this century have added to the numbers of known physically and mentally handicapped, as a direct result of combat involvement, poor post-service adjustment, or discovery of disabilities as soldiers were examined for active duty.

4. A civil rights philosophy now fosters the concept that the physically or mentally impaired are also human beings whose capacities should be developed to their fullest potential and satisfaction.

5. Professionals in other disciplines who work with the handicapped are now more aware of the potential contribution of appropriate recreation choices to the lives of those who are institutionalized and those who, though disabled, can live in communities that have some support systems for their needs.

6. Recent legislation has mandated equal opportunity for disabled individuals. On April 28, 1977, Joseph Califano, then Secretary of Health, Education, and Welfare, signed into law a regulation requiring recipients of HEW funds to provide equal access for their services and employment or risk losing their federal grants.[2]

Other pertinent legislation that focused dramatic attention on the rights of the disabled included the Education of All Handicapped Act (PL 94-142), Section 504 of the Rehabilitation Act of 1973, and the Tax Incentive for Barrier Removal legislation.

Types of Disability

There are many types of impairment with which the therapeutic recreation professional may come in contact within the community or within special institutions.

The blind and the deaf. Frequently not institutionalized, those who have lost their sight or hearing may need special equipment or activity modification. The story of Sonny Yates, a blind skydiver, refutes the restrictive views of recreation for the sightless.

The cardiac, the diabetic, and the tubercular. These chronic ailments do not necessarily incapacitate the individual but may limit the type or degree of the recreation experience.

The orthopedically impaired. The adjustment of those with obvious crippling of limbs is often made more difficult because of their treatment by others. Rejection all too often creates an emotional adjustment to add to the physical adjustment.

The neurologically handicapped. Handicaps caused by cerebral palsy, brain injury, multiple sclerosis, spinal nerve injury, and similar disorders are complex because they involve impairment of sensory, motor, intellectual, and emotional capacities.

The mentally retarded. For most of the retarded, recreation gives opportunities for learning and for social adjustment. The focus of the Kennedy Foundation on the special rights of the retarded has greatly improved their status in the last decades.

The mentally ill.   The term *mentally ill* encompasses a wide variety of mental disorders, which range from slight emotional disturbances to severe psychoses. Although the numbers who seek psychiatric help have increased, signs indicate that rehabilitation in this area has moved farther faster than in almost any other.

The physically ill.   Those with physical illness of short- or long-term duration may be homebound or hospitalized. General hospitals are giving increased attention to the therapeutic effects of involvement in interesting recreation experiences.

The Challenge to Recreation

The increasing numbers of the ill and the disabled provide a threefold challenge for the park and recreation profession. The first challenge comes in offering satisfying recreation experiences that will relieve tensions, provide substitute activities for meeting basic needs, and act as a positive force in maintaining good physical and mental health so that there may be fewer ill and handicapped.

Second, when a person is incapacitated because of physical or mental difficulties, recreation can keep mind and body occupied with satisfying experiences within the limits of his or her capacities and, in short, contribute to the person's feelings of worth as well as pleasure.

The third challenge is to use recreation experiences to help bridge the gap between the handicapped and the community. If the individual has been institutionalized, then professionals in the hospital and in the community must work to help the patient return to the mainstream of life in a manner that will not pose stresses great enough to cause a retreat. All too often, the patient who has regained

equilibrium in the hospital returns to the kind of environment that made the hospitalization necessary in the beginning—and the cycle repeats itself.

In summary, recreation can be regarded as clinical treatment or, in a nonclinical sense, as simply a positive force to enrich the lives of these special people. Recreation, in providing human satisfactions, can help keep individuals from illness, can help make life bearable during illness, and can help in readjustment to normal life demands after illness.

A Look at History

Providing recreation for the ill and disabled is not a new idea. Florence Nightingale made efforts to ease the life of injured soldiers during the Crimean War with reading rooms, lectures, games, social hours, and concerts. What *is* comparatively new is the broad attention that therapeutic recreation has received during the last five decades. The following list is illustrative, not inclusive, of the enlarged focus:

1930s

Beginning of recreation service at St. Elizabeth's Hospital in Washington, D.C.

Menninger Clinic's stress on recreation as an aid to mental health

1940s

Expansion of recreation in military hospitals

Addition of Hospital Special Services Division to Veterans' Administration Recreation Service

Founding of Hospital Recreation Section of American Recreation Society

Formation of Leisure Time Committee in American Psychiatric Association

1950s

Establishment of Recreation Section of American Association for Health, Physical Education, and Recreation

Founding of National Association of Recreation Therapists

Creation of Council for Advancement of Hospital Recreation

Initiation of National Recreation Association's Consulting Service on Recreation for the Ill and Handicapped

Initiation of voluntary registration program for therapeutic recreation workers (over 1,500 now registered)

1960s

First President's Panel on Mental Retardation

Formation of National Therapeutic Recreation Society as branch of newly merged NRPA

Passage of Public Law 90–170, which resulted in training grants and research for therapeutic recreation

Creation of Bureau of Education for Handicapped in Office of Education

First Special Olympics (Olympics for retarded)

1970s

Education of the Handicapped Act (PL 91–230)

Information and Research Utilization Center in Physical Education and Recreation for the Handicapped (IRUC), a service of AAHPER

Rehabilitation Act of 1973 (PL 93–113)

Education for All Handicapped Act (PL 94–142), which involves leisure education

National Therapeutic Recreation Society 750-hour training program

Standards for therapeutic recreation in psychiatric facilities through joint Commission on Accreditation of Hospitals

Trends

1. Leisure counseling is becoming an important tool in helping the ill and disabled to choose among desirable recreation alternatives.

2. Mental health centers, halfway houses, and sheltered workshops are being used to keep within their communities, in sheltered atmospheres, individuals who formerly would have been institutionalized.

3. There is increased emphasis on the use of recreation to re-engage handicapped individuals in the mainstream of community activity to the extent of their capabilities.

4. Mobile units are being constructed to take recreation experiences to homebound individuals or those who cannot leave their neighborhoods.

5. The direction in programming is toward integration, rather than separation of those who differ from the "norm."

6. There is increased attention to specific research on activity analysis in order to program for behavior modification with special disabilities.

7. Program objectives are being broadened from group activities to individual self-discovery experiences.

8. Certification of therapeutic recreation personnel by state certification units is increasing.

9. Campaigns are being initiated to remove architectural barriers that prevent participation in recreation choices.

Professional Leadership

In the last fifteen years, the scene has changed with regard to the availability of specialized curriculums and the numbers of would-be therapeutic recreation personnel. Fifteen hundred individuals have met voluntary registration criteria, but there are many more professionals who are working in this specialized area. The latest data available from the curriculum studies of the Society of Park and Recreation Educators identified forty-five curriculums that offered specialization in some form of therapeutic recreation.[3] Many others offer fieldwork or special courses without a complete option. Research studies and demonstration projects stimulated by federal funding have increased greatly.

Attention is being focused not only on encouraging professionals to meet registration requirements, but also on actively monitoring curriculums through the evaluative criteria and standards of the National Recreation Accreditation Program (described in Chapter 15).

Many park and recreation professionals still resist the integration of the abnormal with normal populations. An experiment with the mentally ill proved that expressed fears were unfounded: At a therapeutic recreation conference, a social recreation evening was held.[4] Participants included the neighborhood groups who ordinarily frequented the center in which the event was held, the conference participants who were municipal recreation program directors, and two busloads of mental patients who were nearing discharge time from their respective hospitals. What were the results? In the words of one director, "I couldn't tell the patients from us. From now on, they're going to be just human beings to me."

Job Opportunities

Therapeutic recreation personnel find employment in a variety of settings.

Public recreation agencies. Municipal park and recreation agencies are giving increased attention to integration of the disabled in community programs. They are also employing therapeutic recreation personnel for special centers and playgrounds. Special swimming classes for the retarded, social club special programs for returning mental patients, and physical fitness classes for cardiac patients are examples.

Camping. Resident and day camps are available for almost every type of disability. Experiments with integration of the handicapped with all campers have proved rewarding for all participants.

General hospitals. Children's hospitals and psychiatric wards of general hospitals employ therapeutic recreation personnel in their activity therapy programs.

State hospitals. In spite of the trend toward keeping mental patients in their own communities, most state mental hospitals are still overcrowded. The recreation therapy program there is important to the patient's welfare.

Mental health centers. With federal funding, many communities have initiated outpatient programs in these centers. The therapeutic recreation professional is part of the treatment team.

Halfway houses, day centers, and sheltered workshops. These facilities provide a sheltered environment for those who are not yet ready for the stress of social interaction. Recreation experiences usually form a large part of their offerings.

Nursing homes and convalescent centers. Federal legislation is now demanding recreation programming for these institutions.

Drug and alcohol rehabilitation centers. Those centers that provide support services for alcoholics or drug addicts usually provide recreation outlets as part of their program.

Mandatory legislation as well as social conscience has broadened the demand for personnel who are knowledgeable about disabilities, sensitive to the resultant psychological adjustments, aware of the environments in which treatment takes place, and capable of coordinating resources and programs so that the best recreation experiences will result.

The Future

Dr. David Compton, formerly the therapeutic recreation specialist for the National Recreation and Parks Association (NRPA), perhaps best summarized the situation when he said:

> Special populations constitute a major reservoir of human energy which has yet to be tapped. The seventies and eighties pose severe physical energy crises, but our most difficult crises will be with the mobilization and utilization of human energy.
>
> The price we pay for rehabilitation and exclusionary types of programmatic efforts is at best mind-boggling. Pouring money into leisure education, normalization programs, and major preventative efforts may yield much more in the long run for every dollar invested.[5]

The Now Generation—Older Americans

"Old age is the only period of life with no future." So said Dr. Robert Butler in his book *Why Survive?*[6] If we take Dr. Butler at his word, then the aged should truly be the "now" generation. Their present should be infinitely important to them and to society. Dr. Butler's comments, of course, referred to the life cycle patterns, which move from childhood through a variety of stages but always end with old age. Whether old age is satisfying or discouraging is

Figure 13.1. Older people can enjoy many outdoor activities.

inextricably involved with challenges and opportunities in leisure.

For many years the welfare of the aged population in the countries of the world was principally a family affair or an individual responsibility. In a three-generation household and a rural environment, the senior citizen over eighty years old could expect preferential social or family status and possible community deference to his or her years of experience. Since comparatively few persons achieved such an age, they posed no social problem. Today, such community reciprocation for services rendered has become a complex responsibility that has focused dramatic attention on the acute problems of the aged in our country.

In the last eighty years the composition of American society has undergone an accelerated revolution. Since 1900, the number of older Americans has more than quadrupled, while the rest of the population only doubled in size. The changes were even more drastic between 1960 and 1970, when the population over sixty-five increased by twenty-one percent. The combined influences of dropping birth rates and medical technology that keeps people alive longer have created a drastic adjustment in the balance of our age groups. If, as theorized, aging is genetically determined, then it is only a matter of time before scientists discover how to control the clock of aging in our bodies and prolong life-spans well past one hundred years.[7]

A combination of extended life and present compulsory retirement practices will provoke new attention to society's responsibility for improving the quality of life of these individuals who now represent over ten percent of the total population.

The Situation

The reasons for the increased concern for the welfare of older Americans include several factors that must alert the park and recreation profession to the needs of this segment of the nation.

Increase in numbers of persons over sixty-five years of age. Every day, 1,000 persons reach the age of sixty-five. Population predictions indicate that by the year 2000 the aged population will exceed twenty-eight million. These figures become more meaningful when described as percentages of the total population—an increase from four percent in 1900 to more than ten percent in 1977. Better diet, advances in preventive medicine and medical care, better sanitation and health practices, and technological advances that have raised the standard of living and decreased the mortality rate have combined to add years to normal life expectancy. Average life expectancy has increased by more than twenty years for women and seventeen years for men in the

last fifty years. With the advent of the women's liberation movement and more equal necessity for women to cope with stressful situations, the life expectancies for men and women may move closer together in the years to come.

Whatever the future holds, we have right now *more persons* who can expect to live *more years*. There remains a challenge for the park and recreation profession to help to make those additional years meaningful and satisfying. More years to life? Yes, but also more life to those years.

Decrease in work opportunities and increase in compulsory retirement. In spite of attempts to legislate against age discrimination in the employment arena, several factors continue to keep the older worker from job opportunities. Stereotypes of absenteeism and decreased efficiency have been refuted by research, but still abound. Cultural malaise is evident, caused by what Harman calls the "work roles dilemma," which legitimizes social roles only through "holding a job, being married to someone who holds a job, or being a student who is preparing for a career."[8]

Present employment rates indicate that forty-five percent of those now employed work less than full time for the whole year, and that thirty percent of all work is performed by "less than full-time" workers.[9] If our social structure cannot meet the ideal of full employment, and institutions continue to use age as the criterion for compulsory retirement, regardless of economic need, physical ability, mental attitude, or education for leisure use, then we must somehow relinquish our worship of work as the meaning of life and accept and prepare for the leisure ethic.

Signs of struggle against compulsory retirement are already apparent. The American Association of Retired Persons reported a significant victory in their May 1977 *Bulletin,* as Los Angeles voted to prohibit mandatory retirement based on age for their municipal employees. Congress also has had increased concern with mandatory retirement practices, and in 1977 it reversed its decision on mandatory retirement at sixty-five.

Attitudes of and toward the aged. Not the least of the problems blocking fruitful use of leisure in the later years are the attitudes of other generations toward the aged and the negative feelings of the aged about themselves. A 1975 survey by the National Council on Aging indicated, "Compared to the earlier stages of life, the later years are clearly not felt by either the young or the old to be the most desirable time."[10] "The notion of leisure seems to have less relevance among older people . . . with much more free time on their hands."[11]

Other myths and stereotypes tend to increase the psychological impact of the double pressure of withdrawing from the work force and "getting old" in the eyes of others. We must help destroy the current misconceptions.

One of these misconceptions is the belief that chronological years are viable measurements for mental aptitude and physical productivity. Some sixty-five-year-olds are as physically capable and mentally alert as those ten years younger. Some individuals are physiologically old at age fifty.

The idea that old age inevitably ends in senility must be shaken. Research indicates that there are diseases *in* old age but not *of* old age. The deterioration causing senility does not seem to relate merely to having lived a number of years.

The theory of disengagement, that is, the belief that older persons *desire* to *withdraw* from social interaction or responsibility, is detrimental. Although there is no evidence to support it, the myth makes a convenient excuse for those who do not wish to extend their programs to "hard-to-reach" older Americans.

The myth of the "Golden Years"—that old age brings peace, tranquillity, and never-never land—has not been substantiated. Suicide statistics are evidence that, in our society,

stress, grief, loneliness, and helplessness do not miraculously disappear with increasing age.

Ageism is as serious a kind of discrimination as is sexism or racism.

Changing role and status of the aged. As the numbers of aged have increased, their prestige seems to have decreased. The lack of a precise role to play, sudden retirement from the satisfying functions of an occupation, relaxing of family ties with the death of a spouse or the mobility of children, economic inflation which erases the durability of a carefully planned retirement fund, and lack of education for increased leisure all bring psychological impacts that make adjustments painful. Attitudes of society as a whole toward retirement must be changed before the retiree can look forward optimistically to the later years as significant, meaningful, and satisfying.

Financial pressures. Many aged are living on reduced or fixed incomes. Discretionary income for this age bracket does not necessarily correspond to the increase in discretionary time. Many would like to return to work, not only for personal satisfactions derived from their jobs but also for the needed income to meet the necessities of life. The significant increases in Social Security benefits have in many cases been eroded by virulent inflation.

Changing environment. A three-generation household in a rural environment kept the aged of a past generation useful in the daily demands of a rugged existence. The reduction in numbers and proportions of farmers or owners of small businesses has made us a nation of wage earners from whose market the sixty-five-year-old has been banished.

The new trend in homes differs from the rambling farm house in which each of three generations held a useful, interdependent position. The present, smaller, two-generation unit gives the aged person little room, little privacy, and little sense of personal contribution. Rather than face the crises of such an environment, seventy percent of the aged live alone, creating further problems for those who wish to reach them for group activities. The present trend toward congregate housing and communal living may ease that situation.

Providing the aged with housing that is within their financial means and that offers a stimulating, satisfying environment is a challenge to the architects of our time. Many attempts are being made to meet this challenge, both by the federal government and by private agencies.

The living environment for the aged is an individual choice, just as it is for any other age group. Some want group housing; some need institutional life; some prefer housing units integrated with the total community; others seek independent units within a colony of retirees. Among their needs, however, is access to areas and facilities that provide recreation outlets for expanded leisure.

Health of the aged. Maintaining health and vigor in later maturity becomes a problem when diet may be faulty and the opportunity or stimulation of desire for healthful exercise

may be at a minimum. Physical difficulties occur at a more rapid rate than in youth. Susceptibility to mental illness may increase because of organic difficulties or psychological maladjustment resulting from loss of sight or hearing or the decline of meaningful social roles. The "if you don't use it, you lose it" concept applies particularly to the faculties of the aged.

Government intervention. The Older Americans Act and its amendments provided a comprehensive network within each state for the development and monitoring of assorted services for the aged. State commissions through area agencies for each segment of each state assess needs and mete out federal monies for nutrition programs, day-care centers, manpower development, research, housing, transportation, and volunteer service opportunities. Many of these grants have money earmarked for social or educational services that pertain to the use of leisure.

Increase in leisure. Nearly forty percent of the retired, according to a Harris study, were forced to retire. Those who withdraw from the work force through their own decision may have a significantly different attitude toward their retirement than do those

Batters Up

The Kids and Cubs softball teams in St. Petersburg, Florida, will allow no one under age seventy to play in their weekly ball games. One onlooker, aged sixty-eight and now on the "farm" team, wistfully wished away two years of his life so that he could don his Kid or Cub uniform.

Could alternative programs for middle-aged persons gain the same recognition and prestige for younger sports enthusiasts? Must we be "too old for the industrial leagues" and "too young for the Kids and Cubs"?

who must yield to compulsory age regulations. For the majority of the older population, leisure in large blocks is a new experience. The impact of leisure on the elderly is perhaps more potent since they have had little introduction to a leisure ethic and were educated, for the most part, to a philosophy that proclaimed the holiness of work and the sinfulness of nonwork.

Problem or asset? The Harris report makes a concluding observation from its survey:

> Generalizations about the elderly as an economically and socially deprived group can do the old a disservice, for they confront older people with a society who sees them merely as a problem and not as part of the solution to any of society's problems. . . . An exclusive emphasis on the problems of old age can do the young a disservice as well. It might tempt the young to turn their heads away from the elderly, these reminders of what life will be like for them too some day, and to focus their attention instead on a youth-oriented society. In turning away, they would deprive themselves of the contributions that older Americans can make to themselves and to society as a whole.[12]

Concern for the Third Age

In the first part of the twentieth century, there was in the United States a concerted effort to provide better opportunities for youth. The last part of the century may well be spent in showing like concern for the aged. The human life-span seems to be evolving into three phases of emphasis: a first devoted to education, a second involved with family and vocation responsibilities, and a third given to retirement. As one octogenarian commented, "Why do we put all the fun into youth, all the work into middle age, and all the rest into old age?" The third age may well prove to be the longest segment of our lives. Leisure services and recreation choices may contribute to a better quality of life for those added years.

What is it like to be old? The basic psychological needs of the elderly do not differ radically from those of people at any other age. The needs for new experience, social interaction, response, security, self-expression, and the aesthetic or creative are constant. The stimuli resulting in satisfactions of those needs often decrease for the aged because of changes in life situations.

Regardless of the terminology used, most of the literature addresses the role of leisure outlets to provide those stimuli. The contents of the *Senior Citizens' Chapter* from the 1961 White House Conference on Aging were reiterated and reemphasized in the 1971 White House Conference.

The *1976 Bicentennial Charter for Older Americans* restated the charge with the fourth of its nine basic rights: "The right to an opportunity to participate in the widest range of meaningful civic, educational, recreational, and cultural activities. The varying interests and needs of older Americans require programs and activities sensitive to their rich and diverse heritage. There should be opportunities for involvement with persons of all ages in programs which are affordable and accessible."[13]

The goal for this growing segment of the population is to provide an environment that will allow a sense of human worth and dignity. Leisure outlets as well as work involvements must be accepted as meaningful sources of human values by all of society.

A look at history. Although old age has always been with us, the concentration of attention on the elderly in the United States did not mushroom until after World War II. A 1950 national conference was followed by other White House Conferences in 1961 and 1971, and another is scheduled for 1981. The Older Americans Act (1965) and its major amendments (1973) have provided federal funding for education, research, and projects on almost every phase of life support that would enhance the opportunities for older Americans. In 1977, the Labor–HEW Appropriations Act provided some $401.6 million to be administered by the Administration on Aging for training, multidisciplinary centers of gerontology, multipurpose centers for communities, social services, nutrition programs, and model projects. Another $22 million was added for 1978 funding. In addition, monies were appropriated to stimulate volunteer services, research, energy conservation, housing, and transportation that pertained to the aged.

Other evidences of the growing focus on older populations include the following:

1. Social Security benefits have increased fifty percent since the 1971 White House Conference.

2. Every state has produced a plan for the delivery of services through Area Agencies on Aging.

3. The National Council on Aging, early in the 1970s, identified over 350 organizations that served the aged.

4. The American Association of Retired Persons and the National Retired Teachers' Association boasted eleven million members in 1978.

5. The National Institute of Senior Centers was formed to aid in the development and management of the increasing numbers of multipurpose centers.

6. Institutes or centers of gerontology have been formed in connection with many institutions of higher learning.

7. Thousands of aged volunteers have participated in the Retired Senior Volunteer Programs, Foster Grandparents, Vista, and other federally sponsored programs.

8. Gerontology as an academic field has come of age. More than 1,300 different programs were identified on college campuses at the 1977 annual meeting of the Association for Gerontology in Higher Education.

9. Nursing home administrators must adhere to standards for programs and facilities as spelled out in the March 29, 1976, *Federal Register*.

10. The National Council on Aging listed 4,704 senior centers and clubs in its 1974 Directory. Only 24.5 percent of those existed before 1965.

11. The National Institute on Aging and a Special Committee on Aging in the Senate are evidences of further emphasis at the federal levels.

12. As one example of the move to educate persons who will be or are working with older Americans, the Ethel Percy Andrus Gerontology Center at the University of Southern California listed forty-eight separate courses during four two-week summer sessions in 1977.

The above list is suggestive rather than inclusive. In general, the present social and funding environments would seem to be favorable for extended recreation services for the aging.

Recreation Programs

Recreation programs for the elderly are currently sponsored by public park and recreation departments, voluntary agencies, private foundations, industries, philanthropic clubs

Figure 13.2. Leisure brings joy to many retired people.

such as Altrusa, fraternal organizations and service clubs such as Kiwanis International, retirement housing developments such as Sun City, or associations of the aged themselves such as the National Retired Teachers' Association.

Types of programs. The programs suitable for the aged somewhat duplicate the interests of any adult age, but needs assessments must be made for this age group as with any other. Ethnic, economic, social, and educational differences must be considered. Present diverse offerings have progressed far from

the old shuffleboard, bingo, and kitchen band smorgasbord of yesterday.

Sports and physical activity. Keeping physically active is a *must* for good health in later maturity. Jogging clubs, bowling, sailing, physical exercise programs, and dancing of all kinds are popular.

Group discussions, forums, and political activism. Increasingly well attended are the opportunities to discuss social and political issues with one another, with political power personnel, or with other generations.

Classes, workshops, and seminars. Machine tool operation, cooking for one person, problems of death and dying, will and estate planning, arts, and nutrition are all possibilities for inclusion. Classes in pre-retirement planning have been especially helpful for the middle-aged individual who is encouraged to anticipate future needs in health, housing, finance, legal aspects of retirement, and leisure.

Information and referral services. Although the senior may come to the senior center for recreation programs, an aware staff will utilize the opportunities to give information or referral on matters of health, housing, employment, finance, and other concerns. Many elderly who would not think of being seen near a welfare office have been helped to understand social services available to them through the center's referral service.

Service activities. The older person needs to be needed. Service to others is a viable recreation outlet in which both the server and those who are served can reap benefits. Through federal programs like Foster Grandparents or through recreation center organized tutoring, transportation service, and telephone alert systems, the elderly are put back into the mainstream of the community.

The Handy Man service, which allows older people to use skills in electrical repair and carpentry to help refurbish appliances or furniture, is a fairly new addition to recreation service ideas. The use of teenagers to do cleaning and yard work for elderly residents gives an opportunity for helpful interaction between two age groups.

Cultural and educational offerings. There is a broad spectrum of choice here: play going, play reading, oil painting, harmonica bands, informal singing around the piano, or a lecture on opera.

Social clubs. Forming a club for those over sixty-five years old has been a starting place for more involved program efforts for the community. The clubs meet in church basements, schools, recreation centers, indus-

trial complexes, retirement communities, or anywhere that appropriate space can be found. They call themselves Keenagers, the Happy Seventies, the Borrowed Timers, the Gay Nineties, or the Senior Citizens, and they band together in community councils and state associations. Unfortunately, most clubs that do not have their own buildings are still forced to limit meetings to once a week or sometimes once a month. For a population that has almost unlimited free time everyday, that is not enough.

Travel. Not every older person is poor. Travel opportunities with the fun of planning left in and the burden of organization eliminated are increasingly popular.

Sample programs. Programs vary with the needs of the individuals involved. A monthly program for one center included: educational lectures, which ranged from food stamps to death and dying; three forums for input on political and social issues; free movies, whose titles ranged from *Audubon Screen Tour* to *Cancer Detection*; lessons in candlemaking, knitting, automotive repair, stage design, belly dancing, and meals for one; a community health service fair; RSVP recognition banquet; hobby show; a trip to Nashville's Opryland; meetings of the Senior Caucus, the Golden Kiwanis Club, and the Community Action Transportation Committee; an eye clinic; three potluck meals per week as a Title VII nutrition site; tutoring classes in remedial reading; and the regular drop-in reading, visiting, and card-playing activities.

Facilities. Whether it is feasible or desirable to have a center for the exclusive use of older Americans is still a question for discussion. Local situations vary. For some, using a wing of an existing community center provides interaction with other age groups. For others, a separate building is necessary for proper expansion of programs.

Two considerations are of utmost importance—the location and the design. Seniors, in most instances, have decreased energies for long-distance walking, and crime in the streets has made them cautious even in broad daylight. They have limited budgets for transportation even if they own cars. Parking sometimes becomes a real hazard in many of the senior centers in the central city.

In addition, good heating and lighting are mandatory, plus accessibility via doors that are wide enough to accommodate a wheelchair, ramp ways, stairs with handrails, floors that are not slippery, and walls and ceilings that absorb noise.

The multipurpose center.   The trend in the development of senior centers is toward a multipurpose approach to services. By definition, the multipurpose center, particularly if it is to be eligible for federal funding, must "provide social, recreational, educational, counseling, health, nutrition, employment, and voluntary community service components."

Waxter Center in Baltimore, Maryland, is an example of one of the newest and most sophisticated multipurpose centers. Located in downtown Baltimore and funded entirely from a public bond issue, it boasts three floors and 55,000 square feet. It houses a lounge, dining room, auditorium, service and program offices, swimming pool, physical therapy area, model apartment, kitchen, dental suite, craft center, first aid room, and an in- and outpatient care facility.

Nursing home facilities.   The days of the dingy, cell-like accommodations for the elderly ill are all but over. In their place, sometimes through government mandate, is the convalescent center that exhorts the patient to be as active as health will allow and to enjoy a clean surrounding with as much freedom of choice in movement as the facility can tolerate. State health regulations, extended care facility federal restrictions, and better architec-

tural understanding of the needs of elderly patients have done much to improve the environment. Activity directors are employed to stimulate both mental and physical involvement, and facilities are designed with space for crafts, cultural programs, and exercise rooms.

Nutrition sites.   Title VII of the Older Americans Act provided monies to make meals available for the elderly. In those provisions were amounts earmarked for recreation and social services. Recreation professionals must be more involved in the development of adequate planning for expanding leisure choices at the meal site, wherever it is located.

Retirement communities.   The Sun City and Leisure World complexes are self-contained units in which the aged may find a variety of living accommodations, experience countless numbers of recreation choices without leaving the confines of the area, and have access to transportation to other areas at will. The high-rise complexes, built primarily for the elderly poor by the federal Housing and Urban Development program, for the most part have had meager space allotments outside or inside for healthful recreation facilities.

Private and religious organizations have created a broad span of living facilities, from trailer parks to condominiums, which maintain excellent recreation facilities and programs. The older person of today has a much wider choice in planning retirement years.

Leadership needs.   State programs for the aged have grown somewhat like the proverbial Topsy. Many who now have the responsibility for serving the elderly have had little background or experience to qualify them for their duties. More attention must be given on an interdisciplinary basis to professional preparation, continuing education, and in-service education for those who serve this segment of the population. Demands for personnel are expanding. More park and recreation curriculums must include the special needs and interests of the senior citizen. Practical fieldwork experience must include interaction with both the well and the ill elderly. Research efforts to explore better means and models for delivery of service to the elderly must be accelerated.

Coordination—Everyone's Finger in the Pie

There are now so many organizations trying to minister to the aged that particular attention must be given at the local level to avoid duplication of effort. In spite of the network of coordinating Area Agencies in each state, there are still many examples of isolation instead of coordination among local, state, or even federal programs. Serving the aged has become a popular philanthropic bandwagon. Each organization must take the initiative to seek a better system for interfacing its contributions with those of other agencies.

An Eye on the Future

Stieglitz informed us that "success or failure in the second forty years, measured in terms of happiness, is determined more by how we use or abuse our leisure than by any other factor."[14] If the recreation needs of future generations of aged are to be met, recreation personnel must:

1. Help to change public attitudes toward retirement so that this period of leisure may be so meaningful and rewarding that it will no longer be dreaded.

2. Help to create social values that will lend social status and prestige to the leisure roles of the aged.

3. Realize that the aged of the future may not duplicate the attributes of the aged of today, since they will have lived through different leisure experiences unknown in the earlier years of our present aged.

4. Recognize that people spanning the years from sixty-five to one hundred cannot be dealt with as one age group. Knowledge of the aging process and its physical and psychological toll is important to program planning.

5. Plan programs that will integrate the aged with other age groups as well as those that will allow peer association.

6. Create a greater variety of program opportunities with increasing emphasis on social, mental, and cultural activities, including classes that will teach new skills.

7. Use every available means of contact to encourage the isolated aged to participate in recreation.

8. Encourage provision for recreation facilities and leadership in retirement communities and homes for the aged.

9. Plan *with*, not *for* this age group.

10. Keep fees and charges low.

11. Get involved in community issues that affect the ability of the aged to move freely—for example, transportation, crime in the streets, ramps, and lighting.

12. Take the leadership in developing curriculums for the preparation of personnel who serve the aged.

Joseph Lee, father of the playground movement, said, "We do not cease playing because we are old; we grow old because we cease playing." The parks and recreation profession must look to the needs of the aged so that they may retire *to*, not *from* life.

The Disadvantaged

The inscription at the base of the Statue of Liberty reads, "Give me your tired, your poor, your huddled masses, yearning to breathe free." And America has obliged.

Today there are more than thirty million people in the United States whose income places them within the official definition of economic poverty. But are these poor Americans the only disadvantaged? Who are they? We've changed their names often—the underprivileged, the impaired, the deprived, the disadvantaged. We have not yet, as a profession or as a nation, improved drastically their circumstances, although social conscience and federally funded crash programs have spotlighted their concerns.

By definition, the disadvantaged are those who have been denied the ability to meet their potential because of social or environmental circumstances, rather than personal actions. The inference is clear; their situation is not a direct result of their own decision or indecision.

The terms *disadvantaged* and *minority* are not synonymous, although the chances of being disadvantaged often seem to increase if an individual is a member of a minority group. All too frequently the linking of these labels results in excessive concern for some who can operate very well independently (all blacks, for instance, are not poor or culturally deprived) or in overlooking some who are not considered minorities yet are educationally, socially, economically, or culturally disadvantaged (for example, the illiterate aged or foreign-born whites).

Types of Disadvantage

We are dealing primarily with four types of deprivation, although they may, at times, overlap.

Economically deprived. By 1976 data, the majority of the poor lived in central cities or in rural areas, were either under age eighteen or over age sixty-four, and, surprisingly enough, were white rather than nonwhite.[15]

Educationally disadvantaged. Lack of education handicaps adults and is transferred to their children. Not all of the educationally deprived are economically poor, yet research indicates that, "Education—not jobs—is the single most important factor in determining whether a family is poor."[16]

Culturally deprived. Individuals who, because of ethnic or geographic circumstances, are isolated in urban ghettos or inaccessible rural areas have special problems in meeting leisure needs. Lack of mobility, negative environments, and language barriers narrow their opportunities and reduce their ability to be comfortable in programs designed for the predominant culture.

Socially disadvantaged. Social deprivation is often a result of a combination of poverty, ethnic, educational, or geographic circumstances. Many are shortchanged both by birth and by their environment. Discrimination because of age, sex, race, religion, or ethnic prejudices often closes recreation doors in spite of affirmative action or equal opportunity mandates.

Recurring Situations

Historically, both the depression of the 1930s and the social unrest of the 1960s evolved an increased attention to and funding for park and recreation programs for the less fortunate. The WPA (Works Progress Administration) playground offerings and the PWA (Public Works Administration) and CCC (Civilian Conservation Corps) parks of the depression years had their counterparts in the hastily formed, federally funded leisure opportunities initiated to cool the heat of the 1960s riots in areas like Detroit and Watts.

By the late 1970s, the CETA (Comprehensive Employment Training Act) and the YACC (Young Adult Conservation Corps) programs were being used to provide personnel for park, recreation, and conservation jobs. President Carter's welfare program of the late 1970s earmarked over 4,000 jobs that could be directly related to park and recreation concerns.

Challenges

As the park and recreation profession in a democratic nation seeks to serve the disadvantaged populace, it faces several of the barriers listed here.

Current stereotypes. All too often, we equate skin color (black, red, any nonwhite) with poverty, aggression, poor educational background, and/or potential delinquency. The foreign-born is typecast; age and sex stereotypes abound.

Discrimination practices. In spite of equal opportunity directives and monitoring, economic status, social position, ethnic affiliation, age, or sex often deter the disadvantaged from recreation programs because of others' negative attitudes.

Isolation. "The definitive characteristic of poverty and racism is isolation—the inability of too many of their victims to find any escape other than through alcohol and narcotics."[17] Transportation needs are great both in rural and in urban poverty pockets.

Negative environments. Ghetto slums, language inadequacies, and surroundings that are not stimulating or are overstimulating (crowded, noisy) provide backgrounds for discomfort as the individual moves into leisure experiences provided for the dominant culture.

Lack of indigenous leadership. The disadvantaged, and especially the youth, need models. Godbey's 1972 study of *Participation of Minority and Disadvantaged Students in Recreation and Park Curricula* indicated gross underrepresentation of the disadvantaged in 137 colleges surveyed.[18] The mandate to recruit leaders who have experienced the problems of the disadvantaged is obvious.

Roles for Recreation

Faced with existing situations, the park and recreation profession has an obligation to expand its role to include at least the following:

Advocacy. If we are to meet the recreation needs of the disadvantaged, we must play an advocacy role in issues such as education, nutrition, energy, housing redevelopment, crime control, transportation systems, greenbelts, drugs, and delinquency control. Participation in and satisfaction from leisure programs are greatly dependent upon these other life-sustaining factors.

Availability. Often mobile units can be used to take programs to an isolated environment to which the individual feels accustomed and in which he is comfortable. Special transportation to recreation facilities is often needed to stimulate participation.

Leadership. The outreach leaders have proved effective in meeting the disadvantaged in their own environments. Greater attention to recruiting the disadvantaged in park and recreation curriculums and possible relaxing of some restrictive admissions requirements may be necessary to attract suitable leadership personnel.

Broadened program philosophy. Perhaps the greatest boon to increased participation would be the acceptance of a variety of seemingly nonconformist activities without imposition of middle-class judgments. Before we can broaden recreation horizons, we must accept and not criticize people's present leisure choices. Pitching at rats in the alley may offend leadership sensibilities but has provided a very practical leisure pastime for many ghetto youngsters for years.

Organization of effort. The National Recreation Association created a Special Bureau of Colored Work as early as 1919. More recently the NRPA Ethnic Minority Society has attempted to organize the states to concentrate on the needs of minority and disadvantaged groups. Such unification of effort is a first step in improving existing conditions.

A Lost Cause?

Ralph Abernathy, former president of the Southern Christian Leadership Conference, has indicated that the poor "have no leisure, that their total existence is concentrated on survival."[19] Yet other authors picture them with long hours to spend before a television set, which all too often depicts a life-style that seems highly unattainable. In our judgment, the economically disadvantaged, in particular those without jobs, have large segments of free time. What is missing is the availability of meaningful, accessible opportunities for recreation in that time. Cohen pictured the young in these words: "Faced by leisure goals he cannot reach, with little commitment or attachment to others, and lacking any sense of control over his future, his situation contains an edge of desperation."[20]

Abernathy advised, "Right now there are two major barriers to the achievement of equality of leisure for the poor people of America: lack of equal justice and lack of quality education. Anyone who talks about leisure for poor people must first deal with these two issues realistically."[21]

Can the park and recreation profession help improve conditions in both of these categories? Many of the same kinds of challenges created by the disadvantaged apply also to other segments of the population treated in this chapter. With unification of effort, acceptance of a vigorous activist role, and expanded concentration of concern, we should be able to provide more equality of opportunity, if not more equality of results.

Penal and Correctional Institutions

Despite the many social forces that have attempted to stamp out the causes of delinquency, there are still individuals of varied ages who find themselves barred from society because they committed some antisocial act. The old-fashioned penal and correctional institution, the reform school, and the federal penitentiary fostered the concept that the inmates had given up their rights as citizens and had lost all privileges except those that would keep them physically alive. The best treatment that the first-time offender or the hardened criminal could expect was a marching drill in the yard or hours of sitting.

Fortunately, the modern philosophy of treatment for those who have been deprived of their freedom in society shows more enlightened thinking. In spite of insufficient funds, lack of trained leadership, and sometimes adverse public opinion, prison administrators are consistently making efforts to provide meaningful activities for the leisure of prisoners.

Need for Recreation Programs

Recreation programs are far from being a luxury in the prison. Recreation is being offered, in most instances, not so much to relieve the boredom of the inmates, but to help them in the process of again becoming contributing, law-abiding citizens. More and more prison officials view recreation programs as a basic right and necessity rather than as a luxury and privilege.

The values of recreation to the prisoner or to the confined juvenile delinquent are the same as those for any individual. For the prisoner, physical recreation affords stimulating exercise, a release of energies, and a safety valve or sublimation of aggressive urges. Team activities may teach a prisoner new lessons in self-control, cooperation, the assumption of responsibility, and an awareness of limitations. Prisoners may learn skills in art, music, or other areas, which will broaden their horizons for future recreation choices. New interests are awakened; new insights are gained; new skills are learned to assist in rehabilitation.

For the prison administration, recreation activities seem to cut down on needs for disciplinary measures. Maintaining order is easier; control through taking away recreation privileges is often more successful than more drastic forms of punishment. Recreation is, quite frankly, used by some prison authorities as a method of "keeping the lid on."

For society as a whole, rewards come in two ways. Inmates who have been successfully rehabilitated are less apt to return to prison as a continued tax burden. Lessons learned may not only divert them from further misdemeanors but will help them adjust as contributing members of society.

Programs and Facilities

The recreation needs of individuals behind bars are as varied as those of their counterparts outside prison. Unfortunately, their choice is much more confined. Usual offerings consist of team sports, cards, checkers, chess, reading, some music activities such as choral and instrumental groups, hobby pursuits, and second-rate films. Programs are dependent upon available facilities and leadership.

The reasons most often cited by authorities for poor programs include: lack of professional recreation staff, lack of proper facilities, too strong an emphasis on custodial care and security, and administrative authority's general resistance to change. However, because of the efforts of a few enlightened prison officials, some innovative programs have been initiated. Richard W. Velde describes the vast pool of creative resources within our prisons that, until recently, have been virtually ignored.[22] He cites Leavenworth prison as having had

very successful one-day art shows annually since 1972, when 500 works of art were sold for $11,000. The money is used to purchase additional paints and supplies. Also mentioned by Velde is a professional theater company at San Quentin and other dramatic and artistic groups from prisons in New York, Minnesota, and Idaho.

Existing facilities in penal institutions are varied in scope and extent. Most have some provisions for recreation programming. Many prisons have limited outdoor areas for sports activities. There is a serious need for more space to be allocated for both indoor and outdoor activities. There is evidence, however, that this lack of space may not be as valid an excuse as it was once thought. Edith E. Flynn, Associate Director of the National Clearinghouse for Criminal Justice Planning and Architecture, says:

> An active reading program does not require a great amount of space. All it takes is the administrator's willingness to permit access to local public library services that are readily available to his facility. Unfortunately, the number of institutions, and particularly jails, featuring such a program is limited indeed. Further, most arts and crafts do not require much space. They can be conducted in cell or day room areas. What they do require is the willingness on the part of the administrative staff to admit volunteer workers to their facility, with private citizens and interested organizations donating the required material or equipment. Physical exercise and conditioning programs likewise do not require great amounts of space. They need only the concern of a staff member to plan, develop, and conduct the exercises on a regular basis. The great diversity of leisure-time recreation activities that are available to jails and prisons do not depend on space.[23]

Leadership

Few correctional or penal institutions have adequate recreation leadership. Such deficiencies seriously curtail program opportunities. The meagerness of the offerings is explained by the fact that money from the canteen provides the principal source of recreation funds in many instances. Until such time as the general public, who support these institutions through their taxes, can be made more aware of the need for expanded recreation leadership, facilities, and programs, much that could help rehabilitate the delinquent will be impossible.

What Lies Ahead

One of the most promising methods of dealing with the complex problem of rehabilitating criminals is called *community-based corrections*. It is described by Flynn as using, to the fullest extent possible, community-based programs and resources to re-educate, rehabilitate, and redirect the attitudes and behavior of offenders in order to make them self-sufficient and productive members of society. Such programs include residential and nonresidential activities that do not endanger the safety of local citizens.

Various types of offenders are treated with a wide range of programs, with recreation and leisure counseling playing important roles in helping them to rebuild their lives with the family and community. In this way, offenders can avoid the "social shock" that takes place after months or years of incarceration.

Implicit in this concept is the need for community correctional centers, regional facilities, halfway houses, and prerelease centers. It will be expensive, but so is the present method of containment, which offers very little hope. It is estimated that eighty percent of all crimes today are committed by those who have previously been through the criminal justice system. There will still be a need to house the hard-core offenders in facilities similar to prisons of today, but the promise of better opportunities for those capable of adjustment rings eternal.

Selected References

Adler, Joan. *The Retirement Book.* New York: William Morrow and Company, 1975.

Atchley, Robert C. *The Sociology of Retirement.* Cambridge, Mass: Schenkman Publishing Co., Inc., 1976.

Avedon, Elliott. *Therapeutic Recreation Service.* Englewood Cliffs, N.J.: Prentice-Hall, Inc., 1974.

Bannon, Joseph J., ed. *Outreach.* Springfield, Ill.: Charles C. Thomas, Publisher, 1973.

Butler, Robert N. *Why Survive?* New York: Harper & Row Publishers, 1975.

Carp, Frances M. *Retirement.* New York: Human Sciences Press, Behavioral Publications, Inc., 1972.

Fain, Gerald S., and Hitzhusen, Gerald L., eds. *Therapeutic Recreation: State of the Art.* National Therapeutic Recreation Society, 1978.

Fogel, David, ed. "Special Issue—Recreation in Corrections," *Parks & Recreation* 9, no. 9 (September 1974).

Frye, Virginia, and Peters, Martha. *Therapeutic Recreation: Its Theory, Philosophy and Practice.* Harrisburg, Pa.: Stackpole Books, 1972.

Grabowski, Stanley M., and Mason, W. Dean, eds. *Education for the Aging.* Syracuse, N.Y.: Eric Clearing House on Adult Education, 1975.

Incani, Albert; Seward, Barry L.; and Sigler, Jack E. *Coordinated Activity Programs for the Aged.* Chicago: American Hospital Association, 1975.

Johnson, Kenneth R. *Culturally Disadvantaged.* Palo Alto, Cal.: Science Research Associates, Inc., 1970.

Kraus, Richard. *Therapeutic Recreation Service.* Philadelphia: W. B. Saunders Co., 1973.

May, Elizabeth E.; Waggoner, Neva R.; and Hotte, Eleanor B. *Independent Living for the Handicapped and the Elderly.* Boston: Houghton Mifflin Company, 1974.

Murray, Albert. *The Omni-Americans.* New York: Outerbridge & Dienstfrey, 1970.

The National Council on the Aging, Inc. *Senior Centers.* Washington, D.C., 1975.

Nesbitt, John A.; Brown, Paul D.; and Murphy, James F., eds. *Recreation and Leisure Service for the Disadvantaged.* Philadelphia: Lea & Febiger, 1970.

O'Morrow, Gerald. *Therapeutic Recreation.* Reston, Virginia: Reston Publishing Co., 1976.

Puner, Morton. *To the Good Long Life.* New York: Universe Books, 1974.

Rosow, Irving. *Socialization to Old Age.* Los Angeles: University of California Press, 1974.

Sherrill, Claudine. *Adapted Physical Education and Recreation.* Dubuque, Iowa: William C. Brown Company, Publishers, 1976.

Shivers, Jay S., and Fait, Hollis F. *Therapeutic and Adapted Recreational Services.* Philadelphia: Lea & Febiger, 1975.

Stein, Thomas A., and Sessoms, H. Douglas. *Recreation and Special Populations.* Boston: Holbrook Press, Inc., 1973.

Ward, Colin, ed. *Vandalism.* New York: Van Nostrand Reinhold Company, 1973.

Woodruff, Diana S., and Birren, James E. *Aging, Scientific Perspectives and Social Issues.* New York: D. Van Nostrand Company, 1975.

Part Five
Leadership—The Key to Quality

The final test of a leader is that he leave behind him in other men the conviction and the will to carry on.

Walter Lippmann

No social movement is born and progresses without both human recognition of needs and the implementation of a plan to satisfy those needs. The park and recreation movement is a social movement. It grew out of social changes that influenced the directions of human energies, talents, and expectations.

Part Five explores the rationale for leadership in leisure services and then describes the concerns, successes, and disappointments of the profession that emerged to meet the leadership demands. It takes a direct look at professional problems. Yet the future is optimistic. Goals have been set, and the wheels of progress are grinding more rapidly. The responsibilities are great, but rewards in human satisfaction make the acceptance of those responsibilities exciting, challenging, and worthwhile.

14
Leadership—Who's at the Helm?

If the trumpet give an uncertain sound, then who shall prepare for the battle?

Corinthians 14:8.

Human leadership, even in a technological age, is still the most essential tool in work and in leisure. Conditioned by, but more essential than finance, facilities, or program offerings, is the importance of one human being's impact upon another. The power of leadership is one of the great mysteries of human nature, although there has been accelerated effort to study its origins and effects in the last ten years, particularly as leadership styles affect production or worker satisfaction in business and industry.

There is always a need for inspired, creative leadership in the park and recreation profession, but there is no room for complacency. Park and recreation leadership, in order to survive, must adapt to changing life-styles and values, inspire, open new and exciting doors to human growth and development, stimulate active involvement, supervise, guide, or simply provide a place in which an individual may choose a leisure outlet. It must, at different times, levels, and circumstances, be a planner, advocate, catalyst, and provider.

The Need for Leadership

Thoreau once observed, "Americans know a great deal about making a living, but very little about making a life." As a society, we give a great deal of attention to education and guidance for career goals, and we somehow think that we will automatically learn how to use our leisure. However, qualified and competent leadership is needed not only to plan ahead for finance and environment, but also to help develop appropriate skills, appreciations, and attitudes that will allow the citizenry to live fully in their discretionary time.

Charles Brightbill emphasized the need for quality leadership with his comment: "Because leisure will impose challenges heretofore unknown to free men, because its impact upon the social fabric can either be a generating influence or a devastating force, and because recreative living requires human perceptions different from the traditional, the finest kind of leadership is needed."[1]

At the White House Conferences on Children and Youth (1960, 1971) and the White House Conferences on the Aged (1961, 1971), both lay and professional leaders stressed the importance of professional leadership in meeting recreation needs for all ages.

One can cite a host of examples of communities, large and small, that sought to erect beautiful facilities without adequate provision for leadership for programming. The outcomes have been essentially the same—meager use of the facility and a disappointing response to the recreation offerings. The addition of a dynamic, professional leader has increased the use of an area by as much as 500 percent. That leader does not necessarily direct every activity but makes it possible to choose among exciting alternatives.

Changing Concepts of Leadership

The twentieth century has seen a changing attitude toward the need for and importance of leadership in park and recreation experiences for all ages. Millions of dollars of public tax monies are spent on the provision of leisure offerings. It would be irresponsible to minimize the importance of competent planning, direction, supervision, and evaluation of the results of those expenditures.

For many years, the literature about recreation leadership confined itself primarily to the direct, face-to-face context. There were many protests, such as: "Why teach a child to play? No one ever taught me." "Swimming lessons? I just fell into the swimming hole and started paddling." "Adults can certainly take care of their own fun." The old attitude still prevails in statements similar to those of Robert Smith: "When I was a kid, the way we got to play baseball was this: school was out, we ran home and hooked a handful of cookies, hollered 'I'm home, goin' out on the block' and met a friend who had an old first baseman's mitt and a ball, went down the block a little and hollered at the kid who had the bat . . . . We went to the vacant lot and played a game resembling major league baseball only in that it was played with a bat and bases. It was fun."[2] The game probably was fun for those who could find a vacant playing area, who were aggressive enough to insist on being part of the team, or who played by right of ownership of equipment.

But what about the ones left out? The old idea that leadership or direction will thwart freedom of play is fortunately giving way to the newer concept that a certain amount of direction and control is necessary and inevitable and that it is imperative that we get the right kind of control. The impulse to play is natural for children or adults. The form of play is not innate; the opportunity for recreation in a crowded America does not materialize magically when needed. Our American capacity to misuse the new hours of leisure is evidence of the fact that all ages, from the nursery-school cherub to the retired senior citizen, need inspired leadership to stimulate interest in satisfying outlets.

Freedom of choice in recreation pursuits demands leadership to provide creative opportunities and to give guidance by direct or indirect methods. The competent park and recreation professionals of today are agents for change in the total community at several levels in the leadership structure. They have *technical* and *conceptual* skills. Most importantly, they are skilled in *human relationships*, for, to a great extent, the park and recreation province is a people province. Today's leaders do not thwart those who are ready to engage in recreation without direction, but they create an environment that may give wider opportunities in self-directed outlets. On the other hand, leaders are prepared to direct those activities and persons who need or want guidance and instruction.

L. H. Weir, the first field representative for the National Recreation Association, stated, "It is plain common sense to order the use of leisure just as it is needful to order work and to order the relationships of people to each other in modern society."[3] That statement was made more than forty years ago. His views are even more forceful in the complexity of today's environments.

The Nature of Leadership

What is a leader? Who qualifies?

Theories

Several theories of leadership have evolved over the years. They can be loosely categorized according to emphasis as trait, situation, and relationship.

Trait theory. Prior to 1930, the prevalent belief was that leadership was the property of the individual. The leader emerged at birth with the right combination of genes that would make for skilled and inspired leadership. The trait theories were backed by research that tried to isolate universal characteristics among those who were recognized as successful leaders. Early literature proposed that a limited number of individuals inherited certain personality characteristics that gave them a "corner" on leadership capabilities. Later thinking indicated that such traits could be acquired through proper education and opportunity.

Stogdill, in studying personal factors associated with leadership, concluded that the average person who occupied a position of leadership surpassed the norm in intelligence, scholarship, dependability in exercising responsibility, activity and social participation, and socioeconomic status.[4] He also observed that the leader exceeded the average in sociability, initiative, persistence, self-confidence, alertness, cooperativeness, popularity, adaptability, and verbal facility. Hemphill, investigating the situational factors in leadership, found that the leader had to be a member of a group, have prestige, have knowledge of the existing field structure of the situation, and have a vision of the long-time trends of the organization.[5] His research formed a transition to the situation theories.

Although we discuss general qualities that have seemed to be helpful in park and recreation leadership roles, there is no valid proof that a particular combination of personality traits can assure successful leadership in the field. Leaders work within a variety of situations and among constantly changing group interactions. What they are as individuals will *influence* those variables, but will not always *control* the outcomes. Eugene E. Jennings, after a review of the literature that failed to produce consistent findings on the trait theory, stated, "Fifty years of study have failed to produce one personality trait or set of qualities that can be used to discriminate leaders and nonleaders."[6]

Situation theory.   In contrast to the trait theory, which focuses attention primarily on the individual who is trying to lead, the emphasis in the situational approach is on behavior—what is happening both to the leader and to the group. In this concept, leadership is a dynamic process in which different situations evoke different leaders and different group followers. In recreation, the person who emerges as an attractive motivator for the Little Theater group may play a rather insignificant role as decisions and directions are being formed for tennis tournaments. By the same token, even within the same group, leadership changes as crises or unexpected situations evolve. When the fire breaks out at camp, it may be a camper, not the counselor, who maintains the stability of the group.

If we accept the emphasis on behavior and environment, then there is certainly more room for the belief that the effectiveness of leadership can be increased through education.

Relationship theory.   A combination of the first two theories has been described by Douglas McGregor and has, perhaps, the greatest implications for the tasks of leadership in the park and recreation profession. "There are at least four variables now known to be involved in leadership:

1. The characteristics of the leader

2. The attitudes, needs, and other characteristics of the followers

3. Characteristics of the organization, such as its purpose, its structure, the nature of the tasks to be performed

4. The social, economic, and political milieu"[7]

This concept of leadership allows for the varied situations and groups that are encountered by the park and recreation leader. It also allows for the dynamic and changing social, moral, and political environments involved in the recreation function.

Definitions of Leadership

A look at the literature of parks and recreation and other professions will support the idea of changing concepts and definitions of leadership and leaders.

> Terry: "Leadership is the activity of influencing people to strive willingly for group objectives."[8]

> Overstreet and Overstreet: "A leader is one person who counts as more than one."[9]

> Tead: "Leadership is the activity of influencing people to cooperate toward some goal which they come to find desirable."[10]

> Douglass: "A leader is the catalyst who provides opportunity for everybody to be at his best. The creative leader is the kind of human being who dreams, pioneers, invents, acts, and leads."[11]

> Wolf: "Leadership is the art, or science, or gift by which a man is enabled and privileged to direct the thoughts, plans, and actions of his fellow men by honorable and legitimate means, for noble and altruistic ends."[12]

> Stone and Stone: "A leader is a person with a magnet in his heart and a compass in his head."[13]

The Stones' definition of the kind of person who makes a good leader connotes many qualifications for leadership that are desirable in the recreation professional. Within the magnet and the compass can be found most of the components for inspired guidance. The magnet has drawing power; if the leader does not possess enough personal magnetism to attract others, there will be no one to lead in recre-

Figure 14.1. Faith in leadership is essential in the blind-fold hike held as part of sensitivity training.

ation. The magnet also holds; the leader must be skilled enough to wear well with people, to offer varied opportunities, and to perpetuate enthusiasm. It is no accident that the magnet is located in the leader's heart; the issues of inspired leadership are always of the heart. Unfortunately, at some time, we have all found those persons who could attract people as a garbage truck attracts flies, but the magnetism was of no avail, since the attractor had no sense of direction. The compass in the head conveys the idea that the leader has enough skill, knowledge, and common sense to delineate possible and desirable objectives toward which to guide the group.

In short, leaders are people who are perceived as ones who can theorize, analyze, organize, improvise, synthesize, harmonize, summarize, and, if necessary, compromise.

Types of Leadership

Much attention has been given in the last decade to leadership styles. Although there are modifications of each, they fall mainly into the categories of authoritarian, participatory, and enabling styles.

Authoritarian

We all know the authoritarian, line-staff approach. The leader knows the rules, gives the orders, and metes out rewards and punishments. Decisions are made on a *dripolator* basis. The flow is unidirectional from the top to the bottom of the hierarchy. This type of leadership is exemplified by the crafts instructor who allows no creativity in choice or structure of the ceramic piece, or the playground supervisor who demands neatness even on the adventure playground.

Participatory

The participatory or democratic leader tries to get the group involved in decision-making processes—the *percolator* approach, if you will. There is a free flow of ideas from leader to follower and vice versa. In recreation situations, there are some decisions that must be made by the leader on the basis of knowledges and skills not yet acquired by the group. For the most part, however, since recreation involvements are voluntary, there must be input from the group in order to meet expressed interests and needs. The Girl Scout troop leader may have to guide the choice of where to build the campfire on the basis of what she knows of the restrictions of the area, but the girls will be involved with what food was brought to prepare on the fire. The team concept in leadership has been highly successful in industry experiments.

Enabling

The enabling style of leadership has emerged in the park and recreation profession as a viable alternative in a world of rising expectations for widened recreation opportunities and decreasing financial resources for direct leadership. The enabler creates an environment in which choices can be made: packaged programs for individual consumption without direction or supervision, facilities in which groups can manage their own involvements, or information dissemination to whet appetites or give instruction to broaden choices of participation.

Many enthusiasts in clubs, sports, drama, or dance, for instance, do not need either instruction or supervision. They need only a place. Others need to know from someone how they can use the rivers for rafting or what mountains are safe to climb. The trends of the future indicate that we may find information packs in television discs that will be as easy to buy in the local supermarket as the eight-track tape is today. The leader's role may be less in personal contact, instruction, and direction than in the opening of environmental, personal, or informational "doors."

Is There a Right Style?

Is there a best style of leadership? Is it possible to prescribe models that park and recreation personnel can follow with some expectation of success? Some researchers have focused primarily on *tasks* to be performed as opposed to the *relationships* of people involved. It is possible that in the park maintenance areas, a task orientation would be prominent. Others have contended that leaders put their energies on one of two things: routing followers toward some agreed-upon goal and keeping them on target; or focusing on keeping interpersonal relationships pleasant, letting minorities be heard, and increasing interdependence among members.

The optimum probably lies in a combination of these ideas. Good leadership must make it possible for goals to be reached, but there can be no sacrifice in human relationships along the way.

The focus in recreation is on people—what happens to them; how they feel; how they respond to changing situations; and how their expectations, needs, and desires are met. The efficiency expert's philosophy of leadership is hard, for instance, to apply to the enjoyment of a symphony (why repeat with the violins what has already been adequately performed by the brass?) or the exhilaration of a downhill ski run (why make so many turns when the shortest route to the bottom of the hill is obviously a straight line?). The examples are facetious, but the point is obvious. The recreation journey is often more important than the destination.

Aims and Functions of Leadership

In a profession in which thousands of persons are employed in programming, maintaining environments, or planning and researching, an inspection of overall objectives is important. Objectives define the field of desire and delineate the direction of effort. Management by objectives has emerged as a viable process in managing recreation resources as well as in other careers.

The Overall Aim

What is the raison d'être for the park superintendent, the drama specialist, or the recreation therapist? Each is after one tremendously important goal—human happiness. The park and recreation profession is the only profession that has personal enjoyment as its basic goal. But we cannot let it go at that. In a world in which fun (by whatever name you try to embellish it) is not a prestigious goal, we must learn to focus on the potential concomitant values of recreation as people seek and attain their enjoyment.

People gain enjoyment in a variety of ways and environments. What is tremendously enjoyable for one may erase the opportunity for enjoyment for someone in the immediate vicinity. For example, sailboat racing and speeding motorboats do not provide fun for both outdoor enthusiasts in the same body of water, particu-

larly on a windless day. The roar from the speeding cyclist detracts from the picnicker who wants a quiet family meal in the seclusion of the park.

In order to reach the overall aim, we have to teach skills, develop appreciations, provide complementary environments, and encourage more desirable human interactions. In order to stimulate the individual participant or the financial backer of the recreation function, it is important to focus on what values can accrue in addition to the enjoyment factor. The goal of enriched life is closely tied to a person's use or misuse of leisure.

Functions

Many lists of leadership functions have been devised. Whether we are talking about executive leadership, park maintenance supervision, or adventure playground innovative planning, it is important to remember first that the functions of leadership are always exercised with relation to people, rather than primarily to materials, activities, or places. Even the avid protector of the environment makes a plea largely on the basis of what destruction of the environment does or will do to people.

The basic functions of leadership remain essentially the same even in changing settings and can be organized into approximately six categories: planning, information, inspiration, organization, guidance, and evaluation.

Planning. Good recreation experiences don't just happen, although some seem to be spontaneous. Even the tot-lot leader needs to plan smooth transitions from one activity to another if attention spans and enthusiasm are to be kept at optimal levels. The executive's plan for both programs and facilities must fit into overall community projections.

Information. Communicating to the clientele what is available and how it can be obtained is part of the leadership role. People do not shoot the rapids if they do not know the river exists. By the same token, one is not apt to choose that experience at all if nothing is known about a canoe, a raft, or a kayak. The leader represents the undertaking and gives information concerning the purpose of the activity. The leader informs, interprets, develops skills, and teaches youngsters and adults media for recreation. By instruction and information, the leader makes possible increased enjoyment and attempts purposely and purposefully to broaden recreation horizons.

Inspiration. Leaders create an environment for individual or group ideation. Leaders whet the recreation appetite and stimulate a desire to try new offerings. They function as examples in their own choice of recreation menu. They inveigle, stimulate, motivate, and inspire with a wide range of interesting choices made appealing for the novice and challenging for the experienced or the talented.

Organization. The leader insures the success of a program by creating the proper environment. In some cases, the proper environment will include only the availability of essential equipment and materials; in other cases, the activities will demand more extensive initial measures before people, setting, and atmosphere for activity can be brought together. For example, the space set aside on the playground with swings and slides may be adequate organization for some physical recreation. On the other hand, to insure opportunities for all to participate in a drama festival or the league ball games, it may be necessary for the leader to extend energies far past the point of merely providing an area. Organization implies and involves inauguration of programs, control of planning, and delegation of responsibility for execution of plans.

Guidance. Leaders help to identify and select feasible goals, which the group comes to find worthy of its attention. They help the individual or the group to make timely and wise decisions; they are a resource from whom factors conditioning decisions can be learned. They help to administer the undertaking or draw leadership from the group. Once action is taking place, leaders supervise; they are aware of reactions; they confer and suggest; they feel the pulse of the group; they counsel individually.

Evaluation. People who lead others must objectively and effectively interpret and evaluate the paths that have been taken. They have a responsibility not only to study their own progress toward their goals but also to give those whom they lead an opportunity to analyze the efforts made, the decisions that have succeeded or failed, and the goals that have been reached or lost.

A recreation experience can be a learning experience. Growth in learning how to achieve the goals enhances the enjoyment of the activity the next time the individual or group may choose to participate. Evaluation also involves the selection and distribution of appropriate honors. Such honors do not necessarily mean tangible trophies or blue ribbons. To the leader steeped in the values of human relations, an honor may confine itself merely to a casual, "That was a much better job," to the small child who is trying his hand at candlemaking.

Hazards of Leadership

Leadership in any endeavor is a sacred trust, but for the park and recreation profession it is doubly important to maintain responsible leadership, for the very nature of the recreation experience puts potential followers in a receptive environment for leadership influences. What are some hazards and abuses to be avoided; some concerns?

Leading Selfishly

The leader who unites followers so that his or her personal goals may be accomplished has fallen into a hazard of leadership. The Little League coach who inspires and drills his team so that he may emerge the victorious mentor is abusing his sacred trust of leadership. If the entire playground population must work all summer toward a grandiose special event, which the leader may flaunt at the end of the season as her personal triumph, then the leadership role has been violated.

Demands for Excellence

The leader who pushes followers to attain the best possible athletic prowess, dramatic performance, or musical accomplishment may be destroying, not enhancing, the recreation outlet. Although it may be laudable to encourage an individual to excellence in recreation experiences, it is a mistake to push insistently for perfection. Sir Francis Bacon once said, "Some books are to be tasted; others chewed; and still others swallowed and digested." So it is with leisure experiences. It should be possible to perform some recreation choices to their fullest capacity, to engage in others with moderate effort, and to just "do" others. The key factor is that the participant, not the leader, will decide how much effort will go into which pursuit at which time. Leaders who demand excellence in every undertaking discourage those who feel they may never attain excellence and turn off those who do not wish to feel guilty if they have not chosen to perform at expected levels. A sailing friend aptly portrays the problem when she says, "Sailing just isn't fun anymore. Every time we leave the shore, my husband demands maximum performance."

Inability to Delegate

Many leaders fall into the self-fulfilling concept that only they can get the job done properly. The park manager who must oversee even the garbage disposal system and the playground supervisor who must check each item that appears on the bulletin board are both destined to failure. Such thinking keeps the mind of the leader so filled with minor details that there is no time or energy to properly perform the broader responsibilities. Secure leaders are willing to relinquish some of their

Leadership Lost

The superintendent of parks and recreation was well educated, intelligent, forceful, honest, and articulate. In his nineteen years as superintendent, he had skillfully maneuvered the consolidation of parks with recreation, established cooperative relationships with the schools, tripled the recreation land and facility holdings of the city, and raised the quality of both leadership and program.

Yesterday the board fired him. Why? Consider some of these comments about him.

"Too hard to get to see." "Never gives anybody else credit for knowing anything." "Never thanks volunteers or staff for doing a good job." "Sheer politics." "High-handed." "Talks too much. Never listens, even to his own board." "Has to have his own way about everything." "Doesn't go after federal money." "Not interested in the poor." "Has an advisory board but never asks its advice." "Seeks too much power." "Gets paid too much." "Never in his office." "Unsympathetic."

Would these traits justify his dismissal? Could he have avoided his difficulties? What other difficulties might topple a qualified executive from power?

power, to delegate both the responsibility and the authority to meet the responsibility delegated.

Superimposed Value Judgments

The recreation experience is a highly personal involvement. It is often denied because of value judgments superimposed by well-intentioned but poor leadership. Too often, in the process of trying to broaden individual recreation horizons or improve social conditions, leaders may give the impression that cultural activities are *better* than physical sports, intellectual involvements are more *prestigious* than large muscle performance, participating is always *better* than just watching, anything done outdoors is *superior* to indoor activity. Such inferences leave the bookworm who is avidly devouring the latest novel with a guilt complex for not exercising. They relegate the aged or disadvantaged who, for financial or physical reasons, must remain in a city to the "second-class citizen" category because they are not participating in nature's rural grandeur.

Balance is important. Education for broadening opportunities is important; illegal and deteriorating choices should be discouraged, but only the individual can judge what is the best or most rewarding participation at any given time. If society's philosophy or the leadership imposes values that deter us from our chosen leisure pursuits, then we have no freedom of choice.

Concern for Indigenous Leadership

"Only the old can lead the older American programs." "You can't use a white leader in the predominantly black neighborhoods." "Men shouldn't coach the girls' softball team." "You're not going to let a woman call the football game." "He's from the wrong side of the tracks to work with the country club group."

These are just a few of the attitudes that sometimes prevent the most capable potential leaders from getting the job done. The problem lies not in the capabilities of the leaders or even in the situations into which they move, but in the prejudices of the groups with which they must work.

There are some hopeful indications that more and more people are willing to look at their fellow human beings not as stereotypes, but as individuals with strengths and weaknesses, positives and negatives, that may be assets or liabilities with particular populations. Recreation experiences have a potential for integration and for erasure of stultifying stereotypes, but only if they are planned and implemented with such purposes in mind.

Types of Professional Park and Recreation Leaders

The types of park and recreation leaders fall generally and logically into three categories: the executive, the supervisor, and the face-to-face leader. In addition, there are specialists and technicians who serve in special capacities, and volunteer leaders who perform valuable services.

Executive or Administrator

The executive, whether the executive secretary of a youth organization, the head of the state natural resources department, or the superintendent of parks and recreation in a large city, has several functions, which are listed here.

Planning. Good long-range planning and definition of policies under which plans can be made grease the administrative wheels and allow the executive to fit each part of the program effort into a workable whole. Planning involves facilities and personnel, as well as programming. Freedom of choice in recreation offering is impossible without some planned order, consistency, and regularity.

Organization and coordination. The executive, seeing the whole plan, orders and coordinates existing facilities, programs, and personnel, or initiates new areas so that maximum program offerings will be facilitated. The executive leads personnel by organizing them. Accurate job descriptions keep clearly in mind the responsibilities of internal personnel, and proper coordination with other agencies eliminates duplication of effort.

Control. The executive must set a framework for controlling subordinates, although they must have input into the control system. A gathering of talented musicians may make a farce out of a symphony if no leader directs their energies toward desired results. Some measure of common control is necessary to protect the reputation of the organization in the eyes of the public it serves. Control can insure fair working conditions, opportunities, status for employees, or safety for participants.

Reporting. The recreation executive is responsible for reporting to the advisory board and to the public, in intelligible and attractive media, the workings of the organization and its accomplishments. Interpretation of goals and their implementation are important.

Finance and budgeting. The financial plan and its efficient administration again lie usually within the functions of the recreation executive. Justification of and accounting for the expenditure of public or private monies loom large in the success or failure of a department.

Evaluation. An important function is to study existing conditions, interests, opinions, and attitudes, in order to improve services, bolster employee morale, evaluate existing program offerings, equalize job loads, or simply as a public-relations tool for letting the public know what the organization is doing.

Personnel management. Recruiting, orienting, guiding, supervising, and evaluating employees and keeping harmony within the organization are also functions of the recreation executive.

Public relations. The executive, in the last analysis, is responsible for the two-way street that brings about harmony between the organization and the publics it serves. The administrator must interpret the organization to the advisory board, employed staff, participants, and the public at large, and must be ever alert to their attitudes, opinions, and ideas so that the organization, as measured by its quality of service, may be above reproach. The human relations movement has accentuated the need for interpretation of values and contributions of the recreation experience to societal welfare.

Cooperation. The executive should understand the role of the agency in relation to total community needs and should seek to establish within the agency policies of cooperation whereby those needs may be met most effectively.

Resource management. Development, protection, and management of physical environments pertinent to recreation needs are basic to the success of service offerings.

Supervisor

The supervisor in the recreation profession may be responsible for a particular program area, such as drama or arts and crafts, or may serve as a deputy officer in a particular geographic area. As a supervisor for a special activity, he or she is responsible for the planning, promotion, development, and supervision of a special phase of the total community program. The specialty must interrelate with other program offerings and must be administered within the policies of the organization.

The general supervisor, therefore, has the following functions:

Interpret the aims, objectives, and policies of the organization. The executive must depend upon the supervisor to inform subordinates with regard to operating aims and policies.

Act as liaison between staff and executive. Two-way communication between personnel and administration is provided by the supervisor, who interprets the wishes of the administrator to the staff and the reactions or ideas of the employees to the executive.

Aid in formulating and interpreting job descriptions. The immediate supervisor clarifies the responsibilities of the personnel, so that they may know what is expected of them.

Guide leaders to attain expected accomplishments. As part of the administrative staff, the supervisor, through interpersonal relationships with those for whom he or she is responsible, insures that the objectives of the organization will be attained. Such guidance may involve teaching skills, encouraging initiative, or motivating action through individual conferences, in-service training, or observation of active leadership.

Assist in the management process. The supervisor aids in the planning of program, budget, or facilities, after careful observation of the needs.

Evaluate. Measuring the efficiency or progress of those persons or programs with which he or she is directly involved is an important role in supervision.

Build creative human relationships. In the last analysis, the supervisor must make possible an environment in which creative human relationships can take place for the good of the total organization. A supervisor is, literally, a person with an abundance of vision, who sees the total plan of the administration and stimulates action to make that plan materialize.

The Face-to-Face Leader

The leader dealing with the participating public on the playground, in the hospital, in the center, or at the camp is aided by the executive and the supervisor—their administration, organization, and supervision. In turn, the face-to-face leader carries out policies and procedures within the framework of the organization and feeds back information through proper channels so that the executive may be informed of current successes, problems, or interests. The face-to-face leader teaches skills, stimulates activities, guides action, and observes results.

The person who has direct contact with the participating public is in a position to enhance or destroy the best efforts of those who supervise or administer the program. The callous industrial arts instructor in the Handy Man program of the Older American Center can destroy the ego of the would-be electrician. The groundskeeper in the park who shouts obscenities at the jogger who crossed the flower bed reflects the image of the organization.

With the full realization, as previously discussed, that combinations of character traits do not necessarily determine leadership, except in a particular environment, in a particular set of circumstances, or with a particular group of participants or followers; and with the full realization that successful leadership is not so much a matter of characteristics of the leader as it is a matter of working relationships, let's look at some attributes that seem to be prominent in those persons who have found some success in direct leadership roles in recreation experiences.

Love of people. Basic to leadership or any involvement dealing with human nature is a sincere interest in people, an acceptance of them as they are, and an acknowledgment, in practice and feeling, of the dignity and worth of each individual.

Enthusiasm. The recreation leader needs enthusiasm that at times must approach missionary zeal. Ralph Waldo Emerson once said, "Every great and commanding movement in the annals of the world was the product of enthusiasm. Nothing great was ever accomplished without it." Enthusiasm is essential, but we hasten to add that the enthusiasm must be sincere, and it must be competent. The leader does not put on a false show. Sincerity is the basis upon which trust and confidence are built. Without it, there is no great leadership.

Competent enthusiasm implies a knowledge of things to do and the ability to define feasible goals. Sometimes the most important single thing a leader can do with a group is to guide it toward suitable objectives. Enthusiasm also implies vitality, a dynamic energy, which, in turn, suggests good physical and mental health. Lack of enthusiasm for the job may be merely the outward manifestation of too little sleep, too much worry, or a malfunctioning liver. Enthusiasm stems from a peaceful inner zest, although the outward show of enthusiasm does not necessarily have to bubble and fume. The leader knows when to enthuse dramatically and forcefully and when to let quiet sincerity stimulate interest for productive action.

Awareness—empathy. A two-way hookup must exist between the leader and the group. Such a communication system implies that the leader is sensitive to the reactions of the group, can tell when interest is waning, can sense when to tighten and when to ease the reins. Awareness implies that the leader is an engineer in human relations. In short, he must be able to "walk in the shoes of his clientele."

Intellectual capacity. A leader needs, in addition to awareness of the reactions of others, a mind that can grasp knowledges, skills, and understandings. This single quality is the only one that experimental research tells us cannot be learned.

Initiative, imagination, and vision. Vital to the essence of leadership is the courage to start something new; fear stifles initiative. Vital, also, are the imagination to conceive untried and intriguing activities that whet the recreation appetite and the vision to anticipate consequences. Osborne puts tremendous emphasis on the leader's need for creative imagination as he discusses the coined word "imagineering," which means that you "let your imagination soar and then engineer it down to earth."[14] This kind of intelligent, creative vision is mandatory in a field in which people participate in activity, not through compulsion, but through attractive persuasion.

Humility, self-confidence, and self-significance. To link these three traits may seem paradoxical, yet all are found in good leaders. All are needed and must be in balance. The true leaders know the things they can do, their own importance and the influence they possess; yet they fully realize that no one is infallible and no one is indispensable to any organization. The great leader is humble. Donald Laird, noted authority in human relations, writes of Abraham Lincoln that it would have been impossible for Lincoln to have had a valet; the servant would have been, instead, Lincoln's companion.

Sense of humor, sense of the dramatic, and sense of timing. The ability to laugh even when the joke is on you is essential, if you work with people. Seeing the funny side will often ease a tense moment and will bring unity to a situation in which controversy is running high. Humans are the only animals that can laugh; it is one of our happiest attributes, a privilege of nature to be used frequently.

Comparable in importance to this sense of humor is the sense of the dramatic. A good leader capitalizes upon emotional reactions. Look back on the memorable moments of your life. They came in the dramatic situations: the times when you caught your breath at the fiery sunset, the "almost made" stolen base, the first emergence of your print in the photography lab. Being sensitive to those teachable moments and capitalizing on them make inspired leadership.

The third sense, timing, can make success or failure in a leader. When to command, when to cajole, when to be silent, when to be direct, when to initiate a new idea, when to give credit—all are important. Time is a natural resource available to all. The leader learns to work with time.

Persistence and flexibility. Again, the leader seems to embody a paradox. Enough persistency is necessary to prevent easy discouragement, but flexibility that allows one to know when to bend is just as important.

Strangely enough, the ability to learn depends in part upon the ability to relinquish what has already been learned. However well trained the leader is for today, tomorrow may bring new situations. The wise leader adopts and adapts, rearranges, modifies, or substitutes.

Fairness and consistency. You can be extremely firm if you are fair. The leader must be an objective, impartial observer. Disciplinary measures and restrictions for young or old are much more readily accepted if the leader is consistent. Children and adults need to know what to expect. Impartiality is essential. "A favorite has no friends."

Patience and optimism. People are human. Patience with their frailties is mandatory for good human relations. A leader cannot expect a perfect contribution from followers. If such were the case, there would be no followers. An optimistic outlook helps in difficult times. Optimism does not mean the unrealistic approach of a Pollyanna. The good leader knows the facts, plans within that knowledge, and hopes for good things to evolve. Leaders expect the best, but if the results in followers or programs are less than the best, they are patient and try again; or, better still, they try a different method.

Judgment, dependability, and responsibility. Rarely does a person rise to heights of leadership without the ability to see the whole situation and to judge its merits. Followers are attracted to those who will take major responsibilities and make decisions, those on whom they can depend for vision and courage. Implied in the term *judgment* is plain, old-fashioned common sense. The leader must be extroverted enough to know when to take the spotlight and sensible enough to know when the best results will come from a quiet, rearguard instigation.

Integrity. Last, but by no means least, on the list of essential character traits in a leader is integrity, upon which all other traits are based. Leaders who do not have basic personal honesty will be a menace, for they provide examples to their followers. If the pat-tern is faulty, the possibility of perfected products is remote.

Abilities, Knowledges, and Skills for Leaders

What kind of things must a successful recreation leader know? There is no magic in leadership, no sleight-of-hand tricks. Leadership in recreation is based firmly on specific, trainable skills, concepts, and abilities that must be used in concrete situations.

Knowledge of self and others. Knowing ourselves implies that we know our abilities, our strengths, and our weaknesses, and that we allow for them. Knowing others involves an understanding of human behavior, an ability to read and interpret people. The recreation leader understands the importance of human relationships and the total community process.

Knowledge of the organization and its purposes. Basic to leadership are a sound philosophy of recreation and a cognizance of the aims of the profession and the organization to which loyalty is owed. An abiding faith in those aims is essential if others are to be convinced that the goals are feasible and desirable. A recreation leader must know the why of the program as well as the how.

Ability to plan and organize. The leader learns to visualize, then organize toward objectives, learns to discriminate intelligently, to encourage the group toward attainable goals. The next step, the one most difficult for many leaders, is to assign tasks to move toward those objectives and then to allow the followers time and environment for accomplishing the desired ends. The final step in the process is to follow up the action of others to the successful conclusion of the effort. This step is all too frequently ignored.

Ability to encourage initiative. The intelligent, far-sighted leader trains other leaders. The real test for leadership is found in the ability to inspire action. Leadership, it is said, rises to its greatest height when it "sets men on fire."

Ability to work democratically. Building group morale, enlisting cooperation, sharing the task, and learning to give credit where credit is due blend in fostering democratic working relationships within a group. There are no easy formulas for group morale, but the leader who creates an environment in which people may share plans, decisions, problems, success, and achievements with a sincere respect for the contribution of each person is well on the way to cementing relationships that make a "group" from an assortment of individual personalities.

Ability to observe and be sensitive. Leaders are trained to be keen observers, to be sensitive to the reactions of people. They know how to stretch the members of a group; they are well aware that persons stretched to extended capacities never return to their original dimension. They are sensitive to the touchy spots; they handle situations so that the child or the adult does not lose face in difficulty or grow unduly boastful in success.

Ability to make decisions. Leadership, at times, demands action. The leader accepts the responsibility for making decisions. When quick decisions must be made, a leader has the courage to take action. When the situation affords time for more leisurely decision making, the wise leader takes time to weigh all aspects before plunging into motion. The executive may be involved with more numerous and consequential decisions, but the face-to-face program leader must learn that decisive choices are also necessary.

Ability to communicate. The ability to communicate, so necessary to leadership, insures that the spirit as well as the intent of ideas is shared with the group. A pleasant approach, a lively voice, and an infectious personality ease the road to communication, but certain knowledges and skills are needed also.

Ability to act, not react. Leaders do not allow other people to sway their action against their better judgment. A strong person does not wait for someone else to act and then retaliate in kind. Instead, a leader innovates, creates, and instigates.

The Roving Leader

The roving leader is one kind of face-to-face leader. The role emerged because of increasing situations in which participants could not attend a recreation or park area because of immobility caused by age, handicap, or lack of transportation; insecurity which prevented them from leaving home neighborhoods; or gang attachments in the inner city.

The mobile unit in Florida, which brings recreation outlets to the homebound; the library bookmobiles, which provide reading for rural adults and youngsters; and the New York City recreation leaders assigned to neighborhood gangs are examples of outreach work so necessary if the goal of recreation for all is to be achieved. *Outreach*, edited by Joseph Bannon, explores these special programs.[15]

The Technician and the Specialist

More and more park and recreation agencies are employing technicians or professionals with special skills. Examples include the horticulturist, the planner, the media specialist, the landscape architect, and the computer programmer. Each must be carefully oriented to the philosophy, goals, and thrusts of the organization.

The Volunteer Leader

In addition to the professional leaders, efficient and intelligent use of volunteers has been beneficial in the park and recreation field. The rewards are twofold: in good situations, both the volunteer and the recipient of the service receive benefits. With the formation of the National Center for Voluntary Action in 1970, the national spotlight was focused on the use of volunteers in a myriad of roles. The National Center is a nonprofit, private, nonpartisan organization, which has as its main goal the "stimulation and strengthening of problem solving by volunteers and voluntary organizations, alone or in concert with other institutions." It has spawned many local volunteer centers that cooperate in recruiting and educating those who wish to give service.

The Volunteers in Parks (VIP) of the National Park Service, funded in 1970, has been highly successful in giving its participants firsthand involvement with the operation of the system. Service time for one year has reached as many as 300,000 hours. The National Recreation and Park Association Board and Commission Branch has provided in-service workshops and promoted better understanding of the recreation and park functions for hundreds of volunteers who work on advisory or policy-making boards.

Reasons for use of volunteers. The philosophies concerning the balance of advantages and disadvantages in the use of volunteers are varied. With federal government monies stimulating voluntarism, the pendulum seems to be swinging heavily in favor of increased use.

The vote is "aye." Let's first take a look at the positive side of volunteer participation.

1. First and foremost, the volunteer not only expands the services of the agency, but also receives rewards and satisfactions according to the individual's motivations or desired results. Some want public recognition, some want merely to be needed, and some want social interaction.

2. Public recreation agencies have been unable for financial reasons to employ the number of leaders needed to program adequately for today's expanded leisure demands. Economy and personnel freezes during inflationary periods make the use of volunteers very attractive.

3. A special area such as oil painting, dramatic production, music instruction, and facility planning is sometimes handled by a volunteer whose talent is of such caliber that the fees for it would be beyond reach.

4. Good public relations are fostered by properly oriented volunteers. They become liaisons between the organization and the public, interpret offerings, and act as sounding boards for public opinion and interest. The use of volunteers invites participation of the total community. An active volunteer has a personal stake in the success of the program.

5. The volunteer, as a differently trained individual, may bring a fresh enthusiasm and different point of view to the activities.

6. Work as a volunteer offers self-realization and a feeling of service for the volunteer. Many aged people in the community have time, experience, and talent left unused.

7. The use of the volunteer often augments interest in adult recreation programs. Leaders in the community who are volunteering bring with them many followers who otherwise might not have embarked on any given program.

8. Interested lay citizens are influential in moving the electorate to improve parks and recreation in the community.

The "no's" have it. The use of volunteers is not without drawbacks. Following is a list of difficulties often discussed by professionals.

1. The recreation leadership task is, to the volunteer, a secondary job. The full-time job at the school, office, or home must, of necessity, come first. The executive cannot *demand* time, excellence of performance, or long-range commitments.

2. Lack of dependability is sometimes experienced within the ranks of volunteers.

3. The volunteer must be oriented and trained. Such training takes precious time from the schedule of the professional. Frequently, just as the volunteer is thoroughly trained and oriented, he or she drops out of the program.

4. Volunteers sometimes give difficulty because of vested interests in some particular area of the program. The person who offers service so that his daughter may star in the play, his son may make the team, or his friend may be soloist in the glee club must be tactfully handled.

5. The volunteer who refuses to gain knowledge of the entire community program will sometimes hinder good public relations, as the volunteer is often mistaken for the professional leader.

6. The complaint that the volunteer is actually doing more work than the paid leader may sometimes be a realistic observation, which causes unrest. Volunteers frequently feel that they should be hired after they have worked without pay for a period of time.

7. Professionals who have had poor experiences with volunteers often maintain that the biggest source of difficulty is getting rid of the undesirable volunteer. Proper selection practices could perhaps avoid the need for the dismissal, but it is difficult to refuse an offer of volunteer service. It requires the utmost tact to refuse, without giving offense, a person who is eager to serve your objectives.

8. In years of "down" markets for placing professionals in appropriate jobs, there is real concern on the part of those who are starting out in the field that volunteers who do not need monetary rewards are absorbing positions that could be better filled by jobless park and recreation professionals.

Development of volunteer service. How do we balance the positives and negatives? The solution is carefully to select, train, supervise, and evaluate the volunteer as well as the professional. Such effort takes time but will produce payoffs in recreation service to the volunteer, goodwill in the community, and improved understanding of the park and recreation mission.

Selection. Recruiting individuals, analyzing their talents, and screening them for the tasks they will be assigned are the first important steps in successful voluntarism. Although specific abilities and skills are appreciated, the novice volunteer may hold an important role in handling operational details in order to free highly skilled professionals for more demanding assignments.

Sources of volunteers. How do we entice the volunteer? Where can we search? Here is a list of suggestions for volunteer sources.

Interest surveys made in clubs, church groups, schools, neighborhood centers, and service organizations.

Talks before civic groups, PTAs, Junior League, and similar organizations, with an invitation to participate.

High school guidance programs that explore career choices.

Investigation of the rosters of those retiring from business, industry, or the professions.

Perusal of newspaper articles to get names of hobbyists.

Observation of active participants skilled enough to be used in leadership positions.

Establishment of a citywide volunteer bureau. Such centralization may evolve from volunteer centers, community service councils, or other coordinating bodies.

Federal ACTION programs, which in 1976 sponsored some thirty-seven million volunteers who worked an average of nine hours a week for a total of more than seventeen billion hours, or an estimated financial worth of $34 billion of time.

Advisory Councils, such as Robert Crawford's Council in Philadelphia, which is an excellent recruiting unit.

Assignment of volunteers.

Special orientation. No volunteer should be assigned to any task in an organization without a thorough orientation to the aims, philosophy, and policies under which the agency operates; the breadth and patterns of program capabilities; the facility availability and restrictions; and the personnel with whom the volunteer will work. All too often the volunteer is not aware of what is expected, who makes which decisions, what materials or equipment are accessible, what records must be kept, and what evaluations will be made.

Types of assignments. Robert Banes, a volunteer in the park and recreation movement for more than twenty-five years in California, indicated four categories of assignment for volunteers.[16]

Administrative volunteers—Individuals who serve in a policy making capacity—boards, commissions, committees, study groups, task forces, etc. Their contribution is primarily in decision making and the peripheral activities necessary to gather data or information for the decision (recommendation) process. There is little or no involvement in carrying out the decision objective.

Participative volunteers—Individuals who are involved in doing a task, activity or program. This would include, for example, a baseball coach, helper at a carnival, typist in the office, ticket taker at a special event, etc.

Special resource volunteers—Individuals with a special knowledge or skill who contribute that resource. An insurance expert reviews a policy for content, an industrial relations manager assists staff with the development of personnel policies, an electrician inspects lighting at a new ball park. In most instances, these are services which the public agency could buy but is receiving at no cost through donated services.

In-lieu-of-staff volunteers—A volunteer may become an unpaid staff member with full operational or management responsibilities. This usually occurs when resources such as money or people are not available to an agency. A volunteer may fill the position until the needed resources are available. An example would be the volunteer who hires personnel and supervises a summer recreation or aquatic program.

Principles for working with volunteers.

In the discussion of the role of the volunteer, certain basic principles evolve as guidelines for action.

1. Volunteer leaders can make important contributions, but the volunteer should supplement, not replace, the professional leadership.

2. In selecting volunteers, get to know the volunteer's personality and abilities before accepting the services. Careful screening will avoid future headaches. The quality of volunteers is more important than the quantity.

3. The volunteer must be oriented to the procedures and the policies of the or-

ganization in order to work within them. Volunteers must be given not only information, but inspiration—a sense of loyalty, of belonging.

4. The volunteer needs to see specific objectives. Volunteer jobs must fit into a long-range pattern, but, at the same time, must involve short-term successes and aims.

5. For best mutual satisfaction, the talents of the volunteer must be matched against the needs of the job; the tasks to be accomplished must be definite and specific.

6. Proper attention to assignment, training, supervision, and guidance must be given if the volunteer is to grow with the experience. Training institutes, staff meetings attended by volunteers, individual conferences, and encouragement of attendance at professional conferences are rewarded by more and better service from the volunteer. Manuals tailored to the needs of the volunteer have been found to add information and incentive.

7. Volunteers should be included in the planning of assignments and program events.

8. The contributions made by volunteers must be properly evaluated and recognized for satisfactory relationships. Recognition may come in many ways. Agencies present certificates, service buttons, or invitations to represent the agency at conferences or official meetings, but volunteers must know along the way that their services are observed, evaluated, and appreciated.

9. Opportunities should be given for the volunteer to improve and advance to greater responsibilities.

10. A good volunteer should not be abused by overwork.

Need for Creative Leadership

In the last quarter of the twentieth century, there is a critical need for inspired recreation leadership to stimulate and motivate satisfying use of the expanded leisure of all age groups. No longer will the laissez faire or caretaker leader meet the ever-widening demands of a more sophisticated public. Professionally educated men and women, informed in the understanding of people and their needs and skilled in a breadth of recreation outlets, must meet the challenge.

Creative leadership is required in the park and recreation profession. Paul Douglass defined the creative process as the "inner illumination which lights the path to productive action into hitherto unexplored territories."[17] Such fires must be cultivated in leadership for leisure experiences.

The park and recreation profession must continue to seek out and recruit intelligent youth to lead the parade toward enriched living in leisure. Educational curriculums must be visionary enough to inspire in new leaders the courage to evaluate the past and the present and to anticipate the future.

To the park and recreation leader goes a twofold challenge: guiding and educating the spontaneous enthusiasms of young and old. There is no more exciting incentive.

Selected References

Bannon, Joseph J. *Leisure Resources: Its Comprehensive Planning.* Englewood Cliffs, N.J.: Prentice-Hall, Inc., 1976.

Bannon, Joseph J., ed. *Outreach, Extending Community Service in Urban Areas.* Springfield, Ill.: Charles C. Thomas, Publisher, 1973.

Christiansen, Monty L. *Park Planning Handbook.* New York: John Wiley & Sons, 1977.

Cosgrove, Frank D. "Leadership" *Creative Programming, Leisure Today, Journal of Health, Physical Education, and Recreation,* (December 1973): 53.

Eppley, Garrett G. *Improve Your Public Relations.* Arlington, Virginia: National Recreation and Park Association, 1977.

Goble, Frank. *Excellence in Leadership.* New York: American Management Association, 1972.

Haimann, Theo. *Supervision: Concepts and Practices of Management.* Cincinnati, Ohio: Western Publishing Co., 1977.

Hemphill, John K. *Situational Factors in Leadership, Monograph 32.* Columbus: Bureau of

Educational Research, The Ohio State University, 1949.

Hersey, Paul, and Blanchard, Kenneth H. *Management of Organizational Behavior, Utilizing Human Resources.* Englewood Cliffs, N.J.: Prentice-Hall, Inc., 1972.

Kraus, Richard G., and Bates, Barbara J. *Recreation Leadership and Supervision.* Philadelphia: W. B. Saunders Company, 1975.

Matteson, Michael T.; Blakeney, Roger N.; and Domm, Donald R. *Contemporary Personnel Management.* San Francisco: Canfield Press, 1972.

McGregor, Douglas. *The Human Side of Enterprise.* New York: McGraw-Hill Book Company, 1960.

Stogdill, Ralph M. *Handbook of Leadership: A Survey of Theory and Research.* New York: Macmillan Publishing Co., 1974.

15
The Recreation and Park Profession

A great pilot can sail even when his canvas is rent.

Seneca

Recreation, like any other social movement, grew out of an expressed need. Changing environments, both social and natural, elicited a demand for more sophistication in the delivery of leisure services, and the park and recreation profession was born. Like other professions, it has experienced growing pains, but the field is emerging as a potent force in contributing to the quality of human life.

Is Recreation a Profession?

Is this comparatively new field of human service a profession? Here are the most commonly described components of a profession, against which we can evaluate the progress of the park and recreation movement.

General acceptance by the public as serving a social need

Basic body of knowledge

Research and literature

Professional education

Personnel standards

Recruitment

Professional organizations

Registration, certification, and accreditation

Code of ethics

General Acceptance by the Public

The services provided by park and recreation professionals have been demanded by minorities, funded by government legislation, and overwhelmed with participation by various segments of the population. In spite of the billions of dollars spent, the media attention, the advocacy emphases, and the diverse agencies offering leisure services, the park and recreation profession has not yet emerged as a clearly defined entity by the general public. Most individuals will react to questions concerning the field on the basis of whatever knowledge they have acquired from their own park and recreation experiences. Broad interpretations of the goals of the total movement are needed before the profession can expect clear understanding from the population. There are, however, hopeful signs as doctors prescribe recreation outlets as therapy, schools start to initiate leisure education, and even rioting prisoners or inner-city protesters demand more recreation as their "human right."

Basic Body of Knowledge

The park and recreation profession, like many others (medicine, engineering), has a core content to which is added information or understanding that deals with specializations. Since recreation professionals deal with human beings in social and physical environments, they must first have a basic understanding of human nature, community organization, and environmental concerns. To the base of a liberal arts education are added special professional courses related to the interpretation, program delivery system, and environment management functions.

The special knowledge base has enlarged considerably in the last ten years. The number of book titles that relate to some phase of leisure service or its values has increased more than fourfold. A most heartening aspect of the literary influx is that many books and research projects are now authored by park and recreation professionals, rather than by writers from related disciplines. Interesting, too, is the proliferation of magazines and media programs dealing with leisure topics. Two Oscars were awarded in 1977 to documentary films depicting leisure and its effects (*Leisure*, an interpretation; and *Numbered Years*, the story of the aged with expanded leisure).

Leisure Today, a magazine supplement in the *Journal of Health and Physical Education*, has been highly successful in dealing with specialized topics.

Research

For many years, recreation as a new discipline relied upon government, education, psychology, sociology, and medicine for information. Recreation research was slow to earn its wings; first, because it was easy for a new profession to rely on closely related disciplines for answers to basic problems; second, because park and recreation education was a comparatively new venture in institutions of higher learning; and third, because those who were involved with serving the public in the park and recreation systems were understaffed and busy giving the service rather than interpreting it or evaluating its outcome.

The last ten years have found increasing attention to all facets of recreation research. Federal funding sources, particularly in the areas of outdoor recreation and special populations; the development of more graduate programs in colleges and universities; and the in-

creased need for professionals to understand cause-and-effect relationships in their planning have been instrumental in the increased efforts.

The *Journal of Leisure Research*, published by the National Recreation and Park Association beginning in 1969, has provided a real stimulus for quality investigation. The journal provides a medium for interdisciplinary exchange. In addition, there have been several efforts to disseminate information through separate research newsletters.

The NRPA held a special research seminar in Denver in 1974 with the purpose of bridging the gap between research results and the application of those results by practitioners. Subsequent efforts have been encouraging. Broader exchange of research information, dissemination of pertinent published data, and informal interaction between practitioner and researcher are hopeful signs.

The NRPA has long had a research focus, beginning with the employment of George Butler by the National Recreation Association. Today there is a special research division in the association office. Significant study has been done in such diverse areas as energy conservation and model cities programs.

Professional Education

Although specialized education of park and recreation personnel has existed for some time, actual professional preparation of recreation personnel by colleges and universities is less than fifty years old. The demand for more, better prepared, and more highly specialized professionals has grown over the years. Specializations or options have now evolved in park management, recreation administration, therapeutic recreation, college union management, industrial recreation, commercial recreation, natural resource administration, outdoor recreation and outdoor education, corrections, gerontology, and youth-serving organizations.

Looking back—origins. Listed here are milestones that give a brief overview of the historical antecedents in today's profession.

National Recreation Association School for Professional Graduate Training (1926–1936)

National Conferences on Professional Preparation of Park and Recreation Personnel

> University of Minnesota, 1937
> University of North Carolina, 1939
> New York University, 1941, 1948
> Washington, D.C., 1954, 1956, 1962

National Conference on Undergraduate Professional Preparation in Health, Physical Education, and Recreation, Jackson's Mills, West Virginia, 1948

National Conference on Graduate Study in Health Education, Physical Education, and Recreation, Pere Marquette State Park, Illinois, 1950

Therapeutic Recreation Curriculum Conference, 1961

Stein Status Study on Park and Recreation Education in the United States and Canada, made every two years by the Society of Park and Recreation Educators

National Forum on Preparing Tomorrow's Park, Recreation, and Conservation Leaders, Washington, D.C., 1968

Conference on Professional Preparation in Physical Education and Recreation for the Handicapped, 1970

Conference on Articulation between Two-Year and Four-Year Curriculums, Denver Congress, 1974

Accreditation Project, 1961 to present

A Career in Parks and Recreation?

The local Rotary Club recently held its annual vocational conference for high school students, during which various professional leaders met with students interested in their particular fields. The superintendent of parks and recreation talked for about an hour with two girls and two boys who were curious about recreation as a career.

Questions came quickly. What kind of education must I have? What are the opportunities for women? salaries? chances for advancement? working conditions? future of the profession? How does the field compare with such fields of service as teaching and social work? The superintendent tried to answer all questions honestly and to indicate disadvantages as well as advantages.

In discussing the interview later, one of the students commented on the newness of the profession and the freedom for creativeness and innovation. Another remembered particularly the superintendent's obvious satisfaction in helping people increase their appreciation and enjoyment of living.

How would you have answered their questions? What do you consider the major advantages and disadvantages of leisure and recreation as a professional career? Does your state have personnel standards for park and recreation employees? What professional organizations are open to you?

Curriculums. Perhaps the best indicator of the changes in professional preparation is the rapid growth of both curriculums and numbers of majors. The demand for better personnel has grown constantly. (See Figure 15.1.) From one curriculum in the late 1930s, we have documentation of 398 curriculums in 1975. The Stein study was, at best, a conservative overview of the present proliferation of curriculums. Dr. Stein could report only those curriculums whose chairpersons responded to his questionnaire.

An informal state-by-state inquiry as the Accreditation Project was evolving in 1973, plus some additions from the Society of Park and Recreation Educators' *Curriculum Catalog,* surfaced another 170 programs either in the planning stages or already "on the books." Numbers of faculty, according to the Stein report, jumped from 369 in 1969 to 841 in 1975. Student majors numbered 35,000 in 1976. This number included two-year, four-year, master's, and doctoral students.

Most of the professional preparation programs started with four-year baccalaureate degree offerings. The master's and doctoral programs were added in fewer numbers.

In the last decade, two-year curriculums have proliferated at an intense rate (only three of the present nearly 200 were in existence in 1968). Junior colleges and community colleges have sought with two-year concentrations to serve the interests of students and the leadership needs of employers. Some two-year programs culminate in an associate terminal degree. Others are intended to form the base for continuation in a four-year curriculum. Articulation between two-year and four-year curriculums has been a source of concern for students, faculty, and potential employers. Discussions of these concerns can be found in the following documents, which are proceedings from NRPA-SPRE meetings: *SPRE Two-Year/Four-Year National Articulation Guidelines,* Society of Park and Recreation Educators, 1976; *California Park and Recreation Education Articula-*tion, Committee Report, March 4, 1972; and *Recreation and the Community College,* Joseph Bannon, University of Illinois, December 1973.

Personnel Standards

Recreation and park administrators and the agencies they represent constantly strive to improve their personnel practices. Several attempts have been made to define standards for various positions in municipal recreation departments. Agencies that work with special populations have defined evaluative measures and expectations for therapeutic recreation specialists. Federal regulations concerning equal employment opportunities and more definitive job specifications have served to place more emphasis on development and maintenance of personnel standards.

Recruitment

The gap between the supply and demand of qualified personnel that existed in the 1960s has reversed itself. Several factors have contributed to such a reversal.

1. Proliferation of park and recreation curriculums

2. Increased awareness of the career possibilities in the park and recreation profession

3. Greater national focus on recreation jobs

4. More literature and media interpretation support

5. Inclusion of park and recreation careers in high school occupation resource booklets and career days

6. Increased trend to use part-time or specialist personnel in some park and recreation departments

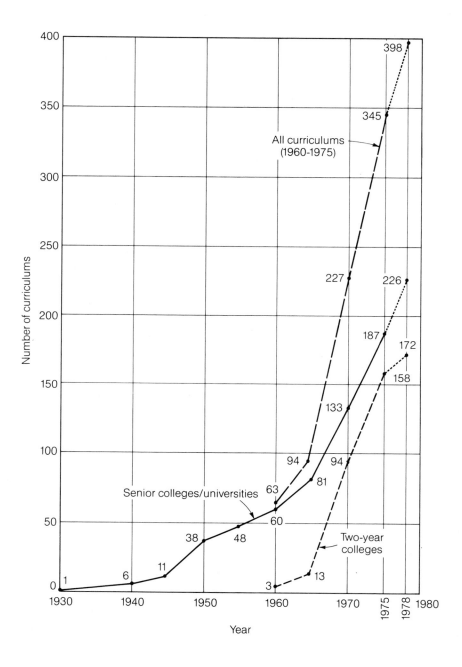

Figure 15.1. Number of park and recreation curriculums, 1930 to 1975. Source: *Thomas Stein,* SPRE Report on the Status of Recreation and Park Education *(1975), p. 4.*

National survey. In a 1977 *National Survey of Selected Public Recreation and Park Personnel*, Dr. Donald Henkel of the National Recreation and Park Association staff and Dr. Geoffrey Godbey of the Pennsylvania State University painted a different picture of personnel status and needs from that of a 1968 study that projected massive recruitment needs to fill the increasing demands for park and recreation expertise.[1]

The 1977 survey was restricted to "full-time, year-round personnel, employed in public, tax-supported municipal, county, special district, and state park and recreation systems."[2] Here are excerpts from the findings.

1. Approximately 85,000 full-time staff were identified, one third of whom were skilled park personnel.

2. Approximately fifteen percent were women and twenty-two percent were ethnic minorities.

3. Only 2.1 percent had primary responsibility in serving the disabled.

4. Only fifty-one percent of the chief executives had a bachelor's or master's degree in recreation and parks.

5. Women and minorities were notably absent from power positions.

The conclusions of the survey left little doubt that the 1970s brought an oversupply of personnel for a depleting job market. What are the solutions?

1. Accreditation and registration demands may eliminate those curriculums and those graduates who have not met minimum standards and should, therefore, not be in competition on the job market.

2. Job freezes mandated by dwindling economies in the tax-supported agen-

cies may ease as the general economy improves.

3. Other job prospects not dealt with in this survey may lead to greater personnel demands in commercial recreation, tourism, international potentials, community education leadership, leisure counseling, and therapeutic recreation jobs.

4. The other obvious solution, of course, is to make professional preparation so pertinent to leisure service needs that both the public and the employer will see the benefits of hiring professionally prepared individuals who will prove their worth in terms of accomplishments.

Placement. In spite of the gloomy outlooks depicted above, there are still exciting and diverse opportunities for those who are interested in employment in the park and recreation field. Here are just a few samples of types of positions or settings open to graduates.

1. Municipal park and recreation agencies—superintendent, community center director, specialist in sports or performing arts, playground supervisor, public relations officer, researcher, director of older Americans center

2. Commercial recreation—resort manager; retirement community program director; sport ranch superintendent; director of program or facilities of golf courses, ski shops, family multirecreation complexes, singles condominiums, tennis complexes, equipment sales and distribution, or experiential villages

3. State and federal agencies—ranger, outdoor education specialist, natu-

ralist, park director, planner, researcher, extension agent, conservationist, forester, wildlife manager, museum director

4. Industrial recreation—program director, facility manager, resort or center director for unions, pre-retirement counselor

5. Armed forces—service club director, special activities supervisor, youth activities director, Red Cross area director, leisure education faculty member

6. Outdoor recreation—researcher, interpreter, outdoor educator, camp counselor, camp manager, trail developer

7. Colleges and universities—faculty member in park, recreation, or leisure services departments; campus recreation director; recreation sports program specialist; recreation extension specialist; college union program director

8. Therapeutic recreation—camp director; activity therapy specialist; worker in research, management, or programs in state hospitals, developmental centers for the retarded, centers for older Americans, rehabilitation centers, or national organizations that pertain to the ill and handicapped

9. Youth-serving agencies—4-H director; program supervisor or facility manager in YMCA, Girl Scouts, Boys' Clubs, etc.

Professional Organizations

A professional organization is the mouthpiece for the profession and serves as the unifying force in professional endeavor. Over the years, a number of professional organizations have promoted the development of park, recreation, leisure, and conservation services. In far too many cases, conflict, competition for membership, and overlapping of services resulted in dividing the profession. The goal of creating a unified national organization representing the park and recreation endeavors, as well as certain aspects of the conservation movement, was finally achieved on January 1, 1966, with the formation of the National Recreation and Park Association. The following five professional and service groups merged: the *American Recreation Society*—founded in 1938 and committed primarily to recreation aspects of the movement; the *American Institute of Park Executives*—founded in 1898 and originally devoted to park resource concerns, although its scope was broadened to program functions in later years; the *American Association of Zoological Parks and Aquariums*—established in 1924 for zoological park personnel; the *National Conference on State Parks*—organized in 1921 and administered primarily by lay and professional state park personnel; and the *National Recreation Association*—established in 1906 as the Playground Association of America. A service organization, NRA boasted a large membership of both lay and professional contributors to the leisure movement.

The National Recreation and Park Association. The present National Recreation and Park Association has moved through many changes in the 1970s. It consists of the following branches, whose titles are self-explanatory:

Society of Park and Recreation Educators

American Park and Recreation Society

Student Branch

Armed Forces Branch

National Therapeutic Recreation Society

National Society of Park Resources

Council of Park and Recreation Consultants, Inc. (affiliate)

Commission and Board Members Branch

Friends of Recreation and Parks

The last two branches on the list are composed of lay members who are serving on park and recreation boards or commissions, or are simply interested enough in the thrust of the leisure services movement to contribute time or financial support.

The NRPA is unique among national organizations. Chartered as a nonprofit educational and service agency, it combines the efforts of lay persons and professionals in promoting the park and recreation cause and the leisure movement. As a result of a Special Goals Committee, chaired by Ralph Wilson, a Soil Conservation Service officer in Washington, D. C., a restatement of NRPA goals and directions was evolved in 1976. Below are excerpts from that report, approved by the policy-making Board of Trustees of NRPA.

> The Goals Committee reaffirms its strong support of the citizen-professional partnership concept on which the National Recreation and Park Association was founded.
>
> The purpose of the NRPA shall be to serve the public in its pursuit of a meaningful leisure experience.
>
> To accomplish this purpose, the Association shall assume a leadership role in the progressive development and wise administration of physical, human, and financial resources, to serve its membership and the public. [3]

The central headquarters is located in Arlington, Virginia. Regional headquarters serve a projected eight districts around the country. The functions and services of the association include:

Annual National Recreation and Park Congress

Regional institutes, workshops, and conferences

Field services to help local groups with special problems

Research development, coordination, and dissemination

Professional development—registration system, internships, accreditation, continuing education

Public information and interpretation

Public policy and trend analysis

Citizen involvement at local and national levels

Job information and referral

Technical assistance

Legislative policy information

Publications

> Parks & Recreation
> Journal of Leisure Research
> Therapeutic Recreation Journal
> Management Aids
> Curriculum Guide
> Monographs on special interests or concerns

The American Association for Leisure and Recreation. This association was formerly called the Recreation Division of the American Alliance for Health, Physical Education, and Recreation. Recreation personnel active in this division come mainly from colleges and universities and from recreation departments in the public schools. The parent association has been involved with functions that include research, professional preparation, workshops and institutes, leisure counseling, and leisure education. Publications include: *Research Quarterly*, the *Journal of Health and Physical Education*, and *Leisure Today*. Central offices are maintained in Washington, D.C.

World Leisure and Recreation Association. This organization, formerly called the International Recreation Association, with headquarters in New York, sees itself as the parent body for the recreation and leisure movement on a global scale. It has been instrumental in building several regional associations, has stimulated interaction among professionals on an international basis, and has been responsible for exchange programs among students and professionals of several countries. The principal publication is the *WLRA Bulletin*, which contains news of park and recreation opportunities and developments around the world.

American Camping Association. The American Camping Association is the national professional camping organization of the organized camping movement. Formed in 1910, it is dedicated to furthering "the interests and welfare of children and adults through camping as an educative and recreative experience." Membership includes camp directors, members of camp staffs, and interested individuals from allied or related fields of education and recreation. The association maintains a national office with professional personnel at Bradford Woods, Martinsville, Indiana.

Other related agencies. Several other organizations play an important role to their respective constituents. They include the American Association of College Unions; the Association of Interpretive Naturalists, Inc.; the Athletic Institute (a service organization); the National Industrial Recreation Association; the National Recreation Sports Association (formerly called the Intramural Sports Associa-

tion); and the National Community Education Association.

Registration, Certification, and Accreditation

If a profession is truly to come of age, it must have control over the quality of professional preparation and development of personnel. Accreditation, registration, and certification are irrevocably interdependent, so we need to look at their definitions before exploring how far the park and recreation profession has come in these areas.

Accreditation is a program under which institutions of higher learning may earn an approved rating from an autonomous council authorized by the Council on Post Secondary Accreditation, if the institution is deemed to have met the minimum standards and evaluative criteria adopted by the council.

The accreditation of curriculums for the preparation of recreation, parks, and leisure services personnel is primarily a means of protecting the consumer public, the employers of park and recreation personnel, and the students who wish to choose a career in this sphere of interest. Accreditation can foster self-evaluation and self-improvement for the institution, define a base below which no recognized curriculum can plunge, and help discourage and reduce substandard curriculum offerings.

Registration is a process through which the park and recreation profession attempts to assure the general public and the employing agency of the competence of park and recreation professionals. It purports to certify that certain individuals have met prescribed standards in education and experience to qualify for specific positions.

Programs for registration of park and recreation personnel have been undertaken and implemented since the 1950s. State societies, led by efforts in California, New York, and North Carolina in the early years, developed voluntary registration plans to upgrade the quality of preparation and experience for those who moved into the park and recreation profession in their states. The American Recreation Society (ARS) created a National Registration Board to administer a national registration program, but this effort was somewhat delayed because of the merger of ARS with the National Recreation and Park Association. Two branches of the new association, namely the Armed Forces Branch and the National Therapeutic Recreation Society, evolved their own registration plans.

Early in 1970, the NRPA Task Force on Registration was formed to explore registration concerns and needs. Out of the recommendations of that task force came the NRPA Registration Board, approved by the NRPA Board of Trustees in the fall of 1970 to "implement a program of professional registration."

By December 1973, a Model Registration Plan for Park and Recreation Personnel had been finalized as a prototype for state registration programs. As of 1977, twenty-three states had had their registration plans approved through the NRPA Registration Board. Others, particularly states that already had clearly defined and operational registration systems, have continued their status quo without application for NRPA Registration Board approval.

Certification involves legal licensing of park and recreation professionals and requires legislation.

As with registration plans, certification documents usually spell out education and experience qualifications for administrators, supervisors, leaders, technicians, and specialists. The first efforts in such legislation came in the 1960s in New Jersey and Georgia. In both cases, the legislation was permissive, not mandatory, but proved beneficial in emphasizing the need for quality performance in park and recreation services.

After polling their membership, the California Park and Recreation Society, which already had an excellent registration system, attempted in 1974 and 1975 to put teeth into their process by introducing a certification bill into the state legislature. It read, in part:

> 5831.3 On and after July 1, 1975, it shall be a misdemeanor for any person to act in the capacity of, or to use the title of park and recreation professional . . . without being licensed pursuant to this chapter, unless exempted under the provisions thereof.
>
> 5831.4 A city, county, district, or state agency shall employ a person licensed under the provisions of this chapter as a prerequisite for state and federal funding in the field of parks and recreation.[4]

The bill did not pass. Certification is not yet a reality, but the efforts to propel the park and recreation movement in that direction have helped to stimulate public interpretation and awareness.

To be accepted as a lawyer, doctor, dentist, nurse, teacher, or architect in most states, practitioners must qualify by education and experience and be duly certified by professional organizations. There are hopeful signs of progress that the park and recreation profession, too, as a human service profession, may adopt certification restrictions in the near future.

Interrelationships. Accreditation refers to standards that apply to the institution offering the professional preparation. Both registration and certification refer to standards that apply to the qualifications of the personnel who perform the park and recreation service. We indicated at the beginning of this discussion that registration, certification, and accreditation are irrevocably interdependent. Why?

Most registration or certification plans describe a professional preparation level as a prerequisite. These descriptions are always couched in terms of "degrees in parks and recreation from an accredited college" or "degrees in related fields plus successful experience in park and recreation positions."

An institution of higher education may have general institutional accreditation for the liberal arts curriculums yet contain a substandard park and recreation curriculum. Without specialized accreditation, there are no penetrating investigations of how the college meets the park and recreation professional needs.

Therefore, if registration is to be meaningful in its relationship to improving personnel qualifications, it must be tied to a recreation education accreditation program that will insure that the degree demanded in the registration plan was arrived at by the individual through acceptable standards of professional preparation.

Thus, the sequence to insure better-qualified recreation and park personnel starts with accreditation of the curriculums that prepare the professionals, then moves through registration and certification to control entry into the job market of only those individuals who meet specified educational and experience standards.

In the last analysis, until we have attained the power of certification or actual licensing to prevent unqualified personnel from performing in park and recreation positions, we must rely on the judgment of those who employ park and recreation workers. They must be convinced of the importance of hiring registered personnel. The best way to convince them is for curricular experiences to produce graduates whose competence exceeds that of those who have had less exposure to the prescribed education.

History of recreation education accreditation. The evolution of the present National Council on Accreditation, an autonomous body sponsored through the joint efforts of the National Recreation and Park Association (NRPA) and the American Alliance for Health, Physical Education, and Recreation (AAHPER), spanned an effort of nearly two decades.

In 1962, a discussion at the Detroit NRA Congress by a handful of professionals, concerned about the proliferation of curriculums with few commonalities, resulted in the formation of the American Recreation Society Professional Development Committee. In 1963, the ARS Committee met and accepted tasks in three broad areas: compilation of a rationale to show the need for specialized accreditation for recreation education, development of standards and evaluative criteria by which to judge existing curriculums or initiate new ones, and identification of potential financial resources to achieve the first two tasks. In 1964, committee materials and responsibilities were absorbed by a committee (chaired by Dr. Edith Ball of New York University) of the Federation of National Professional Organizations for Recreation. This group broadened the base of concern to include all agencies working with park and recreation thrusts. Again, three major tasks were assumed:

1. The refinement of the rationale statement—This statement must explain what ill effects will result to the consumer public and to society's welfare or safety if there is not better monitoring of the professional preparation for park and recreation workers. It justifies why general accreditation of the institution, without special criteria applying to the park and recreation profession, will not suffice.

2. The development of standards and evaluative criteria, an objective measurement tool to apply to the existing efforts of schools to be accredited— Standards and evaluative criteria can be objectively evaluated by a visiting accreditation team. The team makes all of its judgments based on what the

department or school indicates as its purpose. Academic freedom is not restricted, nor does the accreditation superimpose inflexibility. It merely sets forth standards below which the institution may not fall if it wishes to achieve accreditation. Standards are described in the following areas: philosophy and purposes; faculty; administration; research; student services; public service; areas, facilities, equipment, and instructional resources; and curriculum content for undergraduate and graduate degrees.

3. The development of the mechanism or structure by which the process of accreditation would take place and the outlines for a suggested special accrediting agency for parks and recreation—The present accrediting agency or council is composed of nine members: five educators, three practitioners, and one administrator.

In 1968–69, six pilot studies were conducted to test the Standards and Evaluative Criteria documents. In 1970–71, forums were held in each of the NRPA districts to evolve grass roots input and understanding.

In 1970, a Board on Professional Education was created by NRPA "to seek approval from the National Commission on Accrediting for park and recreation curricula."[5] Dr. Janet MacLean of Indiana University was named chairman of the board, which had representation from all branches of the association. The three documents evolved from previous committees were again revised. The principal effort on the rationale statement came from Dr. H. C. Hutchins and Phyllis Lee of the University of Wisconsin, Dr. Edith Ball, and Edward Thacker, Deputy Director of Recreation in Washington, D.C. The Standards and Evaluative Criteria were initiated and revised primar-

ily by Dr. Betty van der Smissen of Pennsylvania State University and Dr. Janet MacLean. Dr. H. Douglas Sessoms of the University of North Carolina formulated the document that described the structure of the proposed accrediting agency and the mechanisms for the process.

In 1972, the Federation of National Professional Recreation Organizations moved to disband and to turn accreditation authority over to the NRPA Board on Professional Education.

In 1972, the American Association for Health, Physical Education, and Recreation, which had in 1956 requested specialized accreditation of recreation education through the National Council on Accreditation for Teacher Education (NCATE), agreed to ask for withdrawal of that responsibility from NCATE at such time as the National Commission on Accrediting would approve the new sponsoring agency proposed by the NRPA Board on Professional Education. It was through the efforts of Dr. Clifford Seymour and Dr. Edward Heath that such action was taken.

In 1973, California initiated state accreditation for park and recreation curriculums.

In 1973 and 1974, the request for specialized accreditation by a separate agency for park and recreation curriculums was twice refused by the National Commission on Accrediting.

In 1974, the NRPA Board of Trustees, in cooperation with the AAHPER, authorized the formation of a National Council on Accreditation in cooperation with the American Association for Leisure and Recreation (AALR). Dr. David Gray, of California State University at Long Beach, was named the first chairman of the council. Council membership included, in addition to the chairman, three educators and three practitioners chosen from the ranks of NRPA, and two educators from AALR.

In 1977, the first schools were accredited by the new council, and two full days of the NRPA Congress were devoted to discussion of accreditation.

The first steps in the accreditation, registration, and certification sequence are well under way. Two documents are available from the National Recreation and Park Association national headquarters for those who are interested in further detail: *Procedural Guidelines for the Accreditation Process,* October 1975; and *Standards and Evaluative Criteria for Recreation, Leisure Services and Resources Curricula, Baccalaureate and Master's Degree Programs,* October 1975.

Code of Ethics

The establishment of a code of ethics by the constituents of an organization is the expression of their desire to adhere to sound practices and relationships that will develop status and integrity for the profession. Several codes have been set forth by the various branches of the NRPA and its antecedents. In 1973, a task force was assigned for evolving a universal code of ethics that could be accepted and enforced by all branches and affiliates.

Dr. Charles Pezoldt, who chaired the national Code of Ethics Committee, reported the results of committee deliberations in a suggested Model Code of Ethics which could be used by any state or any branch of the association.[6] The code includes principles that form the basis for compliance with accepted behavior and also defines different actions for censure if the principles are not followed.

Overview

Since its inception, the park and recreation profession has come a long way. The opportunities are diverse; the responsibilities are significant. In spite of developmental traumas, the environment for exciting contributions to human service still make park and recreation careers most attractive to those who want to deal in human service.

The challenges and advantages outweigh the problems. There is room for competent, dedicated professionals of both sexes, all ethnic minorities, and a variety of age brackets. The goal is a compelling one—a better quality of life through the rewarding uses of leisure.

Part Six
The Years Ahead

. . . we go by the twin assumptions that our future can be understood only by knowing our history, and that the future is in all likelihood etched plainly in the present, if only we knew where to look.

Smithsonian

The past fifty years have seen more unpredictable scientific and social changes than were witnessed in the previous 2,000 years. Events of the next fifty years are even more difficult to predict. Our efforts to peer into the crystal ball can be based only upon observing and interpreting the world today, reflecting upon past experiences, and trying to determine trends.

There are two divergent schools of thought regarding the years to come. One assumes that the population explosion and the depletion of natural resources will result in lower standards of living and restricted life-styles. The other sees a "brave new world" in which technology will solve the problems of energy, food, overcrowding, unemployment, and inflation. Truth may well lie somewhere in between.

No one will deny the burdensome problems of welfare, unemployment, crime and delinquency, fuel shortages, and restless youth. However, we prefer to take the offense with an optimistic note. In just two centuries America has become one of the healthiest, best educated, and most prosperous nations the world has ever known. Because of our technology, we have essentially freed most Americans from demeaning labor and raised the hopes of millions throughout the world who strive to emulate our standard of living.

There are as many opportunities for success in America today as when the Pilgrims landed, not the least of which is the challenge of leisure. Space exploration is just beginning, health care is still in its infancy, and opportunities for service and individual development in our leisure have been barely tapped. In this book we have treated work and leisure as equal dominating forces in today's society.

On the following pages, in which we consider trends and guidelines for the future, we assume that we shall escape the catastrophe of world conflicts, debilitating internal social revolution, and lethal degradation of the environment. If the tremendous burden of armaments could be lifted from the world, the release of monies could propel a great leap forward in social and environmental conditions. All the world must share this hope.

16
Recreation and Leisure—The Third Century

If we change the world, let it bear the mark of our intelligence.

Unknown author

As the United States moves into its third century as a nation, we search for evidence of the directions it will take and how these directions will influence leisure and recreation. How big will our nation be? Where shall we live? How will our population change in age, economic status, and education? What will our life-style be like? How can we plan for leisure services?

Changes in Society and Life-Styles

Population experts tell us that by the year 2000 the United States will be a nation of somewhere between 247 million and 287 million people. A larger percentage of people will be older. Life expectancy at birth, now 74.8 years, is expected to increase, and health and vigor at all ages will improve. The toll taken by most of the major killer diseases has decreased, and it is predicted that even cancer will eventually be conquered. Pressure on open space and energy resources will increase, and crowding will be an even greater problem than it is today (see Figure 16.1).

The surge to the cities has reversed somewhat, and small communities are now increasing in population. The trend of growth in America is to the South, Southwest, and West, while the East and Mideast are growing more slowly. As construction costs and building sites become more expensive, apartments and condominiums will continue to replace separate homes. To compensate for the loss of home yards and gardens, multiple housing units will provide a wide range of recreation facilities and programs.

Family structures are undergoing many alterations. There are many more households made up of singles, and the divorce rate continues to climb. We have become a much more permissive society. Sex roles are changing, and women are assuming an ever-larger place in work outside the home. Leisure needs and services for the future must be reevaluated in terms of this change.

Spending for leisure will doubtless continue to consume a larger proportion of income. Early retirement, shorter working hours, and the higher expectations of people will contribute to this flow of money. Travel will continue to expand. Job enrichment programs with opportunities for personal growth will increase to counteract the boredom of routine tasks in industry and business.

A larger percentage of the population will move up the educational ladder. There will be a new emphasis on education for leisure throughout the educational system. The community school idea will expand and make possible more efficient use of community facilities.

Despite these changes, the human being

Figure 16.1. Can we preserve this serenity?

remains essentially the same. Life-styles may change, some temporarily and some permanently, yet certain verities endure—love, friendship, family, humor, appreciation of beauty, worship, desire for justice and truth, the need to serve, and the thirst for adventure. We strive for individual identity and self-expression. These are constants in human nature that leisure services will continue to consider.

Recreation and Social Problems

History moves from crisis to crisis. Every age has its problems, and ours is no exception. The park and recreation profession is challenged to contribute what it can to the solution of these problems.

When the organized recreation movement began early in this century, its values were promoted in such terms as, "It's better for a boy to be caught stealing first base than caught stealing apples." Today, even though we stress the inherent values of recreation, we still must recognize that it can alleviate certain social problems.

Poverty and Unemployment

Although full employment is a major goal today, poverty may never be completely eliminated. For the jobless and poor, recreation is even more important than for the affluent. It can never be a substitute for a job, but it can give meaning and zest to life, build self-respect, and provide outlets for energy and creativity.

In times of severe unemployment, government has often stepped in with emergency work programs. A fantastic number of jobs can be provided on recreation lands and facilities, in beautification of the country, and in recreation leadership. This is work of lasting value and a source of pride for the worker.

As technology decreases the number of jobs in some fields, the fast-growing service industries, including recreation, may absorb excess workers. Commercial recreation, in particular, promises numerous job opportunities.

Delinquency and Crime

Many delinquent acts are expressions of a lack of vital interests, a revolt against boredom, and a need for excitement. The high rate of youth unemployment, violence on television, and confused standards of morality are given as explanations for the mounting delinquency rate.

We have noted the increase in recreation opportunities of all kinds for youth and adults. Yet, if recreation has any contribution to make to this problem, why are crime and delinquency increasing? Perhaps we must change our programs drastically in order to attract trouble-prone persons. Personal concern and effective counseling to individuals should be emphasized. Some schools and park and recreation agencies retain staff members who specialize in giving personal assistance to those not otherwise reached by their programs.

The fear is sometimes expressed that if delinquents are attracted to recreation programs, regular participants may be driven away. Recreation authorities must therefore have due regard for how programs are conducted for problem youth and how these programs are interpreted to the community.

The Central City

Deteriorating inner-city neighborhoods leave residents with a sense of hopelessness. The central city once more must be made a viable place in which to live and work. A whole new concept of program scheduling will be necessary to help those who do not respond to traditional recreation services.

Inflation and Deficits

In times of financial stress, recreation and park budgets are often cut, while expenditures to care for the unemployed are expanded. Public administrators have a responsibility to see that every public dollar used for parks and recreation is wisely spent.

Trends

The task of separating trends from wishes is difficult. All we can do is look at today and attempt to foresee the directions for tomorrow.

In General

Leisure services have been growing rapidly, with increased numbers of participants, increased financial support, and increased appreciation of their purposes and values.

Community education is gaining acceptance. In some situations it represents a series of comprehensive community centers for all ages.

In spite of financial stringencies, recreation expenditures are rising.

The computer is being used as an aid both in financial management and in program activity analysis.

Although the trend toward combining existing park and recreation departments is leveling off, newly established departments usually combine the two functions.

The number of new park and recreation systems established yearly and financial support for public park and recreation programs continue to grow.

Park and recreation programs are being established on a county or regional basis, cutting across political boundaries.

With federal funds, work and recreation are combined in summer employment experiences offered to young people.

Rapid growth is taking place in the kinds and numbers of commercial recreation enterprises.

The values of leisure are being sought through shorter hours and higher wages on the job. A revolt against dull and routine work is resulting in the search for ways of making work itself more satisfying.

Areas and Facilities

Private recreation centers, including tennis and racquetball centers, health spas, sports clubs, fishing and hunting clubs, and swimming clubs, have increased.

Great success has been achieved by the new amusement complexes, theme parks, and experiential villages.

Shopping centers are cooperating with community groups to offer festivals, hobby shows, musical events, and benefits. Some maintain children's play areas and child-care centers.

Condominiums, apartments, and mobile home parks are providing more and more recreation facilities for their residents.

Family rooms, recreation rooms, backyard play equipment, and other family recreation facilities, common in higher-income homes, are decreasing in new lower-cost homes as construction costs have soared.

The size and numbers of public lands and waters designated for parks and recreation have increased.

Canoe routes, bicycle paths, walking trails, and camping facilities are being enlarged.

Wetlands, beaches, estuaries, natural lakes, and wilderness areas are being expanded and given special protection.

Mobile units and mini-areas are used increasingly to serve congested or remote areas.

More originality in the design of outdoor areas is being exercised; and play equipment for children is becoming more creative.

Youngsters are given freedom to do "their own thing" on adventure playgrounds created by children themselves.

Populations Served

Park and recreation services to the disadvantaged, particularly in the inner city, are being expanded.

Programs for the aging are multiplying.

Recreation services to the disabled are becoming more widespread, both in therapeutic institutions and in the community.

Formerly segregated park and recreation facilities have been integrated.

Special attention is focused on minorities, including blacks, Mexican-Americans, and Indians.

Sex barriers to any form of recreation are being lifted.

Programs

Increased pride in ethnic backgrounds has given rise to ethnic festivals, with songs, dances, parades, and ethnic foods.

A renewed interest in history and genealogy is stimulating the preservation of historical sites and the introduction of interpretive historical programs.

Long-range planning emphasizes recreation uses of many types of land.

Complexes combining music halls, theaters, and other cultural interests are being developed in large cities.

Museums, libraries, and zoos are including innovative recreational features appealing to visitors of all ages.

Participation in most forms of outdoor recreation has increased, abetted by interest in physical and mental fitness and in preventive medicine.

Concern for the environment is reflected in new outdoor programs that blend recreation and education.

More adventurous activities for older youth and adults are being sought.

The Profession

Professional leadership is being upgraded through better salaries, improved status, expanded college and university curriculums, executive development programs, and national efforts toward registration, certification, and accreditation.

Many two-year colleges are inaugurating curriculums in recreation.

Indigenous leaders are being recruited and educated for special social or geographic areas.

More leaders are employed on a part-time basis to make staff available at times of peak loads.

Leisure counseling is an emerging area of leadership. Pre-retirement counseling is offered by many social agencies and industries.

Citizen participation is being emphasized in public recreation and park programs.

Crosscurrents and Contradictions

Trends lead off in all directions, some opposing others. Resolving the conflicts is a challenge to those concerned with leisure.

Environmental crosscurrents. Although many recreation uses of land are in harmony with good environmental practices, others conflict. Overuse of parks and wilderness often ruins the beauty and isolation that were their major attraction. New reservoirs provide water and shoreline recreation but destroy the natural area and the recreation associated with it. A classic example was the flooding of the uniquely beautiful Glen Canyon to create Lake Powell.

Other conflicts pit bird watchers against bird hunters, fishermen against water skiers,

---

New Town

A conglomerate of developers, with some financial help from a large foundation, plans a new town to accommodate 75,000 to 100,000 people. The experience of "new towns" in England and the United States is to be drawn upon to create an ideal self-sufficient community. It is anticipated that at least 25 years will pass before the project reaches fruition.

Political scientists, economists, sociologists, educators, and park and recreation experts are brought into the planning process. Imagine yourself responsible for the park and recreation planning. In the light of present trends, what recommendations would you make relative to the following?

What recreation areas, facilities, and programs should be provided for physical and mental health and for special populations such as the aged? How should responsibility for recreation be apportioned among commercial, voluntary, and tax-supported recreation agencies? What responsibilities might be allocated to schools? How can citizen participation be secured in financing, planning, and conducting recreation programs? How can personal choices and privacy be protected from overzealous efforts to secure conformity? How can programs be made more creative and adventurous than the traditional activities?

wilderness seekers against road builders, snowmobile users against wildlife lovers, off-the-road motor vehicle users against hikers, sailors against motorboat users, and so on. Some of these conflicts can be resolved. Environmental impact studies are increasingly required for proposed developments. Certain zones in a lake are sometimes restricted to canoes, rowboats, and sailboats to help avoid their conflict with speedboats; and limiting motorized vehicles to special forest trails somewhat appeases hikers. Education, so that each user may understand not only the land capacity but also the rights of others, is a potent aid.

The cult of instant gratification. We are faced with two contrary attitudes in our society: "doing your own thing" and being concerned for the welfare of others. There is more effort today than ever before to attain equality for all people, yet we see more selfish desire for the good things in life.

Is this an age of instant gratification? We have instant foods, instant light, instant heat, instant cold, instant cars at our door, and instant sexual freedom. However, self-denial and self-discipline are not dirty words. The search for instant pleasure must not obliterate the satisfaction of working for others and planning for the future. Recreation at its best enriches not only the individual but all aspects of human relationships.

Energy. Although the future may bring solutions of our energy needs, at present it is advisable to reduce consumption. Much recreation depends on energy—for cars, boats, entertainment, and the manufacture of recreation goods. Temporarily, at least, we may need to reduce travel, have our recreation closer to home, reduce lighting, and make other fuel-saving efforts.

Overdependence. Are we being contradictory when we promote participation in

organized recreation while at the same time encouraging the development of individual resourcefulness? The best programmed recreation should help to make a person less dependent on structured leisure pursuits. We have discussed the importance of providing those things that people cannot provide for themselves, but we must not expect society to do for us what we are able to do for ourselves.

Like individuals, communities are often tempted to lean too heavily on assistance (in this case, federal). It is dangerous to accept federal grants for programs that must be dropped as soon as federal money is withdrawn. To counteract overdependence on federal help, communities need much more citizen participation in directing and leading community programs. The development of local leadership is an important goal.

Guidelines for the Future—A Charge to the Profession

Leisure services have now entered the mainstream of American life and assumed their place in the total planning for human welfare. The following are some of the guidelines for these services in contributing to individual happiness and social well-being.

Political activism. Those concerned with recreation and leisure, whether as park and recreation professionals, agency representatives, or private citizens, must become part of the power structure as political activists. They must act as advocates for the fulfillment of leisure service goals. Goals will not be realized without expertise in the means of achieving them.

Broadening and upgrading programs. Recreation must serve all people—all ages, races, economic and social levels, levels of intelligence and physical ability, the typical and the atypical. To accomplish this goal, programs must be more innovative, creative, and adventurous. Greater emphasis must be placed on cultural offerings. Schedules must be arranged with more consideration of those whose leisure hours do not coincide with those of most people.

Leisure education. Education for leisure must assume a larger place in the preparation for living. Only through such education can the full benefit of increased leisure be realized. The day may come when leisure literacy ranks with the three Rs as an essential in education.

Cooperation and coordination. Public, private, voluntary, and commercial recreation agencies must improve their cooperation in order to reduce overlapping and provide for unmet needs. The community education movement should provide a channel for more efficient use of community resources.

Increasing citizen involvement. The participation of citizens in the planning and execution of leisure programs must be encouraged. The use of volunteers on advisory committees and in direct leadership should be increased.

Environmental improvement. Since much recreation will continue to be related to the natural environment, professionals concerned with leisure have an important responsibility in the protection and proper use of natural resources. Recreation and park agencies must unite with other community forces that work for a clean and beautiful environment, open space, the survival of plants and animals, and pollution abatement.

Planning for the future. Without planning today, there can be no orderly future. Recreation and leisure professionals must have a voice in slum elimination, antidiscrimina-

tion efforts, and other social planning for the well-being of society. As land becomes more difficult to secure, the planning for recreation land and facilities becomes a particularly important responsibility.

Professional preparation. Professional preparation must be continually upgraded and modified to meet the needs of the future. It must include education for administration, planning, understanding of human relationships and needs, and knowledge of ways in which the needs may be met. Certification of leaders is essential to insure the meeting of standards for various work responsibilities.

Research. Although progress has been made in recreation research, its quality and extent must be improved. Research in depth must become the underpinning of the recreation movement.

International relations. Leisure can be a unifying force. As the peoples of the world travel more freely, recreation should contribute to their mutual understanding. Music, drama, and arts speak an international language. International sports should also cultivate friendships, but unfortunately competition has too often turned to unfriendly rivalry. The United Nations, through such agencies as UNESCO and UNICEF, must assume greater responsibility for expanding leisure services, with cooperation from the World Leisure and Recreation Association. All agencies concerned with leisure must encourage exchange visits for youth and adults from various countries.

Federal recreation service. For many years there have been sporadic attempts to develop a strong federal recreation service to include all areas of recreation. These efforts must be continued. Eventually there might even be a cabinet-level agency devoted to leisure services.

The Search for Quality in Leisure Pursuits

Many "if's" cloud our vision of the future. If we develop new and abundant sources of energy—such as solar and atomic energy, supplemented by thermal heat, tides, and wind—fantastic possibilities lie ahead. Visionaries foresee bubble cities with climate control, wide travel (including space travel), greatly lengthened life-spans, new food-growing techniques, leisure beyond our dreams, and a whole world open for recreation experiences.

If these marvels come to pass, will our lives necessarily be better? Philosophers and prophets throughout the ages have sought the purposes of life. If the peoples of the future have more leisure and less worry about earning a living, whole new vistas of spiritual, social, and cultural development could lie ahead. If this opportunity is lost in the pursuit of hedonistic pleasures, the pessimists' predictions that our civilization will crumble through internal decay may well come true.

In the past, work has been considered the great good in life. If, by *work*, we mean drudgery and routine tasks, then we must change our thinking; for these tasks are better done by machine. If, however, *work* means creatively contributing to society, then work will continue to be a central purpose for people in occupations where such contributions are possible. For large segments of the population, however, leisure rather than work will offer the major satisfactions of life.

In leisure, each person must make individual choices. How choices are made will depend on many factors, particularly on the standards, attitudes, and skills inculcated in children and youth and on the opportunities available.

The human being wants to *feel useful* and needed. Voluntary service, as well as work, will help us achieve a sense of purpose. The human being is *active*. Mental alertness and physical fitness can be promoted through healthful physical activity. The human being is *creative* and desires opportunities for self-expression. Aesthetic experiences through the arts, literature, and the world of nature will meet deep-seated needs. The human being is *social* and needs the companionship of others. Recreation can help fill these desires. The human being is *spiritual* and searches for meaning in the world. Leisure can afford opportunities for contemplation and wonder.

The leisure and recreation services must help people find the most satisfying uses of leisure, not only as avenues to personal happiness but also as channels to social well-being. This is the challenge of recreation in America's third century.

Selected References

Darling, F. Fraser, and Milton, John P., eds. *Future Environments of North America.* Garden City, N.Y.: Natural History Press, 1966.

"2024 A.D." *Saturday Review/World*, Golden Anniversary issue, pt. II. August 24, 1974.

Appendix

Table A.1. Historical Time Line: Park and Recreation Developments in the United States Compared with Other Events

Year	Government Events Concerned With Recreation and Parks	Political, Military, and Social Bench Marks	Educational and Voluntary Agencies, and Professional Societies
1981	White House Conference on Aging scheduled		
1978	Heritage Conservation and Recreation Service (HCRS) replaced the Bureau of Outdoor Recreation		
1977	President Carter created Department of Energy in his cabinet	President Carter took office	
	Education for All Handicapped Children Act		
	White House Conference on Handicapped		
1976	Federal Land Policy and Management Act	American Revolution Bicentennial Celebration	The National Recreation and Park Association, the National Community Education Association, and the American Association for Leisure and Recreation cooperated to provide services at local level
1975		Arab nations doubled oil prices	First National Leisure Educational Conference
1974	Community Schools Act	President Nixon resigned office	Council on Recreation Education Accreditation formed
			National Conference on State Parks became National Society for Park Resources
1973	Older Americans Act amended		International Recreation Association became World Leisure and Recreation Association
	Job Corps established		
1972	Revenue Sharing began	Nixon in Peking and Moscow	
	Gateway National Recreation Areas, east and west	Watergate coverup disclosed	

Year			
1971	President Nixon announced "Legacy of Parks" Program Second White House Conference on Aging J. F. Kennedy Center for Performing Arts opened ACTION—CAP programs started	Ping-Pong diplomacy Attica Prison revolt Pentagon Papers	American Association of Zoological Parks and Aquariums returned to separate status
1970	White House Conference on Children focused on protection Environmental Protection Agency	Women's liberation movement gained momentum Cambodia and Kent State protests	
1969	Environmental quality control established	Chicago Seven trial Apollo II landed on moon Woodstock	*Journal of Leisure Research* published
1968	Wild and scenic rivers and recreation and scenic trails established National Council for Indian Opportunity President's Council on Physical Fitness established	Robert Kennedy and Martin Luther King died U.S.S. Pueblo lost My Lai massacre	Executive development training for park and recreation personnel began at Indiana University; cosponsored by National Recreation and Park Association
1967	New Jersey approved state certification for recreation personnel	Hippie movement gained attention Ghetto violence topped out	
1966	Appropriation for Land Between the Lakes Recreation Area Historical Preservation Act National Museum Act	Black Power and backlash America scarred by forty-three race riots	First merged Congress of National Recreation and Park Association, Washington, D.C.

Table A.1. Historical Time Line (continued)

Year	Government Events Concerned With Recreation and Parks	Political, Military, and Social Bench Marks	Educational and Voluntary Agencies, and Professional Societies
1965	Older Americans Act National Foundation on the Arts and the Humanities Act Federal Water Project Recreation Act Elementary and Secondary Education Act Land and Water Conservation Fund established	Medicare Selma March, Watts	National Recreation and Park Association formed by merging of National Recreation Association, American Association of Zoological Parks and Aquariums, American Recreation Society, American Institute of Park Executives, and National Conference on State Parks
1964	White House Conference on Natural Beauty National Wilderness Recreation System Act Classification and Multiple Use Act of Bureau of Land Management	First long, hot summer Civil rights murders, Mississippi Vietnam War started	
1963		Wallace stood in school house door March on Washington Death of President Kennedy in Dallas Beatles toured United States	
1962	White House Conference on Conservation Bureau of Outdoor Recreation Created ORRRC report completed	John Glenn orbited earth Cuban missile crisis	
1961	First White House Conference on Aging U.S. Travel Service established	Freedom riders in Dixie Bay of Pigs invasion	
1960	U.S. Forest Service Multiple Purpose Act U.S. Forest Service began visitor information service	Kennedy elected President Black sit-ins, Greensboro, N.C.	

Year			
1959	Open Space Land Grant Program. White House Conference on Children and Youth	Nixon in Moscow; Khrushchev in United States	European Recreation Society established
1958	Outdoor Recreation Resources Review Committee established	Hula hoop craze	
1957		First Russian satellite, Sputnik	
1956	Mission 66 Program: National Park Service. Fish and Wildlife Act created Bureau of Sports Fisheries and Wildlife		International Recreation Association formed
1954		Supreme Court outlawed school segregation	Federation of National Professional Organizations of Recreation established
1953	Department of HEW established	Death of Stalin. End of Korean War	
1952		The hydrogen bomb	
1950	Dingell-Johnson Act Tax on Fishing Tackle for Improvement of Water Habitat	Korean War began	A "Mid-Century Declaration of Recreation Policy" published
1948		The Kinsey Report. Berlin airlift. Truman beat Dewey	National Conference on Graduate Education for Health, Physical Education: Jackson's Mill, West Virginia. Camp standards developed by American Camping Association
1947		Marshall Plan	
1946		Churchill's "Iron Curtain" speech	
1945	First state recreation commission established, North Carolina	Surrender of Germany, May 8; Japan, September 2. Bombs dropped on Hiroshima and Nagasaki. United Nations founded	Girls Clubs of America established

Table A.1. Historical Time Line (continued)

Year	Government Events Concerned With Recreation and Parks	Political, Military, and Social Bench Marks	Educational and Voluntary Agencies, and Professional Societies
1944	Flood Control Act	Battles of Anzio, Normandy, the Bulge, Saipan, and Leyte Gulf	
1941		Japanese attacked Pearl Harbor	Federal Recreation Services established to meet war needs, Special Services, Red Cross, USO
			National Industrial Recreation Association formed
1940	Fish and Wildlife Service formed	Steinbeck won Pulitzer for *Grapes of Wrath*	
1939	Federal Security Agency established	World War II began *Gone with the Wind* released	
1938		Orson Welles's Martian broadcast	
1937	Cape Hatteras National Seashore Pittman-Robertson Act Tax on Firearms for Habitat Improvement	Amelia Earhart vanished in Pacific	American Physical Education Association affiliated with National Educational Association to become American Association for Health, Physical Education, and Recreation The Society of Recreation Workers of America formed, later became the American Recreation Society
1936	Blue Ridge Parkway: first national parkway National Park Service—Recreation Demonstration Areas	FDR won second term	Graduate courses in recreation, New York
1935	Works Progress Administration (WPA) established	Swing music born Social Security Act	Athletic Institute formed
1934			Camping organizations combined to form American Camping Association American Youth Hostels established

Year			
1933	National Parks System reorganized; Tennessee Valley Authority created	Collapse of U.S. banks	American Library Association included recreation in its three-point program
1932	Recreation as a major use of forests made official policy	Fifteen million jobless in United States; Bonus riot in Washington; Amelia Earhart solo flight across the Atlantic	First International Recreation Congress
1930	Veterans Administration created	Television patented	Forest Management Recreation Program, Utah State College; Playground and Recreation Association of America became National Recreation Association
1929		U.S. stock market crash	
1928			Liebert H. Weir: *Manual on Parks*
1927		Lindbergh crossed Atlantic	
1926	Recreation Act passed by Congress		National Recreation School organized; International Federation of Settlements formed
1925		Flappers era	
1924		Death of Lenin	White House Conference on Outdoor Recreation; Camp Directors Association; American Association of Zoological Parks and Aquariums established
1922		Mussolini came to power	
1921			National Conference on State Parks established; American Association of Park Superintendents became American Institute of Park Executives

Table A.1. *Historical Time Line (continued)*

Year	Government Events Concerned With Recreation and Parks	Political, Military, and Social Bench Marks	Educational and Voluntary Agencies, and Professional Societies
1920		League of Nations	
		Marconi developed radio	
		Prohibition began	
		Women suffrage movement	
1919		Treaty of Versailles	
1918	Interpretive Service began in National Park Service	World War I ended	Community Chests and Councils of America organized (now United Way)
			National Education Association's Seven Cardinal Principles adopted
1916	National Park Service established (U.S. Department of Interior)		National Community Center Association formed
1915			Girl Guides became Girl Scouts
1914	U.S.D.A. Cooperative Extension Service established, including 4-H Clubs, by Smith-Lever Act	World War I began	
1912			Girl Guides, later called Girl Scouts of America, formed
1911			Playground Association of America changed name to Playground and Recreation Association of America
			National Federation of Settlements and Neighborhood Centers founded
1910			Boy Scouts of America founded
			Camp Fire Girls founded
			Camp Directors Association organized
1907	4-H programs organized		
	Social and civic centers opened, Rochester schools		

Year	Parks	General	Recreation / Organizations
1906	Yosemite National Park established		National YWCA organized Boys' Clubs federated Playground Association of America formed, Washington, D.C. *Playground Magazine* began, now *Parks & Recreation*
1905	Opening of ten South Side Park Centers, Chicago U.S. Forest Service established	Einstein stated Theory of Relativity	
1904	Board of Playground Commissioners appointed, Los Angeles		New England Park Superintendents became American Association of Park Superintendents
1903	Five million dollars voted for creation of small parks by South Side Park Commissioners, Chicago	First airplane flight—Wright Brothers First baseball world series First motion picture to tell story, *The Great Train Robbery*	
1902	Bureau of Reclamation established		
1898		Spanish-American War	New England Association of Park Superintendents formed
1896		Modern Olympics started	
1895	First county park system established in Essex County, New Jersey	First motor-vehicle race, Chicago	
1894		Haynes Horseless Carriage tested in Kokomo, Indiana	
1893	Park Districts formed, Illinois	Automobile arrived in United States	
1892	First municipal legislation for parks, Boston		Sierra Club of California established Hull House established model playground
1891	Forest reserves became start of Forest Service	Basketball began in Springfield, Massachusetts	

Table A.1. Historical Time Line (continued)

Year	Government Events Concerned With Recreation and Parks	Political, Military, and Social Bench Marks	Educational and Voluntary Agencies, and Professional Societies
1889	Boston converted ten acres into an outdoor gym	Edison invented the kinetoscope	Jane Addams and Ellen Gates Starr opened Hull House, Chicago
1888	New York City appropriated $1 million for park acquisition		
1887			Settlement house movement introduced in New York City from England
1886	U.S. Army protected and managed Yellowstone		
1885	Niagara Falls, New York, public reservation		Boston sandgardens opened
	Fort Mackinac, Michigan		
1876		Bell invented telephone	
		U.S. Centennial celebration	
1875			Forestry College, Cornell
			American Forestry Association formed
1874			Chautauqua movement started in western New York
1873			Forestry Department, Yale
1872	First national park, Yellowstone, established		
	Brookline, Massachusetts, bought land for two playgrounds		
1869		Suez Canal opened	
		Transcontinental railroad completed	
		First intercollegiate football game, Princeton vs. Rutgers	

Year			
1867	Fairmount Park, Philadelphia		Patrons of Husbandry, known as "The Grange," originated
	Commissions established in Wisconsin and Michigan to study conservation practices		
1866			First YWCA established, Boston
			National YMCA formed
1865		Civil War ended	
1864	Yosemite valley granted to California for state recreation purposes		
1862		Homestead Act	
1861		Civil War began	Gunnery School Camp—start of organized camping
1860			Boys' Club organized, Hartford
1859		Darwin published *The Origin of Species*	
1858	Frederick Law Olmsted and Calvert Vaux win competition for design of Central Park		
1857	Frederick Law Olmsted appointed superintendent of Central Park		
1853	Central Park, New York City, land purchase began, first large city park		
1851			YMCA established, Boston
1849		Gold rush to California	
1846	Smithsonian Institution founded		
1839	Old Dearborn Park, Chicago, established	Baseball played in Cooperstown	
1832	Hot Springs National Park, limited in scope, established		
1825		First steam railroad	

Table A.1. Historical Time Line (continued)

Year	Government Events Concerned With Recreation and Parks	Political, Military, and Social Bench Marks	Educational and Voluntary Agencies, and Professional Societies
1824	Congress established Civil Works, function of Army Corps of Engineers		
1823		Monroe Doctrine announced	
1815		Napoleon defeated at Waterloo	
1812–14		War of 1812	
1807		Fulton's steamboat	
1803		Louisiana Purchase	
1793		Whitney's cotton gin	
1791	Major L'Enfant designed parks and pleasure gardens, Washington, D.C.		
1790		First U.S. census	
1789		French Revolution began	
1788	National capital parks		
1776		Declaration of Independence	
1775–83		American Revolution	
1773			Museum movement started in America in Charlestown, S.C.
1769		Watt's steam engine patented	
1733	James Olgethorpe designed public gardens, squares, and open spaces in Savannah, Georgia		
1689		English Bill of Rights	
1687		Newton stated Law of Gravity	
1682	William Penn set aside five open squares in Philadelphia plan		

1653   First library in America believed to have originated in Boston

1640   Massachusetts Bay Colony created ordinance opening bodies of water over ten acres to public

1634   Boston Commons established, first city park in the English colonies

1620   Pilgrims landed on Cape Cod

1609   Galileo invented the telescope

1608   Quebec founded by French

1607   Jamestown founded by English

1565   Plaza in St. Augustine, considered by many as first park in the continental United States

1558–1603   Reign of Queen Elizabeth

1519–22   Magellan circumnavigated the globe

1517   Martin Luther: Protestant revolt in Germany

1492   Columbus discovered America

Four Major Types of Administration of Recreation

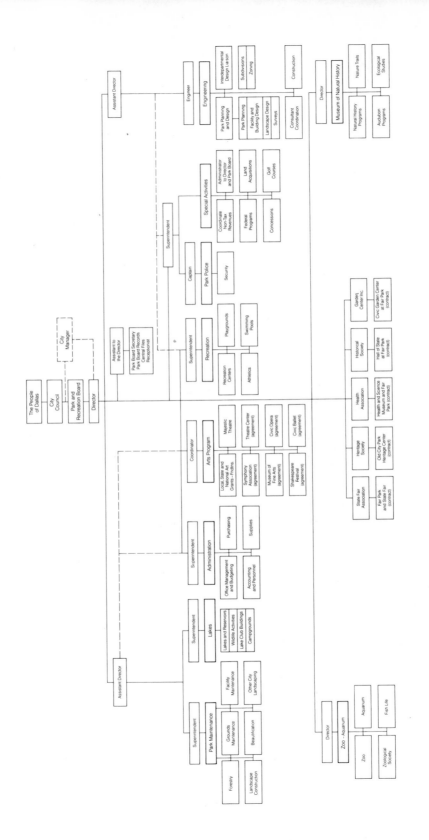

Figure A.1. Combined park and recreation department (Dallas, Texas). Source: Used by permission of the Dallas, Texas, Park and Recreation Board.

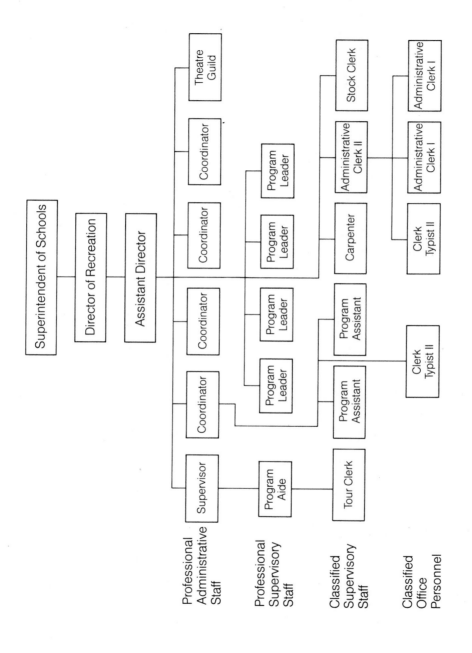

Figure A.2. School-community recreation program (Madison, Wisconsin). Source: Used by permission of the School-Community Recreation Department. Madison Wisconsin Public Schools.

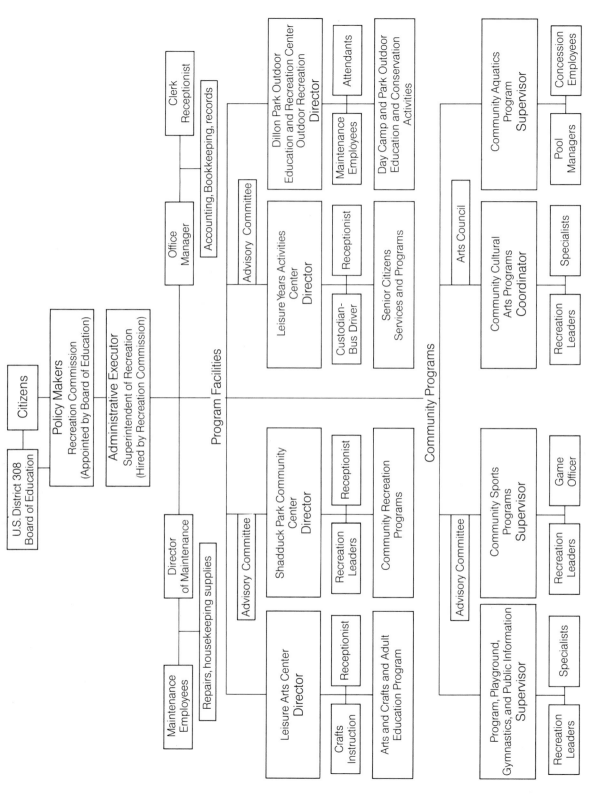

Figure A.3. Separate recreation department (Hutchinson, Kansas). Source: Used by permission of the Hutchinson, Kansas, Recreation Commission.

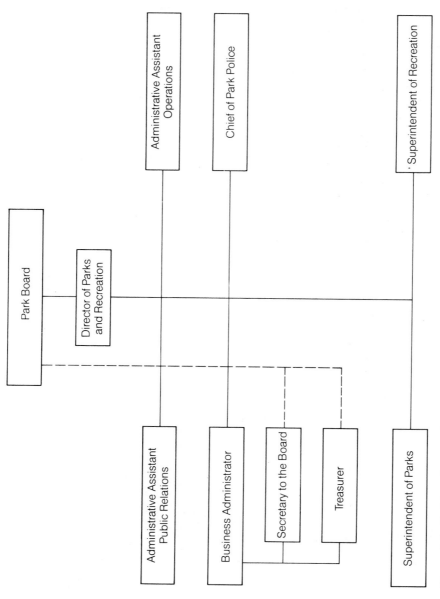

Figure A.4. Park board responsible for recreation (Peoria, Illinois). Source: Used by permission of the Peoria, Illinois, Park District.

Notes

Chapter 1

1. Max Kaplan, *Leisure: Theory and Policy* (New York: John Wiley & Sons, Inc., 1975), p. 18.

2. Sebastian de Grazia, *Of Time, Work, and Leisure* (New York: Twentieth Century Fund, 1962), p. 7.

3. Ibid., p. 15.

4. Josef Pieper, *Leisure, The Basis of Culture* (New York: New American Library, 1963), p. 43.

5. Joffre Dumazedier, *Toward a Society of Leisure* (New York: The Free Press, 1967), pp. 16–17.

6. Max Kaplan, in *The Next Twenty-Five Years*, ed. Andrew Spekke (Washington, D.C.: World Future Society, 1975), p. 177.

7. Walter Kerr, *The Decline of Pleasure* (New York: Simon and Schuster, 1962), p. 182.

8. Martin H. Neumeyer and Esther S. Neumeyer, *Leisure and Recreation* (New York: Ronald Press Company, 1958), p. 15.

9. Charles K. Brightbill and Tony A. Mobley, *Education for Leisure-Centered Living* (New York: John Wiley & Sons, 1977), p. 5.

10. Richard Kraus, *Recreation and Leisure in Modern Society* (Englewood Cliffs, N.J.: Prentice-Hall, Inc., 1971), p. 266.

11. James F. Murphy, *Recreation and Leisure Service* (Dubuque, Iowa: Wm. C. Brown Publishers, 1975), p. 15.

12. Paul F. Douglass in an address given at Milwaukee, Wisconsin. Reprinted by permission.

13. Kaplan, *Leisure: Theory and Policy*, p. 19.

14. John Neulinger, *The Psychology of Leisure: Research Approaches to the Study of Leisure* (Springfield, Ill.: Charles C. Thomas, Publisher, 1974), p. 24.

15. Kaplan, *Leisure: Theory and Policy*, p. 19.

16. S. R. Slavson, *Recreation and the Total Personality* (New York: Association Press, 1948), p. 3.

17. Robert J. Havighurst, "Maturation Through Play and Sport," in *The Humanistic and Mental Health Aspects of Sports, Exercise, and Recreation*, ed. Timothy T. Craig (Chicago: American Medical Association, 1967), p. 13.

18. Johan Huizinga, *Homo Ludens* (London: Routledge and Kegan Paul, Ltd., 1949), p. 7.

19. Michael J. Ellis, *Why People Play* (Englewood Cliffs, N.J.: Prentice-Hall, Inc., 1973), p. 2.

20. Friedrich Froebel, *Education of Man* (New York: Appleton and Company, 1887), p. 55.

21. Plato's *Laws*, ii 667 E.

22. Ott Romney, *Off the Job Living* (New York: A. S. Barnes and Company, 1945), p. 14.

23. De Grazia, *Of Time, Work, and Leisure*, p. 246.

24. Howard Braucher, *A Treasury of Living* (New York: National Recreation Association, 1950), p. 23.

25. *Dictionary of Sociology* (New York: Philosophical Library, 1944), p. 25.

26. Thomas M. Kando, *Leisure and Popular Culture in Transition* (St. Louis: C. V. Mosby Company, 1975), p. 26.

27. Kraus, *Recreation and Leisure*, p. 266.

28. David Gray and Seymour Greben, "Hu-

man Perspectives," *Parks and Recreation* 9, no. 6 (July 1974): 49.

29. Allen V. Sapora and Elmer D. Mitchell, *The Theory of Play and Recreation* (New York: Ronald Press Company, 1961).

30. Kraus, *Recreation and Leisure*.

31. Ellis, *Why People Play*.

32. Richard Grey Sipes, "Sports as a Control for Aggression," in *The Humanistic and Mental Health Aspects of Sports, Exercise, and Recreation*, ed. Timothy T. Craig (Chicago: American Medical Association, 1976), p. 46.

33. Barry Alan Smolev, "The Relationship Between Sports and Aggression," in *The Humanistic and Mental Health Aspects of Sports, Exercise, and Recreation*, ed. Timothy T. Craig (Chicago: American Medical Association, 1976), p. 49.

34. Ellis, *Why People Play*, p. 11.

35. Kaplan, *Leisure: Theory and Policy*.

36. Peter A. Martin, "Work, Leisure and Identity in Adolescence and Adulthood," in *Leisure and Mental Health, A Psychiatric Viewpoint* (Baltimore: Garamond/Pridemark Press, 1967), p. 25.

37. Patrick West and L. C. Merriam, Jr., "Outdoor Recreation and Family Cohesiveness," *Journal of Leisure Research* 2, no. 4 (Fall 1970): 257.

38. Bennett M. Berger, "The Sociology of Leisure," in *Work and Leisure*, ed. Erwin O. Smigel (New Haven, Connecticut: College and University Press, 1963), pp. 21–38; William R. Burch, Jr., "The Social Circles of Leisure, Competing Explanations," *Journal of Leisure Research* 1, no. 2 (Spring 1969): 125–47; Kenneth Keniston, *The Uncommitted* (New York: Harcourt Brace, 1965).

39. Mary Moffitt, "Play as a Medium for Learning," *Leisure Today*, Journal of Physical Education and Recreation (June 1972): 45–47; Jean Piaget, *Play, Dreams, and Imitation in Childhood* (New York: W. W. Norton and Co., 1962); Robert Hutchins, "Implications for Education," in *Technology, Human Values and Leisure*, ed. Max Kaplan and P. Bosserman (New York: Abingdon Press, 1971).

40. John Neulinger and Miranda Breit, "Attitude Dimensions of Leisure: A Replication Study," *Journal of Leisure Research* 3, no. 2 (Spring 1971): 108–15; Jon M. Shepard, "A Status Recognition Model of Work-Leisure Relationships," *Journal of Leisure Research* 6, no. 1 (Winter 1974): 58–63.

41. Abraham Maslow, "Human Needs and Work," in *The Future of Work*, ed. F. Best (Englewood Cliffs, N.J.: Prentice-Hall, Inc., 1973), p. 26.

42. Slavson, *Recreation and the Total Personality*.

43. Don Fabun, ed., "Leisure: Old Rockin' Chair's Got Me," in *Dynamics of Change* (Englewood Cliffs, N.J.: Prentice-Hall, Inc., 1968), p. 18.

44. Daniel Yankelovich, "The Meaning of Work," in *The Worker and the Job*, ed. Jerome M. Rosow (Englewood Cliffs, N.J.: Prentice-Hall, Inc., 1974), p. 23.

45. *Work in America* (Washington, D.C.: Special Task Force to the Secretary of Health, Education and Welfare, 1973), pp. 4–5.

46. Yankelovich, "The Meaning of Work," p. 23.

47. Garrett de Bell, ed., *The Environmental Handbook* (New York: Ballantine Books, Inc., 1970), p. xiii.

48. John Mee, *Perspectives* (Bloomington: Indiana University Committee for Future Studies, 1973), p. 22.

49. David Riesman, *Individualism Reconsidered* (Glencoe, Ill.: The Free Press, 1963), p. 456.

50. Robert Theobald, "Cybernetics and the Problems of Social Reorganization," in *The Social Impact of Cybernetics,* ed. Charles R. Dechert (New York: Simon and Schuster, 1973), p. 46.

Chapter 2

1. John Huizinga, *Homo Ludens* (London: Routledge and Kegan Paul Ltd., 1949). Reprinted by permission.

2. Foster Rhea Dulles, *America Learns to Play* (New York: Appleton-Century Co., Inc., 1940). Reprinted by permission of the publishers, Appleton-Century-Crofts, an affiliate of Meredith Press.

3. Dulles, *America Learns to Play*, p. 221.

4. George D. Butler, *Introduction to Community Recreation*, 5th ed. (New York: McGraw-Hill Book Company, 1976), p. 75. Reprinted by permission.

5. "A Brief History of the Playground Movement in America," *Playground* 9, no. 2 (1915): 41–42.

6. Dulles, *America Learns to Play*, p. 301.

Chapter 3

1. "People Are Shelling Out More Than Ever for a Good Time," *U.S. News & World Report* 82, no. 7 (February 21, 1977): 40.

2. "How Three Amazing Decades Have Transformed America," *U.S. News & World Report* 82, no. 1 (January 10, 1977): 70.

3. James L. Funk, *The Car Culture* (Cambridge: The MIT Press, 1975), p. 211.

4. "Gambling Goes Legit," *Time* 108, no. 23 (December 6, 1976): 54–65.

5. Richard Kraus, "The Economics of Recreation Today," *Parks & Recreation* 5, no. 6 (June 1970): 51.

6. "People Are Shelling Out," *U.S. News & World Report*, p. 41; "How Americans Pursue Happiness," *U.S. News & World Report* 82, no. 20 (May 23, 1977): 62.

7. U.S. Bureau of the Census, *Statistical Abstract of the United States* (Washington, D.C.: U.S. Department of Commerce, 1976), p. 218.

8. *Environmental Quality, The Fifth Annual Report of the Council on Environmental Quality* (Washington, D.C.: U.S. Government Printing Office, 1974), p. xix.

9. *The Recreation Imperative, A Draft of the Nationwide Outdoor Recreation Plan Prepared by the Department of the Interior* (Washington, D.C.: U.S. Government Printing Office, 1974), p. 201.

10. U.S. Bureau of the Census, *Statistical Abstract*, p. 219.

11. Roger A. Lancaster, "Municipal Services," *Parks & Recreation* 11, no. 7 (July 1976): 23.

12. Robert D. Buechner, "State Park Systems," *Parks & Recreation* 11, no. 7 (July 1976): 35–37, 98.

Chapter 4

1. Peter T. White, "This Land of Ours—How Are We Using It?" *National Geographic* 150, no. 1 (July 1976): 41.

2. H. G. James, *Municipal Functions* (New York: D. Appleton and Company, 1917), pp. 18–19.

3. Ibid., p. 150.

4. Roger A. Lancaster, "Municipal Services," *Parks & Recreation* 11, no. 7 (July 1976): 19.

5. *What is an Adventure Playground?* (London: National Playing Fields Association, n.d.)

6. Robert L. Breeden, ed., *Life in Rural America* (National Geographic Society, 1974), chap. 4, p. 135.

Chapter 5

1. *The Recreation Imperative, A Draft of the Nationwide Outdoor Recreation Plan Prepared by the Department of the Interior* (Washington, D.C.: U.S. Government Printing Office, 1974), pp. 179–80.

2. Ibid., p. 38.

3. Charles E. Doell and Gerald B. Fitzgerald, *A Brief History of Parks and Recreation in the United States* (Chicago: The Athletic Institute, 1954), pp. 83–84.

Chapter 6

1. Outdoor Recreation Resources Review Commission, *Outdoor Recreation for America* (Washington, D.C.: U.S. Government Printing Office, 1962).

2. *The Recreation Imperative, A Draft of the Nationwide Outdoor Recreation Plan Prepared by the Department of the Interior* (Washington, D.C.: U.S. Government Printing Office, 1974), p. 4.

3. Bureau of Outdoor Recreation, U.S. Department of the Interior, *Outdoor Recreation: A Legacy for America* (Washington, D.C.: Department of the Interior, November 1973), pp. 27–48.

4. H. Duane Hampton, *How the U.S. Cavalry Saved Our National Parks* (Bloomington: Indiana University Press, 1971).

5. Newton B. Drury, "State Park Philosophy," in *American Planning and Civic Annual* (Washington, D.C.: American Planning and Civic Association, 1957), p. 154.

6. *The Recreation Imperative*, pp. 256 and 266.

7. Ibid., p. 319.

8. *Recreation in the Armed Forces* (Washington, D.C.: Armed Forces Section, American Recreation Society, n.d.), p. 1.

Chapter 7

1. Franklin Bobbitt, *The Curriculum* (Boston: Houghton Mifflin Company, 1918), p. 212.

2. "The Seven Cardinal Principles Revisited," *Today's Education* (September-October 1976), pp. 68–69.

3. Linda Odum and Anne Khanna, *Analysis of National Survey to Determine Extent of Leisure Education Programs*, mimeographed report (Arlington, Virginia: National Recreation and Park Association Leisure Education Advancement Project, March 1975).

4. Jean Mundy, *A Systems Approach to Leisure Education*, mimeographed material (March 1975).

5. Roger Lancaster, *Report to Lilly Endowment, Inc. Leisure Education Advancement Project*, mimeographed material (January 1977).

6. *General Learning Objectives for Leisure Education in Grades K–12* (Arlington, Virginia: National Recreation and Park Association, February 1976), pp. 3–4, reprinted by permission.

7. Tay Green, *Guidelines for Political Action in Leisure Education*, mimeographed report (Ar-

lington, Virginia: Society of Park and Recreation Educators Leisure Education Committee, 1974).

8. Ibid.

9. George T. Wilson, "Leisure Counseling," in *Proceedings of the Third National Leisure Education Conference, Accent on Coordination,* ed. Janet R. MacLean (Arlington, Virginia: National Recreation and Park Association, January 1977), pp. 81–83.

10. Ibid., p. 81.

11. Peter J. Verhoven and Dennis A. Vinton, *Career Education for Leisure Occupations* (Lexington: University of Kentucky, 1972), p. 2.

12. Casmer Heilman, "Leisure Education—Career Education," in *Proceedings of the Third National Leisure Education Conference, Accent on Coordination,* ed. Janet R. MacLean (Arlington, Virginia: National Recreation and Park Association, January 1977), p. 75.

13. Larry E. Decker, "Community Education," in *Leisure Today* (Washington, D.C.: American Association for Health, Physical Education, and Recreation, April 1974), p. 7.

14. Robert M. Artz, ed., *The Ultimate to Serve* (Arlington, Virginia: National Recreation and Park Association, July 1976), p. 12.

15. *Guiding Policies for the Cooperative Use, Planning and Development of School and Park District Facilities,* mimeographed material (Peoria, Ill.: Peoria School District 150, Peoria Park District, 1975), pp. 1–2, reprinted by permission.

16. *Irving, Texas, School-Community Agreement,* mimeographed material (1969), reprinted by permission.

17. Lloyd B. Sharp, "Introduction," in *Outdoor Education for American Youth* (Washington, D.C.: American Association for Health, Physical Education, and Recreation, 1957).

Chapter 8

1. *UWASIS II, A Taxonomy of Social Goals & Human Service Programs,* second edition of *UWASIS*—United Way of America Services Identification System (Alexandria, Va.: United Way of America, November 1976), pp. 7–8, reprinted by permission.

2. From *Constitution of Girl Scouts of the U.S.A.* Used by permission.

3. "Relevance and Vigor Reflected in Programs and Services, Survey Results," *Keynote, The Quarterly Magazine of Boys' Clubs of America* 5, no. 1 (Winter 1976–77): 3.

4. Letter from Camp Fire Girls national office to Reynold E. Carlson.

5. *Why Girls Clubs?* (New York: Girls Clubs of America, Inc.), brochure.

6. Statement by the International and National Council of the YMCAs of the U.S. 1957 (Revision of statement adopted in 1931.)

Chapter 9

1. "Behind the Sharp Increase in Two-Breadwinner Families," *U.S. News & World Report* 82, no. 5 (February 7, 1977): 54.

2. *The Recreation Imperative, A Draft of the Nationwide Outdoor Recreation Plan Prepared by the Department of the Interior* (Washington, D.C.: U.S. Government Printing Office, 1974), p. 193.

3. United States Travel Service, *USA Plant Visits—1977–78* (Washington, D.C.: U.S. Government Printing Office, 1977).

4. John J. Bullaro, "Career Potential in Commercial Recreation," *Journal of Physical Education and Recreation* 46, no. 9 (November–December 1975): 36.

5. Arlin Epperson, "Opportunities for Recreation Students in the Travel and Tourism Industry," *Journal of Physical Education and Recreation* 46, no. 9 (November–December 1975): 38.

Chapter 10

1. The Editors, "Working Together," *California Parks and Recreation* 32, no. 5 (December/January 1976–77): 11.

2. George Hjelte and Jay S. Shivers, *Public Administration of Recreational Services* (Philadelphia: Lea & Febiger, 1972), p. 55.

3. Diana R. Dunn and Lamarr A. Phillips, "Synergetic Programming or 2 + 2 = 5," *Parks & Recreation* 10, no. 3 (March 1975): 24–25.

4. John F. Mee, "Ideational Items—A Collection," *Business Horizons* (June 1969).

5. Larry Lunch, "Irvine's Heritage Park: A Product of Cooperation," *California Parks and Recreation* 32, no. 5 (December/January 1976–77): 19.

6. Richard C. Trudeau, "Ways and Means to Stretch Tax Dollars," *Trends, Park Practice Program* (October, November, December 1976): 9.

7. Sterling S. Winans, writing in *Managing Municipal Leisure Services*, ed. Sidney G. Lutzin and Edward H. Storey. (Washington, D.C.: International City Management Association, 1973) p. 259.

Chapter 11

1. Bennett Schiff, "The Arts, Parks, and Leisure Project," *Parks & Recreation* 8, no. 3 (March 1973): 46.

2. Raymond Forsberg, "It's High Time," *Parks & Recreation* 9, no. 6 (June 1974): 94–95.

3. Bernice Reed, "Culture Comes of Age in America," *Trends, Park Practice Program* (July, August, September 1973).

4. Viscount Grey of Fallodon, *Recreation* (New York: National Recreation Association, 1920), pp. 10–11, reprinted by permission.

5. Donna M. Gelfand and Donald R. Hartman, "Some Detrimental Effects of Competitive Sports on Children's Behavior," in *The Humanistic and Mental Health Aspects of Sports, Exercise and Recreation* (Chicago: American Medical Association, 1976).

6. Gelfand and Hartman, pp. 135–136.

7. Tim Berry, "Competition in Recreation Sports Programs," *Leisure Lines*, California Park and Recreation Society, Inc. 3, no. 3 (April 1977), reprinted by permission.

Chapter 12

1. Joseph J. Bannon, *Leisure Resources: Its Comprehensive Planning* (Englewood Cliffs, N.J.: Prentice-Hall, 1976), p. 3.

2. Patricia Farrell and Herberta M. Lundegren, *The Process of Recreation Programming* (New York: John Wiley & Sons, Inc., copyright 1977) and reprinted by permission of John Wiley & Sons, Inc.

3. Adah Parker Strobell," Modernizing Evaluation Techniques," *Parks and Recreation* 12, no. 6 (June 1977): 31.

Chapter 13

1. *Employ* 2, no. 7, (March 1976): 1.

2. "Rights for the Handicapped—New Rules

Stir Turmoil," *U.S. News & World Report* (May 9, 1977): 84.

3. Thomas Stein, *Report on the State of Recreation and Park Education in Canada and the United States* (Arlington, Virginia: National Recreation and Park Association, 1975).

4. Janet R. MacLean, ed., *Therapeutic Recreation in the Community* (Bloomington: Indiana University Press, 1963).

5. "The Untapped Reservoir of Human Energy," paper delivered at the University of Waterloo, December 1974.

6. Robert N. Butler, *Why Survive?* (New York: Harper & Row Publishers, 1975), p. 409.

7. Albert Rosenfeld, *Prolongevity* (New York: Alfred A. Knopf, 1976).

8. Willis W. Harman, "The Coming Transformation," *The Futurist* (February 1977): 6.

9. William Abbott, "Work in the Year 2000," *The Futurist* (February 1977): 25.

10. Louis Harris and Associates, Inc., *The Myth and Reality of Aging in America* (Washington, D.C.: National Council on Aging, 1975), p. 5.

11. Ibid., p. 10.

12. Ibid., p. 38.

13. *Annual Report to the President* (Washington, D.C.: Federal Council on Aging, January 1976), p. 43.

14. Edward J. Stieglitz, *The Second Forty Years* (Philadelphia: J. B. Lippincott Company, 1946), p. 260.

15. "A Surprising Profile of America's Poor," *U.S. News & World Report* 81, no. 19 (November 8, 1976): 58.

16. Ibid., p. 57.

17. Fred R. Harris, "Man Must Laugh," in *Recreation and Leisure Service for the Disadvantaged*, ed. John A. Nesbitt, Paul D. Brown, and James F. Murphy (Philadelphia: Lea & Febiger, 1970), p. viii.

18. Geoffrey Godbey, *Participation of Minority and Disadvantaged Students in Recreation and Park Curricula*, mimeographed report (1972), p. 5.

19. Ralph D. Abernathy, "Leisure Time for the Poor," in *Spectrum* (New York: National Council of Churches, 1976), p. 11.

20. Stanley Cohen, "Property Destruction: Motives and Meanings," in *Vandalism*, ed. Colin Ward (New York: Van Nostrand, Reinhold Company, 1973), p. 53.

21. Abernathy, "Leisure Time for the Poor," p. 112.

22. Richard W. Velde, "Master Craftsman Inside," *Parks & Recreation* 9, no. 9 (September 1974): 30.

23. Edith E. Flynn, "Recreation—A Privilege or a Necessity?" *Parks and Recreation* 9, no. 9 (September 1974): 57, reprinted by permission.

Chapter 14

1. Charles K. Brightbill, *Man and Leisure* (Englewood Cliffs, N.J.: Prentice-Hall, Inc., 1961), p. 281.

2. Robert Smith, "Let Your Kids Alone," *Life* 44 (January 1958): 103–4.

3. Lebert H. Weir, *Europe at Play* (New York: A. S. Barnes and Company, 1937), p. 1.

4. Ralph Stogdill, "Personal Factors Associated with Leadership," *Journal of Psychology* 25 (1948).

5. John K. Hemphill, *Situational Factors in Leadership* (Columbus: Ohio State University, 1949), p. 9.

6. Eugene E. Jennings, "The Anatomy of Leadership," *Management of Personnel Quarterly* 1, no. 1 (1961): 13.

7. Douglas McGregor, *The Human Side of Enterprise* (New York: McGraw-Hill Book Company, 1960), p. 182.

8. George R. Terry, *Principles of Management* (Homewood, Ill.: Richard D. Irwin, Inc., 1960), p. 5.

9. Harry A. Overstreet and Bonaro W. Overstreet, *Leaders for Adult Education* (New York: American Association for Adult Education, 1941), p. 1.

10. Ordway Tead, *The Art of Leadership* (New York: McGraw-Hill Book Company, 1935), p. 20.

11. Paul Douglass, unpublished speech at National Recreation Congress, Long Beach, California, October 1957.

12. Frederick E. Wolf, *Leadership in the New Age* (Rutland, Vt.: Tuttle Publishing Co., 1937), introduction.

13. Walter L. Stone and Charles G. Stone, *Recreation Leadership* (New York: William-Frederick Press, 1952), p. 19.

14. Alex F. Osborne, *Applied Imagination* (New York: Charles Scribner's Sons, 1953).

15. Joseph Bannon, ed., *Outreach* (Springfield, Ill.: Charles C. Thomas Publishing Co., 1973).

16. Robert Banes, "Maximizing Human Resources," *Parks & Recreation* 10, no. 12 (December 1975): 29.

17. Paul Douglass, unpublished speech on creative leaders, given at the Great Lakes Park Training Institute, Pokagon, Indiana, February 1957. Quoted by permission.

Chapter 15

1. Donald Hawkins and Peter Verhoven, *NRPA Supply/Demand Study: Professional Recreation and Park Occupations* (Arlington, Virginia: National Recreation and Park Association, 1968).

2. Donald D. Henkel and Geoffrey C. Godbey, *Parks, Recreation, and Leisure Services, Employment in the Public Sector: Status and Trends* (Arlington, Virginia: National Recreation and Park Association, 1977).

3. *Report, Special Goals Committee*, mimeographed material (Arlington, Virginia: National Recreation and Park Association, 1976), pp. 2–3.

4. Public Resources Code Memo, February 1974.

5. Minutes of Board of Trustees, National Recreation and Park Association, September 29, 1970.

6. Charles W. Pezoldt, "A Code to Work By," *Parks & Recreation* 12, no. 1 (January 1977): 32–34.

INDEX